Junior Illustrated Dictionary

Chambers

CHAMBERS
An imprint of Chambers Harrap Publishers Ltd
7 Hopetoun Crescent, Edinburgh, EH7 4AY

Chambers Harrap is an Hachette UK company

© Chambers Harrap Publishers Ltd 2009

Illustrations © Rosie Brooks (Beehive Illustration) 2009

Chambers® is a registered trademark of Chambers Harrap Publishers Ltd

First published by Chambers Harrap Publishers Ltd 2009

Database right Chambers Harrap Publishers Ltd

A CIP catalogue record for this book is available from the British Library.

ISBN 978 0550 10477 9 (main edition)

ISBN 978 0550 10694 0 (paperback edition – not available in UK and Ireland)

10 9 8 7 6 5 4 3 2 1

We have made every effort to mark as such all words which we believe to be trademarks.
We should also like to make it clear that the presence of a word in the dictionary, whether
marked or unmarked, in no way affects its legal status as a trademark

Every reasonable effort has been made by the author and the publishers to trace the
copyright holders of material quoted in this book. Any errors or omissions should be
notified in writing to the publishers, who will endeavour to rectify the situation for any
reprints and future editions

Contributors

Publishing Manager
Morven Dooner

Editor
Elspeth Summers

www.chambers.co.uk

Designed by Chambers Harrap Publishers Ltd, Edinburgh
Typeset in VAG Rounded by Chambers Harrap Publishers Ltd, Edinburgh
Printed and bound in Italy by Legoprint

What is Chambers Junior Dictionary?

Chambers Junior Dictionary has been specially written for use by primary school pupils aged 5-7. It has been compiled with the benefit of advice from a number of primary school teachers, ensuring that the book provides all the information a pupil at this level needs in the most straightforward terms.

To encourage young dictionary users, definitions are worded so that all children can easily understand them, and examples have been carefully selected to make the meaning and use of the words even more clear. In many cases, these examples have been taken directly from our corpus of children's literature, a resource which has helped the editors to make informed decisions about the words a child is likely to meet in his or her reading.

Further assistance with language is provided by clear, coloured word class labels (noun, verb, etc). The inclusion of full-out forms such as the plurals of nouns and past tenses of verbs makes such forms easy to identify and spell. Extra pieces of important and interesting information, such as homophones that can be confused and word histories, are included in short, eye-catching boxes. It is all these features that make *Chambers Junior Dictionary* an invaluable resource for primary school pupils, for dictionary work and everyday reference.

For lots of classroom activities that can be used in conjunction with the dictionary, visit our website at **www.chamberslearning.co.uk**

Contents

How do I use my Junior Dictionary?

A **dictionary** is a book that contains lists of words and their meanings, in alphabetical order.

You can use a dictionary to find out what a word means, but there are other things you can use it for. For example, you can use a dictionary to check that you have spelt a word properly or said it properly.

How do I find a word?

Imagine that you want to look up the word *balloon*.

1 The alphabet down the side of the page will show you the letter that begins the words on that page, so you look for the pages where **Bb** is marked.

2 The red word at the top of a left page shows you which is the first word on that page, while the red word on a right page shows you which is the last word on that page. If you're looking for the word **balloon** you know it comes before banana, so you know to look for it on that page.

3 The first words in an entry are the main words that you look up, so these words are large and coloured blue so it is easy to find them.

ballet   balloon

Each main word and the block of information below it is called a dictionary **entry**.

4 You might find the word you want marked with a blue arrow like this [▶].

A word in **blue** after a blue arrow is part of the **word family** of the main word. It will be in alphabetical order after the main word.

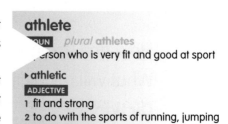

What will my dictionary tell me?

1 If it is hard to guess how to say the word from its spelling, the dictionary will tell you how to say it.

> **chef** said "**shef**"

The word is shown in sounds you will recognize from the spelling.

ai is the sound your hear in the words pain, train
ay is the sound your hear in the words **day, play**
ie is the sound your hear in the words lie, tie
o is the sound your hear in the words cot, stop
oa is the sound your hear in the words loan, moat
oeis the sound your hear in the words **no, th**ough
oi is the sound your hear in the words **b**oy, **s**oil
ow is the sound your hear in the words **n**ow, **plough**
u is the sound your hear in the words bus, tub

2 The word in CAPITAL LETTERS tells you the **word class** the entry word is. This is simply the type of word it is, and the job that it does.

NOUN   A noun names people or things.

VERB   A verb is used to tell what people are doing or what is happening.

ADJECTIVE   An adjective describes people or things.

ADVERB   An adverb describes the way something is done.

PRONOUN   A pronoun is used to replace a noun so that you do not repeat the noun over and over again.

PREPOSITION   A preposition is placed before a noun to tell you where some thing is or where it is moving to.

CONJUNCTION   A conjunction joins two parts of a sentence together.

3 A word in yellow after NOUN is the **plural** of the noun. This is the word you use when you are talking about more than one of something.

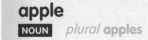
apple
NOUN *plural apples*

4 Words in yellow after **VERB** show you how to spell the different **forms** of the verb. The one you use depends on who did the action or when it happened.

apologize *or* **apologise**
VERB apologizes, apologizing, apologized

5 Words in yellow after **ADJECTIVE** are the ones you use when you are making a **comparison** and you want to say something is *more* or *the most… .*

bad
ADJECTIVE worse, worst

6 Numbers show you that there are different meanings of the word. Each meaning has a different number.

accident
NOUN *plural* accidents
1 a bad thing that happens by chance ⋛ *We had an accident with the glue and now it's everywhere.* ⋚
2 a road accident is when a vehicle crashes into something on a road

7 The meaning of the word is explained after this. This is called the **definition**.

8 The words with ⋛ ⋚ around them after some of the meanings **are examples** to show you how you might use the main word, and they help explain the meaning.

a *or* **an**
ADJECTIVE
1 one ⋛ *a hundred miles* ⋚
2 any ⋛ *I need a pen.* ⋚
3 each ⋛ *Tommy gets £5 pocket money a week.* ⋚

9 Sometimes you will see a small box that looks like this:

> If you write *all ready* as two words, then it means 'completely prepared'. For example: *Are you all ready to go?*

These boxes might tell you how to spell or use a word properly, for example by not getting the word mixed up with another one that sounds the same.

a *or* an

ADJECTIVE

1 one ⋟ *a hundred miles* ⋞
2 any ⋟ *I need a pen.* ⋞
3 each ⋟ *Tommy gets £5 pocket money a week.* ⋞

> You use **a** before words that begin with a consonant, for example *a horse*. You also use **a** before words that begin with **u** if they are pronounced like 'you', for example *a uniform*. You use **an** before words that begin with a vowel (**a, e, i, o, u**), for example *an eye*. You also use **an** before the letter **h** when it is not pronounced, for example *an honest man, an hour*.

able

ADJECTIVE abler, ablest

1 if you are able to do something, you can do it ⋟ *He wasn't able to run fast enough.* ⋞ ⋟ *Will you be able to help me?* ⋞
2 an able person is good at doing something ⋟ *a very able singer* ⋞

about

PREPOSITION

1 to do with ⋟ *a book about bats* ⋞
2 not exactly but nearly the number given ⋟ *about five years ago* ⋞ ⋟ *about four centimetres* ⋞
3 around ⋟ *books scattered about the room* ⋞

ADVERB

1 in or to one place and then another ⋟ *move things about* ⋞ ⋟ *running about all day* ⋞

2 in the opposite direction ⋟ *He turned about and walked away.* ⋞
▸ **about to**
just going to ⋟ *I was about to leave when the phone rang.* ⋞ ⋟ *I think it's about to rain.* ⋞

above

PREPOSITION

in a higher position ⋟ *the shelf above the sink* ⋞ ⋟ *two degrees above zero* ⋞ ⋟ *in the class above me* ⋞

ADVERB

1 higher up ⋟ *clouds in the sky above* ⋞
2 earlier in a piece of writing ⋟ *See instruction 5 above.* ⋞
▸ **above all**
more than anything else ⋟ *We were, above all, hungry.* ⋞

accident

NOUN *plural* accidents

1 a bad thing that happens by chance ⋟ *We had an accident with the glue and now it's everywhere.* ⋞
2 a road accident is when a vehicle crashes into something on a road
▸ **by accident**
by chance ⋟ *I dropped the glass by accident and it smashed.* ⋞

▸ **accidental**

ADJECTIVE

if something is accidental, it happens by mistake

▸ **accidentally**

ADVERB

by accident ⋟ *I accidentally shut the door on my brother's hand.* ⋞

ache

NOUN *plural* **aches**

a pain that goes on and on ⋛ *an ache behind my eyes* ⋛

VERB aches, aching, ached

if part of your body aches, it hurts for a long time, especially in a dull, heavy sort of way ⋛*My arm aches from playing too much tennis.* ⋛

acorn

NOUN *plural* **acorns**

the fruit of the oak tree

act

VERB acts, acting, acted

1 to perform in a play or film
2 to behave in a certain way ⋛ *Stop acting like a baby.* ⋛
3 to do something ⋛ *We must act now to save the planet!* ⋛

▸ **act up**
to behave badly

NOUN *plural* **acts**

1 something that someone does ⋛ *a brave act* ⋛
2 a piece of entertainment in a show ⋛ *a comedy act* ⋛

add

VERB

1 to put things together ⋛ *Add two and two.* ⋛ ⋛ *Add the milk and sugar to the mixture.* ⋛
2 to say or write something else ⋛ *'If you don't mind?' he added.* ⋛

▸ **add up**
1 to find the total of numbers put together ⋛ *Can you add these numbers up in your head?*⋛
2 if things add up, they grow into a large amount ⋛ *£1 a week soon adds up.* ⋛

▸ **addition**
NOUN *plural* **additions**

1 addition is adding up numbers

2 an addition is something that has been added ⋛ *a new addition to the collection* ⋛

address

NOUN *plural* **addresses**

1 your address is the name or number of the house, street and town where you live ⋛ *Please write down your address for me.* ⋛
2 a speech ⋛ *a powerful address given to all the governments involved* ⋛
3 **ICT** a group of letters and numbers that you can send emails to ⋛ *I have a new email address.* ⋛

VERB addresses, addressing, addressed

1 **formal** to speak to someone ⋛ *Were you addressing me?*⋛
2 to write an address on something like an envelope

Adi-Granth said "u-dee-**grunt**"

NOUN

the Guru Granth Sahib, the holy book of the Sikh religion

adjective

WORD CLASS *plural* **adjectives**

a word that tells you something about a noun. For example, *difficult*, *good* and *stupid* are adjectives

adult

NOUN *plural* **adults**

a grown-up

ADJECTIVE

to do with or for grown-ups ⋛ *adult sizes* ⋛

▸ **adulthood**
NOUN

the period of time in your life when you are an adult

adventure

NOUN *plural* **adventures**

something exciting that you do ⋛ *Going into space would be a real adventure.* ⋛

▸ **adventurous**

ADJECTIVE

an adventurous person likes to do exciting new things

adverb

WORD CLASS *plural* adverbs

a word that you use to describe verbs, adjectives or other adverbs. For example, *really*, *badly* and *often* are adverbs

advert

NOUN *plural* adverts

a notice or short film about something that somebody is trying to sell

advice

NOUN

someone who gives you advice tells you what they think you should do

Remember that **advice** with a **c** is a noun: *Can you give me some advice?* **Advise** with an **s** is a verb: *Can you advise me?*

advise

VERB advises, advising, advised

to tell someone what you think they should do

▸ **adviser** *or* **advisor**

NOUN *plural* advisers *or* advisors

a person who tells people what to do

aeroplane

NOUN *plural* aeroplanes

a machine for flying that has fixed wings.

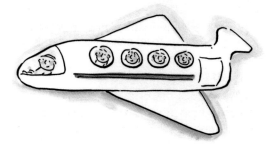

Aer is the Greek word for *air*. If a word starts with **aero**, you can guess that it has something to do with air or flying. Other examples are **aerobics** and **aerosol**.

afford

VERB affords, affording, afforded

1 to have enough money to pay for something ⋝ *We can't afford to go on holiday.* ⋜
2 to have enough time to do something ⋝ *I can't afford to stay any longer or I'll be late.* ⋜

▸ **affordable**

ADJECTIVE

at a low enough price to buy

afraid

ADJECTIVE

frightened ⋝ *There's no need to be afraid.* ⋜ ⋝ *Small children are often afraid of dogs.* ⋜

▸ **I'm afraid**

if you say 'I'm afraid' you mean you are sorry ⋝ *I'm afraid I don't know the answer.* ⋜

after

PREPOSITION

1 following ⋝ *I'll do it after dinner.* ⋜ ⋝ *Your name's after mine on the list.* ⋜
2 if you were named after someone, you were given their name ⋝ *Gordon was named after his uncle.* ⋜
3 to ask after someone is to ask how they are ⋝ *Mrs Young was asking after you.* ⋜

▸ **after all**

anyway ⋝ *I went after all.* ⋜

ADVERB

later ⋝ *Can you come the week after?* ⋜

CONJUNCTION

following in time ⋝ *Mrs Shaw died after we moved.* ⋜ ⋝ *After we'd said goodbye, we felt awfully sad.* ⋜

afternoon

NOUN *plural* **afternoons**

the time between midday and the evening

again

ADVERB

1 once more ⧽ *Do it again!* ⧽
2 to the place you started from or the way you were before ⧽ *Can we go home again now?* ⧽ ⧽ *Grandad would like to be young again.* ⧽
▸ **again and again**
lots of times

age

NOUN *plural* **ages**

1 a person's age is how old they are
2 **informal** an age is a very long time ⧽ *We had to wait an age for him to come out.* ⧽
3 a time in history ⧽ *the Stone Age* ⧽

▸ **ages**
informal a long time ⧽ *You took ages to finish.* ⧽

VERB **ages, aging** *or* **ageing, aged**

1 to get older
2 to look older ⧽ *She's aged a lot recently.* ⧽

▸ **aged**
ADJECTIVE

1 said "aijd"
having the age of ⧽ *a boy aged 10* ⧽
2 said "**aij**-id"
old

ago

ADVERB

in the past ⧽ *Lily was born ten years ago.* ⧽

agree

VERB **agrees, agreeing, agreed**

1 to agree with someone is to think the same as them about something ⧽ *Don't you agree?* ⧽ ⧽ *I agree with everything you've said.* ⧽
2 to agree to do what someone has asked

you to is to say that you will do it ⧽ *I only agreed to come if you came too.* ⧽
3 if some food or drink does not agree with you, it upsets your stomach

▸ **agreeable**
ADJECTIVE

1 something that is agreeable is pleasant or enjoyable
2 someone who is agreeable is willing to do something ⧽ *If you're agreeable, we'll leave at about 3 o'clock.* ⧽

▸ **agreement**
NOUN *plural* **agreements**

1 an agreement is something that people have decided together that they will do ⧽ *These countries have made an agreement not to fight.* ⧽
2 agreement is when things such as opinions or answers are the same ⧽ *We are in complete agreement about this.* ⧽

air

NOUN

1 air is the gases around us that we breathe in ⧽ *Kelly left the room to get some air.* ⧽ ⧽ *The air carries the seeds for miles.* ⧽
2 an air of secrecy or mystery is a feeling that there is a secret or mystery
▸ **by air**
in an aeroplane or helicopter
▸ **on the air**
broadcasting a radio or television programme
▸ **up in the air**
not yet definite or decided ⧽ *Our holiday plans are still up in the air.* ⧽

VERB **airs, airing, aired**

1 to air washing is to make it completely dry
2 to air a room is to let some fresh air into it

airport

NOUN *plural* **airports**

a place where passengers can get on and off aeroplanes

a b c d e f g h i j k l m n o p q r s t u v w x y z

alarm

NOUN *plural* alarms

1 an alarm is a signal to warn people ⋝ *The ringing sound is the fire alarm.* ⋜
2 alarm is a sudden feeling of fear ⋝ *Freddie jumped back in alarm.* ⋜

VERB alarms, alarming, alarmed
to frighten someone, especially suddenly

▸ **alarming**
ADJECTIVE
frightening ⋝ *an alarming sight* ⋜

alive

ADJECTIVE

1 living ⋝ *the greatest ballerina alive* ⋜
2 lively ⋝ *The town comes alive at night.* ⋜

all

ADJECTIVE

1 every one ⋝ *All the children stood up.* ⋜
2 every part ⋝ *We ate all the cake.* ⋜

▸ **all in**
informal tired out ⋝ *We were all in after the race.* ⋜

ADVERB
completely ⋝ *all dirty* ⋜

PRONOUN

1 every one ⋝ *I want to see them all.* ⋜
2 every part of something ⋝ *Don't spend it all.* ⋜

Allah

NOUN
the Muslim name for the creator of the world

alligator

NOUN *plural* alligators
a large reptile like a crocodile, with thick skin, a long tail and large jaws

almost

ADVERB
very nearly but not quite ⋝ *She is almost ten years old.* ⋜

alone

ADJECTIVE
without anyone else ⋝ *I was alone in the house.* ⋜

ADVERB

1 not with others ⋝ *I live alone.* ⋜
2 without other things ⋝ *The ticket alone will use up all my money.* ⋜

along

PREPOSITION

1 from one end to the other ⋝ *Shona walked along the street.* ⋜
2 on the length of ⋝ *Harry's house is somewhere along this street.* ⋜

ADVERB

1 onwards ⋝ *Move along please.* ⋜
2 to a particular place ⋝ *I'll come along later.* ⋜

▸ **along with**
together with ⋝ *We'd packed drinks along with the sandwiches.* ⋜

alphabet

NOUN *plural* alphabets
all the letters of a language arranged in a particular order

▸ **alphabetical**
ADJECTIVE

1 to do with the alphabet
2 arranged in the order of an alphabet ⋝ *an alphabetical index* ⋜

▸ **alphabetical order**
something that is arranged in alphabetical order is arranged so that words beginning with **a** come first, then **b** and so on ⋝ *You can see that this dictionary is in alphabetical order.* ⋜

a b c d e f g h i j k l m n o p q r s t u v w x y z

▶ **alphabetically**

ADVERB

with the letters in the order of the alphabet ⪧ *The list has been arranged alphabetically.*

> **Alphabet** comes from the Greek word **alphabetos**, which is made up of the first two Greek letters – these are **alpha** (a) and **beta** (b).

already

ADVERB

1 before a particular time ⪧ *I had already gone when Bob arrived.*
2 now, before the expected time ⪧ *Is he here already?*

> If you write *all ready* as two words, then it means 'completely prepared'. For example: *Are you all ready to go?*

also

ADVERB

in addition ⪧ *Bernie speaks French and also some Italian.* ⪧ *My sister also attends this school.*

although

CONJUNCTION

in spite of the fact that ⪧ *He was late for school although he'd hurried.*

always

ADVERB

1 at all times ⪧ *I always work hard.*
2 continually or often ⪧ *I'm always getting this wrong.*
3 forever ⪧ *I'll always remember that day.*

am

VERB

1 the form of the verb **be** that you use with I ⪧ *I am happy.*

2 **am** is also used as a helping verb along with a main verb ⪧ *I am going out.*

ambulance

NOUN   *plural* **ambulances**

a vehicle for taking sick or injured people to hospital

amount

NOUN   *plural* **amounts**

a quantity ⪧ *a small amount of money* ⪧ *large amounts of land*

VERB   **amounts, amounting, amounted**

to amount to a particular number is to add up to that much ⪧ *What I've spent amounts to exactly £10.*

amrit

NOUN

a Sikh ceremony where someone drinks amrit, a special mixture of water and sugar, as a sign that they are joining the body of Sikhs

an

ADJECTIVE

you use **an** instead of **a** before words beginning with a vowel or before the letter 'h' when it is not pronounced ⪧ *an honest person*

ancient

ADJECTIVE

1 belonging to a very long time ago ⪧ *the ancient people who once lived here*
2 very old

and

CONJUNCTION

1 a word that is used to join parts of sentences ⪧ *We'll have bread and butter.* ⪧ *Go and get ready.*
2 plus ⪧ *Two and two make four.*

angel

NOUN   *plural* **angels**

1 a messenger from God

2 a very good person ⋛ *You are an angel to help me like this.* ⋛

▸ **angelic**
ADJECTIVE
very beautiful and good

▸ **angelically**
ADVERB
very sweetly ⋛ *They sang angelically.* ⋛

> **Angel** comes from the Greek word **angelos,** which means *messenger.*

angry
ADJECTIVE angrier, angriest
cross or very cross ⋛ *Mum got very angry.* ⋛ ⋛ *an angry crowd* ⋛

▸ **angrily**
ADVERB
in a very cross way ⋛ *A young girl came in, crying angrily.* ⋛

animal
NOUN *plural* animals
a living being that can feel and move

> This word comes from the Latin word **anima,** which means *life.* The word **animation** is also linked to the Latin word **anima.**

ankle
NOUN *plural* ankles
the place where your foot joins your leg

annoy
VERB annoys, annoying, annoyed
to annoy someone is to make them feel rather angry ⋛ *The way she never listens to me really annoys me.* ⋛

▸ **annoyance**
NOUN *plural* annoyances
1 annoyance is a feeling of irritation ⋛ *a look of annoyance* ⋛

2 an annoyance is something that irritates you

▸ **annoyed**
ADJECTIVE
rather angry

anorak
NOUN *plural* anoraks
a waterproof jacket, usually with a hood

another
ADJECTIVE
1 one more ⋛ *Have another piece of cake.* ⋛
2 a different one ⋛ *Another day we'll walk further.* ⋛

PRONOUN
1 one more ⋛ *He had two gold medals and now he has another.* ⋛
2 a different one ⋛ *If that pencil is broken, use another.* ⋛

answer
NOUN *plural* answers
1 an answer is what you reply when someone asks you a question
2 the answer to a problem is the thing that solves it

VERB answers, answering, answered
1 to reply when someone asks you a question
2 to answer the telephone is to speak to the person calling when it rings
3 to open the door when someone rings or knocks ⋛ *Would you answer the door please?* ⋛

ant
NOUN *plural* ants
a tiny insect

any
ADJECTIVE
1 every ⋛ *Any child would know that answer.* ⋛

a b c d e f g h i j k l m n o p q r s t u v w x y z

2 one, but not a particular one ⋛ *It'll be here any day now.* ⋚
3 some ⋛ *Have we got any sweets?* ⋚

ADVERB

at all ⋛ *I can't go on any longer.* ⋚

PRONOUN

1 one ⋛ *Ask any of them.* ⋚
2 some ⋛ *We haven't got any left.* ⋚

anybody
PRONOUN

any person at all ⋛ *Anyone can come.* ⋚

anyone
PRONOUN

any person at all ⋛ *There isn't anyone left in the playground.* ⋚

anything
PRONOUN

something of any kind ⋛ *He hasn't eaten anything.* ⋚ ⋛ *Has anything happened?* ⋚

anywhere
ADVERB

in or to any place ⋛ *I'm not going anywhere.* ⋚ ⋛ *I can't find my keys anywhere.* ⋚

PRONOUN

any place ⋛ *Anywhere would be better than this.* ⋚

apart
ADVERB

1 separated by distance or time ⋛ *Stand with your feet apart.* ⋚ ⋛ *two classes, a week apart* ⋚
2 into pieces ⋛ *My brother took my doll apart.* ⋚

PREPOSITION

except for ⋛ *Apart from us, nobody's interested.* ⋚

ape
NOUN *plural* **apes**

a kind of monkey that is large and has no tail

VERB *apes, aping, aped*

to ape someone is to copy what they do

apologize *or* apologise
VERB *apologizes, apologizing, apologized*

to say sorry for doing something wrong ⋛ *I had to apologize for being so rude.* ⋚

▶ **apology**
NOUN *plural* **apologies**

an apology is when you say sorry for something you have done

apple
NOUN *plural* **apples**

a hard, round fruit with red, green or yellow skin

April
NOUN

the fourth month of the year, after March and before May

> **April** comes from the Latin word **aperire**, which means *to open*, because the spring flowers start to open around this time.

apron
NOUN *plural* **aprons**

a piece of cloth you wear over the front of your clothes to keep them clean or dry

aquarium
NOUN *plural* **aquariums** *or* **aquaria**

a glass tank or a building, for example in a

zoo, for keeping fish or water animals in

> **Aqua** is the Latin word for *water*. If a word starts with **aqua**, you can guess that it has something to do with water.

are
VERB
1 the form of the verb **be** in the present tense that is used with **you**, **we**, **they** and plural nouns ⇒ *We are all here today.* ⇒ *Where are the best places to visit?*
2 **are** is also used as a helping verb along with a main verb ⇒ *We are leaving tomorrow.*

argue
VERB   argues, arguing, argued
1 to quarrel ⇒ *The children never stop arguing with each other.*
2 to argue with someone is to tell them you disagree with what they have said

▶ **argument**
NOUN   *plural* **arguments**
1 a discussion where people do not agree with each other ⇒ *There was a loud argument going on next door.*
2 the reasons for having or doing something ⇒ *My argument against the trip is that we don't have enough money.*

arm
NOUN   *plural* **arms**
1 the part of your body between your shoulder and your hand ⇒ *Judy has broken her arm in two places.*
2 the arm of a piece of clothing is a sleeve
3 a part of something that sticks out of its side, usually with a bend or angle in it ⇒ *the arm of a chair*

armpit
NOUN   *plural* **armpits**
the angle where your arm joins your body under your shoulder

army
NOUN   *plural* **armies**
an organization of many soldiers, who will fight against an enemy

arrive
VERB   arrives, arriving, arrived
1 to arrive is to reach a place ⇒ *Please arrive at the station by 5.30.* ⇒ *If they don't arrive soon, we'll have to go without them.*
2 when a time or event arrives, it happens ⇒ *Would her birthday ever arrive?*

art
NOUN   *plural* **arts**
1 art is the beautiful things that people do and invent in painting, sculpture, music and literature
2 an art is a skill that you use to do or make something beautiful
3 arts are subjects that you can study that are not sciences

▶ **artist**
NOUN   *plural* **artists**
1 a person who paints, draws or makes sculptures
2 a person who does something very skilfully, especially some kind of performing

▶ **artistic**
ADJECTIVE
1 an artistic person is creative and enjoys art
2 something artistic is creative and skilful ⇒ *a very artistic use of colours*

as
CONJUNCTION
1 a word you use when you compare things or people ⇒ *Are you as tall as me?*
2 while ⇒ *As we climbed, the air got colder.*
3 because ⇒ *I went first as I was the youngest.*
4 like ⇒ *As I thought, most people had already left.*

a
b
c
d
e
f
g
h
i
j
k
l
m
n
o
p
q
r
s
t
u
v
w
x
y
z

ash¹

NOUN   *plural* ashes

the white powder that remains after something is burnt

ash²

NOUN   *plural* ashes

a tree with a silvery-grey bark

ask

VERB   asks, asking, asked

1 to say a question so that you get information from someone ⋛ *They asked me about my family.* ⋚
2 to ask someone for something is to tell them that you would like them to give it to you ⋛ *Ask your brother for a sweet.* ⋚
3 to ask someone to an event like a party is to invite them ⋛ *We've asked twenty people but they won't all turn up.* ⋚

▸ **ask for it**

to do something that will definitely get you into trouble

asleep

ADJECTIVE

sleeping ⋛ *Don't wake her if she's asleep.* ⋚

ADVERB

into sleep ⋛ *I fell asleep after a while.* ⋚

assembly

NOUN   *plural* assemblies

1 putting something together from different parts ⋛ *assembly instructions* ⋚
2 coming together to form a group ⋛ *the morning assembly at school* ⋚

at

PREPOSITION

1 showing where or when you mean ⋛ *Look at me!* ⋚ ⋛ *School finishes at noon.* ⋚
2 costing ⋛ *four bottles at 75p each* ⋚

ate

VERB

a way of changing the verb **eat** to make a past tense ⋛ *The dog ate most of my dinner last night.* ⋚

athlete

NOUN   *plural* athletes

a person who is very fit and good at sport

▸ **athletic**

ADJECTIVE

1 fit and strong
2 to do with the sports of running, jumping and throwing

▸ **athletics**

PLURAL NOUN

the group of sports that include running, jumping and throwing

atlas

NOUN   *plural* atlases

a book of maps

This word comes from the name of a character in Greek mythology, **Atlas**. He was forced by the Greek gods to carry the universe on his shoulders as a punishment.

audience

NOUN   *plural* audiences

1 the people who listen to or watch a performance ⋛ *The audience cheered then the band appeared.* ⋚
2 an interview with an important person ⋛ *an audience with the Queen* ⋚

August

NOUN

the eighth month of the year, after July and before September

August comes from the Latin word for this month, **Augustus**, which was named after the Roman emperor *Augustus Caesar*.

aunt

NOUN   *plural* aunts

1 the sister of one of your parents
2 your uncle's wife

author

NOUN   *plural* authors

a writer of something such as a book

autumn

NOUN   *plural* autumns

the season of the year between summer and winter when the leaves change colour and fall, and it gets dark earlier

awake

ADJECTIVE

not sleeping ⇒ *Are you still awake?*

VERB   awakes, awaking, awoke, awoken

to wake up ⇒ *Gloria awoke early.*

⇒ *Grandma awoke the whole family in the night.*

▶ awaken

VERB   awakens, awakening, awakened

to wake up ⇒ *We were awakened by the bombs.*

away

ADVERB

1 somewhere else ⇒ *Go away!* ⇒ *Throw that away.*
2 at a distance ⇒ *How far away is the school?* ⇒ *only a week away*
3 in the opposite direction ⇒ *Peter turned away.* ⇒ *Remember to put all the toys away again.*

ADJECTIVE

an away game or match is one that is played on an opponent's ground and that a team has to travel to

a b c d e f g h i j k l m n o p q r s t u v w x y z

a b c d e f g h i j k l m n o p q r s t u v w x y z

baby

NOUN *plural* **babies**

1 a very young child

2 a young animal ⋧ *a baby elephant* ⋧

▸ **babyish**

ADJECTIVE

1 like a baby ⋧ *He had a smooth babyish face.* ⋧

2 suitable for babies or younger children ⋧ *This game is probably too babyish for ten-year-olds.* ⋧

back

NOUN *plural* **backs**

1 the back of something is the side that is opposite to or furthest away from its front ⋧ *The socks were at the back of the drawer.* ⋧

2 the part of your body that stretches from the back of your neck to your bottom ⋧ *I always sleep on my back.* ⋧

▸ **back to front**

with the back part wrongly at the front ⋧ *Your T-shirt's on back to front.* ⋧

ADJECTIVE

behind or opposite the front ⋧ *He's had one of his back teeth out.* ⋧

ADVERB

1 farther away in distance ⋧ *Stand back while Dad lights the fireworks.* ⋧

2 to the place, person or state from which someone or something came ⋧ *I'm taking these books back to the library.* ⋧

3 in or to an earlier time ⋧ *Think back and try to remember exactly what happened.* ⋧

VERB backs, backing, backed

1 to move backwards ⋧ *The dog growled and the boys backed away in fear.* ⋧

2 to back someone is to give them support or help, often money ⋧ *A local shopkeeper has offered to back our football team.* ⋧

▸ **back down**

someone backs down when they admit they are beaten or have lost an argument

▸ **back someone up**

to back someone up is to support them

bad

ADJECTIVE worse, worst

1 wicked or naughty ⋧ *Tony and Harry have been very bad boys today.* ⋧ ⋧ *Don't jump up on me, you bad dog!* ⋧

2 not of a good standard ⋧ *His handwriting is bad, and his spelling is worse.* ⋧

3 nasty or upsetting ⋧ *a bad storm* ⋧ ⋧ *very bad news* ⋧

4 harmful to your health ⋧ *Eating too many fatty foods can be bad for you.* ⋧

5 if someone is bad at doing something they do not do it well ⋧ *I'm very bad at maths.* ⋧

6 something is bad or has gone bad if it is rotten or decaying ⋧ *Don't eat that pear – it's bad.* ⋧ ⋧ *Your teeth will go bad if you don't brush them regularly.* ⋧

▸ **not bad** *or* **not too bad**

you say 'not bad' or 'not too bad' to mean quite good ⋧ *'How are you feeling today?' 'Not too bad, thanks'.* ⋧

▸ **badly**

ADVERB

1 not well ⋧ *The work was done very badly.* ⋧

2 seriously ⋧ *The car was badly damaged in the crash.* ⋧

3 very much ⋧ *I badly wanted a new pair of trainers.* ⋧

> Comparing how **bad** things are: *The weather was* bad *yesterday, it was* worse *the day before and last Friday was* worst *of all.*

badge

NOUN *plural* **badges**

a small object with words or pictures printed on it that you pin or sew on to your clothing to show, for example, that you are a member of a group or club

bag

NOUN *plural* **bags**

an object used for carrying things in, made of paper, plastic, cloth or leather

▶ **bags of**

informal lots of ⋛ *We've got bags of time before the bus comes.* ⋚

VERB **bags, bagging, bagged**

1 **informal** to claim something as your own ⋛ *I bagged the best seat.* ⋚
2 to put things into a bag or bags ⋛ *We helped Dad bag all the garden rubbish and put it in the bins.* ⋚

Baisakhi said "bie-**sak**-i"

NOUN

1 a Sikh festival celebrating the new year
2 a Hindu festival to celebrate the new year or the harvest, or to honour a god

bake

VERB **bakes, baking, baked**

1 to cook something such as bread or a cake in an oven ⋛ *Mum does a lot of cooking but she doesn't bake very often.* ⋚
2 to bake food is to cook it in an oven ⋛ *Bake the lasagne in the oven until it is golden brown.* ⋚
3 to bake things that are soft is to harden them in the sun or in an oven ⋛ *The clay hardens when it is baked in a kiln.* ⋚

ball¹

NOUN *plural* **balls**

1 a round object that you use for playing games like football, hockey, cricket and tennis
2 anything that has a round shape ⋛ *a ball of string* ⋚ ⋛ *The hedgehog had rolled itself into a tight ball.* ⋚

> The words **ball** and **bawl** sound the same, but remember that they have different spellings. To **bawl** is to cry out.

ball²

NOUN *plural* **balls**

a big formal party where people dance ⋛ *Cinderella couldn't go to the ball.* ⋚

ballet

NOUN *plural* **ballets**

1 a type of dancing that uses graceful steps and movements ⋛ *Emily prefers ballet to tap dancing.* ⋚
2 a ballet is a story told using dance ⋛ *My favourite ballet is Swan Lake.* ⋚

balloon

NOUN *plural* **balloons**

a very light object made of thin rubber that expands and floats when it is filled with air or gas

VERB **balloons, ballooning, ballooned**

to balloon is to swell like a balloon does when it is filled with air or gas ⋛ *The sail ballooned out in the breeze.* ⋚

banana

NOUN *plural* **bananas**

a long, yellow, very soft fruit that you peel to eat and that grows in hot countries

a b c d e f g h i j k l m n o p q r s t u v w x y z

a b c d e f g h i j k l m n o p q r s t u v w x y z

band

NOUN *plural* **bands**

1 a group of musicians who play together ⋰ *My big brother has formed a rock band with some of his school friends.* ⋰
2 a group ⋰ *a band of robbers* ⋰
3 a strip of material to put round something ⋰ *a rubber band* ⋰ *a headband* ⋰

VERB bands, banding, banded

▸ **band together**
to band together is to join together to do something as a group ⋰ *All the parents banded together to campaign for a new school crossing.* ⋰

bandage

NOUN *plural* **bandages**

a strip of cloth for wrapping round a part of your body that has been cut or hurt

VERB bandages, bandaging, bandaged
to bandage a part of the body is to wrap it in a bandage

bang

NOUN *plural* **bangs**

1 a sudden loud noise ⋰ *There was a loud bang and all the lights went out.* ⋰
2 a hard knock ⋰ *She's had a bang on the head and is feeling a bit dizzy.* ⋰

VERB bangs, banging, banged

1 a door or window bangs when it closes or is shut roughly so that it makes a loud noise ⋰ *The door banged shut in the wind.* ⋰
2 to bang something is to knock it hard against something else ⋰ *Neil banged his books down on the table.* ⋰

bank

NOUN *plural* **banks**

1 a business that looks after and lends money ⋰ *He puts his pocket money in the bank every month.* ⋰
2 a place where a particular thing is stored so that it can be used later ⋰ *a blood bank* ⋰
3 the banks of a river or a lake are the areas of ground beside it ⋰ *We camped on the banks of Loch Lomond.* ⋰

VERB banks, banking, banked

1 to bank money is to put it in a bank
2 an aeroplane banks when it tips over to one side as it changes direction

▸ **bank on something**
to depend on something happening ⋰ *You can't bank on the weather staying dry, so take an umbrella.* ⋰

bar

NOUN *plural* **bars**

1 a piece of hard material ⋰ *an iron bar* ⋰
2 a bar of something is a solid piece of it ⋰ *a bar of soap* ⋰
3 a room or counter serving drinks or food ⋰ *a burger bar* ⋰
4 one of the sections of equal time into which a piece of music is divided ⋰ *four beats to the bar* ⋰

VERB bars, barring, barred

1 to bar a door, a window or a gate is to put metal or wooden bars across it so that no one can get in or out
2 if people are barred from a place or from doing something, they are not allowed in or are not allowed to do it ⋰ *Anyone over the age of 12 is barred from the competition.* ⋰

barbecue

NOUN *plural* **barbecues**

1 a grill used for cooking food outdoors
2 an outdoor party where food is grilled on a barbecue

VERB barbecues, barbecuing, barbecued
to barbecue food is to grill it on a barbecue

bare

ADJECTIVE barer, barest
naked or without any covering ⋰ *It's a*

*bit too cold to be going out with bare
legs.* ⟩ ⟩ *Without the posters on the walls
the bedroom looks really bare.* ⟩

bark¹

NOUN *plural* **barks**

the short loud sound that a dog or fox makes

VERB **barks, barking, barked**

animals bark when they make this sound

bark²

NOUN

the bark of a tree is the rough outer covering
of its trunk and branches

bar mitzvah

NOUN *plural* **bar mitzvahs**

a religious ceremony for Jewish boys to mark
the time, at about age 13, when they are
expected to take some of the responsibilities
of an adult

base

NOUN *plural* **bases**

1 the surface or part on which a thing
   rests ⟩ *a bronze statue on a black marble
   base* ⟩
2 the lowest part of something ⟩ *the base of
   the tree* ⟩
3 a place where people work, or where an
   activity happens ⟩ *an army base* ⟩

VERB **bases, basing, based**

to base one thing on another is to create it
using the other thing ⟩ *a film based on a
Roald Dahl book* ⟩

> The words **base** and **bass** sound the
> same but remember that they have
> different spellings. **Bass** is the lowest
> range of musical notes.

basket

NOUN *plural* **baskets**

a container made of strips of wood or canes
woven together

basketball

NOUN *plural* **basketballs**

1 a game played by two teams who try to
   score points by throwing a ball through a
   hoop fixed high above the ground on a post
2 a basketball is a large ball used to play
   basketball

bat¹

NOUN *plural* **bats**

a shaped piece of wood that you use to hit
the ball in games like cricket

VERB **bats, batting, batted**

to use the bat in games like cricket and
rounders ⟩ *It's Gary's turn to bat next.* ⟩

bat²

NOUN *plural* **bats**

a flying animal that comes out at night to feed

bath

NOUN *plural* **baths**

1 a bath is a large container that you sit in
   to wash yourself ⟩ *I think it's your turn to
   clean the bath.* ⟩
2 a bath is a wash in this kind of
   container ⟩ *You're filthy! When did you last
   have a bath?* ⟩
3 baths are a building which contains a public

a
b
c
d
e
f
g
h
i
j
k
l
m
n
o
p
q
r
s
t
u
v
w
x
y
z

a b c d e f g h i j k l m n o p q r s t u v w x y z

swimming pool ⋗ *I learnt to swim in the local baths.* ⋖

VERB baths, bathing, bathed

to bath someone is to wash them in a bath ⋗ *Dad is bathing my baby brother.* ⋖

bat mitzvah

NOUN *plural* **bat mitzvahs**

a religious ceremony for Jewish girls to mark the time, at about age 12, when they are expected to start taking some of the responsibilites of an adult

battle

NOUN *plural* **battles**

1 a fight between two armies ⋗ **the Battle of Hastings** ⋖

2 any fight or struggle ⋗ *It's always been a bit of a battle to get him to do his homework.* ⋖

VERB battles, battling, battled

to battle is to fight or struggle ⋗*The ship battled bravely through the storm.* ⋖

be

VERB

1 to be is to exist ⋗ *There may be a very good reason for it.* ⋖

2 to be something is to have that position or to do that job ⋗ *What do you want to be when you grow up?* ⋖

3 to be a particular thing is to have that feeling or quality ⋗ *Try to be happy.* ⋖ ⋗ *We can't all be as clever as you.* ⋖

beach

NOUN *plural* **beaches**

an area of sand or pebbles at the edge of the sea

beak

NOUN *plural* **beaks**

a bird's beak is the hard, pointed part of its mouth that it uses to pick up food

---

There are many different forms of the verb **be**. If you are talking about something that is happening at this very time, you use the present tense forms. These are *I* am; *you* or *they* are; *he, she* or *it* is. You can also say *I* am being; *you, we* or *they* are being; *he, she* or *it* is being. If you are talking about something that was the case in the past, you use the past tense forms. These are *I, he, she* or *it* was; *you, we* or *they* were. You can also say *I, you, we* or *they* have been; *he, she* or *it* has been.

bean

NOUN *plural* **beans**

a type of seed that grows in a pod and is eaten as a vegetable

▶ **full of beans**

if someone is full of beans, they have lots of energy

bear¹

NOUN *plural* **bears**

a large heavy animal with a thick coat and hooked claws

bear²

VERB bears, bearing, bore, born *or* borne

1 to bear something is to put up with it ⋗ *She couldn't bear the cold winters.* ⋖

2 to bear something is to carry it or have it ⋗ *Three men arrived, bearing gifts.* ⋖ ⋗ *The door bore the family's name.* ⋖

3 women bear children and animals bear young when they give birth to them

▶ **bearable**

ADJECTIVE

if something is bearable, you are able to put up with it ⋗ *'Is the pain bad?' 'It's bearable.'* ⋖

If you are talking about the birth of a child or young animal, you use the spelling **born**: *He was* born *at midnight on New Year's Eve.* If you mean that something is carried, or someone has put up with something, or a woman has given birth to a child, you use the spelling **borne**: *She had* borne *five children.* • *The seeds are* borne *on the wind.*

beard

NOUN   *plural* **beards**

the hair that grows on a man's chin and cheeks ⋛ **He'd shaved off his beard.** ⋚

▸ **bearded**

ADJECTIVE

having a beard ⋛ **a tall bearded man** ⋚

beast

NOUN   *plural* **beasts**

1 a four-footed animal ⋛ **the beasts of the field** ⋚
2 a cruel or nasty person ⋛ **Don't do that, you beast!** ⋚

▸ **beastly**

ADJECTIVE   **beastlier, beastliest**

horrible or nasty ⋛ **my beastly brother** ⋚

beat

VERB   **beats, beating, beat, beaten**

1 to hit over and over again ⋛ **He beat his fists on the table.** ⋚
2 to beat someone is to defeat them or win against them ⋛ **Do you think Manchester United can beat Real Madrid?** ⋚
3 to make a regular sound or movement ⋛ **He could hear his heart beating.** ⋚
4 to beat food is to stir or mix it by making quick regular movements through it with a spoon, fork or whisk

▸ **beat someone up**

to injure someone by hitting them over and over again

NOUN   *plural* **beats**

1 a beat is a regular sound or movement like that made by your heart or your pulse
2 **music** a regular rhythm
3 a police officer's beat is the regular route he or she takes around an area

beautiful

ADJECTIVE

1 a beautiful person is very pretty or handsome
2 very pleasant to see, hear or smell ⋛ **a beautiful sunset** ⋚   ⋛ **a beautiful voice** ⋚ ⋛ **a rose with a beautiful scent** ⋚
3 the weather is beautiful when it is very pleasant, especially if it is bright, dry and sunny ⋛ **It's a beautiful morning.** ⋚

▸ **beautifully**

ADVERB

in a pleasant or attractive way ⋛ **She is always beautifully dressed.** ⋚   ⋛ **He sings beautifully.** ⋚

beauty

NOUN   *plural* **beauties**

1 beauty is the quality of being very attractive, and pleasant to see or hear ⋛ **the beauty of the alpine scenery** ⋚
2 a person who is beautiful to look at ⋛ **Her grandmother was a famous beauty.** ⋚

became

VERB

a way of changing the verb **become** to make a past tense

because

CONJUNCTION

for the reason that ⋛ **You can't borrow my bike because there's something wrong with the brakes.** ⋚   ⋛ **Just because it's raining, it doesn't mean you should do nothing all day.** ⋚

▸ **because of**

as a result of ⋛ **Because of the school holidays, the return match will be delayed for a fortnight.** ⋚

a b c d e f g h i j k l m n o p q r s t u v w x y z

become

VERB becomes, becoming, became

to come to be ⋗ *She'd become old and frail.* ⋖ ⋗ *Tony Blair became prime minister in 1997.* ⋖

bed

NOUN *plural* beds

1 a piece of furniture to sleep on, or any place for sleeping ⋗ *Time to get ready for bed.* ⋖ ⋗ *Each night, chimpanzees make beds of twigs high up in the trees.* ⋖
2 **geography** the bottom of a river, a lake or the sea
3 an area in a garden that contains flowers and other plants ⋗ *a bed of lilies* ⋖ ⋗ *beautiful beds of roses* ⋖

bedroom

NOUN *plural* bedrooms

a room with a bed or beds used for sleeping in

bee

NOUN *plural* bees

a small winged insect that can sting you. Bees fly from flower to flower collecting nectar to make honey

beef

NOUN

meat from a cow

been

VERB

a form of the verb **be** that is used with a helping verb to show that something happened in the past ⋗ *My brother has been very good today.* ⋖

beetle

NOUN *plural* beetles

an insect with two pairs of wings. Its front wings are hard and cover its back wings when the beetle is not flying

before

PREPOSITION

earlier than something ⋗ *Let's go for a walk before lunch.* ⋖ ⋗ *I sent the letter the day before yesterday.* ⋖

ADVERB

at an earlier time ⋗ *I don't think we've met before.* ⋖ ⋗ *We had all been to the beach the day before.* ⋖

CONJUNCTION

1 earlier than the time when something will happen ⋗ *Wash your hands before you come to the table.* ⋖
2 rather than ⋗ *Ali would die before he would admit he was wrong.* ⋖

begin

VERB begins, beginning, began, begun

to start ⋗ *The concert began at 7.30 and finished at about 9.30.* ⋖ ⋗ *Marie had begun to enjoy being at the new school.* ⋖

▸ **beginner**

NOUN *plural* beginners

someone who has only just started to do or to learn something ⋗ *a guitar class for beginners* ⋖

▸ **beginning**

NOUN *plural* beginnings

1 the start of something ⋗ *He led from the beginning of the race.* ⋖
2 the early part of a period of time ⋗ *In the beginning, I didn't like her much.* ⋖ ⋗ *My birthday is at the beginning of July.* ⋖

behave

VERB behaves, behaving, behaved

1 to behave in a certain way is to act in that way ⋗ *If you behave badly today, you won't get sweets.* ⋖
2 if you behave, or behave yourself, you are good and don't do anything that you shouldn't

being

VERB

the form of the verb **be** that is used to make certain tenses ⋟ *I am being good today.* ⋠   ⋟ *He was just being kind.* ⋠

NOUN   *plural* **beings**

a being is something that lives or exists ⋟ *a science fiction story about beings from other planets* ⋠

belief

NOUN   *plural* **beliefs**

something you believe, especially something that you think is true or exists   ⋟ *strong religious beliefs* ⋠

believe

VERB   believes, believing, believed

1 to be sure that something is true or real ⋟ *I believed his story.* ⋠   ⋟ *Do you believe in ghosts?* ⋠
2 to think that something is true though you are not completely sure ⋟ *I believe he was once a famous film star.* ⋠

▸ **make believe**

if you make believe, you pretend something is real when it isn't

▸ **believable**

ADJECTIVE

if something is believable, it can be believed ⋟ *a believable excuse* ⋠

▸ **believer**

NOUN   *plural* **believers**

someone who believes something, especially someone who believes in a particular religion

bell

NOUN   *plural* **bells**

1 a hollow metal object with a long piece of metal inside that swings and hits the sides of the bell making a ringing sound
2 any device that makes a ringing sound ⋟ *a doorbell* ⋠   ⋟ *a bicycle bell* ⋠

belly

NOUN   *plural* **bellies**

1 the front part of your body between your chest and the tops of your legs
2 your stomach
3 the part underneath an animal's body between its front legs and its back legs

belong

VERB   belongs, belonging, belonged

1 if something belongs to you, you own it ⋟ *Who does this suitcase belong to?* ⋠
2 you belong to the place where you feel at home ⋟ *She felt as if she didn't belong there.* ⋠
3 if you belong to a club or organization, you are a member ⋟ *Peter belongs to the local tennis club.* ⋠
4 something belongs in a particular place if that is where it is usually kept ⋟ *That big chair belongs over there by the fireplace.* ⋠
5 people or things that belong with each other match each other, fit together or make a pair ⋟ *These socks don't belong together.* ⋠

a b c d e f g h i j k l m n o p q r s t u v w x y z

▸ **belongings**

PLURAL NOUN

your belongings are the things you own ⋛ *He just packed up all his belongings and moved out.* ⋛

below

PREPOSITION

lower than or under something ⋛ *the cupboard below the stairs* ⋛ *Simon was below me in school.* ⋛

ADVERB

at or in a lower place ⋛ *From the top of the hill, we looked down on the valley below.* ⋛ *Write your name in the box below.* ⋛

belt

NOUN *plural* **belts**

1 a band of leather, cloth or plastic that you wear around your waist
2 a loop of material in a machine that moves round and round ⋛ *a conveyor belt* ⋛ *a fan belt* ⋛

VERB **belts, belting, belted**

1 to belt someone is to hit them hard ⋛ *The branch sprang back and belted him on the nose.* ⋛
2 **informal** to belt is to go very fast ⋛ *The boys came belting down the hill on their bikes.* ⋛

bench

NOUN *plural* **benches**

1 a long seat ⋛ *We sat on a wooden bench in the park.* ⋛
2 a table used to make things on ⋛ *a carpenter's bench* ⋛

bend

VERB **bends, bending, bent**

1 you bend or bend down when you lower your body by making your back curve ⋛ *She bent down to look at the tiny insects.* ⋛
2 to bend is to curve ⋛ *He bent the wire around the post.* ⋛

NOUN *plural* **bends**

a curve ⋛ *a bend in the road* ⋛

▸ **bend the rules**

to break the rules in a way that will not be noticed or is not very important

▸ **bendy**

ADJECTIVE **bendier, bendiest**

1 with bends in it ⋛ *bendy knees* ⋛
2 able to bend easily ⋛ *a bendy piece of rubber* ⋛

bent

VERB

a way of changing the verb **bend** to make a past tense, either with or without a helping verb ⋛ *The striker bent the ball round the defenders.* ⋛ *I have bent this fork. Can I have another one?* ⋛

ADJECTIVE

not straight ⋛ *a bent pin* ⋛

beside

PREPOSITION

1 next to or at the side of someone or something ⋛ *We do like to be beside the sea.* ⋛ *Go and stand beside Billy.* ⋛
2 compared with ⋛ *Beside that tiny kitten the dog looks enormous.* ⋛

▸ **beside yourself**

terribly upset ⋛ *She's beside herself with grief.* ⋛

best

ADJECTIVE

better than all the rest ⋛ *the best film they'd ever seen* ⋛

ADVERB

in the most suitable or pleasing way ⋛ *I know it's difficult but just do it as best you can.* ⋛ *The city is best seen at night when all the skyscrapers are lit up.* ⋛

NOUN

the most excellent things ⋛ *Parents want the best for their children.* ⋛

▸ **do your best**

to do as well as you can

▸ **make the best of something**

to enjoy something, or do as well as you can with it, even if it is not very good ⋝ *Although it was raining, we made the best of our trip to the seaside.* ⋜

better

ADJECTIVE

1 of a higher standard or more excellent ⋝ *This is a better way to do it.* ⋜

2 not as bad or as ill as before ⋝ *My cold's much better today.* ⋜ ⋝ *Don't go back to school until you're better.* ⋜

ADVERB

in a more pleasing or more suitable way ⋝ *Which do you like better, the green one or the blue one?* ⋜ ⋝ *Try to do better next time.* ⋜

▸ **better off**

in a better position ⋝ *We'd be better off taking the plane. We'd get there quicker.* ⋜

▸ **had better do something**

if you say you had better do something, you mean that you ought to do it ⋝ *I had better hurry, or I'll be late.* ⋜

NOUN

something of a higher standard than others ⋝ *Of the two players, Federer is definitely the better.* ⋜

▸ **get the better of someone**

to defeat someone ⋝ *You'll never get the better of him, no matter how long you argue.* ⋜

between

PREPOSITION

1 in the area or space that divides two people, things or places ⋝ *What letter comes between Q and S in the alphabet?* ⋜ ⋝ *the road between San Francisco and Los Angeles* ⋜

2 giving each a part or a piece ⋝ *Colin and Russell divided the work between them.* ⋜

3 including or involving each one ⋝ *They'll have to sort it out between them. We're not getting mixed up in it.* ⋜

4 one and not the other ⋝ *I had to decide between going to the concert or staying to watch the fireworks.* ⋜

ADVERB

things between or in between are in the middle ⋝ *He'd had a big breakfast, an enormous lunch and lots of snacks in between.* ⋜

Bible

NOUN *plural* **Bibles**

the holy book of the Christian and Jewish religions

▸ **biblical**

ADJECTIVE

to do with or in the Bible ⋝ *a biblical character* ⋜

bicycle

NOUN *plural* **bicycles**

a machine you ride on, made up of a metal frame with two wheels which are moved by pressing down on pedals with your feet

big

ADJECTIVE bigger, biggest

1 large ⋝ *a big truck* ⋜ ⋝ *It was the biggest fish he'd ever seen.* ⋜

2 older ⋝ *My big brother is 15.* ⋜ ⋝ *You won't be allowed to walk to school on your own until you're a lot bigger.* ⋜

3 important ⋝ *Are you going to watch the big match on TV?* ⋜

4 successful, popular or famous ⋝ *one of the biggest stars in Hollywood* ⋜

a b c d e f g h i j k l m n o p q r s t u v w x y z

bike

NOUN *plural* bikes

a bicycle

bill¹

NOUN *plural* bills

1 a piece of paper showing how much is owed for something, such as a meal in a restaurant or the supply of goods or services ⋛ *an electricity bill* ⋚
2 a poster or printed sheet listing or advertising something
3 a suggestion for a new law that people in parliament discuss and vote for or against

bill²

NOUN *plural* bills

a bird's beak

bin

NOUN *plural* bins

1 a container for putting rubbish in
2 a container for storing something ⋛ *a bread bin* ⋚

bird

NOUN *plural* birds

a creature with feathers growing on its body and which lays eggs ⋛ *Penguins are flightless birds.* ⋚

birth

NOUN *plural* births

1 birth is the process of being born ⋛ *Life is the time between birth and death.* ⋚
2 a birth is the time when a particular person or animal is born

birthday

NOUN *plural* birthdays

your birthday is the anniversary of the date when you were born

biscuit

NOUN *plural* biscuits

a kind of hard, baked cake made from dough

bit¹

NOUN *plural* bits

1 a piece or a part ⋛ *There was one bit of the book that I really enjoyed.* ⋚ ⋛ *The toy came to bits in my hand.* ⋚
2 a small amount ⋛ *I need a bit of help with this sum.* ⋚
3 a short time ⋛ *Let's wait a bit longer.* ⋚
4 a metal bar on a horse's bridle that the horse holds in its mouth

▸ **bit by bit**
gradually

bit²

VERB

a way of changing the verb **bite** to make a past tense

bite

VERB bites, biting, bit, bitten

1 you bite something when you cut through it by bringing your top and bottom teeth together ⋛ *He stumbled and bit his tongue.* ⋚
2 if an animal bites, it uses its teeth to attack or injure ⋛ *Be careful! The cat sometimes bites.* ⋚

NOUN *plural* bites

a cut or injury made with the teeth, or the part cut off by biting ⋛ *The dog gave the postman a nasty bite.* ⋚ ⋛ *Can I have a bite of your apple?* ⋚

> Be careful not to confuse the spelling of **bite** with **byte**, a unit of computer memory.

bitter

ADJECTIVE

1 bitter things have a sour rather than a sweet taste ⋛ *Lemon juice is bitter.* ⋚
2 if the weather is bitter, it is uncomfortably cold ⋛ *a bitter winter's night* ⋚
3 to be bitter is to be angry and resentful

because of disappointment ⟩ *He turned into a bitter old man who hated the world.* ⟨

black

NOUN

the darkest colour, the colour of coal or a dark night

ADJECTIVE blacker, blackest
of the colour black

VERB blacks, blacking, blacked

▸ **black out**
if someone blacks out, they become unconscious for a short time

blackboard

NOUN *plural* blackboards
a dark board for writing on with chalk

blame

VERB blames, blaming, blamed

1 to blame someone is to say that something is their fault ⟩ *I was nowhere near the window, so don't try to blame me.* ⟨
2 if you say that you do not blame someone, you mean you understand their reasons for doing something ⟩ *We shouldn't blame him for being angry.* ⟨

NOUN

1 blame is responsibility for something bad that has happened ⟩ *They were made to take the blame.* ⟨
2 you are to blame for something bad if you have caused it ⟩ *Who is to blame for this mess?* ⟨

blanket

NOUN *plural* blankets

1 a covering for a bed, usually made of wool or some other warm fabric
2 a layer that covers everything ⟩ *a blanket of snow* ⟨

blend

VERB blends, blending, blended
to put things together so that they are mixed

in with each other ⟩ *Blend the butter and the sugar.* ⟨

▸ **blend in**
if people or things blend in somewhere, they fit in well with the people or things around them

NOUN *plural* blends

a mixture of two or more things ⟩ *Banana milkshake is a blend of milk, banana and ice cream.* ⟨

▸ **blender**

NOUN *plural* blenders

a machine with a blade that turns quickly, used for mixing foods or liquids together ⟩ *Put the ingredients in a blender.* ⟨

blew

VERB

a way of changing the verb **blow** to make a past tense

blind

ADJECTIVE

not able to see ⟩ *New-born kittens are blind.* ⟨

VERB blinds, blinding, blinded
to make someone blind ⟩ *He was blinded in the war.* ⟨ ⟩ *The light blinded me for a moment.* ⟨

NOUN *plural* blinds
a covering for a window, used instead of curtains or to keep out strong sunlight ⟩ *I'll pull down the blinds.* ⟨

blink

VERB blinks, blinking, blinked
to close and open your eyes very quickly ⟩ *She blinked in the strong sunlight.* ⟨

blood

NOUN

the red liquid that carries oxygen and other substances round your body in veins

blouse

NOUN *plural* **blouses**

a shirt for girls or women

blow

VERB blows, blowing, blew, blown

1 wind blows when it moves around ⋗ *a breeze blowing from the west* ⋖
2 to blow something is to force air on to it or into it ⋗ *She managed to blow all the candles out in one go.* ⋖ ⋗ *You'd have to blow hard to inflate a balloon that big.* ⋖
3 to blow a musical instrument is to breathe into it to make a sound

▶ **blow something up**

1 to blow something up is to destroy it with an explosion ⋗ *Guy Fawkes plotted to blow up the Houses of Parliament.* ⋖
2 to inflate something such as a balloon by blowing air into it ⋗ *We got Dad to blow up the balloons.* ⋖

NOUN blows

1 a hard knock ⋗ *a blow to the face* ⋖
2 a sudden piece of bad luck ⋗ *Missing the train was a bit of a blow.* ⋖

blue

NOUN *plural* **blues**

the colour of the sky in the day time if there are no clouds

ADJECTIVE bluer, bluest

of the colour blue

blush

VERB blushes, blushing, blushed

to go pink in the face with embarrassment ⋗ *Everyone turned to look at Philip, who blushed.* ⋖

board

NOUN *plural* **boards**

1 a flat piece of cut wood
2 a flat piece of material with a pattern or divisions marked on it, used to play a game ⋗ *a chess board* ⋖

3 a group of people who manage a business company or other organization ⋗ *She's on the school's board of governors.* ⋖

▶ **on board**

on a ship or aircraft

VERB boards, boarding, boarded

to board a ship or an aircraft is to get on it to make a journey ⋗ *More passengers boarded at Carlisle.* ⋖

boast

VERB boasts, boasting, boasted

to talk proudly about things you own or things you have done, in a way that other people find annoying ⋗ *He's always boasting about his expensive trainers.* ⋖

NOUN *plural* **boasts**

something you say when you boast ⋗ *It was her proud boast that she always got the highest mark in her class.* ⋖

▶ **boastful**

ADJECTIVE

a boastful person is in the habit of talking proudly about what they own or what they have done

boat

NOUN *plural* **boats**

a vehicle for travelling over the surface of water. A boat is smaller than a ship

▶ **in the same boat**

if two or more people are in the same boat, they have the same problems or difficulties

body

NOUN *plural* **bodies**

1 the whole of a human being or an animal ⋗ *I had a rash all over my body.* ⋖
2 a dead person or animal ⋗ *They found the bodies of hundreds of dead birds on the shore.* ⋖

boil[1]

VERB boils, boiling, boiled

1 something boils when it is heated until it

bubbles and turns into gas or vapour ⇒ *Is the water boiling yet?*

2 to boil a liquid is to heat it until it bubbles ⇒ *Boil some water in a saucepan and add the pasta.*

3 to boil food is to cook it in boiling water ⇒ *Are you going to boil or fry the potatoes?*

NOUN

a state of boiling ⇒ *Bring the water to the boil.*

boil²

NOUN *plural* **boils**

a boil is a red painful swelling on the skin caused by an infection

bomb

NOUN *plural* **bombs**

an object that is designed to explode and cause damage or injuries

VERB bombs, bombing, bombed

to bomb a place is to drop bombs on it or explode a bomb in it

bone

NOUN *plural* **bones**

1 bone is the hard substance that forms a skeleton and supports the flesh and muscle in the body

2 a bone is one of the pieces of a skeleton ⇒ *He broke a bone in his arm.*

bonfire

NOUN *plural* **bonfires**

a large fire built outside

book

NOUN *plural* **books**

pages joined together and given a cover

VERB books, booking, booked

if you book something such as tickets for an event or a table in a restaurant, you tell the company that you want it and will pay for it ⇒ *Mum is booking our holiday today.*

boot

NOUN *plural* **boots**

1 a kind of shoe that covers the ankle and often part of the leg

2 the part at the back of a car where you carry things

VERB boots, booting, booted

to boot something is to kick it ⇒ *Georgie booted the ball right over the bar.*

border

NOUN *plural* **borders**

1 the border between two countries or areas is the line on the map which separates them ⇒ *They settled near the Canadian and United States border.*

2 an edge of something or a strip round its edge ⇒ *a pillowcase with a lace border*

VERB borders, bordering, bordered

▸ **border on**

one thing borders on another when the first thing is very close to the second thing ⇒ *Jumping off that wall borders on stupidity.*

bore¹

VERB bores, boring, bored

if something bores you, it makes you feel tired and fed up because it doesn't interest you ⇒ *The speech bored him.*

NOUN *plural* **bores**

someone or something that makes you feel tired and fed up ⇒ *It was a real bore having to sort all the papers.*

> Be careful not to confuse the spelling of **bore** with **boar**, which means a male pig.

bore²

VERB bores, boring, bored

to bore something is to use a drill, or

a b c d e f g h i j k l m n o p q r s t u v w x y z

something that works like a drill, to make a hole in or through that thing ⊰ *The insect bores a tiny hole in the fruit.* ⊱

bore³

VERB

a way of changing the verb **bear** to make a past tense

bored

ADJECTIVE

if you are bored, you feel tired and fed up because you are doing something that isn't interesting, or because you have nothing to do ⊰ *I'm bored. Let's go out and play.* ⊱

boring

ADJECTIVE

not at all interesting ⊰ *a long boring journey* ⊱

born

VERB

1 a form of the verb **bear** that you use if you are talking about the birth of a baby or animal ⊰ *My sister was born three years ago.* ⊱
2 to be born is to come into existence ⊰ *A new star was born.* ⊱

ADJECTIVE

having a talent you seem to have been born with ⊰ *She's a born entertainer.* ⊱

borrow

VERB borrows, borrowing, borrowed

to borrow something is to take it with the owner's permission and give it back to them later ⊰ *Can I borrow your pencil for a minute, please?* ⊱

▶ **borrower**

NOUN *plural* borrowers

a person who borrows something

Try not to confuse **borrowing** and **lending**. If you **borrow** something *from* someone you get it from them and if you **lend** something *to* someone, you give it to them.

bossy

ADJECTIVE bossier, bossiest

someone who is bossy likes telling other people what to do ⊰ *Stop being so bossy. You're not in charge here.* ⊱

both

ADJECTIVE

you use 'both' to refer to two people or things when you mean the one and also the other ⊰ *She ate both cakes, and I didn't get one.* ⊱ ⊰ *Both the boys are good at tennis.* ⊱

PRONOUN

two people or things together ⊰ *John and Andrew are nice boys – I like them both.* ⊱ ⊰ *Both of these chairs are broken.* ⊱

bottle

NOUN *plural* bottles

a container with a narrow neck used for holding liquids like milk, lemonade or wine

VERB bottles, bottling, bottled

to bottle a liquid is to put it in a bottle

▶ **bottle something up**

if someone bottles up unpleasant feelings, they avoid talking about them, even though this might make them feel better

box 27

bottom

NOUN *plural* **bottoms**

1 the lowest part of something ⇒ *the bottom of the stairs* ⇒ *the bottom of the sea*
2 the part of your body that you sit on
3 the lowest position ⇒ *the team at the bottom of the league*

ADJECTIVE

in the lowest position, with other things above ⇒ *the bottom shelf*

bought

VERB

a way of changing the verb **buy** to make a past tense. It can be used with or without a helping verb ⇒ *She bought me an ice cream.* ⇒ *Mum has bought a new car.*

bounce

VERB bounces, bouncing, bounced

1 to bounce is to jump up and down quickly on a springy surface ⇒ *We bounced on the trampoline.*
2 a ball bounces when it hits something hard and moves away again in another direction

▸ **bouncy**

ADJECTIVE bouncier, bounciest

springy and able to move up and down

bound

VERB bounds, bounding, bounded

to run with jumping movements ⇒ *The dogs bounded into the room, barking excitedly.*

NOUN *plural* **bounds**

a leap or jumping movement ⇒ *The deer was over the fence in a single bound.*

bow¹ rhymes with **cow**

VERB bows, bowing, bowed

1 if you bow to someone, you bend your head or the top half of your body forward to greet them or show them respect ⇒ *Everyone bowed to the king and queen.*
2 if you bow your head, you look at the ground because you are ashamed

NOUN *plural* **bows**

a bending of the head or body ⇒ *The pianist took a bow when the audience clapped.*

bow² rhymes with **cow**

NOUN *plural* **bows**

the pointed front part of a ship or boat

bow³ rhymes with **show**

NOUN *plural* **bows**

1 a weapon for shooting arrows, made from a curved piece of wood with a string stretched between its two ends
2 a wooden rod with a string stretched along it, used for playing a musical instrument such as a violin
3 a knot made with loops on either side

bowl

NOUN *plural* **bowls**

1 a wide container open at the top and used for holding various things ⇒ *a soup bowl*
2 anything round and hollow that is shaped like this kind of container, such as a sports stadium

VERB bowls, bowling, bowled

to bowl is to throw the ball towards the person batting in cricket and rounders

box

NOUN *plural* **boxes**

a container, sometimes with a lid, used for holding or storing things

VERB boxes, boxing, boxed

1 to box something is to put it in a box or boxes
2 people box when they hit each other with their fists

▸ **boxer**

NOUN *plural* **boxers**

someone who does the sport of boxing

▸ **boxing**

NOUN

a sport in which two people hit each other

a b c d e f g h i j k l m n o p q r s t u v w x y z

with their fists, usually while wearing heavy leather gloves

boy
NOUN *plural* **boys**

a male child

> Be careful not to confuse the spelling of **boy** with **buoy**, a floating object on the sea.

bracelet
NOUN *plural* **bracelets**

a piece of jewellery that you wear around your wrist

Brahma
NOUN

in Hinduism, Brahma is the god who created the world

brain
NOUN *plural* **brains**

the organ inside your skull that controls all the other parts of your body and with which you think

branch
NOUN *plural* **branches**

1 any of the parts of a tree that grow out from the trunk ⇒ *Rooks build their nests high in the branches of trees.* ⇐
2 one of the shops or businesses that belong to a larger organization ⇒ *the local branch of the bank* ⇐

VERB branches, branching, branched

to form branches or to separate into different parts like the branches of a tree ⇒*The road branches to the north and west.* ⇐

brass
NOUN

a metal made by mixing two other metals, copper and zinc

brave
ADJECTIVE braver, bravest

able to face danger without fear, or able to suffer pain without complaining ⇒ *It was brave of you to chase away that bull.* ⇐

▶ **bravely**
ADVERB

in a brave way ⇒ *She smiled bravely, though she was in pain.* ⇐

▶ **bravery**
NOUN

being brave ⇒ *an award for bravery* ⇐

bread
NOUN

a food whose main ingredient is flour. Bread is baked in an oven and is often cut into slices for making sandwiches and toast

break
VERB breaks, breaking, broke, broken

1 something breaks when it falls to pieces ⇒ *The vase fell over and broke.* ⇐
2 to break something is to cause it to fall to pieces, usually by dropping it or hitting it against something ⇒ *Careful, or you'll break that glass.* ⇐
3 to break a law is to do something that law forbids
4 to break news is to tell it ⇒ *I didn't want to break the bad news to them before they had finished their holiday.* ⇐
5 to break a record is to improve on what the previous record holder has done

▶ **break down**
if a machine breaks down it stops working

▶ **break in**
if someone breaks in to a locked building, they force their way in

▶ **break off**
if you break off what you are doing, you stop doing it for a while

▶ **break out**
fire, fighting or a disease breaks out when it starts suddenly

▸ **break up**

school breaks up when the term finishes and the teachers and pupils go on holiday

NOUN   *plural* **breaks**

1 a opening or crack in something ⋛ *a break in the clouds* ⋚   ⋛ *Colin had a bad break in his leg.* ⋚
2 a pause ⋛ *a break in her studies* ⋚
3 a piece of good luck ⋛ *It was a lucky break finding someone to buy your old bike.* ⋚

▸ **breakable**

ADJECTIVE

something breakable can be broken if you don't handle it carefully

> The words **break** and **brake** sound the same but remember that they have different spellings. To **brake** is to slow down or stop.

breakfast

NOUN   *plural* **breakfasts**

a meal people eat in the morning soon after getting out of bed

breath

NOUN   *plural* **breaths**

1 you take a breath when you fill your lungs with air and then let the air out again ⋛ *Take a few deep breaths.* ⋚
2 your breath is the air that comes out of your mouth ⋛ *We could see our breath in the freezing air.* ⋚

> Remember that the verb **breathe** has an **e** at the end, and the noun **breath** does not. Be careful not to confuse the spelling of the verb **breathes** with **breaths**, which means more than one breath.

breathe

VERB   breathes, breathing, breathed

to take in air through your mouth or nose, and blow air back out through your mouth or nose ⋛ *I found it hard to breathe.* ⋚

brick

NOUN   *plural* **bricks**

a block of baked clay used for building ⋛ *a pile of bricks* ⋚   ⋛ *a wall made of brick, not stone* ⋚

bridge

NOUN   *plural* **bridges**

1 a structure built over a river, road or valley, to allow people or vehicles to cross from one side to the other
2 a platform on a ship where the captain usually stands
3 the bridge of your nose is the bony part

bright

ADJECTIVE   brighter, brightest

1 giving out a lot of light or having a lot of light ⋛ *the bright lights of the city* ⋚   ⋛ *a nice bright bedroom* ⋚
2 a bright colour is strong and clear ⋛ *His eyes were bright blue.* ⋚
3 cheerful, happy and interested in what is going on around you ⋛ *Grandad was a lot brighter this morning.* ⋚
4 a bright person is clever ⋛ *She's bright but she's a bit lazy.* ⋚

▸ **brighten**

VERB   brightens, brightening, brightened

1 to become sunnier ⋛ *The weather had brightened, so we went out for a walk* ⋚
2 to make someone more cheerful and happy ⋛ *This good news brightened everyone up.* ⋚

▸ **brightly**

ADVERB

in a bright way ⇒ *The sun shone brightly.*

▸ **brightness**

NOUN

being bright

bring

VERB brings, bringing, brought

1 to bring is to take, lead or carry a person or thing with you ⇒ *You can bring all your friends to the party.* ⇒ *He'd brought a couple of jigsaws out of the cupboard.*
2 if one thing brings another the first thing causes the second to come ⇒ *The drought brought famine to the area.* ⇒ *Dad's job brings him into contact with a lot of famous people.*

▸ **bring about**

if one event brings about another, the first causes the second ⇒ *Scientists say that changes in climate are brought about by global warming.*

▸ **bring up**

1 to bring up a subject is to mention it ⇒ *You shouldn't have brought up the subject of money.*
2 to bring up children or young animals is to look after them until they are old enough to look after themselves ⇒ *Oliver Twist was brought up in an orphanage.*
3 if someone brings up their food, they vomit

broad

ADJECTIVE broader, broadest

1 wide ⇒ *a broad avenue* ⇒ *My feet are small but broad.*
2 a broad accent or dialect is strong or noticeable ⇒ *He wrote poetry in broad Scots.*

▸ **broaden**

VERB broadens, broadening, broadened

to make something wider ⇒ *They'd broadened the road and made two lanes.*

▸ **broadly**

ADVERB

1 widely ⇒ *Jack was smiling broadly.*
2 generally ⇒ *Your answer is broadly right but a few of the details are incorrect.*

▸ **broadness**

NOUN

being broad

broke[1]

VERB

a way of changing the verb **break** to make a past tense ⇒ *She always broke their toys, but she didn't mean to.*

broke[2]

ADJECTIVE

having no money ⇒ *I can't afford a new game – I'm completely broke.*

broken

VERB

a form of the verb **break** that is used with a helping verb to show that something happened in the past ⇒ *Did you know Alan has broken his leg?*

ADJECTIVE

with a break or breaks ⇒ *a broken window*

broomstick

NOUN plural broomsticks

a long handle with thin sticks tied to one end that witches are supposed to ride on

brother

NOUN plural brothers

your brother is a boy or man who has the same parents as you do

brought

VERB

a way of changing the verb **bring** to make a past tense. It can be used with or without a helping verb ⇒ *Jeremy brought me a cup* *of hot tea.* *I have brought a box of chocolates for you.*

brown

NOUN

the colour of soil and most kinds of wood, made by mixing red, yellow and blue

ADJECTIVE   browner, brownest

of the colour brown

bruise

NOUN   *plural* bruises

a mark on the skin caused by a knock or blow *He's got a big bruise just under his eye.*

VERB   bruises, bruising, bruised

to make a bruise on skin, or to become marked by a bruise *Daniel bruised his knees when he fell.* *These ripe peaches will bruise easily.*

brush

NOUN   *plural* brushes

a device with tufts of bristles used to smooth hair, paint with, or clean dirt or dust away

VERB   brushes, brushing, brushed

1 to make something tidy or clean using a brush *Have you brushed your hair?*
2 to touch something lightly with part of your body *I brushed against the desk on my way past.*

bubble

NOUN   *plural* bubbles

1 a very thin, light ball of liquid filled with air *soap bubbles*
2 a small ball of air inside a liquid *We could see the air bubbles in the water.*

VERB   bubbles, bubbling, bubbled

1 something bubbles when small balls of air form in it *A big pot of soup was bubbling away in the kitchen.*
2 if something bubbles up, it is forced up to the surface like bubbles rising in a liquid *Excitement was bubbling up inside her.*

▶ **bubbly**

ADJECTIVE   bubblier, bubbliest

1 full of bubbles *The paint had gone all bubbly in the heat of the sun.*
2 full of energy and life *She has a bubbly personality.*

bucket

NOUN   *plural* buckets

1 a container, usually with a handle, used for carrying water or things like earth, sand or cement
2 the amount that a bucket will hold *four buckets of water*

bud

NOUN   *plural* buds

the part of a plant from which a leaf or flower develops

VERB   buds, budding, budded

a plant buds when its buds start to show

Buddhism

NOUN

a religion, practised in many parts of the world, that follows the teachings of Buddha

▶ **Buddhist**

NOUN   *plural* Buddhists

someone who follows the teachings of Buddha

ADJECTIVE

to do with Buddhism or Buddhists

bug

NOUN   *plural* bugs

1 a small insect, especially one that bites
2 a germ that causes illness *She had a tummy bug.*
3 a tiny hidden microphone used to record secretly what people say
4 **ICT** a fault in a computer program that stops it working properly

VERB bugs, bugging, bugged

1 **slang** to bug someone is to annoy them
2 to bug a room or a telephone is to put a hidden microphone in it to record what people say

build

VERB builds, building, built

1 to create something is to put together its parts bit by bit ⫸ *He's building a wall.* ⫷ ⫸ *Milk builds healthy teeth and bones.* ⫷
2 to create something by working on it ⫸ *You build close friendships through trust.* ⫷

▸ **build up**

1 if something builds up, it increases ⫸ *If you heat the container, the air pressure builds up inside.* ⫷
2 if something builds you up, it makes you stronger

NOUN

your build is the shape of your body ⫸ *He's got a strong, muscular build.* ⫷

building

NOUN plural buildings

1 building is the trade or action of making houses and other structures ⫸ *There is a lot of building going on in this street.* ⫷
2 a building is a house or other structure ⫸ *New York has lots of tall buildings.* ⫷

bulb

NOUN plural bulbs

1 a glass globe with an electrical part inside that gives out light ⫸ *The bulb's gone in my bedside lamp.* ⫷
2 the rounded part of plants like onions or tulips that the rest grows out of ⫸ *daffodil bulbs* ⫷

bull

NOUN plural bulls

1 a male cow
2 a male elephant or a male whale

bully

NOUN plural bullies

a person who is cruel to people smaller or weaker than they are

VERB bullies, bullying, bullied

to be cruel to smaller or weaker people

bump

NOUN plural bumps

1 a knock or blow ⫸ *a bump on the head* ⫷
2 a raised or swollen part on the surface of something ⫸ *a road with speed bumps to slow the traffic down* ⫷

VERB bumps, bumping, bumped

to bump something is to knock it by accident ⫸ *Try not to bump my arm when I'm writing.* ⫷ ⫸ *The baby bumped her head on the table.* ⫷

▸ **bump into**

if you bump into someone, you meet them by chance ⫸ *I bumped into Helen yesterday.* ⫷

bun

NOUN plural buns

a kind of cake made with sweet dough ⫸ *a currant bun* ⫷

bunch

NOUN plural bunches

1 a group of things tied or growing together ⫸ *a bunch of grapes* ⫷ ⫸ *He carried a big bunch of keys.* ⫷
2 **informal** a group of people ⫸ *Josh's friends are a nice bunch.* ⫷

VERB bunches, bunching, bunched

▸ **bunch together** or **bunch up**

to bunch together, or to bunch up, is to be or move close together ⫸ *Don't all bunch together – keep to your positions on the pitch.* ⫷

burglar

NOUN plural burglars

a criminal who breaks into a house or other building to steal things

▶ **burglary**

NOUN   *plural* **burglaries**

the crime of breaking into houses to steal things

burn

VERB   burns, burning, burnt

1 to burn something is to set fire to it ⫶ *Be careful with that wok or you'll burn the house down.* ⫶
2 to burn is to be on fire ⫶ *We could see the grass burning from miles away.* ⫶
3 if something burns you, it injures you by burning or being very hot ⫶ *The soup burnt his tongue.* ⫶

NOUN   *plural* **burns**

an injury or mark left after touching fire or something very hot

burrow

NOUN   *plural* **burrows**

a hole in the ground made by a rabbit or other animal

VERB   burrows, burrowing, burrowed

to burrow is to make a hole in the ground

burst

VERB   bursts, bursting, burst

to break or tear, especially from being put under too much pressure ⫶ *He blew and blew until the balloon burst.* ⫶

▶ **burst in**

to burst in is to come in suddenly and noisily ⫶ *He burst in just as I was falling asleep.* ⫶

ADJECTIVE

broken or torn ⫶ *a burst tyre* ⫶

NOUN

a short time when you do or feel something a lot ⫶ *a burst of energy* ⫶

bury

VERB   buries, burying, buried

1 to bury a dead person is to put their body in the ground

2 to bury something is to cover or hide it ⫶ *She buried her face in her hands.* ⫶

bus

NOUN   *plural* **buses**

a large vehicle with lots of seats for passengers

bush

NOUN   *plural* **bushes**

1 a plant that has many leaves and is smaller than a tree ⫶ *a rose bush* ⫶
2 **geography** the bush is wild areas in hot countries, where nobody lives and where only wild plants grow ⫶ *walking in the Australian bush* ⫶

▶ **bushy**

ADJECTIVE   bushier, bushiest

1 covered with bushes
2 growing thickly ⫶ *a long bushy tail* ⫶

business

NOUN   *plural* **businesses**

1 business is buying and selling, and the work of producing things that people want to buy ⫶ *Dad has gone into business with Uncle Frank.* ⫶
2 a business is any company that makes and sells goods, or that sells services
3 someone's business is their work or trade ⫶ *What business is Tom's mother in?* ⫶
4 your business is the things that involve you only, which other people should not ask about or become involved in ⫶ *It's none of your business what I spend my pocket money on!* ⫶

busy

ADJECTIVE   busier, busiest

1 someone is busy when they have a lot to do ⫶ *Dad's busy making lunch in the kitchen.* ⫶
2 if a place or a road is busy there are lots of people or a lot of traffic in it ⫶ *London's busy streets* ⫶

a
b
c
d
e
f
g
h
i
j
k
l
m
n
o
p
q
r
s
t
u
v
w
x
y
z

but

CONJUNCTION

1 **but** is used between parts of a sentence to show that there is a difference between the first part and the second part ⋗ *I can write stories but I can't draw very well.* ⋖ ⋗ *I'd like to go to the cinema but I don't have any money.* ⋖

2 **but** is also used between parts of a sentence to mean 'except' ⋗ *You are nothing but a liar.* ⋖

PREPOSITION

except ⋗ *No one but me turned up.* ⋖

butter

NOUN

a yellow fatty food made from milk and used to spread on bread or for cooking

VERB butters, buttering, buttered

to spread butter on bread or toast ⋗ *Mum buttered and filled about two hundred sandwiches for the party.* ⋖

butterfly

NOUN *plural* butterflies

a kind of insect with brightly coloured patterned wings

button

NOUN *plural* buttons

1 a round object used to fasten clothes

2 something you press to make a machine work

3 **ICT** a small shape on a computer screen that you click on with the mouse or the keyboard to make something happen

VERB buttons, buttoning, buttoned

to fasten with buttons

buy

VERB buys, buying, bought

to buy something is to give money so that it becomes yours ⋗ *I've bought all their albums.* ⋖

▶ **buyer**

NOUN *plural* buyers

someone who buys something ⋗ *We couldn't find a buyer for our old computer.* ⋖

by

PREPOSITION

1 near to or next to something ⋗ *the big house by the station* ⋖

2 past someone or something ⋗ *He ran by me.* ⋖

3 through, along or across something ⋗ *We came by the north road.* ⋖

4 something is by someone when they are the person who has created it ⋗ *a painting by Lowry* ⋖

5 something happens or is done by a certain time when it happens or is done no later than that time ⋗ *I'll be home by 7.30.* ⋖

6 by means of something ⋗ *go by train* ⋖

ADVERB

1 near ⋗ *They all stood by, watching but doing nothing to help.* ⋖

2 past ⋗ *The cars went whizzing by.* ⋖

3 aside ⋗ *Try to put some money by for an emergency.* ⋖

▶ **by the way**

something you say when you want to add something to what you have just said ⋗ *I've done my homework and fed the cat. By the way, there's no milk left.* ⋖

bye-bye

INTERJECTION

a more informal way of saying **goodbye**

cage

NOUN *plural* **cages**

a box or enclosure with bars where a bird or animal is kept so that it can't escape

VERB **cages, caging, caged**

to cage an animal or bird is to put it in a cage

▸ **caged**

ADJECTIVE

kept in a cage ⋛ ***caged birds*** ⋚

cake

NOUN *plural* **cakes**

a food made from flour, eggs, sugar and other ingredients mixed together and baked in an oven until they are firm ⋛ ***Do you like cake?*** ⋚ ⋛ ***a Christmas cake*** ⋚

calculator

NOUN *plural* **calculators**

an electric machine that you use to do sums quickly

calendar

NOUN *plural* **calendars**

a table or list that shows the days of the year with their dates, divided into weeks and months

calf¹

NOUN *plural* **calves**

1 a young cow
2 a young elephant, whale or deer

calf²

NOUN *plural* **calves**

the back part of your leg just below the knee where there is a big muscle

call

VERB **calls, calling, called**

1 to call is to shout ⋛ ***I heard him calling my name.*** ⋚
2 to call someone is to ask them to come to you ⋛ ***Mum called us in from the garden.*** ⋚
3 to call someone is to speak to them on the telephone ⋛ ***I'll call you later.*** ⋚
4 to call someone something is to give them that name ⋛ ***He's called Jonathan James.*** ⋚ ⋛ ***How dare you call me a liar.*** ⋚
5 to call at a place is to stop there for a short time ⋛ ***We'll call at the shop on the way home.*** ⋚

NOUN *plural* **calls**

1 a shout ⋛ ***calls for help*** ⋚
2 a telephone conversation ⋛ ***I had a call from David yesterday.*** ⋚
3 a short visit ⋛ ***I've got a couple of calls to make on the way home.*** ⋚

calm

ADJECTIVE **calmer, calmest**

1 still and quiet ⋛ ***a calm sea*** ⋚
2 not worried, excited or upset ⋛ ***I met him before the exam and he seemed very calm.*** ⋚

VERB **calms, calming, calmed**

▸ **calm down**

to calm, or to calm down, is to become quiet and still again after being noisy or disturbed ⋛ ***The boats can sail when the weather calms down.*** ⋚

▸ **calm someone down**

to calm someone down is to stop them being so excited or upset ⋛ ***She took a couple of deep breaths to calm herself down.*** ⋚

a b c d e f g h i j k l m n o p q r s t u v w x y z

▶ **calmly**

ADVERB

without feeling worried or excited ⋛ *Grace walked calmly on to the stage.* ⋚

▶ **calmness**

NOUN

being calm ⋛ *We were impressed by his calmness under pressure.* ⋚

came

VERB

a way of changing the verb **come** to make a past tense ⋛ *They came downstairs, laughing and shouting.* ⋚

camel

NOUN   *plural* **camels**

a desert animal with a long neck and one or two humps on its back for storing water

camera

NOUN   *plural* **cameras**

a device for taking photographs, or for making television programmes or films

camp

NOUN   *plural* **camps**

a place where people live in tents, huts or caravans, usually for a short time ⋛ *a refugee camp* ⋚

VERB   camps, camping, camped

to camp is to stay somewhere for a short time in a tent, hut or caravan ⋛*We camped in a clearing in the woods.* ⋚

▶ **camper**

NOUN   *plural* **campers**

someone who stays in a tent or hut, usually while they are on holiday

▶ **camping**

NOUN

if you go camping you go somewhere where you stay in a shelter like a tent, hut or caravan

can¹

VERB

1 to be able to ⋛ *Can you swim? Yes, I can.* ⋚
2 to be allowed to ⋛ *Can I go swimming? Yes, you can.* ⋚

can²

NOUN   *plural* **cans**

a metal container that food or drink is sold in

candle

NOUN   *plural* **candles**

a stick of wax that you burn to give out light

cannot

VERB

1 **cannot** is used with another verb to say that you are not able to do something ⋛ *I cannot read your writing.* ⋚
2 **cannot** is used with another verb when you are not giving permission for something ⋛ *No, you cannot have another slice of cake.* ⋚

canoe

NOUN   *plural* **canoes**

a light boat that is pointed at both ends and that you move through the water using a paddle

VERB   canoes, canoeing, canoed

to canoe is to paddle, or to travel in, a canoe

cap

NOUN   *plural* **caps**

1 a soft hat that often has a peak at the front

2 a small top for a bottle, tube or pen

VERB caps, capping, capped
to cap something is to put a covering or lid on it ⮞ *mountains capped with snow* ⮜

cape
NOUN *plural* capes
a kind of coat with no sleeves which is tied at the neck

capital
NOUN *plural* capitals
1 the capital of a country or state is the city where its government is based ⮞ *What's the capital of Sweden?* ⮜
2 a capital is a capital letter ⮞ *Write your name in capitals.* ⮜

ADJECTIVE
most important ⮞ *a capital city* ⮜

capital letter
NOUN *plural* capital letters
a letter like THESE LETTERS

captain
NOUN *plural* captains
1 an officer in charge of a ship, an aircraft or a company of soldiers
2 the leader of a sports team or a sports club

VERB captains, captaining, captained
to captain a ship or an aircraft, or a sports team, is to be its captain

car
NOUN *plural* cars
a vehicle with an engine and seats for a small number of passengers

caravan
NOUN *plural* caravans
a vehicle for living in, which can be towed behind a car

card
NOUN *plural* cards
1 card is thick, stiff paper

2 a card is a piece of thick, stiff paper used to give a greeting or information to someone ⮞ *a birthday card* ⮜ ⮞ *a business card* ⮜
3 cards, or playing cards, are a set of pieces of card used for playing games. They have numbers and symbols printed on one side
4 if you play cards, you play games like snap or rummy with a set of playing cards
▸ **on the cards**
something that is on the cards is likely to happen

cardigan
NOUN *plural* cardigans
a piece of knitted clothing worn on the top of the body, which has buttons down the front

Cardigans were named after the Earl of *Cardigan*, whose soldiers in the 19th century wore woollen jackets with buttons.

care
NOUN *plural* cares
1 care is the effort you make to do something well, or to avoid accidents ⮞ *Meg does her school work with great care.* ⮜ ⮞ *Handle these glasses with care.* ⮜
2 a care is something you worry about ⮞ *She doesn't have a care in the world.* ⮜
3 care is worried feelings ⮞ *We all want a life with as little care and trouble as possible.* ⮜

VERB cares, caring, cared
1 to care is to be concerned or interested ⮞ *He said he didn't care what happened.* ⮜ ⮞ *You can't care about the environment if you drop litter.* ⮜
2 to care for a child or an ill person is to look after them ⮞ *She wants to be a vet so that she can care for sick animals.* ⮜
3 if you say you care for something, it is a way of saying that you like it or want it ⮞ *I don't care much for fish.* ⮜

▸ **careless**

ADJECTIVE

not being careful or not paying close attention ⟫ *a careless mistake* ⟫ *He is a bit careless with his money.*

▸ **carelessly**

ADVERB

in a careless or clumsy way ⟫ *He threw his schoolbag carelessly on the ground.*

▸ **careful**

ADJECTIVE

making sure that you do something properly without making a mistake or causing an accident ⟫ *Dad is always careful to lock all the doors.* ⟫ *Be careful when you cross the road.*

▸ **carefully**

ADVERB

without making mistakes or causing damage

▸ **carer**

NOUN *plural* **carers**

1 someone who looks after an old or ill person, especially in their home
2 someone who brings up a child but is not the child's parent, for example a grandparent

career

NOUN *plural* **careers**

a job that someone has trained for and can get better positions as they get more experience ⟫ *She was keen to have a career as a lawyer.*

carpet

NOUN *plural* **carpets**

1 a covering for a floor made of wool or some other soft strong fabric
2 anything that forms a covering on the ground ⟫ *a carpet of primroses and bluebells*

VERB **carpets, carpeting, carpeted**

to carpet a floor is to cover it with a carpet

carrot

NOUN *plural* **carrots**

a long orange vegetable that grows under the ground

> The words **carrot** and **carat** sound the same but remember that they have different spellings. A **carat** measures gold and precious stones.

carry

VERB **carries, carrying, carried**

1 if you carry something, you pick it up and take it somewhere ⟫ *This bag is too heavy for me to carry.*
2 when sound carries, it travels over a long distance ⟫ *He has the sort of voice that carries.*

▸ **carry on**

1 to carry on is to continue ⟫ *Carry on with your work while I go and see the headmaster.*
2 to carry on is to behave badly ⟫ *Will you two stop carrying on like babies, please.*

▸ **carry something out**

to carry something out is to do it

▸ **get carried away**

if someone gets carried away, they get too excited by something ⟫ *He got a bit carried away by the music and started jumping up and down.*

carton

NOUN *plural* **cartons**

a cardboard container that drinks are sometimes sold in

case

NOUN *plural* **cases**

1 a suitcase ⟫ *Have you unpacked your cases yet?*
2 a container or covering ⟫ *The jewels are kept in a glass case.*

castle

NOUN *plural* castles

a type of large house with thick high walls and usually towers and battlements, which was built to protect the people inside from attack

cat

NOUN *plural* cats

1 an animal, often kept as a pet, that has soft fur and claws
2 any animal that belongs to the family of animals that includes cats, lions, leopards and tigers

catch

VERB catches, catching, caught

1 to catch something is to hold it and stop it from escaping ⋝ *Throw the ball and I'll try to catch it.* ⋜ ⋝ *He caught a fish but let it go again.* ⋜
2 to catch an illness is to get it ⋝ *Be careful not to catch a cold.* ⋜
3 to catch a bus or train is to be in time to get on to it ⋝ *Dad left early so that he would catch the 8.30 bus.* ⋜
4 to catch someone doing something bad is to discover them while they are doing it ⋝ *My sister caught me making faces at her.* ⋜
5 if you catch part of your body or your clothing you injure or damage it on something ⋝ *I caught my sleeve on the barbed wire.* ⋜

▸ **catch fire**
to start to burn and produce flames
▸ **catch up**
to catch up, or catch up with people who are ahead of you, is to reach the place where they are

NOUN *plural* catches

1 a fastening ⋝ *The catch on my bracelet has broken.* ⋜
2 a fisherman's catch is the number of fish he has caught
3 something that seems good at first has a catch if it has a disadvantage that you didn't know about ⋝ *The holiday was supposed to be free, but there was a catch, of course.* ⋜

▸ **catching**

ADJECTIVE

if an illness or disease is catching, it is infectious ⋝ *I hope that sore throat you have isn't catching.* ⋜

caterpillar

NOUN *plural* caterpillars

a small creature with a soft body that feeds on plants and leaves and which turns into a moth or butterfly

caught

VERB

a way of changing the verb **catch** to make a past tense. It can be used with or without a helping verb ⋝ *Emily caught a cold.* ⋜ ⋝ *She must have caught it from Sophie.* ⋜

cauliflower

NOUN *plural* cauliflowers

a large, round vegetable with a hard, white middle part made up of pieces that look like small trees

a b c d e f g h i j k l m n o p q r s t u v w x y z

cave

NOUN *plural* caves

a large hole in the side of a hill, cliff or mountain or under the ground

CD

ABBREVIATION CD's *or* CDs

short for **compact disc**, a small metal and plastic disc you can play to listen to music or look at pictures

celebrate

VERB celebrates, celebrating, celebrated

to celebrate something is to have a party or do something special because of it ⋗ **Everyone was celebrating the win.** ⋖

▸ **celebration**

NOUN *plural* celebrations

celebration or a celebration is something done to celebrate an event ⋗ **They've won money and are having a celebration.** ⋖

celebrity

NOUN *plural* celebrities

1 a celebrity is someone who is famous
2 celebrity is fame

cellar

NOUN *plural* cellars

an underground room used for storing things

cello said "**chel**-oh"

NOUN *plural* cellos

an instrument like a large violin that is held upright on the floor and played with a bow

centimetre

NOUN *plural* centimetres

a metric unit for measuring length, equal to one hundredth of a metre. This is often shortened to **cm**

centre

NOUN *plural* centres

1 the centre of something is its middle

point or part ⋗ **the centre of a circle** ⋖ ⋗ **chocolates with soft centres** ⋖
2 a centre is a building or group of buildings used for a particular activity ⋗ **a sports centre** ⋖

VERB centres, centring, centred

to centre something is to put it or place it in the centre

ceremony

NOUN *plural* ceremonies

a ceremony is an event where special forms or customs are used ⋗ **a wedding ceremony** ⋖

chain

NOUN *plural* chains

1 chain, or a chain, is several rings that are linked together
2 a chain of things is several things that are linked or connected ⋗ **a chain of events** ⋖
3 a chain of shops is several similar shops owned by the same person or company

chair

NOUN *plural* chairs

a chair is a piece of furniture with a back on which one person sits

VERB chairs, chairing, chaired

someone chairs a meeting when they are in charge of it

chalk

NOUN *plural* chalks

1 chalk is a kind of soft white stone
2 a chalk is a piece of this, often with a colour mixed through it, that is used to draw with

champion

NOUN *plural* champions

1 someone who has beaten all the others in a contest or competition ⋗ **the world boxing champion** ⋖
2 someone who is a champion of a cause is a strong supporter of that cause ⋗ **the champion of women's right to vote** ⋖

a b c d e f g h i j k l m n o p q r s t u v w x y z

VERB champions, championing, championed

to champion something is to support it strongly

▸ **championship**

NOUN *plural* championships

a competition or contest to decide the champion

chance

NOUN *plural* chances

1 a possibility ⟫ *Is there any chance that I'll be picked for the school team?*
2 an opportunity ⟫ *You didn't give me a chance to answer.*

▸ **by chance**

something that happens by chance happens when you have not planned it ⟫ *I met Alan by chance, when I was playing football in the park.*

▸ **take a chance**

to take a chance is to take a risk ⟫ *We didn't phone – we just took a chance that she'd be in.*

change

VERB changes, changing, changed

1 to change is to become different ⟫ *The leaves changed from green to golden brown.*
2 to change something is to make it different ⟫ *We've changed the garage into an extra bedroom.*
3 if you change, you put on different clothes
4 if you change schools, jobs or houses, you leave one and go to another
5 if you change your mind, your opinion changes

NOUN *plural* changes

1 a change is a difference
2 a change of clothes is a different set of clothes
3 change is money in the form of coins
4 change is the money that a customer gets back because they gave too much money when they paid for something

Chanukah

NOUN

another spelling of **Hanukkah**, a Jewish festival

chapter

NOUN *plural* chapters

one of the sections of a book ⟫ *Turn to chapter three in your history books.*

charity

NOUN *plural* charities

1 a charity is an organization that raises money to improve life for particular people, for example people with a disability
2 charity is kindness, especially in the form of money given to people who need it

chase

VERB chases, chasing, chased

to chase someone or something is to run after them

NOUN *plural* chases

a chase is a hunt for a person, animal or thing

chat

VERB chats, chatting, chatted

people chat when they talk to each other in a friendly way about everyday things

NOUN *plural* chats

a friendly talk

chatty

ADJECTIVE chattier, chattiest

if someone is chatty, they like to talk or chat to other people ⟫ *At first she was shy, but now she's become quite chatty.*

cheap

ADJECTIVE cheaper, cheapest

1 something cheap does not cost a lot ⟫ *a cheap fare*
2 something that is cheap is of little value ⟫ *a cheap imitation diamond*

▶ **cheaply**

ADVERB

without spending a lot of money ⇒ *You can eat quite cheaply at these cafés.*

cheat

VERB cheats, cheating, cheated

1 to cheat someone is to deceive them ⇒ *The man cheated the old lady out of all her savings.*

2 to cheat in a game or exam is to act dishonestly so that you gain an advantage ⇒ *It's cheating to look at someone else's cards.*

NOUN plural cheats

a cheat is someone who deceives people or tries to gain an advantage by behaving dishonestly

check[1]

VERB checks, checking, checked

1 to check something is to make sure that it is correct or that it is working properly ⇒ *Can you check these sums, please.*

2 to check something is to make sure that it is safe, or that it has definitely been done ⇒ *I'll just check that the back door is locked.* ⇒ *Check the soup to make sure it isn't boiling.*

3 to check something is to stop it ⇒ *He tried to check the bleeding by tying a handkerchief round his leg.*

▶ **check something out**

if you check something out, you find out about it ⇒ *Can you check out the times of the trains for me, please?*

NOUN plural checks

a test to see that something is correct or is working properly ⇒ *a health check* ⇒ *an oil check*

check[2]

NOUN plural checks

a pattern of squares ⇒ *trousers with a bold check*

▶ **checked**

ADJECTIVE

having a pattern of squares ⇒ *a checked skirt*

cheek

NOUN plural cheeks

1 your cheeks are the two areas of your face that stretch from below your eyes to your chin

2 cheek, or a cheek, is behaviour that people think is rude or offensive ⇒ *He didn't even thank me for the present. What a cheek!*

▶ **cheekily**

ADVERB

rudely and disrespectfully

▶ **cheeky**

ADJECTIVE cheekier, cheekiest

rude and showing lack of respect ⇒ *Don't be cheeky to your father!*

cheer

NOUN plural cheers

1 a cheer is a loud shout to someone to give them encouragement or to show that you think they are doing well

2 formal cheer is happiness and fun

VERB cheers, cheering, cheered

1 to cheer is to shout encouragement or approval ⇒ *They cheered each runner as he ran into the stadium.*

2 to cheer someone is to make them feel happier or more hopeful

▶ **cheer up**

to cheer up is to feel happier

▶ **cheer someone up**

to cheer someone up is to make them feel happier

cheerful

ADJECTIVE

1 a cheerful person behaves in a happy way

2 if a place is cheerful it is bright and pleasant and makes you feel comfortable or happy

cheerio

INTERJECTION

a word people use instead of 'goodbye' when they want to sound informal or friendly ⸲ *Cheerio, hope to see you tomorrow.* ⸴

cheese

NOUN   *plural* cheeses

a white or yellow food made from milk, which can be solid or soft

ADJECTIVE

made with or containing cheese ⸲ *a cheese sandwich* ⸴

chef said "shef"

NOUN   *plural* chefs

a person with special training who cooks in the kitchen of a restaurant or hotel

chemist

NOUN   *plural* chemists

1 someone who studies chemistry
2 someone who makes up medicines and medical prescriptions
3 a chemist's is a shop where medicines and toiletries are sold

cherry

NOUN   *plural* cherries

1 a kind of small, round, red fruit with a large stone inside
2 the tree that this fruit grows on

chew

VERB   chews, chewing, chewed

to chew is to break up food with the teeth before swallowing it

▸ **chew something over**

to think about something carefully for a while

▸ **chewy**

ADJECTIVE   chewier, chewiest

soft and sticky, or needing to be chewed

chicken

NOUN   *plural* chickens

1 a chicken is a hen, especially a young hen
2 chicken is the meat from a hen ⸲ *roast chicken* ⸴
3 **informal** a coward ⸲ *Jump! Don't be such a chicken.* ⸴

chief

NOUN   *plural* chiefs

1 a ruler or leader ⸲ *the chief of an African tribe* ⸴
2 a boss ⸲ *the chiefs of industry* ⸴

ADJECTIVE

main or most important ⸲ *the chief city of the region* ⸴

▸ **chiefly**

ADVERB

mainly ⸲ *They ate some meat but chiefly their diet consisted of roots and berries.* ⸴

child

NOUN   *plural* children

1 a young human being ⸲ *a child's view of the world* ⸴
2 a son or daughter ⸲ *Their children are grown up.* ⸴

▸ **childish**

ADJECTIVE

silly, and not grown-up ⸲ *a childish row* ⸴

▸ **childhood**

NOUN

the period of time in your life when you are a child ⸲ *memories of childhood* ⸴

a b c d e f g h i j k l m n o p q r s t u v w x y z

children

NOUN

the plural of **child** ⋟ *One child was late and the rest of the children had to wait.* ⋜

chilly

ADJECTIVE   chillier, chilliest

cold ⋟ *Shut the window. It's a bit chilly in here.* ⋜

chimney

NOUN   *plural* **chimneys**

a passage above a fire that allows smoke to escape

chimpanzee

NOUN   *plural* **chimpanzees**

a small African ape with black fur, a flat face and large brown eyes

chin

NOUN   *plural* **chins**

your chin is the part of your face that sticks out below your mouth

chip

VERB   chips, chipping, chipped

to chip something is to break a small piece off it ⋟ *Roy chipped one of his teeth playing rugby.* ⋜

▸ **chip in**

if someone chips in, they contribute to a discussion

NOUN   *plural* **chips**

1 chips are potatoes cut into strips and fried ⋟ *fish and chips* ⋜

2 a small piece broken off a hard object, or the place where a small piece has been broken off

chocolate

NOUN   *plural* **chocolates**

1 chocolate is a sweet food made from the beans of the cacao tree ⋟ *a bar of chocolate* ⋜

2 a chocolate is a sweet made with chocolate

choice

NOUN   *plural* **choices**

there is choice, or a choice, when you are able to decide which thing you will have because there is more than one thing available or on offer ⋟ *We were given a choice of meat or fish.* ⋜ ⋟ *He had to do it; he had no choice in the matter.* ⋜

ADJECTIVE   choicer, choicest

choice things are of the best quality available ⋟ *the choicest vegetables* ⋜

choir said "kwire"

NOUN   *plural* **choirs**

1 a group of singers ⋟ *He sings in the church choir.* ⋜

2 part of a church where the choir sings

choose

VERB   chooses, choosing, chose, chosen

to choose a person or thing from a group of people or things is to decide that you want that particular person or thing ⋟ *If you could have only one, which would you choose?* ⋜

chose

VERB

a way of changing the verb **choose** to make a past tense ⋟ *I wasn't made to do it; I chose to do it.* ⋜

chosen

VERB

a form of the verb **choose** that is used with a helping verb to show that something happened in the past ⋟ *John has been chosen for the football team.* ⋜

ADJECTIVE

being your choice ⋟ *your chosen career* ⋜

Christian

NOUN   *plural* **Christians**

someone who is a believer in Christianity and

follows the teachings of Jesus Christ

ADJECTIVE

to do with Christianity or Christians

▸ **Christianity**
NOUN

a religion, practised in many parts of the world, that follows the teachings of Jesus Christ

Christmas
NOUN

a Christian festival celebrating the birth of Christ and held on 25 December each year

church
NOUN   *plural* **churches**

a building where people, especially Christians, go to worship

cinema
NOUN   *plural* **cinemas**

1 a cinema is a place where films are shown on a big screen
2 cinema is films as an industry or an art form ⋛ *a career in cinema* ⋚

circle
NOUN   *plural* **circles**

1 a shape whose outside edge is an endless curving line, which is always the same distance away from a central point ⋛ *Draw one circle for the head and another for the body.* ⋚
2 a circle of people is a group of people who know each other, have something in common or do a particular thing together ⋛ *my circle of friends* ⋚
3 the circle in a theatre is the set of seats in one of the upper floors

VERB   circles, circling, circled

1 to circle is to go round and round ⋛ *vultures circling overhead* ⋚
2 to circle something is to draw a circle round it ⋛ *She circled the area on the map with a red marker.* ⋚

circus
NOUN   *plural* **circuses**

a type of travelling entertainment that usually includes clowns, acrobats, trapeze artistes, and often performing animals

> **Circus** is the Latin word for a *circle* or *ring*, so a circus is so called because it takes place inside a ring.

city
NOUN   *plural* **cities**

a large important town ⋛ *What's the biggest city in Europe?* ⋚

class
NOUN   *plural* **classes**

1 a group of schoolchildren or students who are taught together, or a period of time during which a particular subject is taught ⋛ *It was Megan's first day in Miss Smith's class.* ⋚   ⋛ *Mum is going to her aerobics class tonight.* ⋚
2 a grouping of people who have similar backgrounds or who belong to the same rank in society ⋛ *the working class* ⋚
3 a division of things according to how good they are ⋛ *He's a first-class student.* ⋚

VERB   classes, classing, classed

to class people or things is to put them in a grouping with others of the same type or rank ⋛ *Anyone under 16 is classed as a junior member.* ⋚

a b c d e f g h i j k l m n o p q r s t u v w x y z

classroom

NOUN *plural* classrooms

a room where lessons are given in a school or college

claw

NOUN *plural* claws

1 one of the long pointed nails on some animals' paws
2 a part on the end of a crab's or lobster's leg that it uses for gripping things

VERB claws, clawing, clawed

to claw something is to scratch it with claws or fingernails

clay

NOUN

soft sticky material found in the ground and used for making pottery

clean

ADJECTIVE cleaner, cleanest

1 if something is clean, it has no dirt or germs on or in it ⇒ *a clean face and hands* ⇒ *There was no clean water to drink.*
2 straight, without any jagged or rough edges ⇒ *It is a clean break so the bone should heal well.*
3 unused ⇒ *Take a clean sheet of paper and start again.*
4 fair and honest ⇒ *a clean game of football*

ADVERB

completely ⇒*It went clean through and out the other side.* ⇒ *He's gone clean mad.*

▶ **come clean**

if someone comes clean they tell the truth

VERB cleans, cleaning, cleaned

to clean something is to remove the dirt from it

▶ **clean up**

to clean up is to tidy a place, removing any dirt and rubbish

▶ **cleaner**

NOUN *plural* cleaners

1 a person whose job is to clean houses, offices or other buildings
2 a product for cleaning things ⇒ *lavatory cleaner*

clear

ADJECTIVE clearer, clearest

1 easy to see, hear or understand ⇒ *a clear view* ⇒ *She spoke in a clear voice.* ⇒ *His explanation wasn't very clear.*
2 see-through ⇒ *clear glass*
3 not blocked or marked by anything ⇒ *a clear sky* ⇒ *The road was clear.*
4 without meeting any difficulties or obstacles ⇒ *The way is clear for him to win the title.*

ADVERB

not near something and not touching it ⇒*Stand clear of the gates.*

VERB clears, clearing, cleared

1 to clear is to become clear ⇒ *The sky cleared and the sun came out.*
2 to clear things is to move them or tidy them away ⇒ *Whose turn is it to clear the dirty supper dishes?*
3 if someone is cleared of something, they are found to be not guilty or not to blame
4 to clear something is to jump over it without touching it ⇒ *Janey's pony cleared all the fences.*

▶ **clear off**

informal to clear off is to go right away from somewhere ⇒ *We had wandered on to his land and he told us to clear off.*

▶ **clear up**

if something such as a rash clears up, it goes away

▶ **clearly**

ADVERB

1 in a way that is easy to understand or see ⇒ *The rules are clearly explained.*
2 without any difficulty ⇒ *I can't see it very clearly.*

3 obviously ⇒ *Clearly, we couldn't continue without proper equipment.*

▸ **clearness**

NOUN

being clear

clever

ADJECTIVE cleverer, cleverest

1 quick to learn and understand things ⇒ *He's the cleverest boy in his class.*
2 skilful ⇒ *He's clever with his hands.*

climate

NOUN *plural* climates

geography the usual sort of weather there is in a region or area ⇒ *The Earth's climate is getting warmer.* ⇒ *plants that only grow in warmer climates*

climb

VERB climbs, climbing, climbed

to climb, or climb something, is to go up, or to go towards the top ⇒ *He likes to climb mountains.* ⇒ *We carried on climbing until we reached the top*

NOUN *plural* climbs

an act of climbing ⇒ *We had a steep climb to the top.*

▸ **climber**

NOUN *plural* climbers

1 someone who climbs, often as a pastime or sport
2 a plant that climbs up things like walls and fences

cloak

NOUN *plural* cloaks

1 a piece of clothing without sleeves that is worn over other clothing and hangs down loosely from the shoulders
2 anything that covers or hides ⇒ *the cloak of darkness*

VERB cloaks, cloaking, cloaked

to cloak something is to cover or hide it ⇒ *hills cloaked in mist*

clock

NOUN *plural* clocks

a machine for measuring time

close¹ said "kloas"

ADJECTIVE closer, closest

1 near in distance or time ⇒ *They are quite close in age.*
2 very dear or affectionate ⇒ *a close friendship*
3 tight, with little space ⇒ *a close fit*
4 thorough or careful ⇒ *Pay close attention.*
5 with no fresh air ⇒ *a close atmosphere*

ADVERB closer, closest

near ⇒ *He came close to winning.* ⇒ *She stood close by.*

▸ **closely**

ADVERB

1 at a close distance ⇒ *He came into the room, closely followed by his two friends.*
2 tightly ⇒ *closely packed sardines*

close² said "kloaz"

VERB closes, closing, closed

1 to shut, or shut something ⇒ *I didn't hear the door closing.* ⇒ *Will you close the window, please?*
2 to finish, or finish something ⇒ *They closed the concert by singing the national anthem.* ⇒ *Sports day closed with the boys' race.*

NOUN *plural* closes

1 the end of something ⇒ *at the close of day*
2 said "kloas"
a street that is blocked at one end

cloth

NOUN *plural* cloths

1 cloth is material made by weaving threads of wool, silk, cotton or some other fibre
2 a cloth is a piece of fabric

a b c d e f g h i j k l m n o p q r s t u v w x y z

clothes

PLURAL NOUN

the things that people wear to cover their bodies

cloud

NOUN *plural* clouds

1 clouds are masses of tiny water drops floating in the sky
2 a cloud of something is a mass of it in the air ⋗ *a cloud of dust* ⋖

VERB clouds, clouding, clouded

to become cloudy ⋗*The sky clouded over and it started to rain.* ⋖

clown

NOUN *plural* clowns

someone who works in a circus and does funny acts dressed up in ridiculous clothes

club

NOUN *plural* clubs

1 an organized group of people who meet regularly to take part in an activity, or the place where they meet
2 one of the metal sticks used in golf to hit the ball
3 clubs is one of the four suits of playing cards, which have the symbol ♣ printed on them
4 a place where adults go in the evening to dance and drink
5 a heavy piece of wood or metal used as a weapon

VERB clubs, clubbing, clubbed

▶ **club together**

if people club together, they each put some money in to buy something

clumsy

ADJECTIVE clumsier, clumsiest

a clumsy person often has accidents because they are careless or because they move in an awkward way

coach

NOUN *plural* coaches

1 a single-decker bus used to carry passengers over long distances
2 a person who trains someone in a particular skill or prepares them for a competition or performance ⋗ *a rugby coach* ⋖ ⋗ *a singing coach* ⋖
3 a railway carriage for passengers
4 a type of large four-wheeled carriage pulled by horses and used to carry passengers

VERB coaches, coaching, coached

to coach someone is to prepare them for a competition or performance

coast

NOUN *plural* coasts

geography the coast is the area of land next to the sea

▶ **coastal**

ADJECTIVE

beside the sea

coat

NOUN *plural* coats

1 a piece of clothing that usually reaches to your knees, with sleeves, and that you wear over your other clothes
2 a layer ⋗ *three coats of paint* ⋖

VERB coats, coating, coated

to coat something is to cover it with a layer of something ⋗*They'd coated their bodies with mud.* ⋖

cobweb

NOUN *plural* cobwebs

a criss-cross pattern of thin threads that a spider makes to catch insects

cocoa

NOUN

a hot drink made with the powdered seeds of the cacao plant, which are also used to make chocolate

coin

NOUN *plural* coins

a piece of metal money

cold

ADJECTIVE colder, coldest

1 low in temperature ⋛ *a cold drink* ⋛ ⋛ *It's too cold to go outside.* ⋛
2 unfriendly ⋛ *a cold stare* ⋛

NOUN *plural* colds

1 cold weather ⋛ *I don't like the cold.* ⋛
2 an illness caused by a virus which makes you sneeze and cough, and makes your nose run

▸ **coldly**

ADVERB

in an unfriendly way ⋛ *She treated them coldly.* ⋛

▸ **coldness**

NOUN

being cold

collect

VERB collects, collecting, collected

1 to collect things is to find them and gather them together ⋛ *He collects unusual postcards.* ⋛
2 to collect someone or something from a place is to go there and pick them up ⋛ *My dad collects me from school.* ⋛

▸ **collector**

NOUN *plural* collectors

someone who finds and gathers several things of the same type to make a collection ⋛ *a collector of antiques* ⋛

▸ **collection**

NOUN *plural* collections

a number of things that have been gathered together by one person or in one place ⋛ *a stamp collection* ⋛

colour

NOUN *plural* colours

1 colour, or a colour, is a quality that shows

up when light hits an object, for example, redness, blueness, yellowness, and so on ⋛ *What colour are your eyes?* ⋛ ⋛ *The sea was a lovely greenish-blue colour.* ⋛
2 a person's colour is the shade of their skin

VERB colours, colouring, coloured

to colour a picture is to add colours to it with paints or crayons

▸ **coloured**

ADJECTIVE

having colour ⋛ *a brightly coloured scarf* ⋛

comb

NOUN *plural* combs

1 an object with a row of teeth along one side that you use to make your hair tidy
2 a part that sticks up on the top of some birds' heads

VERB combs, combing, combed

1 to comb hair is to make it tidy using a comb
2 to comb a place is to search it carefully and thoroughly ⋛ *Detectives were combing the area for clues.* ⋛

combine

VERB combines, combining, combined

to combine things is to join or mix them together ⋛ *Combine all the ingredients in a mixing bowl.* ⋛

come

VERB comes, coming, came, come

1 to move towards the person speaking or to move to the place where they are ⋛ *Are you coming with us or not?* ⋛ ⋛ *They came by boat and train.* ⋛
2 to arrive or happen ⋛ *Has my parcel come yet?* ⋛ ⋛ *The mountains came into view.* ⋛ ⋛ *People come in all shapes and sizes.* ⋛

▸ **come about**

to come about is to happen ⋛ *How did this disagreement come about?* ⋛

▸ **come across someone** *or* **something**

to come across a person or thing is to meet

a
b
c
d
e
f
g
h
i
j
k
l
m
n
o
p
q
r
s
t
u
v
w
x
y
z

or find them by accident ﹥ *I came across a letter my great-grandmother had written in 1944.* ﹤

▸ **come by something**

to come by something is to get it ﹥ *Work was becoming harder and harder to come by.* ﹤

comet

NOUN　*plural* comets

a kind of star that travels across the sky trailing a tail of light behind it

comfortable

ADJECTIVE

1 something which is comfortable is pleasant to wear, sit in or be in ﹥ *a comfortable chair* ﹤　﹥ *a comfortable hotel* ﹤
2 someone who is comfortable has no pain, worry or trouble

▸ **comfortably**

ADVERB

in a way that feels pleasant, without any pain or trouble ﹥ *Are you all sitting comfortably?* ﹤

comma

NOUN　*plural* commas

the punctuation mark that looks like a small dot with a tail. You use it to separate parts of a sentence and make it easier to read, for example *Max put on his hat, his gloves, his coat and his scarf.*

Communion

NOUN

in the Christian Church, Communion is the ceremony celebrating the Last Supper of Jesus and his disciples

compare

VERB　compares, comparing, compared

1 to put two or more things together to show how they are similar or different, or which is better ﹥ *The weather today is lovely compared to last week.* ﹤
2 to describe someone or something as like

another person or thing ﹥ *She compared him to a mad dog.* ﹤

▸ **comparison**

NOUN　*plural* comparisons

putting two or more things together to show how they are similar or different

competition

NOUN　*plural* competitions

a contest between people who are each trying to win or be better than the others

▸ **competitive**

ADJECTIVE

a competitive person likes to compete and win against other people

▸ **competitor**

NOUN　*plural* competitors

someone taking part in a competition

complain

VERB　complains, complaining, complained

to say or write that you are not happy or satisfied ﹥ *He complained that it was too hot and that he hated the food.* ﹤

▸ **complaint**

NOUN　*plural* complaints

1 a statement that lets people know that you are not happy or satisfied
2 an illness

complete

VERB　completes, completing, completed

to complete something is to finish it or make it whole ﹥ *He completed the test in time.* ﹤

ADJECTIVE

1 with nothing missing ﹥ *a complete set of golf clubs* ﹤
2 finished ﹥ *When the dam is complete it will be over 150 metres high.* ﹤
3 total ﹥ *I felt a complete fool.* ﹤

▸ **completely**

ADVERB

totally ﹥ *I agree completely.* ﹤

▸ **completion**

NOUN

the process of finishing something, or the state of being finished ⧽ *The filming is nearing completion.* ⧼

computer

NOUN *plural* computers

an electronic machine that can store and work with very large amounts of information

▸ **computerize** *or* **computerise**

VERB computerizes, computerizing, computerized

to computerize a system or a set of information is to organize it so that it can be held in a computer's memory

▸ **computing**

NOUN

the operation of computers or the skill of working with computers

concert

NOUN *plural* concerts

a performance by musicians or singers

▸ **concerted**

ADJECTIVE

done together ⧽ *We must make a concerted effort to win this match.* ⧼

cone

NOUN *plural* cones

1 a solid shape with a round base and sides that slope up to a point at the top
2 a container of this shape made of wafer and used to hold ice cream

3 a fruit of a pine or fir tree containing its seeds

confident

ADJECTIVE

1 sure of yourself or of your ability to do something ⧽ *She's a very confident swimmer.* ⧼
2 sure that something will happen the way you expect it to ⧽ *I'm confident we'll find the lost children safe and well.* ⧼

▸ **confidence**

NOUN

1 confidence is being sure of yourself
2 if you have confidence in someone, you trust them

▸ **in confidence**

if you tell someone something in confidence, you expect them not to tell it to anyone else

confuse

VERB confuses, confusing, confused

1 to confuse things is to mix them up so that you think one thing is the other
2 if something confuses you, you aren't able to think clearly and don't know what to do or say next

▸ **confusing**

ADJECTIVE

difficult to follow or understand

▸ **confusion**

NOUN

being confused or mixed up

conjunction

WORD CLASS *plural* conjunctions

a word that links other words or parts of a sentence. For example, *and*, *but* and *or* are conjunctions

connect

VERB connects, connecting, connected

to connect things is to join them ⧽ *How do you connect the PC to the Internet?* ⧼

a b c d e f g h i j k l m n o p q r s t u v w x y z

▸ **connection**

NOUN *plural* connections

1 something that joins two things together
2 a train, bus or plane that you need to catch so that you can continue a journey ⋗ *We missed our connection to Dover because the train was late.* ⋖

▸ **in connection with**

to do with ⋗ *He is wanted by the police in connection with a theft.* ⋖

content¹ said "kon-**tent**"

ADJECTIVE

to be content is to be happy and satisfied

▸ **contented**

ADJECTIVE

a contented person is happy and satisfied

▸ **contentment**

NOUN

being happy with what you have

content² said "**kon**-tent"

NOUN *plural* contents

the content or contents of something are the things inside it

contest

NOUN *plural* contests

a competition ⋗ *a contest of strength* ⋖

▸ **contestant**

NOUN *plural* contestants

someone involved in a contest

continue

VERB continues, continuing, continued

1 to continue is to go on in the same way or in the same direction as before
2 to continue with something is to go on with it

conversation

NOUN *plural* conversations

talk or a talk between people ⋗ *He's not very good at making conversation.* ⋖ ⋗ *We had a long conversation about music.* ⋖

cook

VERB cooks, cooking, cooked

to cook food is to heat it by baking, frying, roasting or boiling

NOUN *plural* cooks

a cook is someone who prepares and cooks food

▸ **cooker**

NOUN *plural* cookers

a device in kitchens, used for cooking food

▸ **cookery**

NOUN

the skill or activity of cooking food

cookie

NOUN *plural* cookies

a biscuit

cool

ADJECTIVE cooler, coolest

1 slightly cold ⋗ *a cool drink* ⋖
2 calm and controlled ⋗ *If you find yourself in a dangerous situation, try to stay cool.* ⋖
3 not friendly ⋗ *He gave a cool reply.* ⋖
4 **informal** a way of describing someone or something you think is great ⋗ *He has a really cool haircut.* ⋖

copy

VERB copies, copying, copied

1 to copy something is to make another thing that looks exactly the same or nearly the same
2 **ICT** to copy a piece of information or a file on the computer is to make one that is exactly the same, so you can put it into another place as well
3 to copy something down is to write it down
4 to copy someone is to do the same thing that they do ⋗ *He copies everything his big brother does.* ⋖

NOUN *plural* copies

1 a copy is something that has been copied from something else

2 a copy of a book, magazine or newspaper is one of many that have been printed

cord

NOUN *plural* **cords**

1 cord is thin rope or thick string ⋛ *His hands were tied with cord.* ⋚
2 a cord is a thin rope ⋛ *a window cord* ⋚
3 an electric cable or flex

> The words **cord** and **chord** sound the same but remember that they have different spellings. A **chord** is a musical sound made of several notes.

corn

NOUN

wheat or a similar crop grown for food

corner

NOUN *plural* **corners**

1 a point where two roads, walls, edges or lines meet ⋛ *I'll meet you at the corner of George Street and Alexander Road.* ⋚
2 a place away from the main part or far away ⋛ *a secluded corner in the garden* ⋚ ⋛ *travelling to the far corners of the world* ⋚
3 in soccer and hockey, a kick or hit that you take from one of the corners at the opposing team's end of the pitch

VERB *corners, cornering, cornered*

to force a person or animal into a position from which they can't escape

correct

ADJECTIVE

1 right, not wrong ⋛ *The correct answer is 15.* ⋚
2 correct behaviour is the sort of behaviour that people like

VERB *corrects, correcting, corrected*

1 to correct something is to mark or change any mistakes or faults in it ⋛ *The teacher corrects our homework books.* ⋚

2 to correct someone is to tell them that what they have said or done is wrong

▶ **correction**

NOUN *plural* **corrections**

1 a correction is a mark or change made to correct a mistake
2 correction is checking and altering something to make it better or more accurate ⋛ *Hand in your exercise books for correction.* ⋚

corridor

NOUN *plural* **corridors**

a corridor is a passage in a building or train

cost

VERB *costs, costing, cost*

if something costs a certain amount of money, that is the amount you have to pay for it ⋛ *How much does a litre of milk cost?* ⋚

NOUN *plural* **costs**

the cost of something is the amount of money that has to be spent to buy it or make it

▶ **at all costs**

no matter what cost or suffering may be involved

cot

NOUN *plural* **cots**

a bed with high sides for a baby or young child to sleep in

> This word comes from the Hindi language of India. It comes from the word **khat**, which means *bedstead*.

cough

VERB *coughs, coughing, coughed*

you cough when you make a loud rough sound in your throat as you force air out of your lungs

NOUN *plural* **coughs**

1 the noise you make when you cough
2 an illness that causes you to cough

a b c d e f g h i j k l m n o p q r s t u v w x y z

could

VERB

1 you use **could** with another verb to say that something is or might be possible, or to ask politely if something is possible ⇒ *He could do it if he tried hard enough.* ⇒ *Could I have a drink of water, please?*
2 **could** is the past tense form of the verb **can** ⇒ *He could run fast when he was young.*

count

VERB counts, counting, counted

1 to count is to say numbers in order ⇒ *Can you count backwards from 10?*
2 to count something or to count something up is to work out the total ⇒ *He was busy counting his money.*
3 if something counts, it is important or has value ⇒ *Every school day counts.*
▸ **count on someone or something**
if you can count on someone or something, you can rely on them

NOUN plural counts

a count is a number of things to be counted ⇒ *The teacher did a head count before we left.*
▸ **keep count**
to keep count is to know how many things there are or have been
▸ **lose count**
to lose count is to forget how many you have already counted

country

NOUN plural countries

1 a nation or one of the areas of the world controlled by its own government
2 the land where certain people or animals live ⇒ *This is grizzly bear country.*
3 an area ⇒ *the West Country*
4 the country is the parts of the land away from towns and cities ⇒ *They live in the country.*

cousin

NOUN plural cousins

the son or daughter of your aunt or uncle

cover

VERB covers, covering, covered

1 to cover something or cover something up is to put or spread something else on or over it so that it is hidden ⇒ *She'd covered the table with a clean cloth.*
2 to cover a distance or period of time is to travel over that distance or stretch over that period of time ⇒ *We covered ten miles in three hours.* ⇒ *The history book covers the whole of Queen Victoria's reign.*
3 to cover something is to deal with it ⇒ *The local newspaper covered the story.* ⇒ *We'll need some cash to cover our expenses.*
▸ **cover something up**
to cover something up is to stop people from discovering the truth about it ⇒ *His actions since then had been merely to cover up the crime.*

NOUN plural covers

something that covers, hides or protects something else ⇒ *a bed cover*

cow

NOUN plural cows

1 a large animal kept on farms for its milk ⇒ *a dairy cow*
2 a female animal of the ox family or a female elephant or whale

crab

NOUN plural crabs

a sea animal with a broad shell and five pairs of legs. It has claws on its front pair of legs

crack

NOUN plural cracks

1 a narrow break or split
2 a sudden sharp sound ⇒ *the crack of a whip*
▸ **have a crack at something**
to try to do something

VERB cracks, cracking, cracked

1 to crack is to split or break so that a small

gap appears ⋛ *The ice had started to crack.* ⋚

2 to crack something is to split or break it so that a small gap appears ⋛ *She cracked an egg.* ⋚

3 to crack a joke is to make a joke

cradle

NOUN *plural* cradles

a baby's bed, especially one that can be rocked from side to side

VERB cradles, cradling, cradled

to cradle something is to hold it gently ⋛*She cradled his head in her arms.* ⋚

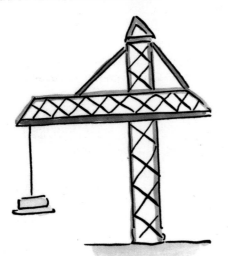

crane

NOUN *plural* cranes

1 a tall machine used to lift heavy weights, such as large boxes that have to be taken off a ship

2 a type of large bird with a long neck and long thin legs

VERB cranes, craning, craned

if you crane your neck, you stretch your neck as far as possible so that you can get a better view of something

crash

NOUN *plural* crashes

1 a loud noise, especially one made when something hard hits another hard thing

causing damage ⋛ *We were woken by a crash from the street.* ⋚

2 a car crash is an accident in which a car hits something else

3 a computer crash is when a computer suddenly stops working properly while you are using it, for example because it can't process the information

VERB crashes, crashing, crashed

1 to crash is to make a loud noise

2 to crash is to be involved in a car crash

3 if a computer crashes it suddenly stops working properly while you are using it, for example because it can't process the information

crawl

VERB crawls, crawling, crawled

1 if a person crawls, they move forwards on their hands and knees ⋛ *Pat had to crawl under the desk to get the pen she'd dropped.* ⋚

2 insects or reptiles crawl when they move about on their legs ⋛ *Look! There's a spider crawling up the wall behind you.* ⋚

3 to move at a very slow pace ⋛ *The traffic was crawling along at about 2 miles an hour.* ⋚

NOUN

1 a very slow pace ⋛ *We were moving forward at a crawl.* ⋚

2 the crawl is a way of swimming where you kick your legs and swing first one arm and then the other into the water ahead of you

crayon

NOUN *plural* crayons

a stick of coloured wax or a coloured pencil for drawing with

crazy

ADJECTIVE crazier, craziest

1 mad ⋛ *a crazy idea* ⋚ ⋛ *He's gone crazy.* ⋚

2 if you are crazy about someone or something, you love them or like them very much

cream

NOUN *plural* **creams**

1 a thick yellowish-white liquid that is separated from milk
2 a yellowish-white colour
3 a thick liquid that you put on your skin or hair ⇒ *suntan cream* ⇐

▶ **creamy**

ADJECTIVE **creamier, creamiest**

containing cream or thick like cream ⇒ *creamy milk* ⇐

create

VERB **creates, creating, created**

to create something is to make it or invent it, or to make it happen or exist ⇒ *They created a big fuss until they got what they wanted.* ⇐

▶ **creation**

NOUN *plural* **creations**

1 the creation of something is making it ⇒ *the creation of the universe* ⇐
2 a creation is something new that has been made ⇒ *one of the designer's latest creations* ⇐

▶ **creative**

ADJECTIVE

a creative person has the skill and imagination to make new things, especially works of art

creature

NOUN *plural* **creatures**

a living thing that is able to move about. Animals are creatures, but plants are not

crew

NOUN *plural* **crews**

a group of people who work together, especially on a ship or aeroplane ⇒ *The lifeboat has a crew of five.* ⇐ ⇒ *The film crew were busy setting up lights and cameras.* ⇐

VERB **crews, crewing, crewed**

to crew a boat or ship is to work as a member of its crew

cricket[1]

NOUN

a game played outdoors between two sides of eleven players with a wooden bat and ball

▶ **cricketer**

NOUN *plural* **cricketers**

someone who plays cricket

cricket[2]

NOUN *plural* **crickets**

a small insect that lives in grass. A cricket makes a high-pitched whirring sound by rubbing its wings together

cried

VERB

a way of changing the verb **cry** to make a past tense. It can be used with or without a helping verb ⇒ *The baby cried and cried.* ⇐ ⇒ *He had cried all day.* ⇐

cries

NOUN

the plural of the noun **cry** ⇒ *No one heard their cries for help.* ⇐

VERB

the form of the verb **cry** in the present tense that you use with **he**, **she** or **it** ⇒ *She always cries when she watches sad films.* ⇐

crime

NOUN *plural* **crimes**

1 a crime is an illegal activity, such as robbery, murder, assault or dangerous driving. Someone who has committed a crime can be punished by law
2 crime is all these activities

▶ **criminal**

NOUN *plural* **criminals**

someone who has committed a crime

ADJECTIVE

1 to do with crime or criminals ⇒ *a criminal court*
2 against the law or very wrong ⇒ *a criminal act*

crisp

ADJECTIVE   crisper, crispest

1 stiff or hard and easily broken ⇒ *nice crisp salad leaves*
2 crisp weather is frosty and dry

NOUN   *plural* crisps

a thin slice of potato that has been fried in oil until it is crisp ⇒ *a bag of crisps*

▶ **crispy**

ADJECTIVE   crispier, crispiest

hard or firm enough to break easily ⇒ *a crispy sugar topping*

croak

VERB   croaks, croaking, croaked

1 to croak is to speak in a hoarse voice because your throat is sore or dry
2 a frog croaks when it makes its deep harsh sound

NOUN   *plural* croaks

1 the sound made by a frog or toad
2 a low hoarse voice

▶ **croaky**

ADJECTIVE   croakier, croakiest

a croaky voice is deep and hoarse

crocodile

NOUN   *plural* crocodiles

a large reptile with thick skin, a long tail and big jaws. Crocodiles are found mainly in Africa and Australia and live in rivers and lakes

crop

NOUN   *plural* crops

1 crops are plants that are gathered or harvested for food from fields, trees or bushes
2 a crop is a particular kind of plant or fruit that grows and is harvested at one time ⇒ *We'll get a good crop of apples this year.*
3 a riding crop is a short whip used by jockeys and horse riders

VERB   crops, cropping, cropped

to crop something is to cut it short

▶ **crop up**

when something crops up, it happens without being expected or planned

cross

NOUN   *plural* crosses

1 a shape made when two straight lines go over each other at a point in the middle, ✕ or ✛
2 a symbol used in the Christian religion to stand for the cross on which Christ was killed
3 a mixture of two things, especially an animal or plant that has been bred from two different animals or plants ⇒ *A mule is a cross between a donkey and a horse.*

VERB   crosses, crossing, crossed

1 to cross something is to go over it from one side to the other ⇒ *cross a bridge*
2 if one thing crosses another, they meet at a certain point and go on beyond it ⇒ *at the place where the road crosses the railway line*
3 to cross things is to put one across and on top of the other ⇒ *cross your fingers*

a b c d e f g h i j k l m n o p q r s t u v w x y z

▸ **cross something out**

to cross something out is to draw a line or lines through it because you want to get rid of it or to replace it with something else ⋮ *He crossed out John's name and wrote in his own.* ⋮

ADJECTIVE crosser, crossest

annoyed or angry ⋮ *I got very cross when he didn't turn up.* ⋮

▸ **crossly**

ADVERB

angrily

crowd

NOUN *plural* **crowds**

a large number of people or things gathered in one place ⋮ *a football crowd* ⋮ ⋮ *crowds of shoppers* ⋮

VERB crowds, crowding, crowded

if people or things crowd in or into a place, they fill it up so that there is hardly any space left

▸ **crowded**

ADJECTIVE

full of people or things ⋮ *a crowded street* ⋮

crown

NOUN *plural* **crowns**

1 an ornament, often made of gold and studded with jewels, worn by a king or queen on their head during formal occasions
2 the top of something, such as your head or a hill

VERB crowns, crowning, crowned

1 a king or queen is crowned when they are made the monarch of a country in a ceremony where a crown is put on their head
2 to crown something is to add something on top ⋮ *We had a very long tiring journey, and to crown it all, our luggage was lost at the airport.* ⋮

cruel

ADJECTIVE crueller, cruellest

someone who is cruel causes pain or suffering to other people without showing any pity

▸ **cruelty**

NOUN

being cruel and having no pity

cry

VERB cries, crying, cried

1 to cry is to shout ⋮ *He cried out in pain.* ⋮
2 you cry when tears fall from your eyes, and often make a sobbing or wailing sound at the same time

NOUN *plural* **cries**

a shout

▸ **a far cry**

if people say that one thing is a far cry from another, they mean it comes nowhere near or is nothing like that other thing

cub

NOUN ·*plural* **cubs**

1 a baby lion, tiger, bear or wolf
2 a member of the Cub Scouts, the junior branch of the Scout Association

cube

NOUN *plural* **cubes**

1 a solid shape with six equally sized square sides
2 **maths** the cube of a number is the number you get when you multiply the number by itself twice. For example, the cube of 2 is $2 \times 2 \times 2$, which is 8. Look up and compare **square**

cup

NOUN *plural* **cups**

1 a small container with a handle that you drink out of ⋮ *cups and saucers* ⋮
2 a decorated metal object or container used as a prize in a competition ⋮ *the World Cup* ⋮

VERB cups, cupping, cupped

to cup your hands is to put them together and bend them into a bowl shape

cupboard said "**kub**-ed"

NOUN *plural* cupboards

a piece of furniture with doors on it and sometimes shelves inside it, used for storing things in

cure

VERB cures, curing, cured

1 to cure a disease or illness is to make it go away
2 to cure a problem is to solve it and make it go away
3 to cure meat is to put salt on it or dry it to make it last longer

NOUN *plural* cures

something that makes a disease or illness go away ⇒ *a cure for cancer*

curl

NOUN *plural* curls

a soft twist or ring of hair ⇒ *blonde curls*

VERB curls, curling, curled

1 to curl hair is to form soft twists or rings in it
2 smoke curls when it moves upwards in twisted or curving shapes

▶ **curl up**

to tuck your legs and arms in close to your body and bend your back in a curve

curly

ADJECTIVE curlier, curliest

having a curl or curls ⇒ *a curly tail* ⇒ *curly hair*

curry

NOUN *plural* curries

a type of food cooked with spices

cushion

NOUN *plural* cushions

1 a soft plump pad of material that you sit on, rest against or kneel on
2 something that gives protection or keeps something off a hard surface

VERB cushions, cushioning, cushioned

to cushion a blow is to make it less painful

custard

NOUN

a thick sauce made from eggs, milk or cream, and sugar

cut

VERB cuts, cutting, cut

1 to cut something is to divide it, separate it, make a hole in it or shape it, using scissors, a knife or some other sharp instrument
2 to make something less ⇒ *My mother cut my pocket money.*
3 ICT to take something from a file on the computer so you can put it into another file, or to take a whole file out of one place so you can put it into another

▶ **cut it out**

if someone tells you to cut it out, they are telling you to stop doing something

▶ **cut off something**

to cut off something such as gas or electricity is to stop it being supplied to a home

NOUN *plural* cuts

1 a split or small wound made by something sharp
2 a share of something

cycle

VERB cycles, cycling, cycled

to cycle is to ride a bicycle

NOUN *plural* cycles

1 a bicycle
2 a series of things that happen one after the other and then start again ⇒ *the cycle of the seasons*

▶ **cyclist**

NOUN *plural* cyclists

someone riding a bicycle

a b c d e f g h i j k l m n o p q r s t u v w x y z

dad or daddy

NOUN *plural* dads *or* daddies

a word that people use for **father**, especially when speaking ⋛ *Thanks to all the mums and dads who have helped.* ⋚

daffodil

NOUN *plural* daffodils

a yellow flower that grows from a bulb and blooms in spring

daily

ADJECTIVE

happening or done every day ⋛ *a daily newspaper* ⋚

ADVERB

every day ⋛ *We met daily for a month.* ⋚

NOUN *plural* dailies

a newspaper that is published every weekday

daisy

NOUN *plural* daisies

a type of small white flower with a yellow centre. Daisies often grow wild in grass

> The word **daisy** has been changed from **day's eye**. It was called this because the flower opens during the day.

damage

NOUN

harm, hurt or injury ⋛ *No lasting damage has been found.* ⋚

VERB damages, damaging, damaged

to hurt, spoil or break something

damp

ADJECTIVE damper, dampest

a bit wet ⋛ *Wipe with a damp cloth.* ⋚

NOUN

slight wetness ⋛ *a patch of damp on the wall* ⋚

▸ **dampen**

VERB dampens, dampening, dampened

to make something a bit wet ⋛ *Dampen the brush before using it.* ⋚

dance

VERB dances, dancing, danced

to move your body in time to music

NOUN *plural* dances

1 a set of steps that you do to some kind of music
2 a party for dancing

▸ **dancer**

NOUN *plural* dancers

someone who dances

danger

NOUN *plural* dangers

something that may harm or injure you ⋛ *the dangers of skiing* ⋚

▸ **dangerous**

ADJECTIVE

1 likely to hurt someone ⋛ *a dangerous substance* ⋜
2 risky ⋛ *It's dangerous to play near the railway.* ⋜

▸ **dangerously**

ADVERB

in a way that could be harmful ⋛ *driving dangerously close to the edge* ⋜

dare

VERB dares, daring, dared

1 to dare someone to do something is to challenge them to do it ⋛ *I dare you to do that again!* ⋜
2 to dare to do something is to be brave enough to do it ⋛ *I wouldn't dare to argue with the headmaster.* ⋜

dark

ADJECTIVE darker, darkest

1 without light ⋛ *a dark room* ⋜
2 strong or deep in colour ⋛ *dark blue* ⋜
3 gloomy, sad or miserable

NOUN

1 where there is no light ⋛ *I'm not afraid of the dark.* ⋜
2 nightfall ⋛ *Don't go out after dark without a torch.* ⋜

▸ **in the dark**

if you are in the dark about something, you know nothing about it

▸ **darkness**

NOUN

where there is no light ⋛ *a tiny point of light in the darkness* ⋜

date¹

NOUN *plural* dates

1 the number of a day of a month or a year ⋛ *The date today is 30 July.* ⋜
2 a particular day of a particular month and year ⋛ *It was on that date that I left home.* ⋜
3 an arrangement to go out with someone

VERB dates, dating, dated

1 to decide how old something is ⋛ *The ring's very old but I couldn't date it exactly.* ⋜
2 to belong to a certain time ⋛ *Our house dates from the nineteenth century.* ⋜

date²

NOUN *plural* dates

a small, dark fruit with a stone that grows on some palm trees

daughter

NOUN *plural* daughters

someone's female child ⋛ *She was the daughter of a poet.* ⋜

day

NOUN *plural* days

1 the time of light between sunrise and sunset
2 the twenty-four hours between one midnight and another ⋛ *There are 365 days in a year.* ⋜
3 a time or period ⋛ *in my grandfather's day* ⋜

dead

ADJECTIVE

1 no longer living ⋛ *a dead body* ⋜
2 no longer working or active ⋛ *The telephone line's dead.* ⋜

ADVERB

1 completely ⋛ *He just stopped dead in front of me.* ⋜

2 exactly ⋗ *standing dead in the centre of the circle* ⋖

NOUN

1 the dead are all the people who have died
2 the dead of night is the quietest part of it

deaf

ADJECTIVE deafer, deafest

not able to hear properly ⋗ *Grandma grew deafer as she got older.* ⋖

▶ **deafening**

ADJECTIVE

unpleasantly loud ⋗ *The music was deafening and we had to leave.* ⋖

▶ **deafness**

NOUN

being unable to hear properly

dear

ADJECTIVE dearer, dearest

1 a thing or person that is dear to you is important because you love them ⋗ *my dear old teddy* ⋖
2 costing a lot of money ⋗ *too dear for me to buy* ⋖
3 the word you use with the name of a person at the beginning of a letter ⋗ *Dear Mary* ⋖

NOUN *plural* dears

a person that is very lovable ⋗ *Nancy is such a dear.* ⋖

December

NOUN

the twelfth month of the year, after November and before January

December was the tenth month of the Roman year and the name comes from the word **decem**, which means *ten* in Latin. Other words in English where you can work out that **dec** means *ten* are **decimal** and **decade**.

decide

VERB decides, deciding, decided

1 to make up your mind to do something ⋗ *Greg decided to work harder at school.* ⋖
2 to choose ⋗ *I can't decide between the blue one and the green one.* ⋖
3 to bring about a result ⋗ *That mistake decided the match.* ⋖

▶ **decision**

NOUN *plural* decisions

something that you have decided ⋗ *It was a very difficult decision to make, and I had to think hard before making a choice.* ⋖

decorate

VERB decorates, decorating, decorated

1 to add something fancy to something to make it look nicer ⋗ *We'll decorate the cake with roses made of sugar.* ⋖
2 to paint or paper the inside of a room
3 to give someone a medal or an award for doing something special ⋗ *He was decorated for bravery in the war.* ⋖

▶ **decoration**

NOUN *plural* decorations

1 decoration is adding things to improve the look of something
2 an ornament that makes something look pretty ⋗ *Christmas decorations* ⋖

deep

ADJECTIVE deeper, deepest

1 going a long way down ⋗ *Is the river very deep?* ⋖
2 very low in tone ⋗ *a deep voice* ⋖
3 reaching a long way back ⋗ *a deep border of roses* ⋖
4 very strong ⋗ *deep blue* ⋖ ⋗ *deep dislike* ⋖

ADVERB deeper, deepest

1 in a downward direction ⋗ *a hole a metre deep* ⋖
2 from front to back ⋗ *rows of soldiers standing four deep* ⋖

deer

NOUN *plural* **deer**

an animal with four thin legs that runs very fast and gracefully. A male deer has antlers like branches that grow on its head

> The singular and plural forms of **deer** are the same: *a deer in the woods* • *two deer in the park.*

defeat

VERB defeats, defeating, defeated

to beat someone in a competition or war

NOUN *plural* **defeats**

1 a defeat is a game or a battle that you have lost
2 defeat is being beaten at something

delete

VERB deletes, deleting, deleted

to cross out or remove something

▸ **deletion**
NOUN *plural* **deletions**

a deletion is something that has been removed, for example from a text

delicious

ADJECTIVE

very good to eat, drink or smell ⇒ *a delicious meal* ⇒

deliver

VERB delivers, delivering, delivered

1 to deliver something is to take it to the door of someone's home or workplace ⇒ *We're delivering leaflets to all the houses in this area.* ⇒
2 to deliver a speech is to say it out loud
3 to deliver a baby is to help with its birth

den

NOUN *plural* **dens**

1 the home of a wild animal ⇒ *a lion's den* ⇒
2 a person's private place where they can get away from other people

dentist

NOUN *plural* **dentists**

a doctor for people's teeth

describe

VERB describes, describing, described

to tell someone what something or someone is like ⇒ *Can you describe what you saw?* ⇒ *The police asked Liz to describe the man who stole her handbag.* ⇒

▸ **description**
NOUN *plural* **descriptions**

1 explaining what someone or something is like ⇒ *an author who's good at description* ⇒
2 the way someone describes a thing, person or event ⇒ *a very funny description of what happened* ⇒

desert

NOUN *plural* **deserts**

an area of land where it does not rain much, so the earth is very dry and not many plants will grow

deserve

VERB deserves, deserving, deserved

to deserve something is to have earned it because of the way you are or something you have done

a b c **d** e f g h i j k l m n o p q r s t u v w x y z

design

VERB designs, designing, designed

1 to plan a building or product before it is built or made
2 if something is designed for someone or for a particular purpose, it is intended for them ⇒ *This dictionary is designed to be used by school pupils.*

NOUN plural **designs**

1 design is planning new shapes and ideas ⇒ *studying craft and design*
2 a design is a plan or diagram of something that could be made ⇒ *a design for a new racing car*
3 a pattern ⇒ *a geometric design*

desk

NOUN plural **desks**

a table for writing at

dessert said "diz-**ut**"

NOUN plural **desserts**

a pudding or sweet at the end of a meal

diamond

NOUN plural **diamonds**

1 a very hard, clear gem that is used for jewellery
2 a four-sided pointed shape
3 diamonds is one of the four suits of playing cards, which have the symbol ◆ printed on them

dice

NOUN plural **dice**

a small cube with different numbers of dots on each face. You throw a dice and use the number of dots as a score when it's your turn in a game

> **Dice** is the plural of **die**. The singular, **die**, is not often used. In fact, **dice** is now used as a singular or a plural noun: *Where are the dice?* • *The dice is on the floor.*

dictionary

NOUN plural **dictionaries**

a book that gives words in alphabetical order and their meanings ⇒ *a French dictionary* ⇒ *a dictionary of medical words*

did

VERB

a way of changing the verb **do** to make a past tense ⇒ *I did the dishes yesterday, it's your turn today.*

die

VERB dies, dying, died

to stop living

▸ **die down**

to die down is to get less ⇒ *Wait for the fuss to die down.*

▸ **die out**

to die out is to disappear gradually ⇒ *More and more species of animal are dying out.*

different

ADJECTIVE

a thing or person is different from another if they are not the same

▸ **difference**

NOUN plural **differences**

1 the way that something is not the same as something else
2 **maths** the amount between two numbers ⇒ *The difference between 6 and 10 is 4.*

> Many people think it is wrong if you say **different to**, so you should say **different from**: *This pencil is different from that one.*

difficult

ADJECTIVE

1 not easy
2 hard to please ⇒ *a difficult customer*

▸ difficulty

NOUN *plural* **difficulties**

1 difficulty is not being easy ⟩ *You should be able to do this without difficulty.* ⟨
2 a difficulty is something that causes a problem ⟩ *We had a few difficulties at the beginning of the day.* ⟨

dig

VERB **digs, digging, dug**

1 to lift up and turn over earth with a spade
2 to make a hole, especially in the ground
3 to poke someone

NOUN *plural* **digs**

1 a poke ⟩ *a dig in the ribs* ⟨
2 a remark that you make to irritate someone deliberately ⟩ *I pretended not to hear her dig about my clothes.* ⟨
3 a place where archaeologists remove earth to look for ancient remains

dinner

NOUN *plural* **dinners**

a main meal in the evening or in the middle of the day

dinosaur

NOUN *plural* **dinosaurs**

an extinct prehistoric giant reptile

> **Dinosaur** comes from the Greek for 'terrible lizard'.

dirt

NOUN

any substance that is not clean or makes something unclean, such as mud or dust

▸ dirty

ADJECTIVE **dirtier, dirtiest**

1 not clean ⟩ *dirty floors* ⟨
2 not polite ⟩ *dirty language* ⟨
3 unfair or dishonest ⟩ *a dirty trick* ⟨

disappear

VERB **disappears, disappearing, disappeared**

to vanish or go out of sight

▸ disappearance

NOUN *plural* **disappearances**

when something or someone vanishes ⟩ *The police are investigating the disappearance of the necklace.* ⟨

disco

NOUN *plural* **discos**

a place or party where people dance to recorded music

discover

VERB **discovers, discovering, discovered**

to find information, a place or an object, especially for the first time ⟩ *The settlers discovered gold in the mountains.* ⟨ ⟩ *We discovered that the ice had melted.* ⟨

discuss

VERB **discusses, discussing, discussed**

to talk about something in detail

▸ discussion

NOUN *plural* **discussions**

1 discussion is talk between people ⟩ *discussion between world leaders* ⟨
2 a discussion is a conversation

disease

NOUN *plural* **diseases**

an illness

▸ diseased

ADJECTIVE

not healthy, especially because of an illness ⟩ *diseased leaves on the roses* ⟨

a b c **d** e f g h i j k l m n o p q r s t u v w x y z

disguise

VERB disguises, disguising, disguised

if you disguise yourself, you wear clothes you would not normally wear or things like make-up or a wig, to hide who you really are

NOUN *plural* disguises

1 a disguise is something you wear to hide who you really are
2 if you are in disguise, you are wearing things like clothes or make-up to hide who you really are

dish

NOUN *plural* dishes

1 a plate or bowl for food
2 food that has been prepared for eating ⇒ *a fish dish* ⋚
3 a large disc that is an aerial for receiving satellite signals, especially for television broadcasts

VERB dishes, dishing, dished

▸ **dish something out**

to give something to a lot of people or in large amounts

distance

NOUN *plural* distances

the space between things ⇒ *Measure the distance between the lines accurately.* ⋚

▸ **in the distance**

a long way off ⇒ *the sound of a train in the distance* ⋚

▸ **distant**

ADJECTIVE

1 far off, not close ⇒ *a distant shout* ⋚ ⇒ *a distant cousin* ⋚
2 cold and unfriendly ⇒ *behaving in a distant manner* ⋚

dive

VERB dives, diving, dived

1 to go into water headfirst
2 to go down steeply and quickly ⇒ *an eagle diving down into a field* ⋚

NOUN *plural* dives

a downwards movement, especially headfirst into water

divide

VERB divides, dividing, divided

1 to separate into parts ⇒ *divide the class into small groups* ⇒ *a single cell that divides and becomes two cells* ⋚
2 **maths** to find how many times one number contains another. For example, if you divide 12 by 3 you get 4, which can be written as $12 \div 3 = 4$

▸ **division**

NOUN *plural* divisions

1 division is dividing things, numbers or people ⇒ *We're learning a different way of doing division sums.* ⋚ ⇒ *the fair division of the money between everyone* ⋚
2 a division is a gap or barrier that separates things ⇒ *The curtain is a division between the two rooms.* ⋚
3 a division is a section of something ⇒ *There are eight teams in our division.* ⋚

Diwali said "di-**wa**-li"

NOUN

the Hindu or Sikh religious festival of lights, which takes place in October or November

dizzy

ADJECTIVE dizzier, dizziest

if you feel dizzy you feel as if you are about to fall over ⇒ *Spinning round will make you dizzy.* ⋚

do

VERB does, doing, did, done

1 to carry out an action or deal with a task ⇒ *do your homework* ⋚
2 to get along or manage ⇒ *How are you doing?* ⋚
3 to be enough ⇒ *Will a pound do?* ⋚

▸ **do away with**

to do away with something or someone is to get rid of them or kill them

▸**do something up**

1 to do something up is to fasten it ⫷ ***Do your jacket up – it's cold out there.*** ⫸

2 to do something up is to decorate it ⫷ ***We're doing up our hall.*** ⫸

NOUN *plural* **dos**

informal a party or celebration

The verb **do** is very important in making English sentences. You use it so you do not repeat a verb: *We rarely have a picnic, but when we do, it always rains.* You often use it with a more important verb: *Do you understand?*
• *I* do *not care.* • *I* do *like chocolate.*

---

dock

NOUN *plural* **docks**

part of a harbour where the things being carried on ships can be lifted on and off

VERB docks, docking, docked

1 to go into, or put a ship into a dock ⫷ ***When we've docked, they'll unload the ship.*** ⫸

2 a spaceship docks when it joins another ship during a flight

doctor

NOUN *plural* **doctors**

someone who has been trained in medicine and treats people who are ill

---

Doctor is the Latin word for *teacher*, but the meaning has changed in English.

---

does

VERB

the form of the verb **do** that is used with **he**, **she** and **it**

dog

NOUN *plural* **dogs**

a four-footed animal that barks and that people often keep as a pet

doll

NOUN *plural* **dolls**

a toy model of a person

dolphin

NOUN *plural* **dolphins**

a very intelligent sea mammal of the whale family that has a long pointed mouth

done

VERB

a form of the verb **do** that is used with a helping verb to make a past tense ⫷ ***I've done my homework and now I'm going out on my bike.*** ⫸

donkey

NOUN *plural* **donkeys**

a type of animal that looks like a small horse with long ears. A donkey may also be called an **ass**

door

NOUN *plural* **doors**

a panel, often on a hinge, that you can open and close. It usually covers the entrance to a building, room or cupboard

dot

NOUN *plural* **dots**

a small round mark

▸**on the dot**

exactly on time ⫷ ***Belinda arrived at three o'clock on the dot, just as she'd promised.*** ⫸

VERB dots, dotting, dotted

1 to dot something is to put a dot or dots on it ⫷ ***Remember to dot the letter 'i'.*** ⫸

2 if people or things are dotted somewhere, they are spread over an area ⫷ ***Cushions were dotted around the floor.*** ⫸

double

ADJECTIVE

1 containing twice as much ⫷ ***a double dose of medicine*** ⫸

a b c **d** e f g h i j k l m n o p q r s t u v w x y z

2 made up of two of the same sort ⊰ **double doors** ⊰

3 suitable for two people ⊰ **a double cabin** ⊰

NOUN *plural* **doubles**

1 twice as much ⊰ **Jan gets double the pocket money I get.** ⊰

2 a thing or person that looks exactly like another one ⊰ **I saw your double in the street yesterday.** ⊰

at the double

very quickly

VERB **doubles, doubling, doubled**

to multiply something by two

▸ **double up**

to bend over in laughter or pain

▸ **doubles**

PLURAL NOUN

in games like tennis, you play doubles when two of you play against two other people

doughnut

NOUN *plural* **doughnuts**

a round cake that is deep-fried. It may have a hole in the middle or be filled with something like jam or chocolate

down¹

ADVERB

1 towards or in a lower position ⊰ **get down** ⊰ ⊰ **sit down** ⊰

2 to a smaller size ⊰ **cut the picture down to fit the frame** ⊰

3 along ⊰ **go down to the post office** ⊰

▸ **go down with**

to become ill with something ⊰ **She's gone down with flu.** ⊰

PREPOSITION

1 towards or in a lower part ⊰ **tears running down his face** ⊰

2 along ⊰ **walking down the road** ⊰

down²

NOUN

light, soft feathers

dragon

NOUN *plural* **dragons**

an imaginary, fire-breathing reptile with wings

drain

VERB **drains, draining, drained**

1 to drain something is to let the water run out of it ⊰ **They must drain the reservoir to repair the dam.** ⊰ ⊰ **Drain the washed cabbage well before cutting it up.** ⊰

2 to drain is to flow away ⊰ **watching the liquid drain down the sink** ⊰

3 to drain a container of drink is to drink it all

NOUN *plural* **drains**

a pipe or ditch for waste water to flow away in

drank

VERB

a way of changing the verb **drink** to make a past tense ⊰ **We drank our tea and left as quickly as possible.** ⊰

draw

VERB **draws, drawing, drew, drawn**

1 to make a picture with a pencil or pen

2 to draw a vehicle is to pull it along behind ⊰ **Horses drew the carriage.** ⊰

3 if something draws people it attracts them ⊰ **The circus always draws huge audiences.** ⊰

4 to draw someone or something to a place is to move them there by pulling them gently ⊰ **Draw your chair up to the table.** ⊰

5 to score equal points in a game ⊰ **This pair have drawn every match they've played so far.** ⊰

NOUN *plural* **draws**

an equal score ⊰ **The game ended in a draw.** ⊰

drawer

NOUN *plural* **drawers**

a sliding box in a table or cupboard

dream

NOUN   *plural* **dreams**

1 the things you think while you are asleep ⇒ *I had a very strange dream last night.*
2 if you are in a dream, you are concentrating on your thoughts and not on what is going on around you
3 a hope or ambition ⇒ *It was always her dream to go to Hollywood.*

VERB   **dreams, dreaming, dreamt** *or* **dreamed**

to imagine something, especially while you are asleep ⇒ *Last night I dreamt that my Mum was having another baby.* ⇒ *Did you say that or did I dream it?*

dress

NOUN   *plural* **dresses**

1 a dress is a piece of clothing for girls or women like a top and skirt joined together
2 dress is clothing ⇒ *dancers in traditional dress*

VERB   **dresses, dressing, dressed**

1 to put clothes on ⇒ *The doorbell rang while I was dressing.* ⇒ *Mum still has to dress my little brother.*
2 to dress a wound is to put a plaster or bandage on it

▸ **dress up**

to put on special clothes ⇒ *Colin always loved to dress up as a pirate.*

drew

VERB

a way of changing the verb **draw** to make a past tense ⇒ *Who drew this face on the board?*

drink

VERB   **drinks, drinking, drank, drunk**

1 to swallow a liquid
2 to drink alcohol ⇒ *My Dad refused the wine because he doesn't drink.*

NOUN   *plural* **drinks**

1 a drink is a liquid that you swallow when you are thirsty

2 drink is alcoholic liquids ⇒ *Please do not bring drink into the hostel.*

drip

NOUN   *plural* **drips**

1 a drop of liquid ⇒ *We're trying to catch the drips in a bucket.*
2 a series of falling drops of liquid ⇒ *I could hear the drip of the bathroom tap all night.*
3 a piece of equipment for slowly giving a hospital patient a liquid that their body needs

VERB   **drips, dripping, dripped**

1 to fall in drops ⇒ *water dripping from the trees*
2 to let a liquid fall in drops ⇒ *I can hear a tap dripping somewhere.*

drive

VERB   **drives, driving, drove, driven**

1 to control a vehicle such as a car
2 to hit a ball very hard, especially in golf
3 to force someone into a certain state ⇒ *That tune's driving me crazy.*

NOUN   *plural* **drives**

1 a journey in a car ⇒ *Let's go for a drive.*
2 a private road up to a house ⇒ *a car parked in the drive*
3 drive is energy and enthusiasm ⇒ *someone with a lot of drive*

drop

NOUN   *plural* **drops**

1 a small blob of liquid ⇒ *drops of water on the window*
2 a small quantity ⇒ *only a drop of milk left in the bottle*
3 a fall or decrease ⇒ *Kevin's new job will mean a drop in pay.*

VERB   **drops, dropping, dropped**

1 to fall or to let something fall ⇒ *Drop the gun now!* ⇒ *An apple dropped from the tree.*
2 to become lower or less ⇒ *The temperature drops a lot in the evening.*

a
b
c
d
e
f
g
h
i
j
k
l
m
n
o
p
q
r
s
t
u
v
w
x
y
z

drove

VERB

a way of changing the verb **drive** to make a past tense ⇥ *We drove to London down the M1.*

drum

NOUN *plural* **drums**

1 an instrument that is round and has a skin stretched over it that you hit to make a rhythm
2 a container in the shape of a cylinder ⇥ *an oil drum*

VERB drums, drumming, drummed

1 to beat a drum
2 to tap your fingers repeatedly

▸ **drummer**

NOUN *plural* **drummers**

a person who plays the drums

dry

ADJECTIVE drier, driest

1 not wet or damp
2 not lively or interesting ⇥ *a dry book*
3 dry humour is funny in a way that is not obvious

VERB dries, drying, dried

to remove or lose all the liquid from something

▸ **dryness**

NOUN

being dry

duck

NOUN *plural* **ducks**

a water bird with webbed feet, short legs and a wide, flat beak

VERB ducks, ducking, ducked

to duck is to lower your head quickly, as if you were avoiding being hit

dug

VERB

a way of changing the verb **dig** to make a past tense. It can be used with or without a helping verb ⇥ *The children dug a hole under the apple tree.* ⇥ *A huge hole had been dug.*

dust

NOUN

a fine powder of something, especially household dirt

VERB dusts, dusting, dusted

1 to clean dry dirt from surfaces ⇥ *The books have to be dusted regularly.*
2 to cover something with a fine powder ⇥ *Dust the cake with icing sugar.*

DVD

ABBREVIATION DVD's or DVDs

short for **digital versatile disk** or **digital video disk**, a type of disk that pictures and sounds can be recorded on, and which can hold more information than a CD

E

each

ADJECTIVE

each person or thing in a group or pair is every one as an individual ⟩ *He had a heavy suitcase in each hand.* ⟨

PRONOUN

every one individually ⟩*Each of the girls had a different costume.* ⟨

▸ **each other**

to, or for, the other ⟩ *The team hugged each other.* ⟨

ear

NOUN *plural* **ears**

your ears are the two parts of your body at each side of your head that you hear with

early

ADJECTIVE AND ADVERB earlier, earliest

1 happening or arriving before others or before the expected or normal time ⟩ *an earlier train* ⟨ ⟩ *I'm going to bed early.* ⟨
2 near the beginning of something ⟩ *the early morning* ⟨ ⟩ *early in life* ⟨

earn

VERB earns, earning, earned

1 to earn is to get money in return for work ⟩ *My brother earns a bit of money from his Saturday job.* ⟨
2 to earn something good, such as praise, is to get it because you have done something well

earth

NOUN *plural* **earths**

1 the Earth is the planet we live on
2 earth is the ground or soil ⟩ *digging in the earth* ⟨

east

NOUN

1 the direction where you see the sun rising in the morning, opposite to west
2 the East and the Far East are the countries in Asia

ADJECTIVE

in, from, or towards the east ⟩ *an east wind* ⟨ ⟩ *East London* ⟨

ADVERB

to the east ⟩*We headed east.* ⟨

Easter

NOUN

a Christian festival commemorating Christ's rising from the dead, celebrated in spring

easy

ADJECTIVE easier, easiest

not difficult or hard to do ⟩ *an easy sum* ⟨
▸ **take it easy**

you take it easy when you relax or don't work too hard

eat

VERB eats, eating, ate, eaten

1 to eat food is to chew and swallow it
2 to eat is to have a meal ⟩ *What time would you like to eat?* ⟨
▸ **eat something away**

to eat something away is to destroy it gradually ⟩ *The cliffs were being eaten away by the sea.* ⟨
▸ **eat something up**

to eat something up is to eat it all or to use it all up ⟩ *Eat up your greens.* ⟨ ⟩ *Buying a computer game had eaten up all my pocket money.* ⟨

a b c d e f g h i j k l m n o p q r s t u v w x y z

a b c d **e** f g h i j k l m n o p q r s t u v w x y z

echo

NOUN *plural* **echoes**

an echo happens when a sound travelling away from you bounces off a surface and comes back towards you, so you hear it for a second time

VERB echoes, echoing, echoed

1 a sound echoes when it is comes back and you hear it again
2 to echo what someone has said is to repeat it

> **Echo** is the Greek word for *sound*.

edge

NOUN *plural* **edges**

1 the side or end of something ⋗ *the edge of the cliff* ⋖ ⋗ *A square has four edges.* ⋖
2 a side of something that is sharp enough to cut ⋗ *The knives have sharp edges.* ⋖
▸ **on edge**
nervous and easily irritated ⋗ *I'm on edge because I'm waiting for my exam results.* ⋖

VERB edges, edging, edged

1 to edge something is to border it ⋗ *pillowcases edged with lace* ⋖
2 to move slowly and carefully ⋗ *Harry edged along the narrow ledge.* ⋖

▸ **edging**
NOUN
the border round the outside of something

educate

VERB educates, educating, educated

to educate people is to teach them and to give them knowledge

▸ **education**
NOUN
education is teaching, especially in schools or colleges

▸ **educational**
ADJECTIVE
to do with teaching and learning

egg

NOUN *plural* **eggs**

1 an egg is a shell or case with a developing baby bird, reptile or fish inside
2 an egg is one of these laid by a hen or other bird that we eat as food ⋗ *a hard-boiled egg* ⋖

Eid-ul-Adha *said* "eed-ul-**ad**-ha"

NOUN

a Muslim festival held to celebrate how the prophet Abraham was willing to sacrifice his son

Eid-ul-Fitr *said* "eed-ul-**fee**-tir"

NOUN

a Muslim festival held to celebrate the end of **Ramadan**

> **Eid** is an Arabic word meaning *festival*.

eight

NOUN *plural* **eights**

the number 8

eighteen

NOUN

the number 18

eighty

NOUN *plural* **eighties**

the number 80

either

ADJECTIVE

1 the one or the other ⋗ *She can write with either hand.* ⋖
2 both ⋗ *There are goalposts at either end of the pitch.* ⋖

PRONOUN

the one or the other of two ⋗ *He can't afford either of them.* ⋖

a b c d **e** f g h i j k l m n o p q r s t u v w x y z

ADVERB

as well ⹂*If you don't go, I won't go either.*⹂

CONJUNCTION

either is used with **or** to show a choice or alternative ⹂*You can have either a video game or a CD.*⹂

elbow

NOUN   *plural* **elbows**

the joint in the middle of your arm that bends

VERB   elbows, elbowing, elbowed

to elbow someone is to poke or push them with your elbow

election

NOUN   *plural* **elections**

the choosing of someone by voting ⹂*standing for election*⹂ ⹂*a presidential election*⹂

electric

ADJECTIVE

made or worked by electricity ⹂*an electric spark*⹂ ⹂*an electric light*⹂

▸ **electrical**

ADJECTIVE

carrying or producing electricity ⹂*an electrical circuit*⹂ ⹂*an electrical storm*⹂

electricity

NOUN

a form of energy used to make light and heat and to give power to machinery

> **Electric** comes from the Greek word **elektron**, which means *amber*. This is because amber makes electricity when it is rubbed.

electronic

ADJECTIVE

electronic equipment uses very small electrical circuits in order to work

tusk
trunk

elephant

NOUN   *plural* **elephants**

a very large grey animal with a long trunk, large flapping ears, and tusks made of ivory

eleven

NOUN   *plural* **elevens**

the number 11

else

ADVERB

other than or besides the thing or person already talked about ⹂*They didn't have anywhere else to go.*⹂

email *or* e-mail

NOUN   *plural* **emails** *or* **e-mails**

short for **electronic mail**, a message or messages that are sent between computers ⹂*They keep in touch by email.*⹂

VERB   emails, emailing, emailed *or* e-mails, e-mailing, e-mailed

to email someone is to send them an email

embarrass

VERB   embarrasses, embarrassing, embarrassed

to embarrass someone is to make them feel uncomfortable or ashamed

▸ **embarrassed**

ADJECTIVE

looking or feeling ashamed or self-conscious ⹂*Susan was embarrassed by all the attention she was receiving.*⹂

▸ **embarrassing**

ADJECTIVE

causing embarrassment ⇝ *an embarrassing mistake* ⇜

▸ **embarrassment**

NOUN

a feeling of discomfort and shame

emergency

NOUN   *plural* **emergencies**

an emergency is a sudden, unexpected event, often one that puts people's lives or property in danger

emotion

NOUN   *plural* **emotions**

emotions are strong feelings, such as love, hate, fear, jealousy or anger ⇝ *He showed no emotion as he was sentenced to jail.* ⇜

▸ **emotional**

ADJECTIVE

showing or having strong feelings ⇝ *an emotional farewell* ⇜

empty

ADJECTIVE   **emptier, emptiest**

having nothing or no one inside ⇝ *an empty glass* ⇜   ⇝ *an empty classroom* ⇜

VERB   **empties, emptying, emptied**

1 to empty is to make or become empty ⇝ *Empty your pockets.* ⇜
2 to empty something is to tip or pour it out of a container ⇝ *The dustmen were emptying the rubbish out of the bins.* ⇜

▸ **emptiness**

NOUN

being empty

encourage

VERB   encourages, encouraging, encouraged

1 to encourage someone is to support them and make them feel confident about what they are doing or are planning to do

2 to encourage something is to do something that will make it more likely to happen

▸ **encouragement**

NOUN

supporting or giving confidence to someone or something ⇝ *The crowd was shouting encouragement to the team.* ⇜

end

NOUN   *plural* **ends**

1 the end of something is its last part or the place where it finishes ⇝ *the end of the day* ⇜   ⇝ *I read the book from beginning to end.* ⇜
2 the ends of something are the parts farthest away from the middle ⇝ *He was running from one end of the pitch to the other.* ⇜
3 an end is a result that you aim for or a purpose that you have ⇝ *They used their power for their own private ends.* ⇜

▸ **on end**

without a stop ⇝ *The rain continued for days and weeks on end.* ⇜

VERB   ends, ending, ended

to finish ⇝ *Our holiday ends tomorrow.* ⇜ ⇝ *He ended his speech with a joke.* ⇜

▸ **end up**

to be in a particular place or situation that you were not expecting ⇝ *The illness got worse and he ended up in hospital.* ⇜   ⇝ *My Mum was out so I ended up going to Jack's.* ⇜

enemy

NOUN   *plural* **enemies**

1 someone or something that is against you or wants to do you harm
2 in a war, the enemy is the people or country you are fighting against

energy

NOUN   *plural* **energies**

1 the strength or power to work or be active ⇝ *He's got bags of energy.* ⇜
2 a form of power, such as heat or electricity ⇝ *trying to save energy* ⇜ ⇝ *nuclear energy* ⇜

engine

NOUN *plural* **engines**

1 a machine that turns energy into movement by burning fuel
2 the vehicle at the front of a train that pulls the coaches

enjoy

VERB enjoys, enjoying, enjoyed

1 to enjoy something is to get a feeling of pleasure from it ⋛ *They seemed to enjoy the concert.* ⋚
2 to enjoy yourself is to have a good time ⋛ *We enjoyed ourselves at the party.* ⋚

▸ **enjoyable**
ADJECTIVE
giving a feeling of pleasure

▸ **enjoyment**
NOUN
pleasure

enormous

ADJECTIVE
very big ⋛ *an enormous tree* ⋚

▸ **enormously**
ADVERB

1 very greatly ⋛ *They all enjoyed themselves enormously.* ⋚
2 extremely ⋛ *enormously grateful* ⋚

> This word comes from the Latin word **enormis**, which means *unusual* or *not normal*.

enough

ADJECTIVE
as much or as many as you need, want or can put up with ⋛ *I've got enough problems without this!* ⋚

PRONOUN
as much as you need, want or can put up with ⋛ *Have you all had enough to eat?* ⋚

ADVERB
as much as is needed or wanted ⋛ *You've gone far enough.* ⋚

enter

VERB enters, entering, entered

1 to enter, or enter a place, is to go in, or to go into it
2 to enter a competition is to take part in it
3 to enter something in a book or list is to write it in the book or list
4 **ICT** to enter data into a computer is to key it in

enthusiastic

ADJECTIVE
eager and showing keenness ⋛ *enthusiastic applause* ⋚

envelope

NOUN *plural* **envelopes**
a folded paper covering for a letter or other document, especially one that is to be sent by post

environment

NOUN *plural* **environments**

1 a person's or animal's environment is their surroundings where they live
2 the environment is all the things, such as air, land, sea, animals and plants, that make up the natural world around us

envy

NOUN
if you feel envy, you want what someone else has

VERB envies, envying, envied
to envy someone is to want what they have

equipment

NOUN
equipment is a set of tools and special clothing needed to do a particular activity or job ⋛ *camping equipment* ⋚

a b c d **e** f g h i j k l m n o p q r s t u v w x y z

escape

VERB escapes, escaping, escaped

1 to escape is to get out or away to safety or freedom ⇒ *The lion had escaped from its cage.*
2 to escape something is to avoid it ⇒ *You're lucky to have escaped punishment.*
3 if something escapes you, it slips from your memory

NOUN plural escapes

1 getting free ⇒ *a failed escape from prison*
2 a way to get free or get away to safety ⇒ *I only had thirty minutes to plan my escape.*

especially

ADVERB

particularly ⇒ *It was especially cold that morning.*

> Remember the difference between **especially** and **specially**. **Especially** means 'particularly': *I like all of the characters, especially Harry.* **Specially** means 'for a special purpose': *I cooked this meal specially for you.*

even

ADJECTIVE

1 an even surface is level and smooth
2 things are even when they are equal ⇒ *The scores were even.*
3 an even number is one that can be divided by 2 without a remainder, for example 12, 104 and 6000. Look up and compare **odd**
4 someone who has an even temper is calm and doesn't suddenly change their mood

ADVERB

even is used to emphasize another word ⇒ *It was even colder the next morning.*
▶ **even so**
though that may be true ⇒ *It looks like the right one, but even so, I'd like to check.*

evening

NOUN plural evenings

evening is the last part of the day and the early part of the night

event

NOUN plural events

1 a happening that stands out or is important for some reason ⇒ *events in history*
2 one of the items in a programme of sports or entertainment ⇒ *The next event is the sack race.*

▶ **eventful**
ADJECTIVE
full of action, excitement and important events ⇒ *She's led an eventful life.*

ever

ADVERB

1 at any time or at all ⇒ *Have you ever been to France?*
2 always ⇒ *ever ready to help*
3 of all time or on record ⇒ *the biggest pizza ever*

every

ADJECTIVE

all the people or things of a particular kind without leaving any out ⇒ *Every runner will get a medal for taking part.* ⇒ *Every day, he does 200 press-ups.*

everybody

PRONOUN

all people or every person ⇒ *I thought everybody liked ice cream.*

everyone

PRONOUN

every person or all people ⇒ *Everyone looks happy today.*

everything

PRONOUN

all things ⇒ *Everything in the room was covered in dust.*

everywhere

ADVERB

in every place ⋟ *We looked for him everywhere.* ⋞

evil

ADJECTIVE

an evil person or an evil act is wicked and causes great harm

NOUN *plural* evils

1 wickedness
2 something that causes great harm or destruction

example

NOUN *plural* examples

1 an example of something is a thing of that kind
2 if someone is or sets a good example, they behave in a way that others should copy

excellent

ADJECTIVE

extremely good or of a very high standard

▸ **excellence**
NOUN

excellence is very high quality or great ability

except

PREPOSITION AND CONJUNCTION

other than, apart from, or not including ⋟ *He works every day except Sunday.* ⋞

exercise

NOUN *plural* exercises

1 exercise is movements or games done to keep your body fit and healthy
2 an exercise is something you do to practise something

VERB exercises, exercising, exercised

to exercise is to move around and be active so that you use your muscles and keep fit and healthy

exhibition

NOUN *plural* exhibitions

a public show or open display ⋟ *an exhibition of modern art* ⋞

exit

VERB exits, exiting, exited

to exit is to go out ⋟ *They exited the stadium by the west gate.* ⋞

NOUN *plural* exits

1 a way out of somewhere ⋟ *Leave the motorway by the next exit.* ⋞
2 to make an exit is to leave ⋟ *He made a hasty exit.* ⋞

expensive

ADJECTIVE

costing a lot of money

experiment

NOUN *plural* experiments

1 a scientific test to discover something unknown or to check that an idea is true
2 something done to find out what will happen or what its effect will be

VERB experiments, experimenting, experimented

1 to experiment is to carry out scientific experiments
2 to try something to find out what the result will be

▸ **experimental**
ADJECTIVE
as a test or trial

expert

NOUN *plural* experts

someone who knows a lot about a particular subject

ADJECTIVE

very knowledgeable or skilled at something

▸ **expertise**
NOUN

skill or knowledge

a b c d e f g h i j k l m n o p q r s t u v w x y z

explain

VERB explains, explaining, explained

1 to explain something is to give more or simpler information or instructions so that it is easier to understand or do
2 to explain yourself is to give someone reasons for your behaviour

▸ **explanation**

NOUN plural **explanations**

1 something that explains
2 a piece of writing that tells you how something works or how it happens

explode

VERB explodes, exploding, exploded

1 to explode is to blow up like a bomb with a loud noise
2 if someone explodes they suddenly lose their temper

▸ **explosion**

NOUN plural **explosions**

a very loud noise made, for example, when a bomb goes off or something is blown up

explore

VERB explores, exploring, explored

1 to explore a place is to look around it and find out what it is like
2 to explore something is to study it to discover things about it or find out how good it might be

▸ **explorer**

NOUN plural **explorers**

someone who travels to a remote or unknown place to find out what it is like

extra

ADJECTIVE

an extra thing or amount is more than usual or necessary

ADVERB

very ⋛ **extra large** ⋛

NOUN plural **extras**

1 something extra, especially a charge that is not included in the original price
2 an actor who appears for a short time in a film as one of a crowd in the background

eye

NOUN plural **eyes**

your eyes are the two parts of your body at the front of your head that you see with

VERB eyes, eyeing, eyed

to eye someone or something is to look at them, especially because you are interested in them

eyeball

NOUN plural **eyeballs**

the round part that makes up your whole eye

eyebrow

NOUN plural **eyebrows**

your eyebrows are the lines of hair above your eyes

eyelash

NOUN plural **eyelashes**

your eyelashes are the hairs round the edges of your eyes

eyelid

NOUN plural **eyelids**

your eyelids are the pieces of skin that cover your eyes when your eyes are closed

face

NOUN *plural* faces

1 the front of your head where your eyes, nose and mouth are
2 the part of a clock or watch where the numbers are
3 the steep side of a mountain or cliff
4 one of the flat outside surfaces of a shape

VERB faces, facing, faced

1 to be opposite someone or something ⋟ *My house faces the park.* ⋞
2 to look or turn in the direction of someone or something ⋟ *They turned and faced each other.* ⋞
3 to have to deal with a difficult situation ⋟ *She faced many difficulties.* ⋞

fact

NOUN *plural* facts

something that you know is true

▸ **in fact**

you say 'in fact' when you are going to give more exact information ⋟ *They know each other; in fact, they are neighbours.* ⋞

factory

NOUN *plural* factories

a building where something is made in large amounts ⋟ *a chocolate factory* ⋞

fade

VERB fades, fading, faded

1 to disappear gradually
2 to lose colour and brightness ⋟ *The jeans had faded.* ⋞

fail

VERB fails, failing, failed

1 to not pass an exam or test ⋟ *My brother failed his driving test four times.* ⋞
2 to be unsuccessful in what you are trying to do ⋟ *They failed in their attempt to sail round the world.* ⋞
3 to not do what is expected or needed ⋟ *The parcel failed to arrive.* ⋞ ⋟ *The brakes failed.* ⋞

▸ **failure**

NOUN *plural* failures

1 someone or something that is not successful ⋟ *She felt like a failure.* ⋞
2 the act of failing ⋟ *Their first attempt ended in failure.* ⋞

fair¹

ADJECTIVE fairer, fairest

1 treating everyone equally ⋟ *It's not fair that my brother can stay up later than me.* ⋞
2 fair skin or hair is very light in colour
3 fair weather is very pleasant, with no rain ⋟ *Tuesday will be fair.* ⋞
4 quite good but not very good ⋟ *a fair attempt* ⋞
5 quite large in size or amount ⋟ *He lives a fair distance away from here.* ⋞

▸ **fairly**

ADVERB

1 quite ⋟ *I was fairly nervous about the test.* ⋞
2 in a way that is reasonable ⋟ *We were treated fairly.* ⋞

▸ **fairness**

NOUN

being fair

fair²

NOUN *plural* fairs

1 an event with lots of stalls where you can buy things

2 a collection of rides that you can go on for entertainment, which moves from town to town

fairy

NOUN *plural* fairies

an imaginary creature that has magical powers and looks like a small person

faith

NOUN *plural* faiths

1 great trust ⋗ *I have a lot of faith in him.* ⋖
2 religious belief ⋗ *people of different faiths* ⋖

fall

VERB falls, falling, fell, fallen

1 to drop down to the ground ⋗ *The apples fell from the tree.* ⋖
2 if you fall, you have an accident and hit the ground ⋗ *Ben fell downstairs.* ⋖
3 if an amount, price or temperature falls, it goes down

▸ **fall out**
to fall out is to stop being friends with someone

NOUN *plural* falls

1 an accident in which you hit the ground ⋗ *My grandmother had a fall last week.* ⋖
2 a drop in a price, amount or temperature ⋗ *a fall in prices* ⋖
3 the American English word for **autumn**

family

NOUN *plural* families

1 a group of people who are related to each other ⋗ *Most people in my family have brown hair.* ⋖
2 a group of animals, plants or languages that are related to each other ⋗ *the cat family* ⋖

famous

ADJECTIVE

known by many people ⋗ *a famous actor* ⋖

fan¹

NOUN *plural* fans

someone who likes a person or thing very much ⋗ *football fans* ⋖

fan²

NOUN *plural* fans

1 a machine with thin blades that spin round and make the air cooler
2 something that you hold and wave in front of your face to make you feel cooler

VERB fans, fanning, fanned

to fan yourself is to use a fan to cool yourself down

far

ADVERB farther or further, farthest or furthest

1 a long distance ⋗ *We have walked quite far.* ⋖
2 much ⋗ *She's a far better swimmer than I am.* ⋖
3 a lot of progress ⋗ *I haven't got very far with my maths homework.* ⋖

▸ **so far**
until now ⋗ *I've only read ten pages so far.* ⋖

ADJECTIVE

the far part of something is the greatest distance from you ⋗ *a house on the far side of the lake* ⋖

farm

NOUN *plural* farms

an area of land where crops are grown and animals are kept

▸ **farmer**
NOUN *plural* farmers

someone who owns and works on a farm

fashionable

ADJECTIVE

liked by many people at a particular time ⋗ *a fashionable restaurant* ⋖

fast

ADJECTIVE   faster, fastest

1 moving or happening at great speed ⋗ *a fast car* ⋖
2 if a clock or watch is fast, it shows a time that is later than the correct time

ADVERB   faster, fastest

at great speed ⋗*She can run very fast.* ⋖

fasten

VERB   fastens, fastening, fastened

to join or tie two things together

▸**fastener**

NOUN   *plural* fasteners

something that is used to join two things together

fat

ADJECTIVE   fatter, fattest

a fat person has a wide round body

NOUN   *plural* fats

1 an oily substance that forms a layer under your skin which keeps you warm
2 an oily substance in food that gives you energy but can be unhealthy if you eat too much ⋗ *foods with a high fat content* ⋖
3 oil from animals or plants that is used for frying food ⋗ *You need more fat in the pan.* ⋖

father

NOUN   *plural* fathers

your male parent

fault

NOUN   *plural* faults

1 a mistake or something that is wrong ⋗ *There's a fault in the engine.* ⋖
2 if something bad is your fault, you are responsible for it ⋗ *Whose fault is it that we lost the keys?* ⋖

favourite

ADJECTIVE

your favourite person or thing is the one you like best ⋗ *My favourite colour is purple.* ⋖ ⋗ *Who's your favourite teacher?* ⋖

▸**favouritism**

NOUN

favouritism is unfairly treating one person or group better than others

fawn

NOUN   *plural* fawns

a young deer

fear

NOUN   *plural* fears

1 a feeling of being very frightened ⋗ *She was shaking with fear.* ⋖
2 a frightened feeling that you have about something ⋗ *John has a fear of spiders and beetles.* ⋖

VERB   fears, fearing, feared

to be afraid of someone or something

feast

NOUN   *plural* feasts

a large meal for a special occasion ⋗ *a wedding feast* ⋖

> This word comes from the Latin word **festum**, which means *holiday*. The word **festival** also comes from the word **festum**.

feather

NOUN   *plural* feathers

one of the long light things that cover a bird's body

a b c d e f g h i j k l m n o p q r s t u v w x y z

February

NOUN

the second month of the year, after January and before March

> **February** comes from the Latin word **Februarius**, which was a Roman festival.

fed

VERB

a way of changing the verb **feed** to make a past tense. It can be used with or without a helping verb ⋩ *Anna fed the dog.* ⋨ ⋩ *Have you fed the cat?* ⋨

feed

VERB feeds, feeding, fed

1 to give food to a person or animal ⋩ *Dad was feeding the baby.* ⋨
2 animals feed when they eat food ⋩ *Don't disturb the dog when he's feeding.* ⋨ ⋩ *Rabbits feed on grass.* ⋨

feel

VERB feels, feeling, felt

1 to have a particular feeling ⋩ *I feel tired.* ⋨ ⋩ *Do you feel better today?* ⋨
2 to touch something with your fingers to see what it is like
3 to experience something touching you or happening to you ⋩ *Suddenly, she felt a hand on her shoulder.* ⋨ ⋩ *He could feel himself falling.* ⋨
4 if something feels hot, smooth, dry etc, that is how it seems when you touch it ⋩ *Your forehead feels hot.* ⋨
5 to think or believe something ⋩ *I feel he should have asked my opinion first.* ⋨
6 if you feel like something, you want it or want to do it ⋩ *I feel like going for a swim.* ⋨

▸ **feeler**

NOUN *plural* **feelers**

one of the two long things on an insect's head, which it uses to sense things

▸ **feeling**

NOUN *plural* **feelings**

something that you experience in your mind or body ⋩ *a feeling of excitement* ⋨

feet

NOUN

the plural of **foot**

fell

VERB

a way of changing the verb **fall** to make a past tense ⋩ *She fell off the chair.* ⋨

felt[1]

NOUN

a type of cloth made of rolled and pressed wool

felt[2]

VERB

a way of changing the verb **feel** to make a past tense. It can be used with or without a helping verb ⋩ *He felt very tired.* ⋨ ⋩ *Have you felt how soft this fur is?* ⋨

female

ADJECTIVE

belonging to the sex that can give birth or lay eggs ⋩ *A female lion is called a lioness.* ⋨

NOUN *plural* **females**
a female animal or person

fence

NOUN *plural* **fences**
a wooden or metal barrier

ferry

NOUN *plural* **ferries**
a boat that carries people and vehicles

festival

NOUN *plural* **festivals**

1 a special time when people have a holiday

to celebrate something ⇒ *a religious festival* ⇒

2 a time when there are a lot of special events of a particular type ⇒ *a film festival* ⇒

▸ **festive**

ADJECTIVE

relating to happy celebrations

fetch

VERB fetches, fetching, fetched

to go somewhere and bring something or someone back with you ⇒ *Could you fetch the newspaper for me, please?* ⇒

few

ADJECTIVE fewer, fewest

not many ⇒ *She has few friends.* ⇒

NOUN

a small number ⇒ *'Did you take any photos?' 'Only a few.'* ⇒

field

NOUN plural fields

1 an area of ground used for growing crops or keeping animals on

2 an area of grass used for playing sport on ⇒ *a football field* ⇒

VERB fields, fielding, fielded

in games like cricket, to be the person or team that throws the ball back after someone has hit it

fierce

ADJECTIVE fiercer, fiercest

1 violent and angry ⇒ *a fierce animal* ⇒

2 strong or intense ⇒ *a fierce storm* ⇒ ⇒ *fierce emotions* ⇒

▸ **fiercely**

ADVERB

in a violent or angry way

fifteen

NOUN

the number 15

fifty

NOUN plural fifties

the number 50

fight

VERB fights, fighting, fought

1 to use your body or weapons to try to hurt someone who is doing the same to you

2 to argue with someone

NOUN plural fights

the act of fighting with someone ⇒ *They had a fight in the playground.* ⇒

▸ **fighter**

NOUN plural fighters

someone who is fighting

fill

VERB fills, filling, filled

1 to make a container full ⇒ *He filled our glasses with water.* ⇒

2 to become full ⇒ *The concert hall quickly filled with people.* ⇒

film

NOUN plural films

1 a story that you watch in a cinema or on television

2 something you put inside a camera so you can take photographs

VERB films, filming, filmed

to make a film of something

fin

NOUN plural fins

one of the parts on a fish that help it to swim

final

ADJECTIVE

coming at the end ⇒ *the final chapter of a book* ⇒

NOUN plural finals

the last game in a competition, which decides who will win

a b c d e **f** g h i j k l m n o p q r s t u v w x y z

find

VERB finds, finding, found

1 to get or see something accidentally, or after you have been looking for it ⟩ *I can't find my pencil case.* ⟩ *I found a £10 note in the street.*
2 to discover something ⟩ *Have you found the answer yet?*
3 to have a particular opinion about someone or something ⟩ *I found him very rude.*

▶ **find something out**
to find something out is to discover information about it ⟩ *I'll try and find out the train times.*

fine¹

NOUN plural fines

money that someone must pay as a punishment

VERB fines, fined, fining

to make someone pay a fine ⟩ *He was fined £100 for parking illegally.*

fine²

ADJECTIVE finer, finest

1 if you are fine, you are healthy and well ⟩ *'How are you?' 'Fine, thanks.'*
2 good or acceptable ⟩ *'Shall we meet at 4 o'clock?' 'Yes, that's fine.'*
3 very thin or delicate ⟩ *fine lines*

▶ **finely**
ADVERB

1 in very thin small pieces ⟩ *Chop the onion finely.*
2 in a beautiful or impressive way ⟩ *a finely decorated room*

finger

NOUN plural fingers

one of the long parts at the end of your hand

finish

VERB finishes, finishing, finished

1 to come to an end ⟩ *What time did the film finish?*
2 to stop doing something or complete it ⟩ *Have you finished your homework?* ⟩ *I'll just finish my drink.*

fire

NOUN plural fires

1 flames and heat that burn and destroy something ⟩ *The building was destroyed by fire.* ⟩ *There was a fire at the school last night.*
2 a pile of wood or coal that is burning to give heat ⟩ *Dad put another log on the fire.*
3 a device that heats a room using gas or electricity

▶ **on fire**
burning and producing flames ⟩ *The house was on fire.*

VERB fires, firing, fired

1 to fire a gun is to shoot a bullet from it
2 to fire someone from their job is to make them leave so they no longer have it

firework

NOUN plural fireworks

a device that can be lit so that it flies into the sky and explodes, making bright lights

firm

ADJECTIVE firmer, firmest

1 not soft ⟩ *a firm bed*
2 strict and not changing your mind ⟩ *a very firm teacher*

first

ADJECTIVE

coming before everything else ⟩ *the first name on the list*

ADVERB

1 before anyone or anything else ⟩ *I finished the exam first.* ⟩ *Finish your dinner first.*
2 doing better than everyone else ⟩ *Philip came first in the cookery competition.*

PRONOUN

the person or thing that comes before all

others ⟩ ***Who is first in the queue?**⟨*

▶ **at first**

at the start of a period of time ⟩ ***At first, I hated school, but I like it now.**⟨*

fish

NOUN   *plural* **fish** *or* **fishes**

a creature that lives and swims in water. People often eat fish as food.

VERB   **fishes, fishing, fished**

to catch fish

fist

NOUN   *plural* **fists**

your hand when it is closed tightly

fit

ADJECTIVE   **fitter, fittest**

1 healthy and active because you do exercise ⟩ ***I'm trying to get fit.**⟨*
2 good enough ⟩ ***This food isn't fit to eat.**⟨*

VERB   **fits, fitting, fitted**

1 to be the right size for someone or something ⟩ ***The dress fits you perfectly.**⟨ ⟩ **The cupboard will fit in the corner.**⟨*
2 to fix something in a place ⟩ ***We're having new kitchen units fitted next week.**⟨*
3 to have space to put people or things ⟩ ***I can't fit any more into the suitcase.**⟨*
4 if something is fitted with particular equipment, it has that equipment ⟩ ***Most bikes are fitted with front and back brakes.**⟨*

▶ **fitness**

NOUN

how healthy and well someone is ⟩ ***exercises to improve fitness**⟨*

five

NOUN   *plural* **fives**

the number 5

fix

VERB   **fixes, fixing, fixed**

1 to attach something to something else ⟩ ***She fixed the shelves to the wall.**⟨*
2 to mend something ⟩ ***He's trying to fix my computer.**⟨*
3 to arrange something ⟩ ***Have you fixed a time for your friends to come over?**⟨*

flag

NOUN   *plural* **flags**

a piece of cloth with a pattern on it, used as the symbol of a country or organization ⟩ ***The American flag has stars and stripes on it.**⟨*

flame

NOUN   *plural* **flames**

the bright burning gas that you see in a fire

flat

ADJECTIVE   **flatter, flattest**

1 level and not sloping ⟩ ***a flat roof**⟨*
2 a flat tyre does not have any air in it
3 a flat battery has no more power in it

▶ **flat out**

as quickly as possible ⟩ ***Mum worked flat out to get the decorating finished.**⟨*

NOUN   *plural* **flats**

a set of rooms that someone lives in, which are part of a larger building

▶ **flatten**

VERB   **flattens, flattening, flattened**

to make something become flat

flavour

NOUN   *plural* **flavours**

the taste that something has ⟩ ***Chocolate is my favourite ice-cream flavour.**⟨*

▶ **flavouring**

NOUN   *plural* **flavourings**

something added to food to give it a

particular taste ⋛ *peppermint flavouring* ⋛

flea

NOUN   *plural* **fleas**

a very small insect that jumps and bites people or animals

flee

VERB   **flees, fleeing, fled**

to run away or escape ⋛ *She turned and fled.* ⋛

flew

VERB

a way of changing the verb **fly** to make a past tense ⋛ *When I opened the door, the bird flew away.* ⋛

flies

NOUN

the plural of the noun **fly**

VERB

the form of the verb **fly** in the present tense that you use with **he**, **she** or **it** ⋛ *I like watching Superman when he flies through the air.* ⋛

flight

NOUN   *plural* **flights**

1 a journey in an aeroplane or helicopter
2 the action of flying ⋛ *a flock of geese in flight* ⋛
3 a flight of stairs is a set of stairs

float

VERB   **floats, floating, floated**

to move along or stay on the surface of water and not sink

NOUN   *plural* **floats**

1 something that is designed to float, for example an object you hold when you are learning to swim
2 a decorated platform that is pulled along by a vehicle in a parade

flood

NOUN   *plural* **floods**

1 a lot of water in a place that is usually dry
2 a large number of people or things ⋛ *a flood of complaints about the noise* ⋛

VERB   **floods, flooding, flooded**

1 if water floods a place, it covers it in large amounts
2 if people flood into a place, they arrive there in large numbers

floor

NOUN   *plural* **floors**

1 the surface that you stand on in a room ⋛ *There were lots of toys on the bedroom floor.* ⋛
2 one of the levels in a building ⋛ *Which floor is your apartment on?* ⋛

flour

NOUN

powder made from wheat, used for making bread and cakes

> The words **flour** and **flower** sound the same, but remember that they have different spellings. A **flower** is a bloom on a plant.

flow

VERB   **flows, flowing, flowed**

if a liquid flows, it moves along ⋛ *The River Thames flows through London.* ⋛

NOUN   *plural* **flows**

a steady movement of something

flower

NOUN   *plural* **flowers**

the part of a plant that has coloured petals ⋛ *Tulips and daffodils are my favourite flowers.* ⋛

VERB   **flowers, flowering, flowered**

to produce flowers ⋛ *Bluebells usually flower in May.* ⋛

The words **flower** and **flour** sound the same, but remember that they have different spellings. **Flour** is used to make bread and cakes.

flown
VERB

a way of changing the verb **fly** to make it past tense ⇒ *The birds had flown south for the winter.*

flu
NOUN

an illness like a very bad cold with muscle pains and weakness. Flu is short for **influenza**

fly
VERB   flies, flying, flew, flown
1 to move through the air ⇒ *The bird flew across the garden.*
2 to travel in an aeroplane ⇒ *We're flying to Spain tomorrow.*
3 **informal** to move very quickly ⇒ *Tom came flying down the street on his bike.*

NOUN   *plural* **flies**
a small insect that flies

fog
NOUN

thick cloud near the ground that makes it difficult to see

▸ **foggy**
ADJECTIVE   foggier, foggiest
having a lot of fog ⇒ *a foggy day*

follow
VERB   follows, following, followed
1 to go after someone or something ⇒ *He followed her down the street*
2 to happen after something ⇒ *The meal was followed by a dance.*
3 if you follow a road, you go in the same direction as it ⇒ *Follow the path to the end and turn right.*

4 to understand what someone is saying ⇒ *Do you follow me?*
5 to obey instructions or advice ⇒ *I followed his advice.*

▸ **follower**
NOUN   *plural* **followers**
someone who supports or admires someone or something

▸ **following**
ADJECTIVE
the following day, week etc is the next one ⇒ *School finished on Friday and we went on holiday the following Wednesday.*

food
NOUN

things that you eat to stay alive ⇒ *What's your favourite food?*

foot
NOUN   *plural* **feet**
1 your feet are the parts of your body that you stand on
2 the bottom of something ⇒ *the foot of a mountain*
3 an old unit for measuring length, equal to about 30 centimetres

football
NOUN   *plural* **footballs**
1 a game played by two teams who try to kick a ball into a goal
2 a ball used for playing football

for
PREPOSITION
1 intended to be received by someone ⇒ *There's a letter for you.*
2 intended to do something ⇒ *What's this switch for?*
3 used to show a certain amount ⇒ *I've lived here for eight years.* ⇒ *We walked for two miles.* ⇒ *I got these shoes for £30.*

a b c d e f g h i j k l m n o p q r s t u v w x y z

4 showing who a feeling is about ⋛ *I felt very sorry for him.* ⋚

5 used to show a reason ⋛ *He was told off for running in the corridor.* ⋚

6 meaning ⋛ *What's the word for 'girl' in French?* ⋚

7 in favour of something ⋛ *Are you for or against the new plan?* ⋚

force

VERB forces, forcing, forced

1 to make someone do something ⋛ *The rain forced us to abandon the picnic.* ⋚

2 to make something move by using your strength ⋛ *She forced the door open.* ⋚

NOUN

1 power or strength ⋛ *The force of the explosion damaged many buildings.* ⋚

2 **science** force is something that makes an object move, or changes its speed or direction

3 a group of police, soldiers etc who are trained to work together ⋛ *a peacekeeping force* ⋚

▸ **forceful**

ADJECTIVE

powerful ⋛ *a forceful argument* ⋚

forehead

NOUN *plural* foreheads

the top front part of your head

foreign

ADJECTIVE

from a country that is not your country ⋛ *foreign languages* ⋚

▸ **foreigner**

NOUN *plural* foreigners

someone who comes from a country that is not your country

forest

NOUN *plural* forests

a place where a lot of trees are growing together

forget

VERB forgets, forgetting, forgot, forgotten

not to remember something ⋛ *I forgot to get a birthday card for Dad.* ⋚

▸ **forgetful**

ADJECTIVE

often forgetting things

forgive

VERB forgives, forgiving, forgave, forgiven

to stop being angry with someone ⋛ *Have you forgiven him for breaking your skateboard?* ⋚

▸ **forgiveness**

NOUN

forgiving someone

▸ **forgiving**

ADJECTIVE

willing to forgive other people for their faults ⋛ *a forgiving nature* ⋚

forgot

VERB

a way of changing the verb **forget** to make a past tense ⋛ *I forgot to ask what time the party is.* ⋚

▸ **forgotten**

VERB

a form of the verb **forget** that is used with a helping verb to show that something happened in the past ⋛ *He has forgotten to lock the door.* ⋚

ADJECTIVE

not remembered by anyone ⋛ *forgotten heroes of the war* ⋚

fork

NOUN *plural* forks

1 something with a handle and points that you use for lifting food to your mouth

2 a point where a road or river divides and goes off in two different directions

form

NOUN   *plural* **forms**

1 a type of something ⇒ *trains, planes and other forms of transport*
2 a piece of paper with questions and spaces to write your answers ⇒ *You have to fill in a form to get a passport.*
3 a shape something has or makes ⇒ *The chairs had been arranged in the form of a circle.*
4 the year someone is in at school ⇒ *My sister's in the sixth form.*

VERB   forms, forming, formed

1 to start, or make something start, to appear or exist ⇒ *How was the Earth formed?*
2 to make a particular shape ⇒ *The children held hands and formed a circle.*

fortune

NOUN   *plural* **fortunes**

1 a fortune is a lot of money ⇒ *His uncle died and left him a fortune.*
2 fortune is luck ⇒ *She had the good fortune to win first prize.*

▸**fortunate**
ADJECTIVE
lucky ⇒ *We arrived at the station late but were fortunate to catch the train.*

forty

NOUN   *plural* **forties**
the number 40

fossil

NOUN   *plural* **fossils**
the remains of an animal or plant that have hardened into rock after a very long time

▸**fossilize** *or* **fossilise**
VERB   fossilizes, fossilizing, fossilized
to become a fossil

fought

VERB
a way of changing the verb **fight** to make a past tense. It can be used with or without a helping verb ⇒ *He fought with his brother.* ⇒ *They had fought for freedom and lost.*

found

VERB   founds, founding, founded
to start an organization ⇒ *The college was founded in 1950.*

four

NOUN   *plural* **fours**
the number 4

fourteen

NOUN
the number 14

fox

NOUN   *plural* **foxes**
a wild animal that looks like a dog, and that has red fur and a thick tail

frame

NOUN   *plural* **frames**

1 a piece of wood or metal around the edge of a picture, mirror etc
2 the part that holds the lenses in a pair of glasses
3 the structure around which something is built or made ⇒ *the frame of a house*

freckle

NOUN   *plural* **freckles**
a small brown mark on your skin, especially your face

▸**freckled**
ADJECTIVE
covered in freckles

a b c d e f g h i j k l m n o p q r s t u v w x y z

a b c d e f g h i j k l m n o p q r s t u v w x y z

free

ADJECTIVE

1 not costing any money ***It's free to get into the museum.***
2 not taken by someone, or not busy ***Is this seat free?*** ***Are you free this evening?***
3 if you are free to do something, you are allowed to do it ***You are free to go anywhere you like.***

VERB frees, freeing, freed

to get someone out of a prison or a place where they are trapped ***Firefighters managed to free the driver from the wreckage.***

▸ **freedom**

NOUN

the right to do what you want ***the freedom to vote***

freeze

VERB freezes, freezing, froze, frozen

1 to turn into ice or become solid
2 to store food at a very cold temperature so it keeps for a long time
3 to stop moving suddenly ***He froze when he saw the big dog.***
4 **ICT** if a computer or other piece of electronic equipment freezes, everything on the screen becomes still because it is not working properly

▸ **freezer**

NOUN *plural* freezers

a machine for keeping food very cold

fresh

ADJECTIVE fresher, freshest

1 just made or collected ***fresh orange juice***
2 clean ***He put fresh sheets on the bed.***

▸ **freshen**

VERB freshens, freshening, freshened

to make something cleaner

▸ **freshly**

ADVERB

only just made or done ***freshly made bread***

Friday

NOUN *plural* Fridays

the day of the week after Thursday and before Saturday ***It's my birthday on Friday.***

> **Friday** comes from the Old English word **Frigedaeg**, which means *Freya's Day*. Freya is the Norse goddess of love.

fridge

NOUN *plural* fridges

a machine for keeping food cool. Fridge is short for **refrigerator**

fried

VERB

a way of changing the verb **fry** to make a past tense. It can be used with or without a helping verb ***Dad fried the fish in butter.*** ***Mum has fried chicken for dinner.***

friend

NOUN *plural* friends

someone who you know and like ***Lindsay is my best friend.***

▸ **friendly**

ADJECTIVE

kind and welcoming ***She's very friendly to everyone.***

▸ **friendship**

NOUN *plural* friendships

the relationship you have with a friend

fries

PLURAL NOUN

long thin pieces of potato that are fried in deep fat

VERB

the form of the verb **fry** in the present tense that you use with **he**, **she**, or **it**

fright

NOUN

a sudden feeling of fear ⋟ **You gave me a fright, jumping out like that!**⋞

▸ **frighten**

VERB frightens, frightening, frightened

to frighten someone is to make them feel scared

▸ **frightened**

ADJECTIVE

scared ⋟ **He's frightened of snakes.** ⋞

▸ **frightening**

ADJECTIVE

something that is frightening makes you feel scared ⋟ **a frightening experience** ⋞

frog

NOUN *plural* **frogs**

a small brown or green animal that can jump and lives near water

from

PREPOSITION

1 showing where something started ⋟ **She's driving up from London.** ⋞ ⋟ **Read the poem from the beginning.** ⋞

2 showing what has made something happen ⋟ **Yogurt is made from milk.** ⋞ ⋟ **He was shivering from the cold.** ⋞

3 showing where someone was born or where they live ⋟ **my cousin from Canada** ⋞ ⋟ **a friend from next door** ⋞

4 out of a place or away ⋟ **He took a notebook from the drawer.** ⋞ ⋟ **Take those sweets from her before she eats them all!**⋞

front

NOUN *plural* **fronts**

1 the front of something is the part of it that faces forwards ⋟ **The front of the house is painted red.** ⋞

2 the part of something that is closest to where you are, or closest to the direction it faces or moves in ⋟ **The teacher asked Amy to come out to the front of the class.** ⋞

3 a seashore or a road or path beside it

ADJECTIVE

at the front of something ⋟ **the front door** ⋞

▸ **in front**

at the front of something ⋟ **There were pots of colourful flowers in front of the house.** ⋞

frost

NOUN

a very thin layer of white ice crystals that forms on surfaces outside when the weather is cold

▸ **frosty**

ADJECTIVE frostier, frostiest

1 when it is frosty, everything is covered in frost

2 not very friendly ⋟ **a frosty welcome** ⋞

frown

VERB frowns, frowning, frowned

to wrinkle your forehead because you are thinking very hard or because you are worried or angry

NOUN *plural* **frowns**

an expression in which your forehead is wrinkled

frozen

VERB

the form of the verb **freeze** that is used with a helping verb to show that something happened in the past ⋟ **It's so cold that the lake has frozen.** ⋞

ADJECTIVE

frozen food is stored at a very cold temperature to make it stay fresh for a long time ⋟ **a packet of frozen peas** ⋞

a b c d e f g h i j k l m n o p q r s t u v w x y z

fruit

NOUN

the fleshy part of a plant, which you can sometimes eat, that holds seeds ***Grapes are my favourite fruit.***

▸ **fruity**

ADJECTIVE fruitier, fruitiest

having the taste of fruit ***a fruity soft drink***

fry

VERB fries, frying, fried

to cook something in hot oil or fat

full

ADJECTIVE fuller, fullest

1 containing as much as possible ***The train was full.*** ***a full bottle of milk*** ***The room was full of children.***

2 if you are full or full up, you cannot eat any more

3 if something is full, it is complete and has nothing missed out ***He told me the full story.*** ***I got full marks in the spelling test.***

▸ **full up**

with no space for anyone or anything else

full stop

NOUN *plural* full stops

the punctuation mark that looks like a small dot. You use it to show where a sentence ends

fun

NOUN

enjoyment and pleasure ***Skateboarding is good fun.*** ***We had a lot of fun at the party.***

▸ **make fun of someone**

to tease someone or make other people laugh at them

funny

ADJECTIVE funnier, funniest

1 a funny person or thing makes you laugh ***a funny story***

2 strange or unusual ***There was a funny noise coming from the engine.***

fur

NOUN

the soft hair on some animals

furniture

NOUN

objects such as beds, tables and chairs that you put in a room

future

NOUN

the future is the time that will come ***You can't know what will happen to you in the future.***

▸ **in future**

from now ***In future, please be more careful.***

gallop

NOUN *plural* **gallops**

a running pace

VERB **gallops, galloping, galloped**

a horse gallops when it runs at its fastest pace with all four feet off the ground at the same time

game

NOUN *plural* **games**

1 a game is any activity or contest with a set of rules in which players try to do better than others or try to get points ⋛ *a computer game* ⋚ ⋛ *card games* ⋚
2 games are all the sports children are taught in school
3 in some sports, a game is one of the parts of a complete match ⋛ *He won the first set 7 games to 5.* ⋚
4 game is wild animals and birds that are hunted for sport

▸ **give the game away**

to give the game away is to let other people know about something you have been trying to hide or keep secret

ADJECTIVE **gamer, gamest**

someone who is game is ready to do things, especially things that involve risk

gang

NOUN *plural* **gangs**

1 a group of friends who meet regularly or go around together
2 a group of criminals or other troublemakers

VERB **gangs, ganging, ganged**

▸ **gang up on someone**

if people gang up on another person they act together against that person

gap

NOUN *plural* **gaps**

1 an opening or space in the middle of something or between things ⋛ *a gap in the wall* ⋚ ⋛ *a gap between his front teeth* ⋚
2 something missing ⋛ *a gap in his memory* ⋚
3 a difference between two things ⋛ *the gap between rich and poor* ⋚

garage

NOUN *plural* **garages**

1 a building, often a small one beside a house, for storing a car or other vehicle
2 a place where vehicles are repaired, or a shop selling petrol and often other items for vehicles or road journeys

> This word comes from the French word **garer**, which means *to shelter*. The word **guard** is also linked to **garer**.

garden

NOUN *plural* **gardens**

an area of land where flowers, trees and vegetables are grown

▸ **gardener**

NOUN *plural* **gardeners**

someone who does gardening

▸ **gardening**

NOUN

working in and taking care of a garden

▸ **gardens**

PLURAL NOUN

a large public park ⋛ *the botanical gardens* ⋚

gas

NOUN *plural* **gases** *or* **gasses**

1 **science** a substance that is not liquid or solid and that moves about like air ⋛ *Oxygen and carbon dioxide are two of the gases that make up air.* ⋛
2 any natural or manufactured gas that burns easily and is used as fuel ⋛ *natural gas* ⋛ ⋛ *coal gas* ⋛
3 gas is short for gasoline, the name used in North America for petrol

gate

NOUN *plural* **gates**

1 a movable structure with hinges that is used to close an opening in a wall or fence

2 the numbered area where passengers wait before getting on an aeroplane

gave

VERB

a way of changing the verb **give** to make a past tense ⋛ *Jodie gave Robbie some of her sweets.* ⋛

geese

NOUN

the plural of **goose**

gem

NOUN *plural* **gems**

a valuable stone that can be cut and polished and used in jewellery

gentle

ADJECTIVE gentler, gentlest

1 a gentle person is kind and calm ⋛ *a gentle giant* ⋛
2 soft and light ⋛ *a gentle breeze* ⋛ ⋛ *a gentle tap on his shoulder* ⋛

▸ **gentleness**
NOUN
being gentle

▸ **gently**
ADVERB
in a gentle way

> The word **gentle** comes from the French word **gentil**, which means well-bred and polite.

germ

NOUN *plural* **germs**

a tiny living thing that can cause disease

get

VERB gets, getting, got

1 you get something when someone gives it to you or you fetch it ⋛ *Kiera got lots of birthday presents.* ⋛
2 you have got something when you have it or own it ⋛ *Have you got a rubber I could borrow?* ⋛ ⋛ *They haven't got a TV.* ⋛
3 you get someone to do something for you when you ask or persuade them to do it ⋛ *Get Rory to help you lift that big box.* ⋛
4 you get somewhere when you arrive there ⋛ *We got to New York at 5 o'clock in the morning.* ⋛
5 you get a bus or some other form of transport when you travel on it ⋛ *Mum gets the train to work.* ⋛
6 if you get a disease or illness, you catch it ⋛ *I hope your sister doesn't get the measles.* ⋛
7 to be in a particular state, or to put something in a particular state ⋛ *I'm*

getting tired – can we go home now?
Try not to get your new shoes dirty.

▸ **get away with**

to get away with something is to manage to do something wrong or illegal without being caught or punished

▸ **get by**

to get by is to manage, especially with the money you have

▸ **get on**

1 to make progress or to do well *You have to study hard if you want to get on.*

2 if people get on, or get on with each other, they like each other and are friendly to each other *Jake and Mikey seem to get on really well.*

▸ **get out of**

to get out of something is to avoid doing it

▸ **get over**

to get over something is to recover from it *It took her a long time to get over the shock.*

giant

NOUN *plural* **giants**

1 in stories, an imaginary being like a huge person that is often evil or frightening

2 a very large thing *an industrial giant*

ADJECTIVE

huge or bigger than normal *a giant crane* *a giant tortoise*

gift

NOUN *plural* **gifts**

something given to another person because it is a special occasion or because you like them

▸ **gifted**

ADJECTIVE

a gifted person is extremely good at something or extremely clever

gigantic

ADJECTIVE

huge, like a giant

giggle

VERB **giggles, giggling, giggled**

to giggle is to laugh in a silly or nervous way

NOUN *plural* **giggles**

a silly or nervous laugh

giraffe

NOUN *plural* **giraffes**

an African animal with a spotted coat, long legs and a very long neck

girl

NOUN *plural* **girls**

a female child or young woman

give

VERB **gives, giving, gave, given**

1 to give something to someone is to let them have it or to pass it on to them *My brother gave me his old bike.*

2 to make someone feel or believe something *The sudden explosion gave us all a shock.* *John gave me the impression he didn't want to come.*

3 to allow someone to have something *Mum has given us another ten minutes to watch TV.*

4 if someone gives a party or performance, they hold a party or they perform in front of other people

5 to give a cry, shout or laugh is to make that

a b c d e f **g** h i j k l m n o p q r s t u v w x y z

sound out loud ⧽ *He gave a whoop of joy.* ⧼

▸ **give something away**

to give away something, such as a secret, is to tell it to someone without meaning to

▸ **give in**

to give in is to admit that you have been beaten

▸ **give out**

if a machine or a part of your body gives out, it stops working

▸ **give up**

to give up is to stop trying to do something because it has become too difficult

▸ **give way**

something gives way when it breaks or collapses

glad

ADJECTIVE gladder, gladdest

pleased or happy ⧽ *We're very glad you could make it to the party.* ⧼

▸ **gladly**

ADVERB

happily or with pleasure ⧽ *I'll gladly do what you ask.* ⧼

▸ **gladness**

NOUN

a feeling of pleasure or happiness

glass

NOUN *plural* glasses

1 glass is a hard breakable material that lets light through
2 a glass is a container for drinks made of this material, or the amount it will hold ⧽ *a tall glass* ⧼ ⧽ *She drank three glasses of milk.* ⧼

ADJECTIVE

made of glass ⧽ *a glass bowl* ⧼

▸ **glasses**

PLURAL NOUN

glasses are a pair of clear lenses inside a frame that you wear over your eyes to help you see more clearly

glitter

VERB glitters, glittering, glittered

to shine or sparkle with small flashes of light

NOUN

tiny pieces of shiny material for decorating or making pictures

▸ **glittery**

ADJECTIVE

shining with little sparks of light or tiny pieces of shiny material

global warming

NOUN

geography the gradual warming of the Earth's surface and atmosphere, causing rises in sea temperature and weather changes around the world

glove

NOUN *plural* gloves

gloves are two matching pieces of clothing that you wear on your hands

glue

NOUN *plural* glues

a substance used for sticking things together

VERB glues, gluing or glueing, glued

to glue something is to stick it with glue

▸ **gluey**

ADJECTIVE

covered with glue or sticky like glue

go

VERB goes, going, went, gone

1 to go somewhere is to travel or move there ⧽ *I'm going home now.* ⧼
2 to go somewhere is to lead to that place ⧽ *Does this road go to Inverness?* ⧼
3 to leave ⧽ *It's six o'clock. I'll have to go soon.* ⧼
4 the place where something goes is the place where it fits or is kept ⧽ *That piece of the jigsaw goes at the top.* ⧼

5 to become ⋚ *Her face went pale.* ⋚ ⋚ *Your soup's gone cold.* ⋚

▶**go in for**
to go in for something is to take part in it

▶**go off**
food goes off when it becomes bad ⋚ *Put the milk in the fridge before it goes off.* ⋚

▶**go on**
to go on is to continue ⋚ *Go on with your work* ⋚ ⋚ *The baby went on crying.* ⋚

▶**going to**
about to ⋚ *What were you going to say?* ⋚

NOUN   *plural* **goes**

a go is a try or a turn ⋚ *Can I have a go on your bike?* ⋚

▶**on the go**
if someone is on the go, they are busy or active

goal

NOUN   *plural* **goals**

1 in games like football and hockey, the goal is the area where you have to put the ball to score a point
2 a goal is a point scored when a ball goes into this area
3 an aim that you want to achieve

goat

NOUN   *plural* **goats**

an animal with horns and long rough hair

goggles

PLURAL NOUN

people wear goggles over their eyes to protect them, for example when they are swimming underwater or working with materials that might damage their eyes

gold

NOUN

1 a pale yellow precious metal
2 a yellow colour

ADJECTIVE

gold-coloured or made of gold

▶**golden**

ADJECTIVE

gold-coloured or made of gold ⋚ *golden hair* ⋚

goldfish

NOUN   *plural* **goldfish**

a small fish with golden or orange scales that is kept as a pet

gone

VERB

the form of the verb **go** that is used with a helping verb to show that something happened in the past ⋚ *I tried to catch him before he left, but he had gone.* ⋚

good

ADJECTIVE   better, best

1 something good is enjoyable or pleasant, or is of a high standard ⋚ *Did you have a good holiday?* ⋚
2 a good person is kind and thoughtful ⋚ *My grandparents are very good to me.* ⋚
3 good behaviour is correct or proper ⋚ *He has very good manners.* ⋚
4 to be good at something is to be able to do it well ⋚ *Sam's very good at drawing horses.* ⋚
5 giving you the result you want ⋚ *a good way to make Mum happy* ⋚
6 something is good for you when it benefits you in some way, especially by keeping you healthy

NOUN

good is rightness ⋚ *the difference between good and evil* ⋚

▶**for good**
for ever ⋚ *He won't be coming back; he's gone for good.* ⋚

goodbye

INTERJECTION

you say 'goodbye' to people you are leaving or who are leaving you

a b c d e f **g** h i j k l m n o p q r s t u v w x y z

goose

NOUN *plural* **geese**

a bird with a long neck and webbed feet

gorilla

NOUN *plural* **gorillas**

a very large ape with a large head, long arms and a strong heavy body

> Be careful not to confuse the spellings of **gorilla** and **guerilla**. A **guerilla** is a type of fighter.

got

VERB

a way of changing the verb **get** to make a past tense. It can be used with or without a helping verb ⇒ *Katy got a bike for her birthday.* ⇒ *Your brother has already got into the car.*

government

NOUN *plural* **governments**

a government is the group of people who are in charge of running the country

grab

VERB grabs, grabbing, grabbed

1 to grab something is to grasp or take it suddenly or roughly ⇒ *He grabbed my bag and ran away.*
2 to grab something is to take it eagerly or in a hurry ⇒ *Let's stop and grab a bite to eat.*

grand-daughter

NOUN *plural* **grand-daughters**

the daughter of someone's son or daughter

grandfather

NOUN *plural* **grandfathers**

the father of your father or mother

grandmother

NOUN *plural* **grandmothers**

the mother of your father or mother

grandson

NOUN *plural* **grandsons**

the son of someone's son or daughter

Granthi said "**grun**-tee"

NOUN *plural* **Granthis**

the guardian of a Sikh temple and the Guru Granth Sahib

grass

NOUN *plural* **grasses**

a plant with long thin leaves called blades, which grows on lawns and in fields

▶ **grassy**
ADJECTIVE grassier, grassiest
covered with grass ⇒ *a grassy field*

grate

VERB grates, grating, grated

1 to grate food is to cut it into fine strands or shreds using a grater
2 something grates when it makes an unpleasant squeaking or scratching noise as it rubs, or is rubbed, against something

grave

NOUN *plural* **graves**

a place where a dead body is buried

great

ADJECTIVE greater, greatest

1 very important or special ⇒ *a great day for the school*

2 very talented or distinguished ⋗ *one of the greatest scientists of all time* ⋖

3 very large ⋗ *The elephant lifted one of its great feet.* ⋖

4 very enjoyable or very good ⋗ *It was a great film.* ⋖

5 you use the word 'great' to show that a family member is another generation above or below. For example, your *great-grandmother* is the mother of your grandmother or grandfather, and your *great-grandson* is the son of your grandson or granddaughter

NOUN *plural* **greats**

an extremely famous, special or important person or thing ⋗ *one of Hollywood's greats* ⋖

▸ **greatly**

ADVERB

very much ⋗ *She wasn't greatly pleased.* ⋖

▸ **greatness**

NOUN

being very impressive, important or talented

greed

NOUN

great or selfish desire for more of something than you need, especially food or money

▸ **greedily**

ADVERB

in a way that shows greed for food or money ⋗ *My brother ate his lunch greedily.* ⋖

▸ **greedy**

ADJECTIVE greedier, greediest

wanting more of something than you actually need

green

NOUN

the colour of grass and the leaves of most plants

ADJECTIVE greener, greenest

of the colour green

▸ **greenery**

NOUN

green leaves

grew

VERB

a way of changing the verb **grow** to make a past tense ⋗ *Stephen grew three centimetres last summer.* ⋖

grey

NOUN

a colour between black and white

ADJECTIVE greyer, greyest

of the colour grey

grin

VERB grins, grinning, grinned

to grin is to smile broadly showing your teeth

NOUN *plural* grins

a wide smile

grip

VERB grips, gripping, gripped

1 if you grip something, you hold it tightly

2 if something grips you, it holds your attention completely

NOUN *plural* grips

a hold or grasp ⋗ *a tight grip* ⋖　⋗ *in the grip of winter* ⋖

groan

VERB groans, groaning, groaned

1 to make a long deep sound because you are in pain or you think something is bad

2 to make a sound like a groan ⋗ *The trees creaked and groaned.* ⋖

NOUN *plural* groans

a deep moan made in the back of your throat

ground¹

NOUN *plural* grounds

1 the ground is the Earth's surface ⋗ *fall to the ground* ⋖　⋗ *on higher ground* ⋖

2 ground is earth or soil ⦚ *stony ground* ⦚

▸ **grounded**

ADJECTIVE

1 a child is grounded when they aren't allowed out, as a punishment

2 a pilot or plane is grounded when they aren't allowed to fly

▸ **grounds**

PLURAL NOUN

1 the grounds of a large house or building are the areas of land that surround it and are part of the same property

2 to have grounds for doing something is to have reasons for doing it

group

NOUN *plural* groups

a number of people or things that are together or that belong together

VERB groups, grouping, grouped

to bring people or things together in a group or groups

grow

VERB grows, growing, grew, grown

1 to grow is to get bigger, taller, wider or stronger ⦚ *He's grown as tall as his father.* ⦚ ⦚ *The club has grown into a big business.* ⦚

2 to grow plants is to look after them while they grow ⦚ *We grow vegetables in our garden.* ⦚

3 to become ⦚ *It was growing dark.* ⦚

▸ **grow out of something**

to grow out of something you used to do or wear when you were younger is to become too old or big for it

grumpy

ADJECTIVE grumpier, grumpiest

bad-tempered ⦚ *He's grumpy if he has to get up early.* ⦚

grunt

VERB grunts, grunting, grunted

to make a deep snorting noise like a pig

NOUN *plural* grunts

a deep snorting noise

guard

NOUN *plural* guards

1 someone whose job is to protect a person or place, or to make sure that prisoners don't escape

2 something that protects from damage or accidents ⦚ *a gum guard* ⦚ ⦚ *a fire guard* ⦚

3 someone who is in charge of a railway train or coach

▸ **keep guard** *or* **stand guard**

to watch over someone or something

VERB guards, guarding, guarded

to guard a person or place is to watch over them

▸ **guard against**

to guard against something is to take care not to let it happen

guess

VERB guesses, guessing, guessed

to guess is to give an answer or opinion without knowing or being sure of all or any of the facts

NOUN *plural* guesses

an answer or opinion made by guessing

guest

NOUN *plural* guests

1 someone you invite to your house or to a party

2 someone staying in a hotel

guilty

ADJECTIVE guiltier, guiltiest

1 you feel guilty when you feel you have done something wrong

2 if someone is guilty of something, other people think that something they do is wrong

3 someone is found guilty of a crime when a jury or judge decides that they did it

guinea pig

NOUN *plural* guinea pigs

1 a small animal with long soft hair that is kept as a pet
2 someone who is asked to try something new that nobody else has tried yet

guitar

NOUN *plural* guitars

an instrument with a rounded body shaped like a figure of eight, a long neck and strings that you play with your fingers

gulp

VERB gulps, gulping, gulped

to gulp is to swallow air or liquid quickly in large mouthfuls ⋛ *He gulped down his tea.* ⋚

NOUN *plural* gulps

1 the sound made when you gulp

2 a large mouthful ⋛ *a gulp of tea* ⋚

gun

NOUN *plural* guns

a weapon that fires bullets or shells from a metal tube

gurdwara said "**goor**-dwar-a"

NOUN *plural* gurdwaras

a building where Sikhs go to worship

Guru Granth Sahib said "**goo**-roo grunt **sa**-ib"

NOUN

the holy book of the Sikh religion. It is also called the **Adi-Granth**

gust

NOUN *plural* gusts

a sudden strong rush of wind

gym

NOUN *plural* gyms

1 a gym is a large room with special equipment for doing exercises
2 a gym is a hall in a school where you do PE
3 gym is the exercises and games that you do in a school gym

gymnast

NOUN *plural* gymnasts

someone trained to do gymnastics, which are exercises done indoors in a gym using special equipment like bars, ropes and beams

a b c d e f g h i j k l m n o p q r s t u v w x y z

had
VERB
1 a way of changing the verb **have** to make a past tense ⫶ *I had a cold last week.* ⫶
2 **had** is also used as a helping verb along with a main verb ⫶ *I had enjoyed my stay in France.* ⫶ ⫶ *He had had enough.* ⫶

hail
NOUN
small white balls of frozen water that fall in showers from the sky

hair
NOUN *plural* **hairs**
1 a hair is one of the thread-like things that grow on the surface of the skin of animals and humans
2 your hair is the mass of hairs that grow on your head

▸ **hairy**
ADJECTIVE hairier, hairiest
1 covered with hair ⫶ *Most men have hairy legs.* ⫶
2 terrifying or dangerous ⫶ *If it is stormy, the ferry crossing can get a bit hairy.* ⫶

hajj
NOUN
the journey or pilgrimage to Mecca that all Muslims should try to make at least once in their lifetime

▸ **hajji**
NOUN *plural* **hajjis**
a Muslim who has made a pilgrimage to Mecca

halal
ADJECTIVE
halal meat is from animals killed and prepared according to the laws of Islam

half
NOUN *plural* **halves**
1 a half is one of two equal parts that together make up the whole of something ⫶ *He ate half and I ate the other half.* ⫶
2 the fraction ½, equivalent to the decimal fraction 0.5 and equal to one divided by two

ADJECTIVE
1 being one of two equal parts ⫶ *a half brick* ⫶
2 not full or complete ⫶ *a half smile* ⫶

ADVERB
1 to the level or extent of a half ⫶ *This glass is only half full.* ⫶
2 partly or almost ⫶ *a half-open door* ⫶
3 nearly ⫶ *It wasn't half as scary as I expected it to be.* ⫶

hall
NOUN *plural* **halls**
1 an area just inside the entrance to a house from which you can get to other rooms or to the stairs
2 a large building or room where meetings, concerts and other events are held

Hallowe'en
NOUN
October 31, the time when ghosts and witches are traditionally supposed to wander about, and when people get dressed up in costumes and masks

This word comes from the old word **All-Hallow-Even**, which means 'the eve of All Saints' Day'.

ham

NOUN   *plural* hams

ham is smoked and salted meat from the leg of a pig

hammer

NOUN   *plural* hammers

a tool with a heavy metal or wooden head at the end of a handle, used for knocking nails in or for breaking up hard material like stones and concrete

VERB   hammers, hammering, hammered

1 to hit something with a hammer
   ﹥ **hammering the nails in one by one** ﹤
2 to hit something several times, making a lot of noise ﹥ **hammering on the door with his fists** ﹤
3 to hammer someone in a game or competition is to beat them by a lot of points ﹥ **We hammered the other team 10-0.** ﹤
▸ **hammer something out**
to hammer something out is to discuss it until everyone is satisfied ﹥ **hammer out an agreement** ﹤

hamster

NOUN   *plural* hamsters

a small animal with soft fur and a short tail, often kept as a pet

hand

NOUN   *plural* hands

1 your hand is the part of your body at the end of your arm just below your wrist
2 a narrow pointer on a clock or watch that moves round and shows the time
3 if you give someone a hand, you give them your help
4 a unit, equal to about 10 centimetres, used for measuring the height of horses ﹥ **a huge horse of almost 16 hands** ﹤
▸ **at hand**
something that is at hand is available quickly ﹥ **Help is at hand.** ﹤
▸ **by hand**
you do or make something by hand when you use your hands to do or make it
▸ **in hand**
something is in hand when it is being dealt with
▸ **on hand**
if someone or something is on hand, they are ready and available to help or be used
▸ **out of hand**
if things get out of hand, they get out of control
▸ **to hand**
if something is to hand, it is near you and you are able to reach it or use it easily

VERB   hands, handing, handed

to hand something to someone is to pass it to them

handle

NOUN   *plural* handles

1 a part of an object that you use to pick it up and hold it ﹥ **a brush with a long handle** ﹤
2 a lever or knob on a door that you hold when you open and close the door
▸ **fly off the handle**
if someone flies off the handle, they lose their temper

VERB   handles, handling, handled

1 to handle something is to touch or hold it with your hands ﹥ **Try not to handle the fruit too much.** ﹤
2 to handle something is to deal or cope with it ﹥ **Mr Peters is handling all the arrangements for the trip.** ﹤

hang

VERB   hangs, hanging, hung *or* hanged

1 to hang something is to attach it or support it at the top so that it is held above the

ground ⟩ *Hang your jackets up.* ⟨

2 something hangs when it is supported near the top and is held above the ground ⟩ *A picture was hanging on the wall.* ⟨

3 to hang someone is to kill them by tying a rope around their neck and removing a support from under their feet

▸ **hang about** *or* **hang around**

to stay in one place doing nothing ⟩ *Don't let's hang about any more. Let's get started.* ⟨

NOUN

▸ **get the hang of something**

to learn how to do something after a bit of practice

> **Hung** is the usual past tense of the verb **hang**. However, you use **hanged** instead of **hung** about someone who dies by hanging.

Hanukkah said "ha-nu-ka"

NOUN

Hanukkah is a Jewish festival lasting for eight days in December. It is also called the Feast of Dedication or the Festival of Lights because a candle is lit on each of the eight days

happen

VERB happens, happening, happened

1 something happens when it takes place or occurs ⟩ *When did this happen?* ⟨ ⟩ *I rang the bell but nothing happened.* ⟨

2 if something happens to a person or thing, an event or situation affects or involves them ⟩ *Do you know what's happened to the front door key?* ⟨

3 if you happen to do or see something, you do or see it by chance ⟩ *She just happened to be there and saw the whole thing.* ⟨

happy

ADJECTIVE happier, happiest

1 joyful ⟩ *the happiest day of her life* ⟨

2 pleased or contented ⟩ *I'd be happy to help.* ⟨

3 lucky ⟩ *a happy coincidence* ⟨

▸ **happily**

ADVERB

joyfully, contentedly or luckily ⟩ *smiling happily* ⟨ ⟩ *Happily, it all turned out well.* ⟨

▸ **happiness**

NOUN

being happy

hard

ADJECTIVE harder, hardest

1 feeling firm and solid when touched and not easily broken or bent out of shape ⟩ *hard as rock* ⟨ ⟩ *a hard bed* ⟨

2 difficult ⟩ *a very hard sum* ⟨ ⟩ *He's had a hard life.* ⟨

3 needing a lot of effort ⟩ *hard work* ⟨

4 tough or not easy to deal with ⟩ *hard luck* ⟨ ⟩ *They drive a hard bargain.* ⟨

ADVERB harder, hardest

1 strongly or violently ⟩ *It was raining hard when we got there.* ⟨

2 with more effort ⟩ *You must work harder.* ⟨

▸ **hard of hearing**

someone who is hard of hearing is nearly deaf

harm

VERB harms, harming, harmed

to harm someone or something is to hurt or damage them ⟩ *You might harm your eyes if you sit too close to the TV.* ⟨

NOUN

damage or injury ⟩ *No harm will come to you.* ⟨ ⟩ *It would do no harm to ask.* ⟨

▸ **harmful**

ADJECTIVE

causing damage or injury ⟩ *protecting your skin from the sun's harmful rays* ⟨

▸ **harmless**

ADJECTIVE

not dangerous or not causing any damage or annoyance ⸴ *a harmless little insect* ⸴

has

VERB

1 the form of the verb **have** that is used with *he, she* and *it* to make a present tense ⸴ *He has large and dreamy eyes.* ⸴
2 **has** is also used as a helping verb along with a main verb ⸴ *He has gone home.* ⸴

hat

NOUN   *plural* **hats**

a covering for your head

hatch

VERB   hatches, hatching, hatched

1 baby birds and reptiles hatch when they break out of their eggs ⸴ *The eggs should hatch in six to eight days.* ⸴
2 to hatch a plot is to think of it and develop its details, especially in secret

hate

VERB   hates, hating, hated

to hate something or someone is to dislike them very much ⸴ *He hates tidying his bedroom.* ⸴

NOUN

1 hate is very strong dislike ⸴ *Her eyes were full of hate and disappointment.* ⸴
2 your hates are the things that you dislike very much ⸴ *It's one of his pet hates.* ⸴

▸ **hatred**

NOUN

hatred is a very strong feeling of dislike

have

VERB   has, having, had

1 to have something is to own or possess it, or to include it ⸴ *I'll look at your essay when I have a free moment.* ⸴ ⸴ *He has a limp.* ⸴

2 to have an illness is to suffer from it ⸴ *Carol's had chickenpox.* ⸴ ⸴ *Mum has a terrible headache.* ⸴
3 to have something is to get or receive it ⸴ *I had a phone call from him last week.* ⸴
4 to have a baby is to give birth to it ⸴ *The cat had kittens.* ⸴
5 to have food or drink is to eat it or drink it ⸴ *I have lunch at school.* ⸴
6 you have something done when you get it done ⸴ *He's having a tooth out.* ⸴
7 if you have to do something, you must do it ⸴ *You have to tell me what was said.* ⸴
8 have is also used as a helping verb along with a main verb ⸴ *I have left some money for you.* ⸴

▸ **have someone on**

to tell someone something is true when it isn't

▸ **have it out**

to have it out with someone is to talk to them to try to settle a disagreement

he

PRONOUN

a word you use to talk about a man, boy, or male animal that has already been mentioned or pointed out ⸴ *I like Tommy. He is very friendly.* ⸴

head

NOUN   *plural* **heads**

1 the part of a human's or animal's body that contains the brain, eyes and mouth
2 your mind or intelligence ⸴ *The idea just popped into my head.* ⸴
3 the head of a group or organization is the person in charge
4 the top of something ⸴ *the title at the head of the page* ⸴

VERB   heads, heading, headed

1 if you head a group of people, you lead them or are in charge of them
2 to head somewhere is to go towards that place
3 to head a ball is to hit it with your head

a b c d e f g **h** i j k l m n o p q r s t u v w x y z

a b c d e f g **h** i j k l m n o p q r s t u v w x y z

headmaster

NOUN *plural* **headmasters**

a male teacher in charge of a school

headmistress

NOUN *plural* **headmistresses**

a female teacher in charge of a school

health

NOUN

1 your health is the condition of your body or mind, and how well you are ⊰ *His health is not good.* ⊱ ⊰ *mental health* ⊱
2 the health of something is how good or bad its condition is ⊰ *the health of the economy* ⊱

healthy

ADJECTIVE healthier, healthiest

1 fit and well ⊰ *a healthy baby* ⊱
2 good for you ⊰ *lots of healthy exercise* ⊱
3 in a good state or condition ⊰ *a healthy bank balance* ⊱

▸ **healthily**

ADVERB

in a way that is good for you ⊰ *You can live healthily by eating well and getting plenty of sleep.* ⊱

▸ **healthiness**

NOUN

being healthy

hear

VERB hears, hearing, heard

1 to hear sounds is to be aware of them through your ears ⊰ *Can you hear that clicking noise?* ⊱
2 to hear news is to be told it ⊰ *I heard that she had got married.* ⊱
3 to have heard of someone or something is to know that they exist ⊰ *I'd never heard of him before.* ⊱
4 you hear from someone when they get in touch with you ⊰ *We haven't heard from him for over a month.* ⊱

▸ **hearer**

NOUN *plural* **hearers**

your hearers are the people who are listening to you when you are speaking

▸ **hearing**

NOUN *plural* **hearings**

1 your hearing is your ability to hear
2 if something is said in your hearing, you can hear it
3 a hearing is a court trial

heart

NOUN *plural* **hearts**

1 your heart is the hollow muscular organ inside your chest that pumps blood around your body
2 someone's heart is their feelings and emotions ⊰ *She captured the hearts of the audience.* ⊱ ⊰ *He has a kind heart.* ⊱
3 a heart is a shape, ♥, that represents the human heart and human love
4 hearts is one of the four suits of playing cards, which have the symbol ♥ printed on them
5 the heart of something is its central or most important part ⊰ *getting to the heart of the problem* ⊱

▸ **by heart**

if you learn something by heart, you learn it so that you can repeat it exactly

heat

NOUN *plural* **heats**

1 heat is high temperature or the warmth that something hot gives out ⊰ *the heat from the sun* ⊱
2 heat is anger or strong feelings ⊰ *She tried to calm them down and take the heat out of the situation.* ⊱
3 a heat is a round in a competition or race ⊰ *Ian won his heat and went through to the semi-final.* ⊱

VERB heats, heating, heated

1 to heat something, or heat it up, is to raise its temperature or make it warm or hot

2 if something heats up, it becomes warmer or hotter

▸**heater**

NOUN *plural* **heaters**

a device used to heat a room or the inside of a car

▸**heating**

NOUN

the system or machinery used to heat a building

heavy

ADJECTIVE **heavier, heaviest**

1 something that is heavy weighs a lot
2 the amount that something weighs is how heavy it is
3 heavy rain or a heavy blow has a lot of force
4 a heavy smoker smokes a lot and a heavy drinker drinks a lot of alcohol
5 if your heart is heavy, you feel sad

▸**heaviness**

NOUN

the state of being heavy or the weight of something

hedge

NOUN *plural* **hedges**

a line of bushes or small trees that are growing close together and form a boundary

VERB **hedges, hedging, hedged**

to avoid answering a question

hedgehog

NOUN *plural* **hedgehogs**

a small wild mammal with prickles all over its body

heel

NOUN *plural* **heels**

1 your heels are the back parts of your feet
2 the heel of a shoe or boot is the part under the back of your foot
3 the heel of a sock or stocking is the part that covers your heel

height

NOUN *plural* **heights**

1 how tall or high someone or something is ⋛ *What height is Mount Everest?*⋛
2 the height of something is the time or level when it is at its greatest or strongest ⋛ *It is the height of stupidity to throw a lighted firework.* ⋛ ⋛ *50 firefighters were there when the fire was at its height.* ⋛
3 a high place ⋛ *looking down from the heights* ⋛

▸**heighten**

VERB **heightens, heightening, heightened**

1 to heighten something is to make it higher ⋛ *We'll have to heighten the seat of the bike a little.* ⋛
2 something heightens, or is heightened, when it increases or is increased ⋛ *The music heightens the tension of the film.* ⋛

held

VERB

a way of changing the verb **hold** to make a past tense. It can be used with or without a helping verb ⋛ *I held my breath and waited.* ⋛ ⋛ *He had held the job for ten years.* ⋛

helicopter

NOUN *plural* **helicopters**

a flying machine without wings that is lifted into the air by large propellers on top which spin round very fast

a b c d e f g **h** i j k l m n o p q r s t u v w x y z

a
b
c
d
e
f
g
h
i
j
k
l
m
n
o
p
q
r
s
t
u
v
w
x
y
z

hello

INTERJECTION

you say 'hello' as a greeting when you meet someone or begin talking to them

NOUN   *plural* hellos *or* helloes

a greeting ⸶ *We said our hellos.* ⸶

help

VERB   helps, helping, helped

1 to do something useful for someone ⸶ *My Mum helped me with my homework.* ⸶ ⸶ *a rhyme that helps you to remember the colours of the rainbow* ⸶

2 if you cannot help something, you cannot stop yourself from doing it, or you cannot stop it happening

▸ **help yourself**

if you help yourself, you take something without waiting for someone to give it to you

NOUN   *plural* helps

1 you give someone help when you do something useful for them ⸶ *He gave some help with the gardening.* ⸶

2 a help is someone or something that helps ⸶ *Thanks for the tip. It was a great help.* ⸶

INTERJECTION

people shout 'Help!' when they are in danger and want someone to come and help them

▸ **helpless**

ADJECTIVE

not able to protect yourself or look after yourself

▸ **helpful**

ADJECTIVE

willing to help, or giving help

▸ **helper**

NOUN   *plural* helpers

someone who helps another person ⸶ *one of Santa's helpers* ⸶

helpful

ADJECTIVE

someone who is helpful gives help to other

people ⸶ *Sally's mum said that she was very helpful when she fed the dog.* ⸶

helping verb

NOUN   *plural* helping verbs

a short verb like *should, will* or *can* that you use with a main verb to make slight differences of meaning, for example *Have you finished?*

hen

NOUN   *plural* hens

a female chicken

her

PRONOUN

a word you use to talk about a woman, a girl, a female animal or a vehicle or ship that has already been mentioned or pointed out ⸶ *I'm looking for Eve. Have you seen her?* ⸶

ADJECTIVE

belonging to her ⸶ *Her hair is blonde.* ⸶

here

ADVERB

at, in or to this place or time ⸶ *I like it here.* ⸶

▸ **here and there**

things that are here and there are in several different places

INTERJECTION

1 people say 'Here!' to express surprise or anger at something someone is doing ⸶ *Here! You can't sit there!* ⸶

2 you say 'here' when you are offering something to someone ⸶ *Here, take this one. It's better than the one you have.* ⸶

hero

NOUN   *plural* heroes

1 a man or boy who many people admire for his courage and bravery

2 the most important male character in a story or film

▸ **heroic**

ADJECTIVE

1 very brave

2 to do with heroes or heroines

▸ **heroine**

NOUN *plural* **heroines**

1 a woman or girl who many people admire for her courage and bravery
2 the most important female character in a story or film

▸ **heroism**

NOUN

great bravery and courage that many people admire

hers

PRONOUN

a word you use to talk about something belonging to a woman, girl, female animal or a vehicle or ship that has already been mentioned or pointed out ⬩ *I gave Sandra my phone number and she gave me hers.*

> Remember there is no apostrophe between the *r* and the *s* in **hers**.

herself

PRONOUN

1 you use **herself** after a verb or preposition when the woman or girl who performs the action is affected by it ⬩ *Did Barbara hurt herself when she fell down?*
2 **herself** is also used to show that a girl or woman does something without any help from other people ⬩ *She always answers every fan letter herself.*
3 you can use **herself** to show more clearly who you mean ⬩ *I wanted to ask Moira herself, but I couldn't get in touch with her.*

hibernate

VERB **hibernates, hibernating, hibernated**

an animal that hibernates goes into a kind of sleep for long periods during the winter when food is difficult to find

▸ **hibernation**

NOUN

hibernating

hide¹

VERB **hides, hiding, hid, hidden**

to put or keep someone or something in a place where they can't be seen or found easily ⬩ *You hide, and I'll come and look for you.* ⬩ *He hid behind a tree.*

hide²

NOUN *plural* **hides**

the skin of an animal

high

ADJECTIVE AND ADVERB **higher, highest**

1 extending far upwards, or a long way off the ground ⬩ *a high building* ⬩ *diving from the highest board*
2 having a certain height ⬩ *10 metres high* ⬩ *How high is Snowdon?*
3 near the top of a scale of measurement or list ⬩ *high marks* ⬩ *a high temperature*
4 a high sound or musical note is near the top of the range of pitch or musical notes ⬩ *high voices of the children* ⬩ *the highest note you can sing*
5 great or large in amount or importance ⬩ *a high number*

ADVERB **higher, highest**

1 far above in the air or a long way off the ground ⬩ *satellites orbiting high above the Earth.*
2 far up a scale or ranking ⬩ *The temperature rose higher and higher.*

NOUN *plural* **highs**

1 a peak or maximum ⬩ *Confidence was at an all-time high.*
2 if someone is on a high, they are feeling very excited and pleased

high school

NOUN *plural* **high schools**

a secondary school

hill

NOUN *plural* hills

1 a high area of land, smaller than a mountain
2 a mound or heap ⟩ *a molehill* ⟨

▸ **hilly**

ADJECTIVE hillier, hilliest

a hilly area has lots of hills

him

PRONOUN

a word you use to talk about a man, boy or male animal that has already been mentioned or pointed out ⟩ *I'm looking for Mr Peters. Have you seen him anywhere?* ⟨

> Try not to confuse the spellings of **him** and **hymn**. A **hymn** is a song of praise.

himself

PRONOUN

1 you use **himself** after a verb or preposition when the man or boy who performs the action is affected by it ⟩ *He poked himself in the eye by mistake.* ⟨
2 **himself** is also used to show that a boy or man does something without any help from other people ⟩ *He can tie his shoelaces himself.* ⟨
3 you can use **himself** to show more clearly who you mean ⟩ *I was surprised when Mr Brown himself answered the telephone.* ⟨

Hindu

NOUN *plural* Hindus

a person whose religion is Hinduism

ADJECTIVE

to do with Hinduism ⟩ *The main Hindu gods are Brahma, Vishnu and Shiva.* ⟨

▸ **Hinduism**

NOUN

a religion of India and parts of South East Asia, which teaches that by a cycle of birth and rebirth, life continues forever or until the soul can be released from the cycle

hip

NOUN *plural* hips

your hips are the parts at each side of your body, between your waist and the tops of your legs

hippopotamus

NOUN *plural* hippopotamuses *or* hippopotami

a large African animal with a heavy body, a large head, small rounded ears and thick legs. Hippopotamuses live near or in rivers

> This word comes from Greek words that mean *river horse*.

his

PRONOUN

a word you use to talk about something belonging to a man, boy or male animal that has already been mentioned or pointed out ⟩ *I didn't have an umbrella so Grandad lent me his.* ⟨

ADJECTIVE

belonging to him ⟩ *He has left his coat behind.* ⟨ ⟩ *The peacock spread his magnificent tail.* ⟨

history

NOUN *plural* histories

1 history is all the things that happened in the past, or the study of things that happened in the past ⟩ *local history* ⟨ ⟩ *My brother is doing history at university.* ⟨

2 the history of something is where it came from and what has happened to it before now ⋧ **What's the history of this old toy?**⋧

3 a person's history is their past life

▸ **historic**

ADJECTIVE

important and likely to be remembered for a long time

▸ **historical**

ADJECTIVE

to do with history

hit

VERB   hits, hitting, hit

1 to strike someone or something with a blow ⋧ **The lorry hit the car head-on.** ⋧

2 an idea or feeling hits you when you realize it or feel it ⋧ **It suddenly hit me that I was quite alone.** ⋧

▸ **hit it off**

if two people hit it off, they get on well together

▸ **hit on something**

to suddenly have a good idea ⋧ **By sheer accident, he'd hit on the perfect solution to the problem.** ⋧

NOUN   plural hits

1 a blow or stroke ⋧ **That was a great hit by the golfer.** ⋧

2 a shot that strikes a target

3 a success with the public ⋧ **The show was an instant hit.** ⋧

ADJECTIVE

successful ⋧ **a hit song** ⋧

hobby

NOUN   plural hobbies

something you enjoy doing in your spare time

hold

VERB   holds, holding, held

1 to hold something is to have it in your hand or hands ⋧ **He was holding a lovely little puppy.** ⋧

2 to keep something in a certain position for a

while ⋧ **Raise your legs up and hold them there for a count of three.** ⋧

3 to contain something ⋧ **This rack holds my CDs.** ⋧

4 a container that holds a certain amount can have that amount put into it ⋧ **It can hold 50 CDs.** ⋧

5 a place or vehicle that holds a certain number of people has enough room or seats for that number ⋧ **The stadium holds about 70,000 spectators.** ⋧

6 to hold an event or celebration, such as a party, is to organize it ⋧ **Where are the next Olympic Games going to be held?**⋧

▸ **hold on**

to hold on is to wait for a while ⋧ **Can you hold on while I get my coat?**⋧

▸ **hold someone or something up**

1 to hold someone or something up is to delay them or it

2 a robber holds up a person or place when they threaten that person, or the people in that place, with a weapon

▸ **hold something up**

if one thing holds up another thing, it supports it ⋧ **The walls hold the roof up.** ⋧

NOUN   holds

1 the place in a ship or plane where its cargo is stored

2 a grip ⋧ **Take a hold of the railing.** ⋧

hole

NOUN   plural holes

1 an opening, tear or gap in something ⋧ **a hole in my sock** ⋧

2 a pit or burrow in the ground ⋧ **They dug a deep hole to plant the tree in.** ⋧

Holi

NOUN

a Hindu festival held near the end of February

holiday

NOUN   plural holidays

1 a day or period of time when you don't have to work or go to school

a b c d e f g **h** i j k l m n o p q r s t u v w x y z

2 a period of time spent in a place other than where you live, in order to relax or enjoy yourself

> This word comes from the Old English words **halig**, which means *holy*, and **dæg**, which means *day*. A holiday used to be a day when you did not work because it was a religious festival.

holly

NOUN   *plural* **hollies**

an evergreen tree with sharp spiky leaves and red berries

holy

ADJECTIVE   holier, holiest

1 to do with God or religion
2 pure and good and having strong religious feelings

home

NOUN   *plural* **homes**

1 your home is the place where you live or where you were born and brought up
2 the home of something is the place where it began or is based ⇒ *Mumbai, the home of the Indian film industry* ⇐
3 a home is a place where people or animals with no one to look after them live and are cared for

VERB   homes, homing, homed

▸ **home in on something**
to focus very closely on something or move directly towards it

homework

NOUN

school work that you do while you are at home, especially in the evenings or at weekends

honest

ADJECTIVE

an honest person tells the truth and does not cheat or steal

▸ **honestly**

ADVERB

1 truthfully ⇒ *He told me honestly what he thought.* ⇐   ⇒ *Honestly, I didn't realize the door should have been kept locked.* ⇐
2 without cheating, stealing or breaking the law
3 you say 'honestly' to show that you are annoyed or angry ⇒ *Honestly, it just makes me sick!* ⇐

▸ **honesty**

NOUN

being honest, truthful or trustworthy

honey

NOUN

a sweet thick liquid you can eat that bees make from the nectar of flowers and which they store in their hives

hoof

NOUN   *plural* **hooves**

the hard part of the foot of some animals, such as horses, cows or sheep

hooray

INTERJECTION

a word that shows approval or joy ⇒ *Hooray! No more school for three whole days!* ⇐

hoot

NOUN   *plural* **hoots**

1 the sound made by an owl or a car horn
2 a loud, sudden burst of laughter, or

something that you find very amusing

VERB hoots, hooting, hooted

1 to hoot is to make the sound of an owl or a car horn
2 to hoot with laughter is to laugh very loudly in sudden bursts

hop

VERB hops, hopping, hopped

1 to jump on one leg
2 to jump ⋛ *Hop in and I'll give you a lift to the station.* ⋚

NOUN *plural* hops

a jump

hope

VERB hopes, hoping, hoped

to hope for something is to think that it is possible or wish that it would happen

NOUN *plural* hopes

1 hope is the feeling that what you want may happen ⋛ *We're not giving up hope, are we?* ⋚
2 your hopes are the things that you want to happen

▸ **hopeless**

ADJECTIVE

1 without any hope of succeeding ⋛ *a hopeless dream* ⋚
2 very bad ⋛ *He was hopeless in goal.* ⋚

▸ **hopeful**

ADJECTIVE

having or feeling hope ⋛ *He's very hopeful that things will turn out well.* ⋚

horizon

NOUN *plural* horizons

the line where the land and sky seem to meet

horn

NOUN *plural* horns

1 horns are the hard pointed objects that grow out of some animals' heads, such as sheep, goats and cows

2 a device in a vehicle that makes a loud noise as a warning to others

3 a musical instrument that you blow into

horrible

ADJECTIVE

very nasty, ugly or unpleasant

▸ **horribly**

ADVERB

in a way that is very nasty

horse

NOUN *plural* horses

a large animal with long hair on its neck and tail. Horses are used by people to ride on and to pull carts or ploughs

horseshoe

NOUN   *plural* **horseshoes**

a curved piece of iron nailed on to a horse's hoof to stop the hoof from being worn down

hospital

NOUN   *plural* **hospitals**

a building where people who are sick or have been injured can go to be treated

> This word comes from the Latin word **hospes**, which means *guest*. A hospital used to be a place where guests could stay.

hot

ADJECTIVE   **hotter, hottest**

1 feeling very warm ⇒ *Don't touch the oven. It's very hot.*
2 spicy ⇒ *hot curries*

hour

NOUN   *plural* **hours**

a period of time that lasts 60 minutes. There are 24 hours in one day

house

NOUN   said "**hows**"   *plural* **houses**

1 a building in which people, especially one family, live
2 the part of a theatre or cinema where the audience sits
3 one of the groups into which the pupils of a school are sometimes divided so they, for instance, can compete against each other in sports

VERB   said "**howz**"   **houses, housing, housed**

1 to house people is to provide them with houses to live in
2 if a room or building houses something, that thing is kept there or operates from there ⇒ *The extension will house a new bookshop and restaurant.*

how

ADVERB

1 how something is done is the way it is done or the means used to do it ⇒ *I'll show you how to tie a reef knot.* ⇒ *How will we get there?*
2 how is used in questions about measurement, extent, distance, time and age ⇒ *I don't know how old Granny is exactly.* ⇒ *How far is your school?*
3 how you are is how well or ill you feel ⇒ *Hello, how are you today?*
4 how you feel about someone or something is the feelings you have for them
5 you use how to show anger or for emphasis ⇒ *How dare you!* ⇒ *How sad is that?*

howl

NOUN   *plural* **howls**

1 a long, loud, sad sound made by a wolf or dog
2 a loud shout of pain or laughter

VERB   **howls, howling, howled**

1 a dog or wolf howls when it makes a long, loud, sad-sounding noise
2 to shout or cry loudly ⇒ *He was howling with pain.*

hug

VERB   **hugs, hugging, hugged**

two people hug when they put their arms around each other's bodies in an affectionate way

NOUN   *plural* **hugs**

the affectionate action of putting your arms around someone

huge

ADJECTIVE

very big

▶ **hugely**
ADVERB
very, extremely

human

NOUN *plural* **humans**

a human, or a human being, is a person

ADJECTIVE

typical of human beings ⸱ *a very human emotion* ⸱

hundred

NOUN *plural* **hundreds**

the number 100

▸ **hundredth**

ADJECTIVE AND ADVERB

coming last in a series of one hundred things ⸱ *This is my hundredth visit here.* ⸱

NOUN *plural* **hundredths**

one of a hundred equal parts of something ⸱ *A centimetre is a hundredth of a metre.* ⸱

hung

VERB

a way of changing the verb **hang** to make a past tense. It can be used with or without a helping verb ⸱ *I hung the picture on my bedroom wall.* ⸱ ⸱ *He had hung the washing out before it started raining.* ⸱

hunger

NOUN

the feeling you get when you need to eat

VERB hungers, hungering, hungered

to hunger for something is to long for it

hungry

ADJECTIVE hungrier, hungriest

having an empty feeling in your stomach and wanting food

▸ **hungrily**

ADVERB

in a keen way that shows you are hungry ⸱ *The dog devoured his food hungrily.* ⸱

hurry

VERB hurries, hurrying, hurried

to move or go quickly

▸ **hurry up**

to move faster or do something more quickly ⸱ *Hurry up and get dressed.* ⸱

NOUN

hurry is trying or needing to get somewhere or get something done quickly ⸱ *in a hurry to catch the bus* ⸱ ⸱ *There's no hurry.* ⸱

hurt

VERB hurts, hurting, hurt

1 to hurt someone or something is to injure or damage them ⸱ *She hurt her ankle playing hockey.* ⸱ ⸱ *Try not to hurt anyone's feelings.* ⸱

2 if something hurts, or hurts you, it injures you or makes you feel pain

ADJECTIVE

injured or showing pain

NOUN

pain, injury or distress

husband

NOUN *plural* **husbands**

a woman's husband is the man she has married

hut

NOUN *plural* **huts**

a small building or shed made of wood, mud or metal

hygienic

ADJECTIVE

without any dirt or germs ⸱ *Hospitals must be as hygienic as possible.* ⸱

hymn said "**him**"

NOUN *plural* **hymns**

a religious song praising God

hyphen

NOUN *plural* **hyphens**

a punctuation mark that looks like a very short line. You use it to join words together, for example *half-term*

a b c d e f g **h** i j k l m n o p q r s t u v w x y z

I
PRONOUN
a word you use when talking about yourself ⋛ *I like ice cream.* ⋚

ice
NOUN
frozen water

ice cream
NOUN *plural* **ice creams**
a sweet frozen food made from milk or cream ⋛ *strawberry ice cream* ⋚ ⋛ *Would you like an ice cream?* ⋚

icy
ADJECTIVE icier, iciest
1 covered with ice
2 extremely cold ⋛ *an icy wind* ⋚

idea
NOUN *plural* **ideas**
a thought or plan that you have ⋛ *That's a good idea.* ⋚
▸ **have no idea**
not to know something ⋛ *I've no idea where he is.* ⋚

if
CONJUNCTION
1 whether ⋛ *I don't know if I can come on Thursday.* ⋚
2 used when talking about possibilities ⋛ *Drink some water if you get thirsty.* ⋚
3 whenever ⋛ *I always call in at his house if I'm passing.* ⋚

igloo
NOUN *plural* **igloos**
a hut made from blocks of snow

ignore
VERB ignores, ignoring, ignored
to pay no attention to someone or something ⋛ *He ignored all my advice.* ⋚ ⋛ *I said hello, but she just ignored me.* ⋚

ill
ADJECTIVE
not well ⋛ *I was ill yesterday and had the day off school.* ⋚

illness
NOUN *plural* **illnesses**
1 an illness is a disease ⋛ *childhood illnesses* ⋚
2 illness is bad health

imagine
VERB imagines, imagining, imagined
1 to form a picture of someone or something in your mind ⋛ *I tried to imagine what he would look like.* ⋚
2 to think or believe something, especially something that is not true ⋛ *You must be imagining things.* ⋚

imam

NOUN *plural* **imams**

a man who leads the prayers in a mosque

important

ADJECTIVE

1 something is important if it matters a lot ⋧ *an important meeting* ⋦
2 an important person has a lot of power

▶ **importance**

NOUN

being important ⋧ *the importance of education* ⋦

▶ **importantly**

ADVERB

seriously or crucially ⋧ *You must go to school and, more importantly, you must listen.* ⋦

impossible

ADJECTIVE

not possible ⋧ *an impossible task* ⋦

in

PREPOSITION

1 inside something ⋧ *He keeps his keys in the drawer.* ⋦
2 at a place ⋧ *They live in Nottingham.* ⋦
3 at a particular time ⋧ *It's my birthday in May.* ⋦
4 after a period of time ⋧ *I'll be back in a few minutes.* ⋦
5 using a particular thing ⋧ *They were speaking in Japanese.* ⋦ ⋧ *Read the word printed in red.* ⋦
6 wearing particular clothes ⋧ *Who's the boy in the football shirt?* ⋦

ADVERB

1 at your home or place of work ⋧ *I'm sorry, Dad's not in. Can I take a message?* ⋦
2 at or into a place ⋧ *What time does your train get in?* ⋦ ⋧ *Come in!* ⋦

incredible

ADJECTIVE

difficult to believe ⋧ *an incredible story* ⋦

▶ **incredibly**

ADVERB

used for saying that something is difficult to believe ⋧ *Incredibly, no one was injured.* ⋦

infection

NOUN *plural* **infections**

1 an infection is an illness ⋧ *an ear infection* ⋦
2 infection is becoming affected by germs

information

NOUN

knowledge, facts or details ⋧ *We asked for information on things to do in the area.* ⋦

▶ **informative**

ADJECTIVE

giving you a lot of useful information ⋧ *an informative book* ⋦

inhabit

VERB inhabits, inhabiting, inhabited

to live in a particular place ⋧ *the creatures that inhabit our world* ⋦

▶ **inhabitant**

NOUN *plural* **inhabitants**

someone who lives in a place ⋧ *the island's inhabitants* ⋦

injure

VERB injures, injuring, injured

to hurt someone or something ⋧ *He injured his knee in a skiing accident.* ⋦

▶ **injured**

ADJECTIVE

hurt ⋧ *an injured knee* ⋦

▶ **injury**

NOUN *plural* **injuries**

a wound or damage to part of your body ⋧ *head injuries* ⋦

innocent

ADJECTIVE

1 not guilty of a crime

a b c d e f g h i j k l m n o p q r s t u v w x y z

2 not having much experience of life and how cruel people can be

insect

NOUN *plural* insects

a very small creature with six legs, such as an ant or wasp

inside

PREPOSITION

in or into something ⇒ *She put the book inside her bag.*

ADVERB

into a building from outdoors ⇒ *Come inside, it's raining.*

ADJECTIVE

on the inner side, not the outer side ⇒ *the inside walls of the house*

NOUN *plural* insides

the inside of something is the part that is in the middle and not on the outside ⇒ *The inside of his jacket was torn.*

instead

ADVERB

in place of someone or something else ⇒ *Ben was ill so John went instead.* ⇒ *You could use a pencil instead of a pen.*

instrument

NOUN *plural* instruments

1 something used for making music
2 a tool for doing something

interest

NOUN *plural* interests

1 the feeling that you like something and want to know more about it ⇒ *I have no interest in cricket.*

2 something that you enjoy doing ⇒ *My main interests are sport and reading.*

VERB interests, interesting, interested

if something interests you, you like it and want to know more about it

▸ **interested**

ADJECTIVE

having or showing interest ⇒ *Dan is very interested in old cars.*

▸ **interesting**

ADJECTIVE

making you feel interested ⇒ *an interesting story*

interjection

WORD CLASS *plural* interjections

a word or phrase used to express a feeling like anger, or as a greeting. For example, *Hooray!* and *hello* are interjections

Internet

NOUN

the Internet is a computer network that allows people around the world to share information

into

PREPOSITION

1 to the inside of something ⇒ *We went into the house.*

2 used for saying how something changes ⇒ *She cut the cake into four pieces.* ⇒ *The caterpillar changed into a butterfly.*

3 used when talking about dividing one number by another ⇒ *2 into 4 goes twice.*

invent

VERB invents, inventing, invented

1 to design or make something that no one else has ever made ⇒ *Thomas Edison invented the electric light bulb.*

2 to think of a story or excuse that is not true

▸ **invention**

NOUN *plural* inventions

something someone has invented

▸ **inventor**

NOUN *plural* inventors

someone who has invented something new

invisible

ADJECTIVE

impossible to see

▸ **invisibility**

NOUN

being impossible to see

invitation

NOUN *plural* invitations

an offer that asks if you would like to do something or go somewhere ⋛ *I've had an invitation to Helen's birthday party.* ⋚

invite

VERB invites, inviting, invited

to invite someone is to ask them if they would like to do something or go somewhere ⋛ *Clare's invited me for tea at her house.* ⋚

iron

NOUN *plural* irons

1 a hard metal used for making tools ⋛ *an iron bar* ⋚

2 a piece of electrical equipment that you use for pressing the creases out of clothes

VERB irons, ironing, ironed

to make clothes smooth using an iron

is

VERB

1 the form of the verb **be** in the present tense that you use with **he**, **she** or **it** ⋛ *He is a fool.* ⋚ ⋛ *It is raining.* ⋚

2 **is** is also used as a helping verb along with a main verb ⋛ *Lisa's mother is going away for a month.* ⋚

Islam

NOUN

the Muslim religion that was started by Mohammed

▸ **Islamic**

ADJECTIVE

relating to the religion of Islam

island

NOUN *plural* islands

an area of land surrounded by sea

it

PRONOUN

1 a word you use to talk about a thing that has already been mentioned or pointed out ⋛ *I've lost the book. Have you seen it?* ⋚

2 used for talking about the weather, time and dates ⋛ *It rained yesterday.* ⋚ ⋛ *It's 3 o'clock.* ⋚

3 used for talking about a fact or opinion ⋛ *It's expensive to travel by train.* ⋚ ⋛ *It's very quiet here, isn't it?* ⋚

itch

VERB itches, itching, itched

if part of your body itches, you want to scratch it

NOUN *plural* itches

a feeling that you want to scratch part of your body ⋛ *I've got an itch on my back.* ⋚

▸ **itchy**

ADJECTIVE itchier, itchiest

an itchy part of your body makes you feel as

a b c d e f g h i j k l m n o p q r s t u v w x y z

though you want to scratch it ⟩ *My back is really itchy.*

its

ADJECTIVE

belonging to it ⟩ *Keep the watch in its box.*

> Be careful not to confuse the spellings of **its** and **it's**. **Its** tells you something belongs to **it**: *The bird built* its *nest.* **It's** is a short way to write **it is** or **it has**: *I think* it's *going to rain.* • It's *been raining all day.*

itself

PRONOUN

1 you use **itself** after a verb or preposition when the thing that performs the action is affected by it ⟩ *The cat lay in the sun and licked itself.*

2 you use **itself** to show that **it** has done something without any help from others ⟩ *The dog managed to get free all by itself.*

3 you can use **itself** to show more clearly the thing you mean ⟩ *The garden is big but the house itself is quite small.*

it's

a short way to say and write **it is** or **it has** ⟩ *It's raining.* ⟩ *It's been a long time since I saw you.*

ivory

NOUN

the hard white substance that forms the tusks of an elephant

jacket

NOUN *plural* jackets

1 a short coat, usually with long sleeves, that reaches down to your waist or hips
2 a loose paper covering wrapped around a hardback book

jail

NOUN *plural* jails

a prison

VERB jails, jailing, jailed

to jail someone is to put them in prison

▸ **jailer**

NOUN *plural* jailers

someone whose job is to watch over prisoners in a jail

jam

NOUN *plural* jams

1 jam is a thick sticky food made by boiling fruit with sugar
2 a jam happens when lots of vehicles or people are packed close together so that they become stuck and can't move

VERB jams, jamming, jammed

1 to jam something into a space is to push it there so that it fits very tightly or is difficult to get out again
2 something like a door or window jams when it becomes stuck and can't be moved
3 people or vehicles jam a place when they crowd it so that it is difficult for any of them to move

janitor

NOUN *plural* janitors

someone whose job is to look after a building, especially a school

January

NOUN

the first month of the year, after December and before February

> **January** comes from the name of the Roman god **Ianus**, who had two faces. One face was looking into the new year, the other looking back to the old year.

jar

NOUN *plural* jars

1 a cylindrical container that is made of glass and has a lid
2 the amount a jar will hold ⋧ *She made six big jars of marmalade from the oranges.* ⋧
3 a bump or blow that causes an unpleasant or painful shake

VERB jars, jarring, jarred

1 if you jar a part of your body, you hurt it by suddenly shaking it or moving it violently ⋧ *He fell awkwardly, jarring his spine.* ⋧
2 if something jars or it jars on you, it has an unpleasant effect on you ⋧ *The bird's screeching jarred on my ears.* ⋧

jaw

NOUN *plural* jaws

1 your jaw is the lower part of your face around your mouth and chin, made up of two bones that your teeth grow in
2 an animal's jaws are its mouth and teeth ⋧ *The crocodile snapped its jaws shut.* ⋧

a b c d e f g h i j k l m n o p q r s t u v w x y z

jealous
ADJECTIVE

feeling that you don't like someone because they have something that you want or because you are afraid that they will take something away from you ⋛ *He's jealous of his brother's success.* ⋚ ⋛ *She made me jealous by going out with her other friends.* ⋚

▸ **jealousy**
NOUN *plural* jealousies

a feeling of being jealous

jeans
PLURAL NOUN

casual trousers made of denim with pockets at the front and back

jelly
NOUN *plural* jellies

1 a wobbly food made with fruit juice ⋛ *orange jelly* ⋚
2 any wobbly substance

jet
NOUN *plural* jets

1 a powerful stream of liquid or gas forced through a narrow opening ⋛ *A jet of icy water shot up his nostrils.* ⋚
2 a fast aeroplane with powerful engines that drive the plane forward by sucking air in at the front and forcing it out behind

VERB jets, jetting, jetted

to jet somewhere is to travel there on a plane ⋛ *jetting off to sunny holiday destinations* ⋚

jewel
NOUN *plural* jewels

a precious stone, used for decoration or display

▸ **jeweller**
NOUN *plural* jewellers

someone who makes or sells jewellery

▸ **jewellery**
NOUN

things that you wear to decorate your body and clothing, such as rings, earrings, bracelets, necklaces and brooches

Jewish
ADJECTIVE

to do with the Hebrew people or the religion of Judaism

jigsaw
NOUN *plural* jigsaws

1 a puzzle made up of lots of different-shaped pieces that fit together to make a picture
2 a type of electric saw with a very thin blade that can cut curved and rounded shapes

job
NOUN *plural* jobs

1 someone's job is the work they do regularly for pay
2 a job is a task or a piece of work ⋛ *There are plenty of jobs to do about the house.* ⋚

join
VERB joins, joining, joined

1 to join two or more things is to put them together or connect them
2 one thing joins another when they come together or meet ⋛ *The track joins the main road just around this corner.* ⋚
3 you join a club or other organization when you become a member

NOUN *plural* joins

a place where two things are joined

joke
NOUN *plural* jokes

something that is said or done to make people laugh

VERB jokes, joking, joked

to make a joke

▶joker

NOUN *plural* jokers

1 someone who likes telling jokes or doing things to make people laugh
2 one of two cards in a pack of playing cards that have a picture of a clown. The jokers are extra cards and are only used in certain card games

jolly

ADJECTIVE jollier, jolliest

cheerful and happy

ADVERB

very ⇒*That was jolly unfair of you!*⇐

journey

NOUN *plural* journeys

1 you go on a journey when you travel from one place to another
2 a journey is the distance you travel from one place to another ⇒*a long and difficult journey*⇐

judge

VERB judges, judging, judged

1 to judge something is to form an idea or opinion about it
2 to judge a competition is to decide which of the competitors is best
3 to judge a case in a court of law is to hear the evidence and decide on what is to be done or how someone should be punished

NOUN *plural* judges

1 someone who hears cases in a law court and decides what is to be done
2 someone who judges a competition
3 someone who can decide whether something is good or bad ⇒*a good judge of character*⇐

▶judgement *or* **judgment**

NOUN *plural* judgements *or* judgments

1 the ability to make decisions, especially good or sensible decisions
2 the decision made by a judge in a law court

jug

NOUN *plural* jugs

a container for pouring liquids, with a handle and a shaped part at its top edge

juggle

VERB juggles, juggling, juggled

to keep several things in the air by continuously throwing them up and catching them

▶juggler

NOUN *plural* jugglers

someone who entertains people by juggling

juice

NOUN *plural* juices

1 juice is the liquid in fruits or vegetables
2 the juices from meat are the liquids that flow out of it while it is being cooked

▶juicy

ADJECTIVE juicier, juiciest

full of juice

July

NOUN

the seventh month of the year, after June and before August

> **July** comes from the Latin word for this month, **Julius**, which was named after the Roman emperor *Julius Caesar.*

jumble

VERB jumbles, jumbling, jumbled

to jumble things up is to mix them up so that they are out of order or in an untidy mess

NOUN

a jumble is lots of things that have been mixed up in a confused or untidy mess

jumble sale

NOUN *plural* jumble sales

a sale where old or unwanted things are sold to raise money

a b c d e f g h i j k l m n o p q r s t u v w x y z

jump

VERB jumps, jumping, jumped

1 to leap into the air ⇒ *He jumped off the wall.*
2 to jump something is to leap over it
3 to make a sudden movement because you are surprised or frightened ⇒ *I jumped as something crawled out from under the stone.*
4 if you jump to do something or jump at something, you eagerly accept an opportunity ⇒ *I thought you would jump at the chance.*
5 if you jump a queue, you join it in front of other people already in the queue

NOUN plural jumps

1 a leap
2 something to be jumped over, or a distance that has to be jumped
3 a sudden movement because of surprise or fear

jumper

NOUN plural jumpers

a warm piece of clothing for the top part of your body, which you pull on over your head

June

NOUN

the sixth month of the year, after May and before July

> **June** comes from the name of the Roman queen of the gods, **Juno**.

jungle

NOUN plural jungles

trees and plants growing thickly together, especially in tropical areas of the world

just¹

ADJECTIVE

1 fair or showing justice ⇒ *a just decision*
2 deserved ⇒ *It was a just reward for all his efforts.*

just²

ADVERB

1 exactly ⇒ *A cold drink was just what I needed.*
2 barely ⇒ *I could only just see him.*
3 a very short time ago ⇒ *The clock's just struck five.*
4 simply ⇒ *I just want to go home.*
▸ **just about**
more or less ⇒ *I've just about finished here.*

justice

NOUN

justice is fairness in dealing with people and their problems

kangaroo

NOUN *plural* kangaroos

an Australian animal that jumps, and that carries its babies in a pouch at the front of its body

keep

VERB keeps, keeping, kept

1 to continue to have something and not give it to anyone else ⋟ **You can keep the book. I don't want it back.** ⋞
2 to put something in a particular place when you are not using it ⋟ **I keep my toys under the bed.** ⋞
3 to make someone or something stay a particular way ⋟ **Keep the door closed.** ⋞ ⋟ **Keep off the grass.** ⋞
4 if food keeps, it stays fresh ⋟ **Milk doesn't keep for very long.** ⋞
5 if you keep animals, you have them and look after them
6 if you keep doing something, you do it a lot or you do it without stopping ⋟ **I keep forgetting to bring my homework.** ⋞

▶ **keep up**

to keep up with someone or something is to move or do something as fast as they

do ⋟ **He was running so fast that I couldn't keep up.** ⋞

▶ **keeper**

NOUN *plural* keepers

the person who looks after something, especially animals in a zoo

kennel

NOUN *plural* kennels

a hut for a dog

kept

VERB

a way of changing the verb **keep** to make a past tense. It can be used with or without a helping verb ⋟ **He kept all the letters his grandad sent him.** ⋞ ⋟ **I have kept the receipt.** ⋞

kerb

NOUN *plural* kerbs

the edge of a pavement

ketchup

NOUN

thick sauce made from tomatoes, which you eat cold

kettle

NOUN *plural* kettles

a container for boiling water in

key

NOUN *plural* keys

1 something you use for locking and unlocking something such as a door
2 **ICT** a button on a computer keyboard or typewriter

3 **music** one of the white or black parts you press on a piano to make a sound

4 something that makes you able to understand or achieve something ⸱ *Hard work is the key to success.* ⸱ *The key to the map is over the page.*

ADJECTIVE

most important ⸱ *Dean is one of the team's key players.*

keyboard

NOUN *plural* **keyboards**

1 **ICT** the set of keys on a computer or typewriter

2 **music** the set of keys on a musical instrument such as a piano

3 **music** an electronic musical instrument that has keys like a piano

kick

VERB **kicks, kicking, kicked**

1 to hit someone or something with your foot ⸱ *Jane kicked the ball over the fence.*

2 to move your legs strongly, for example when swimming

NOUN *plural* **kicks**

1 a strong movement of your leg or foot

2 **informal** a feeling of pleasure or excitement ⸱ *He gets a kick out of annoying other people.*

kid

NOUN *plural* **kids**

1 **informal** a child

2 a young goat

▸ **with kid gloves**

if you treat someone with kid gloves, you are very careful not to upset them

VERB **kids, kidding, kidded**

to kid, or kid someone, is to trick them for fun

kill

VERB **kills, killing, killed**

to make a person or animal die ⸱ *People were killed in the crash.*

▸ **killer**

NOUN *plural* **killers**

a person who kills someone

kind¹

NOUN *plural* **kinds**

a type of something ⸱ *What kind of dog have you got?*

kind²

ADJECTIVE **kinder, kindest**

nice, generous and wanting to make other people happy

king

NOUN *plural* **kings**

a man who rules a country ⸱ *the King of Norway*

▸ **kingdom**

NOUN *plural* **kingdoms**

a country ruled by a king

kiss

VERB **kisses, kissing, kissed**

to touch someone with your lips as a sign of love ⸱ *Ellie kissed her mother.*

NOUN *plural* **kisses**

the act of kissing someone ⸱ *He gave her a kiss.*

kit

NOUN *plural* **kits**

1 the clothes you need for a certain activity ⸱ *gym kit*

2 a set of parts you can put together to make something

kitchen

NOUN *plural* **kitchens**

a room for preparing and cooking food

kite

NOUN *plural* **kites**

1 a toy that you fly in the air when it is windy

2 a type of bird that kills and eats other small animals and birds

kitten

NOUN *plural* **kittens**

a young cat

knee

NOUN *plural* **knees**

the joint in the middle of your leg where it bends

kneel

VERB kneels, kneeling, knelt

to move down so you are resting on your knees

knew

VERB

a way of changing the verb **know** to make a past tense ⋛ *Lucy knew what to do.* ⋜

knife

NOUN *plural* **knives**

a tool used for cutting something, which has a handle and a blade

VERB knifes, knifing, knifed

to stab someone with a knife

knock

VERB knocks, knocking, knocked

1 to hit something so that it moves or falls ⋛ *The cat knocked the vase off the table.* ⋜
2 to hit a door or window several times with your knuckles or a knocker in order to attract attention ⋛ *Knock before you come in.* ⋜
3 to bump into something ⋛ *I knocked my elbow on the edge of the door.* ⋜
▸ **knock someone out**
to knock someone out is to make someone become unconscious, especially by hitting them

NOUN *plural* **knocks**

1 the sound of someone knocking on a door or window ⋛ *There was a knock at the door.* ⋜
2 a blow or injury caused by hitting something ⋛ *He's had a nasty knock on the head.* ⋜

know

VERB knows, knowing, knew, known

1 to have information about something or be aware of something ⋛ *Do you know where he lives?* ⋜ ⋛ *I didn't know you were Alan's cousin!* ⋜
2 to have learnt about something ⋛ *I don't know much German.* ⋜
3 to be familiar with a person or place ⋛ *I didn't know anyone at the party.* ⋜

▸ **knowledge**

NOUN

1 the information and understanding that you have about something ⋛ *a good knowledge of sport* ⋜
2 the fact that you are aware of something ⋛ *His parents had no knowledge that he hadn't gone to school.* ⋜

knuckle

NOUN *plural* **knuckles**

one of the parts on your hands where your fingers bend

koala

NOUN *plural* **koalas**

an Australian animal that looks like a small bear, climbs trees and eats eucalyptus leaves

Koran

NOUN

the Koran is the holy book of the Islamic religion

kosher

ADJECTIVE

kosher food is prepared according to Jewish law

ladder
NOUN *plural* ladders
1 a set of steps that you can move around to climb up to places that you cannot normally reach
2 a long tear that has started from a hole or broken stitch in a stocking or tights

lady
NOUN *plural* ladies
1 a polite word for a woman ⋛ *Ask that lady if the seat by her is free.* ⋛
2 a woman with good manners ⋛ *Mrs Kingsley was a real lady.* ⋛
3 the title for the wife of a lord or knight or for a woman with a high social rank

ladybird
NOUN *plural* ladybirds
a small beetle that is usually red with black spots

lain
VERB
the form of the verb **lie** that is used with a helping verb to show that something happened in the past ⋛ *I had lain down for a moment and fallen fast asleep.* ⋛

lake
NOUN *plural* lakes
a large stretch of water that has land all around it

lamb
NOUN *plural* lambs
1 a young sheep
2 meat from a young sheep

lamp
NOUN *plural* lamps
a piece of equipment that has a light in it ⋛ *a table lamp* ⋛

land
NOUN *plural* lands
1 the solid parts of the earth's surface ⋛ *the land and the sea* ⋛
2 land is ground ⋛ *good land for growing plants* ⋛ ⋛ *The farmer bought another piece of land.* ⋛
3 a land is a country ⋛ *tales from faraway lands* ⋛

VERB lands, landing, landed
1 to come down to the ground ⋛ *He fell from the tree and landed on the grass.* ⋛
2 to arrive on land or on the shore ⋛ *We landed in Spain at about midnight.* ⋛
3 to land an aircraft is to bring it down to the ground ⋛ *The pilot managed to land the aeroplane safely in a field.* ⋛

language
NOUN *plural* languages
1 communication in speaking and writing
2 the words that one particular group uses, such as the people that live in one country ⋛ *a foreign language* ⋛
3 a system of symbols or signs that give information, for example in computers

large
ADJECTIVE larger, largest
big or bigger than normal ⋛ *a large man* ⋛ ⋛ *a large house* ⋛
▸ at large
1 free, not in captivity ⋛ *There is a wild cat at large in the area.* ⋛

2 in general ⇒ *The public at large do not like the idea.*

last

ADJECTIVE

1 coming after all the others ⇒ *the last bus of the day*
2 the final one remaining ⇒ *my last toffee*
3 most recent ⇒ *on my last birthday*

ADVERB

1 after all the others ⇒ *Who came last in the relay?*
2 after everything else ⇒ *I'll do my maths homework last.*
3 most recently ⇒ *When did you see Anna last?*

VERB lasts, lasting, lasted

1 to continue or go on ⇒ *The lesson seemed to last for ever.*
2 to remain in good condition ⇒ *These boots should last for years.*

NOUN

the final person or thing ⇒*You are always the last to finish.*
▸ **at last**
in the end ⇒ *At last we saw the sea.*

late

ADJECTIVE later, latest

1 coming after the expected time ⇒ *a late arrival*
2 far on in time or in a particular period ⇒ *a late movie* ⇒ *the late 19th century*
3 recently dead ⇒ *our late uncle*

ADVERB later, latest

1 coming after the expected time ⇒ *The train is late every day.*
2 far on in time ⇒ *It's getting late.*

▸ **lately**
ADVERB
recently ⇒ *I haven't been to any parties lately.*

▸ **lateness**
NOUN
being late

laugh

VERB laughs, laughing, laughed
to make a sound of enjoyment when you think something is funny

NOUN *plural* laughs
the sound a person makes when they think something is funny

lay

VERB lays, laying, laid

1 to put something down ⇒ *lay the book on the table*
2 to arrange something ⇒ *lay the table* ⇒ *lay a trap*
3 when a bird or female animal lays an egg, the egg comes out of its body

> Try not to confuse **lay** and **lie**. You **lay** something somewhere, whereas you **lie** somewhere: Lay *your pencils on your desks.* • *I am going to* lie *in bed for a while.* The past tenses can be confusing too. **Lay** is also a past tense of **lie**: *The cat* lay *on the mat.*

layer

NOUN *plural* layers
a covering that lies over something, or a thickness under something ⇒ *grass covered with a layer of snow* ⇒ *a layer of jam in the cake*

lazy

ADJECTIVE lazier, laziest
not wanting to do anything much, especially work ⇒ *You must be the laziest pupil in this school.*

▸ **lazily**
ADVERB
in a slow, unhurried way

▸ **laziness**
NOUN
being lazy and not willing to work

a b c d e f g h i j k l m n o p q r s t u v w x y z

lead¹ said "leed"

VERB leads, leading, led

1 to be winning or be more successful ⇒ *Hoy led the race from the beginning.* ⇐
2 to show someone the way by going first ⇒ *You lead and I'll follow on my bike.* ⇐
3 to direct or control a group of people ⇒ *Kim was leading a discussion on bullying.* ⇐
4 if you lead a busy life, you are always busy
5 a road that leads somewhere goes to that place

NOUN plural leads

1 the first or front place ⇒ *Jenkins has been in the lead for most of the race.* ⇐
2 an electrical wire or cable ⇒ *Someone had cut the lead to the alarm.* ⇐
3 help or guidance ⇒ *Follow my lead and just do what I do.* ⇐ ⇒ *The police are following up several new leads.* ⇐
4 a strap or chain attached to a dog's collar that you can hold when you walk with it ⇒ *Please keep your dog on its lead.* ⇐

lead² said "led"

NOUN plural leads

1 a soft, dark grey metal
2 the inside part of a pencil that writes, made of graphite

leader

NOUN plural leaders

a person who leads ⇒ *the leader of the expedition* ⇐

▸ leadership
NOUN
1 being a leader ⇒ *The team's done well under Sam's leadership.* ⇐
2 the ability to lead ⇒ *If you want to be a prefect, you'll have to show good leadership.* ⇐

leaf

NOUN plural leaves

1 a part of a plant that grows out from the side of the stem and is usually green
2 a page of a book

lean

VERB leans, leaning, leant

1 to rest against something ⇒ *a boy leaning on the wall* ⇐
2 to slope over to one side ⇒ *Lean over and get the salt for me would you?* ⇐
3 to rely on someone ⇒ *You know you can always lean on me.* ⇐

ADJECTIVE leaner, leanest

without any or much fat ⇒ *Models have to look lean these days.* ⇐ ⇒ *I'll only buy lean meat.* ⇐

leap

VERB leaps, leaping, leapt

to jump high or long ⇒ *dolphins leaping out of the water* ⇐

NOUN plural leaps

a big jump ⇒ *a leap over the river* ⇐

learn

VERB learns, learning, learnt *or* learned

to get to know something or how to do something ⇒ *learn your lines for the play* ⇐ ⇒ *learning how to swim* ⇐

▸ learner
NOUN plural learners

a person who is being taught something

least

ADJECTIVE

the smallest amount of anything ⇒ *The person who had the least difficulty was the tallest.* ⇐

ADVERB

the lowest amount ⇒ *Which trousers cost least?* ⇐

▸ at least
1 not less than ⇒ *She must be at least forty years old.* ⇐
2 at any rate ⇒ *John has finished, at least he should have.* ⇐

leave

VERB leaves, leaving, left

1 to go away from someone, something or somewhere ⫽ *I left school early.* ⫽
2 to not take something with you when you go away ⫽ *Mum always leaves her umbrella on the bus.* ⫽
3 to put something somewhere ⫽ *Leave your shoes in the hall.* ⫽
4 to not do something ⫽ *I think I'll leave my French homework until tomorrow.* ⫽
5 to make someone have a particular feeling or thought ⫽ *The poor test result left Josh feeling disappointed.* ⫽
6 to give something to someone in a will ⫽ *Granny left Jodie all her jewellery.* ⫽

NOUN

holiday time from work, especially work in the army, navy or air force ⫽ *a week's leave* ⫽

led

VERB

a way of changing the verb **lead** to make a past tense. It can be used with or without a helping verb ⫽ *Connor led the boys into the wood.* ⫽ ⫽ *Where have you led us?* ⫽

left¹

ADJECTIVE

on the other side from the right side. For example, on the side of a page you usually start reading

ADVERB

on or towards the other side from the right ⫽ *Now turn left.* ⫽

NOUN

the left is the other side from the right side ⫽ *Can we stop just here on the left?* ⫽

left²

VERB

a way of changing the verb **leave** to make a past tense. It can be used with or without a helping verb ⫽ *I have left my book at home.* ⫽ ⫽ *I was glad when they left.* ⫽

leg

NOUN plural legs

1 one of the parts of the body that animals and humans stand and walk on
2 one half of a pair of trousers
3 one of the upright supports of a piece of furniture like a table or chair
4 one stage in a journey or a contest ⫽ *This is the second leg of the race across Europe.* ⫽

lemon

NOUN plural lemons

1 an oval fruit with a hard, yellow skin and very sour juice
2 a pale yellow colour

ADJECTIVE

of the colour lemon

length

NOUN plural lengths

1 how long something is, or how much time something lasts ⫽ *We measured the length of the table.* ⫽ ⫽ *twice the length of a normal lesson* ⫽
2 a piece of something long ⫽ *a length of plastic piping* ⫽

▸ at length

in detail ⫽ *The doctor explained the treatment at length.* ⫽

▸ lengthen

VERB lengthens, lengthening, lengthened

1 to lengthen something is to make it longer ⫽ *Mum's going to lengthen my skirt.* ⫽
2 to lengthen is to grow longer ⫽ *a lengthening queue* ⫽

▸ lengthy

ADJECTIVE lengthier, lengthiest
taking a long time ⫽ *a lengthy delay* ⫽

lent

VERB

a way of changing the verb **lend** to make a

a b c d e f g h i j k l m n o p q r s t u v w x y z

past tense. It can be used with or without a helping verb ⸘ *Here's the book you lent me yesterday.* ⸘ ⸘ *You haven't lent him money, have you?* ⸘

leopard

NOUN *plural* **leopards**

an animal of the cat family with spotted skin

less

ADJECTIVE AND ADVERB

not as much ⸘ *We'll have to spend less money.* ⸘ ⸘ *If you complain less, you enjoy life more.* ⸘

NOUN

a smaller amount ⸘ *I've got less than he has.* ⸘

PREPOSITION

minus ⸘ *That leaves £10, less the money I need for sweets.* ⸘

▸ **lessen**

VERB lessens, lessening, lessened

to make or become smaller ⸘ *The pain in my arm had lessened.* ⸘

lesson

NOUN *plural* **lessons**

1 a period of teaching ⸘ *When's our next lesson?* ⸘
2 something that you learn or that someone teaches you ⸘ *one of the most important lessons about history* ⸘
3 a reading from the Bible in a church service

let

VERB lets, letting, let

1 to let someone do something is to allow them to do it ⸘ *Please let me go!* ⸘
2 to let a house or office is to rent it out

▸ **let someone down**

to let someone down is to disappoint them ⸘ *If she promises me something, she won't let me down.* ⸘

▸ **let someone off**

to let someone off is to not punish them even though they have done something wrong

letter

NOUN *plural* **letters**

1 a message that you write and send to another person
2 one of the written shapes that you combine to write words, like *a*, *b* or *c*

▸ **lettering**

NOUN

writing, especially when it is for decoration ⸘ *The title is on the picture frame in gold lettering.* ⸘

lettuce

NOUN *plural* **lettuces**

a green vegetable whose leaves are used in salads

level

ADJECTIVE

1 flat or horizontal ⸘ *a piece of level ground* ⸘
2 as high as something else or in line with it ⸘ *The picture needs to be level with the mirror next to it.* ⸘

NOUN *plural* **levels**

1 a particular position ⸘ *Pin the notice up at eye level.* ⸘
2 a particular standard or grade ⸘ *It's best to start at beginners' level.* ⸘
3 a tool that shows if a surface is horizontal or vertical

VERB levels, levelling, levelled

1 to level something is to make it flat, smooth or horizontal ⸘ *The ground will have to be levelled before they can build on it.* ⸘
2 to level things is to make them equal ⸘ *Grey scored again to level the scores.* ⸘

liar
NOUN *plural* **liars**
someone who tells lies

library
NOUN *plural* **libraries**
a building or room that has a collection of books or recordings

lick
VERB licks, licking, licked
to move your tongue over something

NOUN *plural* **licks**
1 a movement of your tongue over something ⟩ *Give the spoon one last lick.*
2 a small amount of something ⟩ *This room needs a lick of paint.*

lid
NOUN *plural* **lids**
1 a cover that fits a container like a box
2 an eyelid

lie¹
VERB lies, lying, lied
to say something that is not true ⟩ *We know Auntie May lies about her age.*

NOUN *plural* **lies**
a statement that is not true ⟩ *The boy's story is a pack of lies.*

lie²
VERB lies, lying, lay, laid
1 to rest in a flat position ⟩ *Lie flat on your back.*
2 to be or remain a certain way ⟩ *The buildings lay in ruins.*

> The past tense of **lie** when it means 'to tell an untruth' is **lied**: *I* lied *about passing the test.* The past tense of **lie** when it means 'to rest flat' is **lay**: *I* lay *in bed all day.*

life
NOUN *plural* **lives**
1 a life is the time between being born and dying
2 life is the state of being alive ⟩ *feeling her pulse for any sign of life*
3 life is energy and liveliness ⟩ *Try to put a bit more life into your singing.*
4 your life is the way you live ⟩ *Life on a boat is great fun.*
5 life is all living things ⟩ *a book about pond life*

lift
VERB lifts, lifting, lifted
1 to lift something is to pick it up or raise it ⟩ *She lifted her hand to her forehead.*
2 if something such as fog lifts, it gradually disappears

NOUN *plural* **lifts**
1 a moving platform that can take things or people between the floors of a building
2 a ride in someone's car ⟩ *Do you want a lift home?*
3 a movement upwards ⟩ *ten lifts with each leg*

light¹
NOUN *plural* **lights**
1 light is what allows you to see things. Otherwise, it would be dark ⟩ *The light in this room is good for painting.*
2 a light is something that gives light, such as a lamp or a candle ⟩ *Don't forget to switch off the light.*

ADJECTIVE lighter, lightest
1 not dark ⟩ *Mike got up as soon as it began to get light.*
2 pale in colour ⟩ *light blue*

VERB lights, lighting, lit
1 to light something is to make it burn with a flame ⟩ *Let's light the fire.*
2 to light is to start burning ⟩ *Why won't the cooker light?*
3 to light a place is to make it brighter ⟩ *In the*

a b c d e f g h i j k l m n o p q r s t u v w x y z

past, they lit the stage with candles.

light²

ADJECTIVE lighter, lightest

1 not heavy *a light suitcase*
2 easy, or not too serious *light work* *light music*
3 not large or strong *a light shower*

lighthouse

NOUN *plural* lighthouses

a building like a tower in or at the edge of the sea that has a flashing torch at the top to warn or guide ships

lightning

NOUN

an electric flash in the sky that often happens just before a clap of thunder

like¹

PREPOSITION

1 similar to *Marnie looks just like her mother.*
2 in a similar way to *She dances like a professional.*
3 typical of *It's not like you to be late.*

CONJUNCTION

as if *You look like you've seen a ghost.*

like²

VERB likes, liking, liked

to think that something or someone is nice or good *I like pizza.* *The teacher likes us to work quietly.*

limp

VERB limps, limping, limped

to walk unevenly because of a problem with one leg or foot

NOUN *plural* limps

an uneven walk

ADJECTIVE limper, limpest

not stiff or firm *a limp lettuce* *a limp handshake*

line

NOUN *plural* lines

1 a long thin mark or stripe *a white line in the middle of the road*
2 a row of things or people *lines of marching soldiers*
3 a length of rope, wire or string *hanging the washing on the line*
4 a wrinkle, especially on someone's face
5 a railway *the east coast line*
6 a telephone connection *There's a strange noise on this line.*
7 a short letter *I'll drop you a line to let you know how we get on.*

VERB lines, lining, lined

to line something like a street is to be along both sides of it *Police officers will line the route of the procession.*

▸ **line up**

to line up is to stand in a row *Line up for your dinner.*

lion

NOUN *plural* lions

a powerful animal of the cat family. A male lion has a big shaggy mane

This word comes from the Latin word for a lion, which is **leo**.

lip

NOUN *plural* **lips**

1 either the upper or the lower outside edge of your mouth
2 the shaped part of the outside edge of a container such as a jug ⇒ *a saucepan with a lip for pouring*

liquid

NOUN *plural* **liquids**

a substance that can flow, for example oil or water

list

NOUN *plural* **lists**

a series of things like names, numbers or prices, one after another ⇒ *a shopping list*

VERB **lists, listing, listed**

to say or write a lot of words, such as names, one after another ⇒ *She listed all the books she has.*

listen

VERB **listens, listening, listened**

to pay attention to something that you can hear ⇒ *Listen to me.* ⇒ *I'm listening for the postman.* ⇒ *She's not listening.*

lit

VERB

a way of changing the verb **light** to make a past tense. It can be used with or without a helping verb ⇒ *Her face lit up at the idea.* ⇒ *I haven't lit the candles yet.*

litre

NOUN *plural* **litres**

the basic unit in the metric system for measuring the volume of a liquid. This is often shortened to **l**

little

ADJECTIVE **littler, littlest**

1 small ⇒ *a little child* ⇒ *in a little while*
2 **formal** not much ⇒ *There's little hope that we'll win.*

▸ **a little**

1 a small amount of ⇒ *You'll feel better if you drink a little water.*
2 a bit ⇒ *Jump up and down a little to keep warm.* ⇒ *Dad seems a little tired today.*

live¹ rhymes with **give**

VERB **lives, living, lived**

1 to have your home in a certain place ⇒ *How long have you lived in Bradford?*
2 to pass your life in a certain way ⇒ *She's used to living alone.*
3 to be alive ⇒ *Lord Voldemort lives!*

live² rhymes with **hive**

ADJECTIVE

1 real, not a model ⇒ *The children were handling live snakes.*
2 connected to an electricity supply ⇒ *a live socket*
3 a live broadcast or concert actually happens as you watch or listen to it

living

NOUN *plural* **livings**

a way of earning money ⇒ *What does Sam's dad do for a living?*

ADJECTIVE

alive, not dead ⇒ *all living things*

lizard

NOUN *plural* **lizards**

a four-footed reptile with a long body and tail and a scaly skin

loaf

NOUN *plural* **loaves**

a loaf of bread has been shaped and baked in one piece

lock

NOUN *plural* **locks**

1 a device that you work with a key to fasten things such as doors and drawers

a b c d e f g h i j k l m n o p q r s t u v w x y z

2 a small section of a canal or river with gates at each end. The level of the water in the lock can be changed so that boats can pass to higher or lower sections of the canal or river

VERB locks, locking, locked

1 to lock something like a door is to fasten it with a key

2 something like a door locks if it is possible to fasten it with a key ⋙ *Don't leave valuables in this room because the door doesn't lock.*

▸ **lock something up** or **away**

to lock something up or away is to put it somewhere that can be locked with a key ⋙ *Mum locks all her jewellery away in a box.*

log

NOUN *plural* logs

1 a section of a branch or tree trunk that has been cut up

2 an official record of what happens on a journey, especially of a ship or aeroplane

lollipop

NOUN *plural* lollipops

a hard sticky sweet on a stick

lonely

ADJECTIVE lonelier, loneliest

1 a lonely person feels sad because they are alone, with no friends around them

2 a lonely place has very few people living in it or visiting it ⋙ *a lonely cottage on the hillside*

▸ **loneliness**

NOUN

1 being unhappy because you are alone

2 being a long way from anything or anyone else

long¹

ADJECTIVE longer, longest

1 big from one end to the other ⋙ *a long*

supermarket queue ⋙ ⋙ *a long way home*

2 lasting or taking a lot of time ⋙ *a long delay* ⋙ ⋙ *the long summer holidays*

ADVERB longer, longest

1 for a long time ⋙ *Have you been waiting long?* ⋙ ⋙ *It won't be long till she starts school.*

2 through the whole time ⋙ *I've been looking forward to this all day long.*

long²

VERB longs, longing, longed

to want something very much ⋙ *I was longing to see my friends again.* ⋙ ⋙ *Mum was longing for a rest.*

▸ **longing**

NOUN *plural* longings

a very strong wish for something ⋙ *looking at the food with longing*

look

VERB looks, looking, looked

1 to turn your eyes to see something ⋙ *I looked at my brother.*

2 to appear or seem ⋙ *You look tired.* ⋙ *Dan's sister looks about sixteen.*

3 to try to find something ⋙ *I've looked everywhere but I can't find my calculator.* ⋙ *What are you looking for?*

4 to face a certain direction ⋙ *The window looks south.*

▸ **look after someone** or **something**

to look after something or someone is to take care of them ⋙ *Dad looks after my baby sister during the day.* ⋙ *Will you look after my bag while I go to the toilet?*

▸ **look down on someone**

to think that someone is less important than you or not as good as you ⋙ *She looks down on people who are not as rich as her.*

▸ **look forward to something**

to feel happy because you know you're going to enjoy something ⋙ *I'm looking forward to the holidays.*

▶ **look something up**

to try to find information about something, for example by looking in a book or on the Internet

NOUN   *plural* **looks**

1 a glance at something or an examination of it ⟫ ***Take a look at this.***
2 a certain expression on your face ⟫ ***The teacher has an angry look on her face.***
3 the appearance of a thing or person ⟫ ***I don't like the look of those black clouds.***

lorry

NOUN   *plural* **lorries**

a large motor vehicle for taking heavy loads by road

lose

VERB   loses, losing, lost

1 to forget where you put something ⟫ ***I've lost my keys.***
2 to have something taken away from you ⟫ ***Fifty people have lost their jobs.***
3 to have less of something than you had before ⟫ ***The teacher was losing patience with them.***
4 to be beaten in a contest ⟫ ***I lost by 4 games to 6.***
5 a clock or watch loses time when it goes too slowly ⟫ ***My watch is losing about a minute a day.***

▶ **loser**

NOUN   *plural* **losers**

1 the person who does not win an argument, contest or battle ⟫ ***Even the loser will win a huge amount of money.***
2 someone who never seems to succeed at anything

lost

ADJECTIVE

1 something that is lost is missing ⟫ ***The painting has been lost for centuries.***
2 someone who is lost does not know where

they are ⟫ ***How did you get lost when you had a map?***
3 you are lost when you are confused ⟫ ***I'm lost – can you explain that last bit again?***
4 a person is lost if they are killed ⟫ ***soldiers lost in battle***

lot

NOUN   *plural* **lots**

1 a group of things or people ⟫ ***Another lot of visitors will arrive tomorrow.***
2 an area of land ⟫ ***a parking lot***

▶ **a lot**

a large number or amount ⟫ ***a lot of people*** ⟫ ***I like you a lot.***

▶ **lots**

informal a large number or amount ⟫ ***Lots of people love the programme.*** ⟫ ***She puts lots of sugar on her cereal.***

▶ **the lot**

informal everything ⟫ ***Alice only wanted one but decided to take the lot.***

loud

ADJECTIVE   louder, loudest

1 making a lot of sound ⟫ ***a loud noise***
2 very bright in an unpleasant way ⟫ ***a loud shirt***

ADVERB   louder, loudest

making a lot of sound ⟫ ***Could you speak a little louder please?***

▶ **loudly**

ADVERB

making a lot of sound or noise ⟫ ***crying loudly***

lounge

NOUN   *plural* **lounges**

a room where people can sit down and relax

VERB   lounges, lounging, lounged

to sit or lie around lazily ⟫ ***students lounging around the common room***

a b c d e f g h i j k **l** m n o p q r s t u v w x y z

love

NOUN *plural* loves

1 a deep feeling of liking something or someone very much ⟩ ***my love for my parents*** ⟨

2 something or someone that you like very much ⟩ ***Her great love is music.*** ⟨

3 in a game such as tennis, a score of nothing ⟩ ***The score was now forty-love.*** ⟨

VERB loves, loving, loved

to like someone or something very much ⟩ ***Greg had always loved cricket.*** ⟨

lovely

ADJECTIVE lovelier, loveliest

1 beautiful or attractive ⟩ ***lovely eyes*** ⟨

2 enjoyable or pleasing ⟩ ***It was lovely to see you again.*** ⟨

low

ADJECTIVE AND ADVERB lower, lowest

1 near to the ground ⟩ ***a low hedge*** ⟨ ⟩ ***clouds getting lower and lower*** ⟨

2 near the bottom of something such as a list or a scale of measurement ⟩ ***Your name's quite low on the list.*** ⟨

3 a low sound or musical note is near the bottom of the range of pitch or musical notes ⟩ ***She spoke in a low voice.*** ⟨ ⟩ ***the lowest note you can sing*** ⟨

4 less than usual in amount or importance ⟩ ***low prices*** ⟨ ⟩ ***Soon their supplies began to run low.*** ⟨

5 sad or fed up ⟩ ***Are you feeling a bit low?*** ⟨

lower

VERB lowers, lowering, lowered

to move something to a position nearer the bottom of something or nearer the ground ⟩ ***At the end of the session, the scouts lower the flag.*** ⟨

luck

NOUN

1 the way things happen by chance ⟩ ***What bad luck that it rained all that day!*** ⟨

2 something good that happens by chance ⟩ ***It was a piece of luck that I found the money.*** ⟨

▸**lucky**

ADJECTIVE luckier, luckiest

a lucky person has good things happen to them by chance ⟩ ***You're lucky to live so near the school.*** ⟨

lump

NOUN *plural* lumps

1 a small, shapeless piece of something ⟩ ***a lump of coal*** ⟨ ⟩ ***This custard's got lumps in it.*** ⟨

2 a hard swelling on your body

▸**lumpy**

ADJECTIVE lumpier, lumpiest

full of lumps

lunch

NOUN *plural* lunches

the meal that you eat in the middle of the day between breakfast and dinner

lung

NOUN *plural* lungs

the two bag-like organs inside your chest that you use for breathing

lying

NOUN

a form of the verb **lie** that is used with another verb to make different tenses ⟩ ***Please stop lying to me.*** ⟨ ⟩ ***She has been lying all along.*** ⟨

machine

NOUN *plural* **machines**

a device with moving parts that is operated by some form of power and is designed to do a particular job ⋛ *a washing machine* ⋚

mad

ADJECTIVE **madder, maddest**

1 mentally ill ⋛ *The poor woman went mad with grief.* ⋚
2 foolish or reckless ⋛ *Swimming in shark-infested waters is a mad thing to do.* ⋚
3 very angry ⋛ *Mum will be mad when she sees the state of your clothes.* ⋚
4 to be mad about someone or something is to like them or it very much ⋛ *mad about football* ⋚

made

VERB

a way of changing the verb **make** to form a past tense. It can be used with or without a helping verb ⋛ *When he was on the beach, he made a sandcastle.* ⋚ ⋛ *I think you have made a mistake.* ⋚

magic

NOUN

1 a strange power that causes things to happen that cannot be explained
2 tricks, such as making things disappear, which seem to people watching to be impossible
3 something beautiful or wonderful ⋛ *the island's special magic* ⋚

▸ **magical**

ADJECTIVE

wonderful or charming ⋛ *a magical day* ⋚

▸ **magician**

NOUN *plural* **magicians**

1 a man or boy who has magic powers, especially in stories ⋛ *Harry Potter and Gandalf are magicians.* ⋚
2 someone who does magic tricks to entertain people

magnet

NOUN *plural* **magnets**

a piece of iron or other metal, which has the power to attract other pieces of metal to it and which points north to south when it hangs free

▸ **magnetic**

ADJECTIVE

1 something that is magnetic has the power to attract iron and some other metals towards it
2 someone with a magnetic personality is very popular with other people

mail¹

NOUN

letters or parcels carried by post

VERB **mails, mailing, mailed**

to mail a letter or parcel is to send it by post

main

ADJECTIVE

most important or principal ⋛ *a main road* ⋚ ⋛ *The main thing is to stay calm.* ⋚

NOUN *plural* **mains**

a pipe that carries water or gas into houses or buildings ⋛ *a burst gas main* ⋚

main verb

NOUN *plural* **main verbs**

a verb that does not need a helping verb to go with it, for example *The lion escaped*

make

VERB makes, making, made

1 to create, produce or prepare something ⋺ *She makes all her own clothes.* ⋹ ⋺ *I'm making a cup of coffee.* ⋹ ⋺ *Let's make a den.* ⋹

2 something makes something else happen when it causes or forces that other thing to happen ⋺ *The explosion made the house shake.* ⋹ ⋺ *He made the dog sit and stay.* ⋹ ⋺ *Hay makes me sneeze.* ⋹

3 to make a point, suggestion or promise is to give it

4 you make the answer to a sum a particular amount when that is the amount you calculate it to be ⋺ *I make that £1.20 you owe me.* ⋹ ⋺ *What time do you make it?* ⋹

5 two or more quantities make a certain amount when they add up to that amount ⋺ *Six and six makes twelve.* ⋹

6 to make a particular place or point is to reach that place or point ⋺ *We climbed part of the way but we didn't make the summit.* ⋹ ⋺ *If we hurry, we might just make the earlier train.* ⋹

7 to make money is to earn it

▸ **make up your mind**
to decide

male

ADJECTIVE

1 a male animal is of the sex that fathers children but does not give birth ⋺ *A male swan is called a cob.* ⋹

2 to do with men or boys or the things that involve them ⋺ *It's mostly a male hobby.* ⋹

NOUN plural males

a male animal

man

NOUN plural men

1 an adult male human being

2 man is a word sometimes used for human beings generally ⋺ *Man is closely related to the apes.* ⋹

VERB mans, manning, manned

to man something is to be the person that runs it or operates it

manage

VERB manages, managing, managed

1 to manage to do something is to succeed in doing it

2 to manage something like a shop or business is to be in charge of running it

3 to survive on very little money ⋺ *I don't know how he manages on his student grant.* ⋹

mango

NOUN plural mangos or mangoes

a large pear-shaped fruit with orange sweet-smelling flesh and a large stone in the middle

many

PRONOUN

1 a lot or a large number ⋺ *I've got lots of CD's. Do you have many?* ⋹

2 **how many** means 'what quantity or number' ⋺ *If you take three chairs away how many will be left?* ⋹

ADJECTIVE more, most

a lot or a large number ⋺ *He has many friends.* ⋹ ⋺ *Many people in the world don't have enough to eat.* ⋹

map

NOUN plural maps

a diagram of an area of land showing the position of things like hills, rivers and roads as if you are looking at them from above

march

VERB marches, marching, marched

1 soldiers march when they walk together at the same regular pace
2 people march when they walk in a large group through the streets, usually because they are protesting about something

NOUN *plural* marches

1 a steady walking pace or a distance covered by marching ⋛ *a slow march* ⋛ *a long march* ⋛
2 a piece of music for marching to

March

NOUN

the third month of the year, after February and before April

> **March** comes from the name of the Roman god **Mars**. He was god of war and was also connected with the growing of new crops in spring.

mark

NOUN *plural* marks

1 a spot or stain ⋛ **There's a dirty mark on the sofa.** ⋛
2 a written or printed sign or symbol that stands for something ⋛ **a punctuation mark** ⋛
3 a point or grade given as a reward for good or accurate work ⋛ **He could get much higher marks if he tried harder.** ⋛

VERB marks, marking, marked

1 to mark something is to put a mark, scratch or stain on it
2 to mark someone's work is to look at it and give it points or a grade to show how good or accurate it is
3 in games like football and hockey, you mark a player on the other team when you stay close to them to stop them from getting or passing the ball

▶ **marker**

NOUN *plural* markers

1 something that you use to mark the position of something
2 a pen with a thick point

marry

VERB marries, marrying, married

to make someone your husband or wife in a special ceremony, or to perform the ceremony making two people into husband and wife

▶ **marriage**

NOUN *plural* marriages

1 the ceremony in which a man and woman become husband and wife
2 the period of time when two people are married to each other ⋛ **a long and happy marriage** ⋛

mask

NOUN *plural* masks

a covering that you wear over your face to protect it or as a disguise

massive

ADJECTIVE

very big ⋛ **a massive amount** ⋛ ⋛ **Hyenas have massive jaws for tearing flesh.** ⋛

mat

NOUN *plural* mats

1 a flat piece of material for covering or protecting part of a floor
2 a small piece of material for protecting a table's surface or for resting something on ⋛ **a table mat** ⋛ ⋛ **a mouse mat** ⋛

match¹

NOUN *plural* matches

a short piece of wood or other material tipped with a substance that catches fire when it is rubbed against a rough surface

a b c d e f g h i j k l **m** n o p q r s t u v w x y z

match²

NOUN *plural* **matches**

1 a contest or game between two players or two teams

2 something that is similar to, or the same as, another thing, especially in its colour or pattern ⋧ *This isn't the same make of paint but it's a very good match.* ⋦

3 a person or animal who is able to equal another ⋧ *I could beat him over a mile but I was no match for him when it came to the 100 metres.* ⋦

VERB **matches, matching, matched**

1 two things match when they are similar to or the same as each other

2 to match, or match up to, another person or thing is to be as good as them

mate

NOUN *plural* **mates**

1 a friend or companion

2 an officer on a ship

3 an animal's mate is the male or female it mates with

VERB **mates, mating, mated**

animals mate when a male and a female come together so that they can produce young

material

NOUN *plural* **materials**

1 cloth or fabric ⋧ *I need some material to make a costume for the school play.* ⋦

2 anything used for making something else ⋧ *a shop selling artist's materials* ⋦

maths

NOUN

a short form of the word **mathematics**, the study of measurements, numbers and shapes

matter

NOUN *plural* **matters**

1 matter is any substance that takes up space and is part of the physical universe

2 a subject, situation or issue ⋧ *He wants to see you to discuss a personal matter.* ⋦

3 if something is the matter, something is wrong or someone is ill or has a problem ⋧ *What's the matter with Rachel? She's very quiet.* ⋦

▸ **as a matter of fact**

in fact

VERB **matters, mattering, mattered**

to matter is to be important ⋧ *Winning matters to him more than it should.* ⋦

may

VERB **might**

1 you may do something if there is a possibility you will do it ⋧ *I may go to college to study art.* ⋦

2 you may do something when you have someone's permission to do it ⋧ *You may leave the table now.* ⋦ ⋧ *May I ask what you're doing in my room?* ⋦

May

NOUN

the fifth month of the year, after April and before June

> **May** comes from the name of the Roman earth goddess **Maia**.

maybe

ADVERB

perhaps or possibly ⋧ *Maybe you'd like to come to lunch one day?* ⋦

maze

NOUN   *plural* mazes

a confusing network of paths, each with a high wall or hedge on either side, designed as a puzzle to see how well you can find your way

me

PRONOUN

a word you use to talk about yourself ⋛ *Would you get me a drink, please.* ⋜   ⋛ *Lots of cakes for tea, all for you and me.* ⋜

> In a sentence in which you are doing the action, you use **I** before the verb. You use **me** after the verb: *The teacher gave the best mark to* me. • *The teacher gave the best marks to Emily, Rory and* me.

meal

NOUN   *plural* meals

a meal is food that you eat at one time, for example breakfast, lunch or dinner

mean¹

VERB   means, meaning, meant

1 a word or action means something when it shows something or you understand something from it ⋛ *The definitions in this dictionary tell you what the words mean.* ⋜   ⋛ *Dark clouds mean rain.* ⋜
2 you mean to do something when you intend to do it ⋛ *I'm sorry. I didn't mean to stand on your foot.* ⋜
3 you mean what you say when you aren't joking or telling lies
4 something that means something to you is important to you ⋛ *That puppy means an awful lot to her.* ⋜

mean²

ADJECTIVE   meaner, meanest

1 a mean person won't spend money or share what they have with others

2 if someone is mean to you, they are nasty or unkind

meaning

NOUN   *plural* meanings

what a word or action means

measles

NOUN

an infectious disease mainly affecting children, which causes red spots on the skin and a fever

measure

VERB   measures, measuring, measured

1 to measure something is to find its width, height, length, weight or amount ⋛ *Stand straight against the wall so that I can measure your height.* ⋜
2 if something measures a certain number of units, its size or amount is given in that number of units ⋛ *The room measures 3.5 metres from the door to the window.* ⋜

NOUN   *plural* measures

a unit used in measuring ⋛ *A kilogram is a measure of weight.* ⋜

▸ **measurement**

NOUN   *plural* measurements

a size or amount found by measuring

meat

NOUN   *plural* meats

the flesh of animals used as food, such as pork, lamb or beef

▸ **meaty**

ADJECTIVE   meatier, meatiest

full of meat or tasting of meat ⋛ *I had a nice*

a b c d e f g h i j k l **m** n o p q r s t u v w x y z

meaty pie with a crisp crust for lunch.

medal

NOUN *plural* medals

a metal disc, usually with a design or writing stamped on it, given as a prize in a competition

medicine

NOUN *plural* medicines

1 the science of the treatment of illness and disease ⟩ *studying medicine*
2 any substance used to treat or prevent diseases and illnesses ⟩ *cough medicine*

meet

VERB meets, meeting, met

1 to come face to face with someone by chance ⟩ *I met Helen outside the bank yesterday.*
2 to come together with one other person, or a group of other people, at the same time and in the same place ⟩ *Let's meet outside the cinema.*
3 to be introduced to someone and get to know them for the first time ⟩ *Have you met my big sister, Jane?*
4 two things meet when they come together or touch ⟩ *I've got so fat, my waistband doesn't meet round my middle.*

▶ **meeting**

NOUN *plural* meetings

a gathering of people, usually to discuss something ⟩ *The staff meeting had to be cancelled at the last minute.*

melon

NOUN *plural* melons

a large rounded fruit with a green or yellow skin, yellow or orange sweet-tasting flesh and lots of seeds in the middle

melt

VERB melts, melting, melted

something melts when it becomes soft and runny as it is heated

member

NOUN *plural* members

a person who belongs to a group or club

▶ **membership**

NOUN *plural* memberships

1 being a member ⟩ *He has membership of many clubs.*
2 the membership of a group, club or society is all the people who are its members

memory

NOUN *plural* memories

1 memory is the power of your mind to remember things
2 a memory is something you remember ⟩ *happy memories of his school days*

▶ **memorize** *or* **memorise**

VERB memorizes, memorizing, memorized

to memorize something is to learn it thoroughly so that you can remember it later

▶ **memorial**

NOUN *plural* memorials

a statue or monument put up as a way of remembering and honouring a person or event ⟩ *a war memorial*

ADJECTIVE

acting as a memorial ⟩ *the John Andrews memorial trophy*

▶ **memorable**

ADJECTIVE

a memorable event is one that you can, or will, remember because it is special or important

men

NOUN

the plural of **man**

mention

VERB mentions, mentioning, mentioned

to mention something is to say it to someone

menu

NOUN   *plural* menus

1 a list of the food available in a restaurant
2 **ICT** on a computer, a list of things that you can choose from by clicking with the mouse or scrolling down the list

mermaid

NOUN   *plural* mermaids

in stories, a beautiful creature who lives in the sea and is half woman, half fish

merry

ADJECTIVE   merrier, merriest

happy and cheerful

▸ **merrily**

ADVERB

happily and cheerfully

mess

NOUN   *plural* messes

1 an untidy or dirty state or sight
2 something that is in a confused state or that involves lots of problems

VERB   messes, messing, messed

▸ **mess about** *or* **mess around**
to do silly or annoying things
▸ **mess something up**
to spoil something or damage it

▸ **messy**

ADJECTIVE   messier, messiest

untidy or dirty

message

NOUN   *plural* messages

a piece of news or information sent from one person to another

VERB   messages, messaging, messaged

to message someone is to send them a message using a mobile phone or computer

▸ **messaging**

NOUN

sending and receiving messages using mobile phones or computers

met

VERB

a way of changing the verb **meet** to form a past tense. It can be used with or without a helping verb ⋛ *We met yesterday.* ⋚ ⋛ *I thought you two had met before.* ⋚

metal

NOUN   *plural* metals

a hard shiny material that melts when it is heated, for example iron, gold, silver and tin

▸ **metallic**

ADJECTIVE

hard and shiny like metal, or sounding like metal when it is hit

metre

NOUN   *plural* metres

1 the basic unit in the metric system for measuring length. This is often shortened to **m**
2 the regular rhythm of poetry or music

> The words **metre** and **meter** sound the same but remember that they have different spellings. A **meter** is a device for measuring something.

mice

NOUN

the plural of **mouse**

midday

NOUN

noon, or the middle of the day

middle

NOUN   *plural* middles

1 the point, position or part furthest from the sides or edges ⋛ *an island in the middle of the ocean* ⋚ ⋛ *Let me sit in the middle.* ⋚
2 the point in a period of time that is halfway through that period of time ⋛ *Autumn half-term comes in the middle of October.* ⋚ ⋛ *The teacher fainted in the*

middle of our history lesson.
3 your middle is your waist

ADJECTIVE
between two things or at the halfway
point ⇒ *He's the middle child of a family of
five boys.* ⇒ *the middle bit of the book*

middle school
NOUN *plural* **middle schools**
a school for children between the ages of 8 or
9 and 12 or 13

midnight
NOUN
twelve o'clock at night

might¹
VERB
1 **might** is used as a past tense of **may** ⇒ *John
asked if he might come with us.*
2 **might** is also used if there is a possibility of
something ⇒ *He might stay.* ⇒ *It might
rain.*

might²
NOUN
power or strength ⇒ *He pulled with all his
might.*

▸ **mighty**
ADJECTIVE **mightier, mightiest**
1 powerful ⇒ *Atlas took the weight of the
sky on his mighty shoulders.*
2 very great ⇒ *a mighty effort*

mile
NOUN *plural* **miles**
a unit for measuring distance, equal to 1.6
kilometres

milk
NOUN
1 a white liquid that female mammals make
in their bodies to feed their young
2 this liquid that we get from cows, goats and
sheep and use to drink or to make butter
and cheese

VERB **milks, milking, milked**
1 to milk an animal is to take milk from it
2 to milk a person or a situation is to get as
much as possible from them or it, in a clever
or selfish way

million
NOUN *plural* **millions**
the number 1,000,000, a thousand thousand

mind
NOUN *plural* **minds**
your mind is your brain, or your ability to think,
understand or remember
▸ **make up your mind**
to decide

VERB **minds, minding, minded**
1 you mind something when it upsets or
annoys you ⇒ *I don't mind cold weather.*
2 you ask someone if they would mind doing
something, or if they would mind if you
did something, when you are asking them
politely to do it, or if they object to you
doing it ⇒ *Would you mind opening the
window?*
3 to mind someone or something is to look
after them
4 you tell someone to mind something
when you are telling them to watch out for
some danger ⇒ *Mind your head on that
branch.*

mine¹
PRONOUN
a word you use to talk about something
belonging to **me** ⇒ *Is this book yours or
mine?* ⇒ *a friend of mine*

mine²
NOUN *plural* **mines**
1 a place where things are dug out of the
ground, for example coal, metals and
minerals, or precious stones
2 a type of bomb that is hidden in the ground
or in the sea and which explodes when
someone stands on it or a ship hits it

miniature

ADJECTIVE
very small

NOUN *plural* **miniatures**
a very small copy or model of a larger thing, or a very small portrait of someone

mint

NOUN *plural* **mints**
1 mint is a plant with strong-smelling leaves used as a flavouring in cooking
2 a mint is a sweet flavoured with the mint plant

minus

PREPOSITION
1 **maths** taking away or subtracting ⇒ *8 minus 2 is 6*
2 without ⇒ *He came back home covered in mud and minus one shoe.*

ADJECTIVE
less than zero ⇒ *minus ten degrees*

NOUN *plural* **minuses**
maths a minus, or minus sign (–), is a symbol showing that a number is to be taken away from another, or that a number is less than zero

minute[1] said "min-it"

NOUN *plural* **minutes**
1 sixty seconds or a sixtieth part of an hour
2 **maths** in measuring an angle, the sixtieth part of a degree
3 a moment or very short time ⇒ *Wait a minute while I go back for my bag.*

ADJECTIVE
showing the number of minutes ⇒ *the minute hand of your watch*

minute[2] said "mine-yoot"

ADJECTIVE
tiny ⇒ *a minute amount of gold*

mirror

NOUN *plural* **mirrors**
a piece of glass with a reflective backing

that you can look at yourself in

VERB mirrors, mirroring, mirrored
one thing mirrors another when it looks or behaves exactly like that other thing or like a reflection of it

miss

VERB misses, missing, missed
1 to fail to hit or catch something you are aiming at ⇒ *The arrow missed the target.*
2 to miss an event is to be unable to attend it or watch it ⇒ *Granny never misses this programme.*
3 to miss a train, bus or plane is to not arrive in time to catch it
4 to miss a person or place is to be sad because that person is not with you or you are not at that place

NOUN *plural* **misses**
1 a failure to hit a target ⇒ *He scored two hits and a miss.*
2 to give something a miss is to not do it

Miss

NOUN *plural* **Misses**
1 a title used for girls and unmarried women
2 a word used by schoolchildren when they are talking to a female teacher, whether she is married or not

mist

NOUN *plural* **mists**
a thin fog, made up of tiny water droplets in the air

VERB mists, misting, misted
something mists up, or mists over, when it becomes covered with tiny droplets of water or mist

▸ **misty**
ADJECTIVE mistier, mistiest
the weather is misty when there is mist in the air

mistake

NOUN *plural* **mistakes**
something wrong that you do or say and which you did not mean to do or say

a b c d e f g h i j k l **m** n o p q r s t u v w x y z

VERB mistakes, mistaking, mistook, mistaken

to mistake one person or thing for another person or thing is to think wrongly they are that other person or thing

▸ **mistaken**

ADJECTIVE

you are mistaken if you are wrong about something

mitt or mitten

NOUN plural mitts or mittens

a type of glove without separate parts for the four fingers

mix

VERB mixes, mixing, mixed

1 to mix something is to put two or more things together so that they combine or form a mass ⋽ *Mixing a little black paint into the white will give you a light grey.* ⋽ *We each took a turn to mix the Christmas cake.*

2 things mix when they combine ⋽ *Oil and water don't mix.*

3 you mix with other people when you talk to them or get to know them socially

4 if you mix things up, you confuse them and think one is the other ⋽ *He said he might have got me mixed up with Jim.*

NOUN plural mixes

a mixture ⋽ *an odd mix of comedy and horror*

▸ **mixed**

ADJECTIVE

containing several different things or types of people ⋽ *a mixed grill*

▸ **mixer**

NOUN plural mixers

any machine used for mixing things ⋽ *a cement mixer*

▸ **mixture**

NOUN plural mixtures

a combination of several things ⋽ *cough*

mixture ⋽ *Louise felt a mixture of joy and sadness.*

mob

NOUN plural mobs

a mob is an angry crowd of people

VERB mobs, mobbing, mobbed

people mob someone they want to see or meet when they crowd round that person

▸ **mobbed**

ADJECTIVE

if a place is mobbed, it is very crowded

mobile

ADJECTIVE

something is mobile when it moves or can move around

NOUN plural mobiles

1 a short form of **mobile phone**, a telephone that you can carry around with you

2 a hanging decoration that moves in the air

▸ **mobility**

NOUN

being able to move around

modern

ADJECTIVE

modern things belong to the present or recent times rather than the past

▸ **modernize or modernise**

VERB modernizes, modernizing, modernized

to modernize something is to make it more up to date

mole[1]

NOUN plural moles

a small black or dark brown furry animal that lives underground in tunnels that it digs with its strong claws. Moles have poor eyesight but very good hearing

mole²
NOUN *plural* moles

a small dark-coloured permanent mark or lump on someone's skin

moment
NOUN *plural* moments

1 a short period of time ⇒ **Stop what you're doing for a moment.**
2 a particular point in time ⇒ **Just at that moment, she heard a door slam.**

▶ **momentary**
ADJECTIVE

lasting for only a moment ⇒ **There was a momentary pause and then everyone started talking.**

Monday
NOUN *plural* Mondays

the day of the week after Sunday and before Tuesday

> **Monday** is from the Old English word **Monandæg**, which means *day of the moon.*

money
NOUN

1 money is coins or banknotes used to buy things ⇒ **I don't have enough money to buy the jacket I want.**
2 money is a lot of money ⇒ **Only people with money can afford yachts.**

monkey
NOUN *plural* monkeys

an animal with a long tail that walks on four legs and lives in trees

monster
NOUN *plural* monsters

1 in stories, a huge or frightening creature
2 a cruel or evil person

ADJECTIVE

enormous ⇒ **a monster truck**

month
NOUN *plural* months

1 one of twelve periods that a year is divided into ⇒ **In Britain, the winter months are December, January and February.**
2 any period of approximately four weeks or 30 days ⇒ **We had to wait for months for an appointment.**

▶ **monthly**
ADJECTIVE AND ADVERB

happening once a month or each month ⇒ **a monthly salary** ⇒ **He is paid monthly.**

moo
VERB moos, mooing, mooed

a cow moos when it makes a long low sound

NOUN *plural* moos

the long low sound a cow makes

mood
NOUN *plural* moods

your mood is your feelings or temper at a particular time ⇒ **I woke up in a bad mood this morning.**

▶ **moody**
ADJECTIVE moodier, moodiest

a moody person changes their mood often or suddenly, from cheerful to grumpy and impatient

moon
NOUN *plural* moons

1 the large ball-shaped object that orbits the Earth once a month and which you can see in the night sky as a full circle or a partial circle depending on the time of month
2 a similar body going round certain other planets, such as Saturn

moor¹
NOUN *plural* moors

a large stretch of open land with poor soil and very few, or no, trees

moor²

VERB moors, mooring, moored

to moor a boat is to tie it up using a rope, cable or anchor

more

ADJECTIVE

a greater quantity or amount ⋛ *He has more toys than anyone else I know.* ⋚ ⋛ *Could you get me three more mugs?* ⋚

PRONOUN

1 a greater quantity or amount ⋛ *More than forty people turned up.* ⋚

2 an additional quantity or amount ⋛ *Is there any more jelly?* ⋚

ADVERB

1 **more** is used to make comparative forms of adjectives and adverbs ⋛ *He's more patient than I am.* ⋚

2 **more** is the comparative form of **much** and means 'to a greater degree' ⋛ *At first I didn't like her much but I'm beginning to like her more and more.* ⋚

▸ **moreish**
ADJECTIVE

something is moreish if it makes you want more

morning

NOUN *plural* **mornings**

the part of the day from midnight to midday

mosque

NOUN *plural* **mosques**

a building where Muslims go to worship

moss

NOUN *plural* **mosses**

a small plant found in damp places and forming a soft green mat over the ground

▸ **mossy**
ADJECTIVE mossier, mossiest

covered with moss

most

ADJECTIVE

most is the superlative form of **many** and **much**. It means 'more than other people or things' ⋛ *Who scored most goals last season?* ⋚

PRONOUN

1 nearly all, or the majority ⋛ *Most of my friends are allowed to walk to school.* ⋚

2 the largest amount ⋛ *They both had a lot but who had the most?* ⋚

ADVERB

most is the superlative form of **much** and means 'to the greatest degree' ⋛ *What kind of music do you like most?* ⋚

▸ **mostly**
ADVERB

in most cases or in most parts ⋛ *They mostly play indoors.* ⋚

moth

NOUN *plural* **moths**

a creature similar to a butterfly, but usually active at night, rather than during the day

mother

NOUN *plural* **mothers**

your female parent

VERB mothers, mothering, mothered

to mother someone is to treat them with protective kindness, like a mother does

motorcycle

NOUN *plural* **motorcycles**

a motorbike, which is a two-wheeled vehicle with a powerful engine that you sit on like a bicycle

▸ **motorcyclist**
NOUN
plural **motorcyclists**

someone who rides a motorbike

mould¹

NOUN *plural* moulds

a shaped container that you pour a substance into so that the substance has the shape of the container when it cools and hardens ⇒ *a jelly mould*

VERB moulds, moulding, moulded

1 to form something in a mould ⇒ *The gold is moulded into ingots.*
2 to shape something using your hands ⇒ *Mum moulded the icing into pretty flower shapes.*

mould²

NOUN *plural* moulds

mould is something that forms green or black patches on stale food or on damp walls and ceilings

▶ **mouldy**

ADJECTIVE mouldier, mouldiest

covered with mould ⇒ *a mouldy old loaf*

mountain

NOUN *plural* mountains

a very high hill

▶ **mountaineer**

NOUN *plural* mountaineers

someone who climbs mountains using ropes and other special equipment

▶ **mountainous**

ADJECTIVE

a mountainous area has a lot of mountains

mouse

NOUN *plural* mice

1 a small animal with a long tail, bright eyes and grey or brown fur
2 **ICT** a device that you move with your hand over a flat surface to move the cursor on a computer screen. It has buttons that you press to tell the computer to do something

mouth

NOUN *plural* mouths

1 your mouth is the part of your face that you use to speak and eat and which contains your tongue and teeth
2 **geography** the mouth of a river is the place where it flows into the sea

VERB mouths, mouthing, mouthed

to mouth words is to make the shapes of the words with your mouth without making the sounds

▶ **mouthful**

NOUN *plural* mouthfuls

an amount you put or hold in your mouth at one time ⇒ *He took a mouthful of water.*

move

VERB moves, moving, moved

1 you move something when you take it from one place and put it in another ⇒ *Please move your toys off the kitchen table.*
2 if something moves, it changes its position ⇒ *I saw that curtain move.*
3 to move is to change from one house or place of work to another
4 if something moves you, it has a strong effect on your feelings and emotions

NOUN *plural* moves

1 a change of position ⇒ *They made no move to help.*
2 the moving of a piece in a game such as ludo or chess ⇒ *Come on, it's your move.*
3 a change to another home or another place of work

▶ **movement**

NOUN *plural* movements

1 changing position or a change of position
2 a division in a long piece of classical music
3 an organization or association with a common purpose or aim ⇒ *the Scout movement*

Mr

NOUN *plural* Messrs

short for **Mister**, a title used before a man's name, for example when writing his name on an envelope or at the beginning of a letter

Mrs

NOUN *plural* **Mrs**

short for **Mistress**, a title used before a married woman's name, for example, when writing her name on an envelope or at the beginning of a letter

Ms

NOUN

a title sometimes used before a woman's name, whether she is married or unmarried, for example when writing her name on an envelope or at the beginning of a letter

much

ADJECTIVE

1 a lot or a large amount ⋛ *There was much laughter coming from the girls' room.* ⋚
2 **much** is used in questions about quantities or amounts ⋛ *How much fruit do you eat each day?* ⋚

PRONOUN

a lot or a large amount ⋛ *I usually don't have much to eat at lunchtime.* ⋚

ADVERB

1 about ⋛ *Both books are much the same.* ⋚
2 greatly or a lot ⋛ *Do you miss your old school much?* ⋚

mud

NOUN

soft wet soil that sticks to your clothes and shoes

mug

NOUN *plural* **mugs**

a cup with straight sides and a handle

multiply

VERB multiplies, multiplying, multiplied

1 **maths** to increase a number by adding it to itself a certain number of times. For example, 10 multiplied by 3 is 30, which can be written $10 \times 3 = 30$
2 things multiply when they increase in number

▸ **multiplication**

NOUN *plural* **multiplications**

multiplying numbers or things

mum

NOUN *plural* **mums**

an informal word for **mother**

mummy[1]

NOUN *plural* **mummies**

a child's word for **mother**

mummy[2]

NOUN *plural* **mummies**

a mummy is a dead body that has been preserved and wrapped in bandages

murder

NOUN *plural* **murders**

murder is the crime of killing someone deliberately

VERB murders, murdering, murdered

to murder someone is to kill them deliberately

▸ **murderer**

NOUN *plural* **murderers**

someone who has murdered another person

muscle

NOUN *plural* **muscles**

the parts of your body that move your limbs and organs, which you can make bigger and stronger by exercising

▸ **muscular**

ADJECTIVE

to do with the muscles

museum

NOUN *plural* **museums**

a place where collections of interesting things are displayed for people to see

mushroom

NOUN *plural* **mushrooms**

a type of plant that you can eat, with a round top

VERB mushrooms, mushrooming, mushroomed

something mushrooms when it increases its size very quickly

music

NOUN

sounds arranged or combined in patterns, sung or played by instruments

▸ **musical**

ADJECTIVE

1 to do with music ⇒ *musical training*
2 a musical sound is pleasant to listen to

NOUN *plural* **musicals**

a play or film in which there is lots of singing and dancing

▸ **musician**

NOUN *plural* **musicians**

someone who plays music on an instrument

Muslim

NOUN *plural* **Muslims**

a person who is a follower of Islam

ADJECTIVE

to do with Islam ⇒ *Friday is the Muslim holy day.*

must

VERB

must is used with another verb to show that you have to do something or that something is certain or very likely ⇒ *You must finish your homework before you go out.* ⇒ *I saw it on the telly so it must be true.*

my

ADJECTIVE

belonging to me ⇒ *There's my Mum and Dad.* ⇒ *Have you seen my boots?*

myself

PRONOUN

1 you use **myself** after a verb or preposition when **I** is the subject of the action and is also affected by it ⇒ *I've washed myself all over, even behind my ears.* ⇒ *I felt rather proud of myself.*

2 you also use **myself** to show that you do something without any help from anyone else ⇒ *I suppose I'll have to do it myself if no one else can be bothered.*

3 you can use the word **myself** to show more clearly who you mean ⇒ *I have not seen the film myself.*

a b c d e f g h i j k l **m** n o p q r s t u v w x y z

nail

NOUN *plural* **nails**

1 a thin pointed piece of metal that you hit into a surface with a hammer
2 the hard covering on top of the ends of your fingers and toes

VERB nails, nailing, nailed

to attach or join something by hammering it with nails ⇒ *Nail the number on the door.*

name

NOUN *plural* **names**

the word or words that you always call a certain person, place or thing ⇒ *What's your name?* ⇒ *I can't remember the name of the street.*

VERB names, naming, named

to name a person, place or thing is to decide on a certain word to call them ⇒ *They've named their son Samuel.*

nappy

NOUN *plural* **nappies**

a pad for fastening around a baby's bottom

narrow

ADJECTIVE narrower, narrowest

1 not very wide ⇒ *a narrow path* ⇒ *The road was too narrow for lorries.*
2 only just happening, with hardly any room or time to spare ⇒ *a narrow escape*

natural

ADJECTIVE

1 to do with or made by nature, not by people or machines ⇒ *the natural world* ⇒ *An earthquake is a natural disaster.*
2 natural behaviour is what you do normally without thinking ⇒ *It's only natural to be a little nervous before a test.*

nature

NOUN *plural* **natures**

1 everything in the world that was not made or changed by people ⇒ *I love those nature programmes about animals.*
2 what something is basically like ⇒ *questions of a difficult nature*
3 the kind of person someone is ⇒ *It's not in her nature to be unkind.*

naughty

ADJECTIVE naughtier, naughtiest

a naughty child does things they should not do

▸ **naughtiness**

NOUN

bad behaviour or not doing as you are told

near

PREPOSITION

not far away ⇒ *the shop near our house*

ADVERB nearer, nearest

close by a thing or person ⇒ *Stand a little nearer and you'll be able to see better.*

ADJECTIVE nearer, nearest

not far away ⇒ *the near future* ⇒ *a near neighbour*

VERB nears, nearing, neared

to approach or get close ⇒ *As we neared the building, the faces became clearer.*

neat

ADJECTIVE   neater, neatest

1 clean and tidy ⟩ *a neat bedroom*
2 done skilfully ⟩ *a neat shot into the corner of the goal*

necessary

ADJECTIVE

needed in order to get a result ⟩ *Is it necessary for everyone to fill in their own form?* ⟩ *We can stay a bit longer if necessary.*

neck

NOUN   *plural* **necks**

1 the part of the body between the head and the shoulders
2 the opening in a piece of clothing that you put your head through

necklace

NOUN   *plural* **necklaces**

a piece of jewellery for wearing around your neck, such as a string of beads or jewels, or a chain

need

VERB   needs, needing, needed

1 to have to do something ⟩ *We all need to eat and drink.*
2 to be without something that would be helpful or useful ⟩ *What I need here is a sharp knife.*

NOUN   *plural* **needs**

1 you have a need for something when you want it but do not have it ⟩ *If you feel the need of some company, just call me.*
2 if there is no need to do something, it is not necessary ⟩ *There's no need to shout.*
3 your needs are the things that it is necessary for you to have

needle

NOUN   *plural* **needles**

1 a small pointed piece of metal for sewing

2 a long thin piece of wood, metal or plastic that is used for knitting
3 a sharp instrument for giving injections of medicine

neighbour

NOUN   *plural* **neighbours**

a person who lives near you

▶ **neighbourhood**

NOUN   *plural* **neighbourhoods**

an area of a town or city ⟩ *This is a pretty neighbourhood with a lot of trees.*

▶ **neighbouring**

ADJECTIVE

next or nearby ⟩ *a neighbouring town*

> **Neighbour** comes from the Old English words **neach**, which means *near*, and **gebure**, which means 'a person living in (a place)'. **Neachgebur** means 'someone living nearby'.

neither

ADJECTIVE AND PRONOUN

not either ⟩ *Neither woman seemed to understand.* ⟩ *Neither of us can go.*

CONJUNCTION

neither is often used with **nor** to show negative possibilities ⟩ *I neither know, nor care, where he is.*

nephew

NOUN   *plural* **nephews**

your nephew is the son of your brother or sister

nerve

NOUN   *plural* **nerves**

1 a nerve is one of the tiny thread-like connections that carry messages about feelings and movements between your brain and other parts of your body
2 nerve is a kind of boldness or courage ⟩ *I didn't have the nerve to jump.*

a b c d e f g h i j k l m **n** o p q r s t u v w x y z

a
b
c
d
e
f
g
h
i
j
k
l
m
n
o
p
q
r
s
t
u
v
w
x
y
z

▸ **get on someone's nerves**
to annoy someone

nervous

ADJECTIVE

1 worried or frightened ⇒ *I get really nervous just before an exam.*
2 to do with the body's nerves ⇒ *an infection that affects the nervous system*

▸ **nervously**
ADVERB
in a worried, rather scared way

▸ **nervousness**
NOUN
a worried, rather scared feeling

nest

NOUN *plural* **nests**

a place where birds or some kinds of insects and animals live and bring up their young

VERB **nests, nesting, nested**

to build a place to live, especially from twigs and leaves, in a tree

net

NOUN *plural* **nets**

1 net is a material made by crossing and knotting threads and making a pattern of holes
2 a net is made from crossed and knotted threads and is used for catching things like fish or in sports like tennis or football

netball

NOUN

a game where teams of players throw a ball to each other and try to score goals by putting the ball through a high loop surrounded by a net at the end of a court

never

ADVERB

not ever, or not at any time ⇒ *I've never been abroad.* ⇒ *It's never too late to learn.*

new

ADJECTIVE newer, newest

1 not existing or known about before ⇒ *a new discovery*
2 just bought, made or received ⇒ *a new jacket*
3 different ⇒ *Take this book back and get a new one from the library.*

news

PLURAL NOUN

information about something that has just happened

NOUN

a radio or television report about recent events ⇒ *listening to the news at 9 o'clock*

newspaper

NOUN *plural* **newspapers**

a collection of reports and pictures about recent events that is published daily or weekly on a set of folded sheets of paper

next

ADJECTIVE

the one that follows immediately after ⇒ *What's the next name on the list?* ⇒ *Let's meet next week.*

ADVERB

after the present thing, person or time ⇒ *Who's next?* ⇒ *What will happen next?*

nibble

VERB nibbles, nibbling, nibbled

to take little bites of something ⇒ *A mouse had nibbled right through the wires.*

nice

ADJECTIVE nicer, nicest

1 pleasant, good or attractive ⇒ *We'll find somewhere nice to sit, outside.*
2 kind or friendly ⇒ *James is quite nice really, once you get used to him.*

▸ **nicely**

ADVERB

1 in a pleasant way ⟩ *Ask the lady nicely.* ⟨
2 well ⟩ *She's settled in nicely at school.* ⟨

nickname

NOUN *plural* **nicknames**

a name that you use for someone that is not their real name

niece

NOUN *plural* **nieces**

your niece is the daughter of your brother or sister

night

NOUN *plural* **nights**

the time of darkness between the sun going down in the evening and rising again in the morning

nightmare

NOUN *plural* **nightmares**

1 a frightening dream
2 a very unpleasant experience ⟩ *The journey turned out to be a complete nightmare.* ⟨

> The ending of this word comes from the Old English word **mare**, which means *evil spirit*. It used to be believed that bad dreams at night were caused by evil spirits.

nine

NOUN *plural* **nines**

the number 9

nineteen

NOUN

the number 19

ninety

NOUN *plural* **nineties**

the number 90

no

INTERJECTION

a word that you use to express things like refusing, denying or disagreeing ⟩ *'Are you alright?' 'No, my leg's hurting'.* ⟨

ADJECTIVE

not any ⟩ *They have no money.* ⟨

ADVERB

not at all ⟩ *She's no better.* ⟨

nobody

PRONOUN

not any person ⟩ *Nobody tells me what to do!* ⟨ ⟩ *There was nobody at home.* ⟨

NOUN *plural* **nobodies**

a person who is not at all important ⟩ *He's just a nobody who thinks he's somebody.* ⟨

nod

VERB **nods, nodding, nodded**

to move your head up and down as if you were agreeing or saying 'yes'

NOUN *plural* **nods**

an up-and-down movement of your head

noise

NOUN *plural* **noises**

1 a noise is a sound ⟩ *Did you hear a noise outside?* ⟨
2 noise is sound that you do not like ⟩ *Could you please make a little less noise?* ⟨

▸ **noisy**

ADJECTIVE **noisier, noisiest**

making a lot of sound that you do not like ⟩ *a noisy party* ⟨

> This word comes an old French word that means an *uproar.*

none

PRONOUN

not one ⟩ *None of them are going to admit to being wrong.* ⟨ ⟩ *We looked for more biscuits but there were none left.* ⟨

ADVERB

not at all ⇒ *I heard the answer but I'm none the wiser.*

nonsense

NOUN

1 something that does not make sense ⇒ *His theory is a load of nonsense.*
2 silly behaviour ⇒ *Stop your nonsense now please.*

noon

NOUN

twelve o'clock in the day ⇒ *We'll have our lunch at noon.*

no one *or* no-one

PRONOUN

not any person ⇒ *No one's in just now.*

normal

ADJECTIVE

usual and expected ⇒ *It's normal to feel hungry at lunchtime.*

north

NOUN

1 the direction a compass needle points, opposite to south
2 the part of a country or the world that is in the north

ADJECTIVE

in, from, or towards the north ⇒ *the cold north wind* ⇒ *the north wall of the building*

ADVERB

to the north ⇒ *The house faces north.*

nose

NOUN *plural* **noses**

1 the part of your face that you breathe and smell through
2 the front part of something that sticks out, for example the front of an aircraft

nostril

NOUN *plural* **nostrils**

your nostrils are the two openings in your nose that you breathe and smell through

> This word comes from the Old English words **nosu**, which means *nose*, and **thyrel**, which means *hole*, so together they mean 'a hole in the nose'.

not

ADVERB

a word that is used to express negatives and opposites. It often becomes **n't** when it is added to verbs ⇒ *I did not see him.* ⇒ *It isn't fair.* ⇒ *I can't hear you.*

note

NOUN *plural* **notes**

1 a word or sentence to tell or remind someone of something ⇒ *They've left a note to say that dinner's in the oven.*
2 a short letter ⇒ *This is just a quick note to let you know we're well.*
3 a written comment ⇒ *a note at the bottom of the page*
4 a piece of paper money ⇒ *a five pound note*
5 **music** a single musical sound or the sign that stands for it

nothing

PRONOUN

not anything ⇒ *There was nothing in the cupboard.* ⇒ *Nothing's the matter with me.*

notice

VERB notices, noticing, noticed

to realize something because you see, hear, feel, smell or taste it ⇒ *I noticed a funny smell in the hall.* ⇒ *Did you notice the way George was looking at Emily?*

NOUN *plural* **notices**

a notice is a written or printed announcement ⇒ *a notice on the board*

noun

WORD CLASS *plural* **nouns**

a word that refers to a person or thing. For example, *tree*, *Sue* and *idea* are nouns

November

NOUN

the eleventh month of the year, after October and before December

> **November** was the ninth month of the Roman year and the name comes from the word **novem**, which means *nine* in Latin.

now

ADVERB

1 at the present time ⦚ *It is now five o'clock.* ⦚

2 immediately ⦚ *I'll do it now.* ⦚

▸ **now and again** *or* **now and then** from time to time

numb said "num"

ADJECTIVE **number, numbest**

a part of your body is numb when you cannot feel it properly ⦚ *I was so cold my hands had gone completely numb.* ⦚

▸ **numbness**

NOUN

when you lose the feeling in a part of your body

number

NOUN *plural* **numbers**

1 a word or figure showing how many or a position in a series ⦚ *the number four* ⦚ ⦚ *Please write down any three figure number.* ⦚

2 a group or collection of people or things ⦚ *a large number of animals* ⦚

3 a popular song or piece of music ⦚ *a catchy number* ⦚

VERB **numbers, numbering, numbered**

1 to number a group of things or people is to give them all a number ⦚ *The boxes are all clearly numbered.* ⦚

2 a group that numbers a certain quantity is made up of that many ⦚ *The crowd numbered many thousands.* ⦚

nurse

NOUN *plural* **nurses**

a person whose job is to look after people when they are ill or injured, especially in a hospital

VERB **nurses, nursing, nursed**

to nurse someone is to look after them when they are ill or injured ⦚ *He had nursed her back to health over several weeks.* ⦚

nursery

NOUN *plural* **nurseries**

1 a place where parents can take their children to be looked after while they are at work

2 a room for young children

3 a place where plants are grown and sold

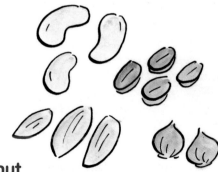

nut

NOUN *plural* **nuts**

a fruit from certain trees that has a hard shell and a firm inside that you can eat

a b c d e f g h i j k l m n o p q r s t u v w x y z

oar

NOUN   *plural* oars

a long piece of wood with a flat end, used for rowing a boat

obey

VERB   obeys, obeying, obeyed

to do what you are told to do ⟩ *I obeyed the order.* ⟨

object

NOUN   said "**ob**-jikt"   *plural* objects

1 something that you can see and touch ⟩ *There were various objects on the table.* ⟨

2 an aim or purpose ⟩ *His main object in life was to become rich.* ⟨

3 **grammar** the word or words in a sentence that stand for the person or thing that the verb affects, for example *me* in *He hit me*

VERB   said "ob-**jekt**"   objects, objecting, objected

to object to someone or something is to say that you do not like them or do not agree with them ⟩ *I object to her rudeness.* ⟨ ⟩ *Jack objected to going to bed so early.* ⟨

▸ **objection**

NOUN   *plural* objections

1 objecting to something ⟩ *His view is open to objection.* ⟨

2 a reason for objecting ⟩ *My objection is that he is too young.* ⟨

ocean

NOUN   *plural* oceans

1 the ocean is the salt water that covers most of the Earth's surface

2 an ocean is one of the five large areas of sea in the world, for example the Atlantic Ocean

October

NOUN

the tenth month of the year, after September and before November

> **October** was the eighth month of the Roman year and the name comes from the word **octo**, which means *eight* in Latin. Another word in English where you can work out that **octo** means *eight* is **octopus**.

octopus

NOUN   *plural* octopuses

a sea creature with eight arms that are called tentacles

> This word comes from the Greek words **octo**, which means *eight*, and **pous**, which means *feet*.

odd

ADJECTIVE   odder, oddest

1 unusual or strange ⟩ *He's wearing very odd clothes.* ⟨

2 an odd number is one that cannot be divided exactly by 2 ⇒ *5 and 7 are odd numbers.*

3 not one of a matching pair or group ⇒ *an odd shoe*

4 left over ⇒ *Have you got any odd bits of wood I could use?*

of

PREPOSITION

1 belonging to ⇒ *a friend of mine* ⇒ *Where is the lid of this box?*

2 away from ⇒ *within two miles of his home*

3 from among ⇒ *one of my friends*

4 made from or out of ⇒ *a house of bricks*

5 used to show an amount or measurement of something ⇒ *a gallon of petrol*

6 about ⇒ *the story of his adventures*

7 containing ⇒ *a box of chocolates*

off

ADVERB

1 away from a place or position ⇒ *He marched off down the road.* ⇒ *Take your shoes off.*

2 not working or in use ⇒ *Switch off the light.*

3 completely ⇒ *Finish off your work.*

ADJECTIVE

1 cancelled ⇒ *The holiday is off.*

2 gone sour or rotten ⇒ *This milk is off.*

3 not switched on ⇒ *The radio was off.*

PREPOSITION

1 away from or down from ⇒ *a mile off the coast* ⇒ *It fell off the table.*

2 out of a vehicle ⇒ *We got off the bus.*

3 taken away from ⇒ *There is £10 off the usual price.*

4 not wanting something ⇒ *Jane is not well and is off her food.*

office

NOUN *plural* offices

1 a building or set of rooms in which the business of a company is done ⇒ *Our head offices are in London.*

2 the room in which a particular person works ⇒ *the bank manager's office*

3 a room or building used for a particular purpose ⇒ *lost property office*

4 an important job or position ⇒ *the office of President*

often

ADVERB

many times ⇒ *I often go to the cinema.*

oil

NOUN *plural* oils

1 a greasy liquid that will not mix with water ⇒ *olive oil* ⇒ *vegetable oil*

2 a substance made from the remains of dead animals and plants. It can be taken out of the ground and used as fuel

VERB oils, oiling, oiled

to oil something is to put oil on or into it ⇒ *The machine will work better if it's oiled.*

OK *or* okay

INTERJECTION, ADJECTIVE AND ADVERB

an informal way of saying 'all right' ⇒ *OK! I'll do it!* ⇒ *an okay song* ⇒ *Do I look OK?*

> **OK** probably comes from an American advertisement from the past, in which 'all correct' was spelt *oll korrect* as a joke.

old

ADJECTIVE older, oldest

1 having lived or existed a long time ⇒ *an old man* ⇒ *an old building*

2 having a particular age ⇒ *nine years old*

3 belonging to times long ago ⇒ *the good old days*

4 worn-out, or no longer used ⇒ *She threw away her old clothes.*

5 former or previous ⇒ *I preferred my old school to this one.*

a b c d e f g h i j k l m n o p q r s t u v w x y z

on

PREPOSITION

1 touching, fixed to or covering the upper or outer side of something ⋧ *on the table* ⋧
2 supported by ⋧ *standing on one leg* ⋧
3 during a certain day ⋧ *on Friday* ⋧
4 about ⋧ *a book on Scottish history* ⋧

ADVERB

1 so as to be touching, fixed to or covering the upper or outer side of something ⋧ *Put your coat on.* ⋧
2 forwards or onwards ⋧ *They moved on.* ⋧
3 working or being used ⋧ *Switch the light on.* ⋧

ADJECTIVE

1 working or being used ⋧ *The television is on.* ⋧
2 planned ⋧ *Do you have anything on this evening?* ⋧
3 not cancelled ⋧ *Is the party still on?* ⋧

once

ADVERB

1 a single time ⋧ *He did it once.* ⋧
2 at a time in the past ⋧ *People once lived in caves.* ⋧

CONJUNCTION

when or as soon as ⋧ *Once you've finished, you can go.* ⋧

one

NOUN *plural* **ones**

the number 1 ⋧ *One and one is two.* ⋧

PRONOUN

1 a single person or thing ⋧ *One of my friends called round.* ⋧
2 a rather formal word for **anyone** or **you** ⋧ *One can see the sea from here.* ⋧

ADJECTIVE

a single ⋧ *We had only one reply.* ⋧

▸ **one another**

used when an action takes place between two or more people ⋧ *They looked at one another.* ⋧

onion

NOUN *plural* **onions**

a round vegetable that has a strong taste and smell

only

ADVERB

1 not more than ⋧ *There are only two weeks until the holiday.* ⋧
2 alone ⋧ *Only you can do it.* ⋧
3 not longer ago than ⋧ *I saw her only yesterday.* ⋧

ADJECTIVE

without any others of the same type ⋧ *the only book of its kind* ⋧

CONJUNCTION

but or however ⋧ *I'd like to come, only I have to do my homework.* ⋧

onto

PREPOSITION

to a place or position on ⋧ *The fans ran onto the pitch.* ⋧

open

ADJECTIVE

1 not shut ⋧ *The door is wide open.* ⋧
2 allowing the inside to be seen ⋧ *an open book* ⋧
3 not enclosed ⋧ *open countryside* ⋧

VERB **opens, opening, opened**

1 to open something is to make it open ⋧ *He opened the door.* ⋧
2 to open is to become open ⋧ *The door opened.* ⋧
3 to open something is to begin it ⋧ *He opened the meeting with a joke.* ⋧

▸ **opener**

NOUN *plural* **openers**

something that opens something else ⋧ *a tin opener* ⋧

▸ **opening**

NOUN *plural* **openings**

1 a hole or space ⋧ *an opening in the fence* ⋧

2 a beginning ⋗ *the opening of the film* ⋖

3 a chance, especially for a job ⋗ *There are few openings for ex-footballers.* ⋖

operate

VERB operates, operating, operated

1 to work, or make work

2 to perform an operation on someone's body

▶ **operation**

NOUN *plural* operations

1 a carefully planned action ⋗ *a rescue operation* ⋖

2 an occasion when a doctor cuts into someone's body in order to remove part of it or treat a disease

opposite

ADJECTIVE

1 on the other side of something ⋗ *on the opposite side of town* ⋖

2 completely different ⋗ *They walked off in opposite directions.* ⋖

PREPOSITION AND ADVERB

facing ⋗ *the house opposite mine*   ⋗ *Who lives in the house opposite?* ⋖

NOUN *plural* opposites

one thing is the opposite of another if it is completely different from it ⋗ *Hot is the opposite of cold.* ⋖

optician

NOUN *plural* opticians

someone who tests your eyesight and makes and sells glasses

or

CONJUNCTION

1 used to show choices ⋗ *Would you prefer tea or coffee?* ⋖

2 because if not ⋗ *You'd better go or you'll miss your bus.* ⋖

orange

NOUN *plural* oranges

1 an orange is a juicy citrus fruit with a thick skin of a colour between red and yellow

2 orange is the colour of this fruit

ADJECTIVE

of the colour orange

orchestra

NOUN *plural* orchestras

a large group of musicians playing together ⋗ *The Boston Symphony Orchestra.* ⋖

order

NOUN *plural* orders

1 an instruction to do something ⋗ *The soldier was given the order to shoot.* ⋖

2 an instruction to supply something ⋗ *The waiter came to take our order.* ⋖

3 the way things are arranged ⋗ *alphabetical order* ⋖

4 peaceful conditions and behaviour ⋗ *law and order* ⋖

5 an organized state when things are in their proper places ⋗ *It was time to bring some order into my life.* ⋖

VERB orders, ordering, ordered

1 to order someone to do something is to tell them to do it ⋗ *The doctor ordered her to rest for a few days.* ⋖

2 to order something is to ask for it to be supplied ⋗ *I ordered some magazines.* ⋖

ordinary

ADJECTIVE

normal and not very special ⋗ *an ordinary Monday morning* ⋖

orphan

NOUN *plural* orphans

a child whose parents are both dead

▶ **orphanage**

NOUN *plural* orphanages

a home for orphans

other

ADJECTIVE

1 the second of two ⋗ *Where is the other glove?* ⋖

a b c d e f g h i j k l m n o p q r s t u v w x y z

2 the rest ⇒ *Jack is here and the other children are at school.*

3 different or extra ⇒ *There must be some other reason.*

4 recently past ⇒ *I was thinking about you just the other day.*

PRONOUN

1 the second of two ⇒ *Here's one sock but where is the other?*

2 the rest ⇒ *Joe is here but where are the others?*

▸ **other than**

except ⇒ *There was no one there other than an old woman.*

ought

VERB

1 **ought** is used to show what you should do ⇒ *You ought to help them.* ⇒ *I ought to go home now.*

2 **ought** is also used to show what is likely to happen ⇒ *The weather ought to be fine.*

our

ADJECTIVE

belonging to us ⇒ *That is our car.*

ours

PRONOUN

a word you use to talk about something belonging to us ⇒ *That car is ours.* ⇒ *These books are ours.*

ourselves

PRONOUN

1 you use **ourselves** after a verb or preposition when **we** is the subject of the action and is also affected by it ⇒ *We saw ourselves in the mirror.*

2 **ourselves** is also used to show that you have done something without any help from other people ⇒ *We painted the room ourselves.*

3 you can use **ourselves** to show more clearly who you mean ⇒ *We ourselves played no part in this.*

out

ADVERB

1 into or towards the open air ⇒ *go out for a walk*

2 from inside something ⇒ *She opened her bag and took out an umbrella.*

3 away from a place, such as home or from the office ⇒ *I'm afraid he's out at the moment.*

4 loudly ⇒ *shout out the answer*

5 completely ⇒ *tired out*

▸ **out of date**

old or old-fashioned ⇒ *This telephone directory is out of date.*

outside

NOUN *plural* **outsides**

the outer surface of something ⇒ *The outside of the house was painted white.*

ADJECTIVE

1 of, on or near the outer part of anything ⇒ *the outside edge*

2 an outside chance is a slight chance ⇒ *an outside chance of winning*

ADVERB

on or to the outside, outdoors ⇒ *Let's eat outside.*

PREPOSITION

on the outer side of, not inside ⇒ *He was standing outside the gate.*

▸ **outsider**

NOUN *plural* **outsiders**

someone not included in a particular group ⇒ *The new boy felt like an outsider.*

oval

ADJECTIVE

shaped like an egg but flat ⇒ *an oval table*

NOUN *plural* **ovals**

an oval shape

> This word comes from the Latin word **ovalis**, which means *like an egg*.

oven

NOUN *plural* ovens

an enclosed space, usually part of a cooker, for cooking and heating food

over

PREPOSITION

1 higher than, above ⹂ *Hang that picture over the fireplace.* ⹁
2 more than ⹂ *He's over 90 years old.* ⹁
3 across ⹂ *We ran over the bridge.* ⹁
4 about ⹂ *They quarrelled over the children.* ⹁
5 by means of ⹂ *We often talk over the telephone.* ⹁

ADVERB

1 across ⹂ *He walked over to speak to them.* ⹁
2 downwards ⹂ *The baby's fallen over.* ⹁
3 above in number ⹂ *children aged seven and over* ⹁
4 left or remaining ⹂ *two cakes each, and two over* ⹁
5 through ⹂ *read the passage over* ⹁

ADJECTIVE

finished ⹂*The match is already over.* ⹁

overseas

ADJECTIVE and ADVERB

abroad ⹂ *overseas property for sale* ⹁ ⹂ *My father works overseas a lot.* ⹁

owe

VERB owes, owing, owed

1 to owe someone something is to be in debt to them ⹂ *I owe Val £10.* ⹁
2 to owe something to someone is to have them to thank for it ⹂ *He owes his success to his family.* ⹁

owl

NOUN *plural* owls

a bird that hunts at night and feeds on small birds and animals

own

VERB owns, owning, owned

you own something if it belongs to you ⹂ *I own a bicycle.* ⹁

▶ own up

to admit that you did something ⹂ *No one owned up to breaking the window.* ⹁

ADJECTIVE

belonging to the person mentioned ⹂ *all his own work* ⹁

PRONOUN

own is used for something belonging to another person ⹂*I lent him a pencil because he forgot to bring his own.* ⹁

▶ get your own back

to have revenge

▶ on your own

1 without help ⹂ *Did he do it all on his own?* ⹁
2 alone ⹂ *Don't leave me on my own.* ⹁

▶ owner

NOUN *plural* owners

a person who owns something

▶ ownership

NOUN

owning something

oxygen

NOUN

a gas that has no taste, colour or smell, and forms part of the air

pack

NOUN *plural* **packs**

1 things that are wrapped together or put in a bag so that you can carry them
2 a packet ⋗ *a pack of baby wipes* ⋖
3 a set of 52 playing cards
4 a group of certain animals ⋗ *a pack of wolves* ⋖

VERB **packs, packing, packed**

to pack or to pack a bag is to put your belongings into a bag or suitcase for a journey ⋗ *She packed hurriedly and caught the next train.* ⋖

packet

NOUN *plural* **packets**

a container made of paper or cardboard, or the container with its contents ⋗ *a packet of biscuits* ⋖

paddle

VERB **paddles, paddling, paddled**

you paddle when you walk about in shallow water

NOUN *plural* **paddles**

a short oar used to make a small boat or canoe move through water

page

NOUN *plural* **pages**

one side of a sheet of paper in a book, newspaper or magazine, or one of the sheets of paper that make up a book, newspaper or magazine ⋗ *page 135 in the history book* ⋖

paid

VERB

a way of changing the verb **pay** to make a past tense. It can be used with or without a helping verb ⋗ *I already paid for this.* ⋖ ⋗ *John has paid the bill.* ⋖

pain

NOUN *plural* **pains**

an unpleasant uncomfortable feeling in your body or mind, because you have been hurt ⋗ *He's broken his leg and is in great pain.* ⋖ ⋗ *the pain of leaving* ⋖

▸ **painless**
ADJECTIVE
causing no pain

▸ **painful**
ADJECTIVE
1 sore, or causing pain or distress ⋗ *Is your knee still painful?* ⋖
2 involving a lot of hard work or effort

paint

NOUN *plural* **paints**

a colouring substance to be put on surfaces in the form of liquid or paste

VERB **paints, painting, painted**
1 to put paint on walls and other parts of a building
2 to make a picture, or pictures, using paint

▸ **painter**
NOUN *plural* **painters**
1 a person whose job is to put paint on walls and other parts of buildings
2 an artist who makes pictures using paint

▸ **painting**
NOUN *plural* **paintings**
1 painting is the activity of painting walls or pictures
2 a painting is a picture made using paints

pair

NOUN   *plural* **pairs**

1 two things of the same kind used or kept together ⋛ *a pair of socks* ⋚   ⋛ *a pair of china dogs* ⋚
2 a single thing made up of two parts ⋛ *a pair of shears* ⋚

> The words **pair** and **pear** sound the same but remember that they have different spellings. A **pear** is a fruit.

palace

NOUN   *plural* **palaces**

a large and magnificent house, especially one for a king, queen or emperor

palm

NOUN   *plural* **palms**

1 the inner surface of your hand between your wrist and fingers
2 a tree with very large leaves which spread out from the top of the trunk

pancake

NOUN   *plural* **pancakes**

a thin cake made by frying a mixture of milk, flour and eggs in a pan

panda

NOUN   *plural* **pandas**

a large and rare black and white bear-like animal that lives in the mountains of China

pants

PLURAL NOUN

a piece of underwear that covers your bottom

paper

NOUN   *plural* **papers**

1 paper is a material made from wood pulp or rags and is used for writing, printing and wrapping things in ⋛ *a piece of paper* ⋚
2 a newspaper ⋛ *Have you read today's paper?* ⋚

3 a piece of paper with things written or printed on it ⋛ *an examination paper* ⋚

parent

NOUN   *plural* **parents**

your parents are your mother and father

▸ **parental**
ADJECTIVE
to do with a parent or parents

park

NOUN   *plural* **parks**

a piece of land in a town or city that has grass and trees, where people can go for fresh air

VERB   **parks, parking, parked**

to park a vehicle is to stop it somewhere, for example by the side of the road

parrot

NOUN   *plural* **parrots**

a bird with a strong curved beak, beady eyes and brightly-coloured or grey feathers. Parrots can be taught to imitate human speech and are often kept as pets

part

NOUN   *plural* **parts**

1 a division or piece of something ⋛ *The pizza is cut into six equal parts.* ⋚
2 a character in a play or film, or the words or actions that a character has to say or do in a play or film ⋛ *a part in the film* ⋚

party

NOUN   *plural* **parties**

1 a party is an event where people gather to celebrate something or to enjoy each other's company
2 a political party is an organized group of people who share the same political beliefs
3 a party of people is a group of people travelling or doing something together

pass

VERB passes, passing, passed

1 to move towards and then go beyond something ⊃ **The lorry passed us on a bend.** ⊰
2 to pass something to someone is to hand it to them ⊃ **Pass me the butter, please.** ⊰
3 to pass a test is to be successful in it

NOUN *plural* **passes**

1 a ticket or card that allows you to get into a place or to travel somewhere
2 in games like football and hockey, a pass is a kick, hit or throw that sends the ball from one player to another in the same team
3 a successful result in an exam

passenger

NOUN *plural* **passengers**

someone travelling in a car, bus, ship or plane who is not the driver or one of the crew

Passover

NOUN

a Jewish festival held in March or April celebrating the freeing of the Jews from slavery in Egypt

password

NOUN *plural* **passwords**

a secret word or phrase that you have to know before you are allowed into a place, or which you must type into a computer before you can see the information in it

past

NOUN

1 the past is the time before the present
2 someone's past is what they have done in their life before the present time

ADJECTIVE

over or ended ⊃ **in the past year** ⊰

PREPOSITION

1 up to and beyond ⊃ **She dashed past me, gasping as she ran.** ⊰
2 later than **It's past eight o'clock.** ⊰

pasta

NOUN

a food made from a special type of flour, water and eggs and formed into lots of different shapes

paste

NOUN *plural* **paste**

a type of glue for sticking paper together

VERB pastes. pasting, pasted

1 to paste something is to stick it with glue
2 **ICT** to paste a piece of information or a file on the computer is to put it somewhere, after you have copied or cut it from another place

path

NOUN *plural* **paths**

a track across a piece of land made or used by people or animals walking

patient

ADJECTIVE

a patient person is able to stay calm and self-controlled, especially when they have to wait a long time for something

NOUN *plural* **patients**

someone being seen or treated by a doctor, or being treated for a particular illness ⊃ **kidney patients** ⊰

▸ **patience**
NOUN

1 the ability or willingness to stay calm ⊃ **Mr Green lost patience with him.** ⊰
2 a card game played by one person

▸ **patiently**
ADVERB

in a patient way ⊃ **waiting patiently for a bus** ⊰

pattern

NOUN *plural* **patterns**

1 a guide used for making something ⊃ **a sewing pattern** ⊰

a b c d e f g h i j k l m n o p q r s t u v w x y z

2 a design that is repeated over and over again, for example on a piece of fabric

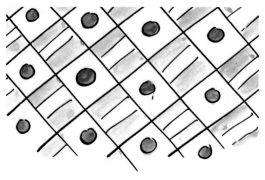

▸ **patterned**

ADJECTIVE

having a pattern

pause

VERB pauses, pausing, paused

to stop what you are doing for a short time

NOUN *plural* pauses

a short stop

pavement

NOUN *plural* pavements

a raised path beside a road, for people to walk on

paw

NOUN *plural* paws

an animal's foot

pay

VERB pays, paying, paid

1 to pay for something is to give money in exchange for it

2 to pay someone is to give them money for something or for doing something for you

NOUN

someone's pay is the amount of money they get for doing their job

▸ **payment**

NOUN *plural* payments

1 an amount of money paid for something

2 paying money or being paid

PE

ABBREVIATION

short for **physical education**, a school subject in which you learn sports, games and exercises and how to keep your body fit

pea

NOUN *plural* peas

a small, round, green vegetable that grows in pods on a climbing plant

peace

NOUN

there is peace when there is no war, or everything is quiet and calm ⋛ *The two countries have been at peace for years.* ⋛ ⋛ *I want a little peace to read my book.* ⋛

▸ **peaceful**

ADJECTIVE

a peaceful place is quiet and calm

▸ **peacefully**

ADVERB

quietly and calmly

> The words **peace** and **piece** sound the same but remember that they have different spellings. A **piece** is a bit of something.

peach

NOUN *plural* peaches

a soft round fruit with a velvety skin, pale orange flesh and a large stone inside

peacock

NOUN *plural* peacocks

a type of large bird. The male bird's tail has long blue and green feathers with round black markings at the ends

peanut

NOUN *plural* peanuts

a nut that grows underground in a shell

a b c d e f g h i j k l m n o **p** q r s t u v w x y z

pear
NOUN *plural* **pears**
a fruit which is round at the bottom and narrows towards the stem at the top

> The words **pear** and **pair** sound the same but remember that they have different spellings. A **pair** is a set of two things.

pebble
NOUN *plural* **pebbles**
a small smooth stone

pedal
NOUN *plural* **pedals**
a lever worked by the foot, such as on a bicycle or piano

peel
VERB **peels, peeling, peeled**
to peel a fruit or vegetable is to take off its skin or outer covering

NOUN
peel is the skin of certain fruits and vegetables

peg
NOUN *plural* **pegs**
1 a wooden, plastic or metal clip used for hanging clothes on a washing line
2 a hook for hanging coats, hats or jackets on

pen¹
NOUN *plural* **pens**
an instrument for writing or drawing in ink

pen²
NOUN *plural* **pens**
a female swan

pence
NOUN
the plural of **penny**

pencil
NOUN *plural* **pencils**
something you use for writing or drawing, which has a stick of graphite or a coloured stick through the middle of it

penguin
NOUN *plural* **penguins**
a bird that cannot fly but which uses its wings like flippers to swim underwater. Penguins are found in the Antarctic

penny
NOUN *plural* **pennies**
a small bronze British coin worth one hundredth of £1

people
NOUN *plural* **peoples**
1 people are men, women and children
2 the plural of **person** ⋗ *one person or many people* ⋖

pepper
NOUN *plural* **peppers**
1 pepper is a hot-tasting powder made by grinding dried seeds called peppercorns
2 a pepper is a red, yellow, orange or green hollow fruit used as a vegetable

perfect
ADJECTIVE said "per-**fikt**"
1 without any mistakes or faults ⋗ *a perfect score* ⋖
2 exact ⋗ *a perfect circle* ⋖
3 complete ⋗ *a perfect stranger* ⋖

▸ **perfection**
NOUN
making perfect or being perfect

▸ **perfectly**
ADVERB
1 without any mistakes or faults ⋗ *She did the pirouette perfectly.* ⋖

2 exactly ⇒ *perfectly square*

3 completely ⇒ *perfectly ridiculous*

perhaps
ADVERB

possibly or maybe ⇒ *The bus is late – perhaps it has broken down again.*

person
NOUN   *plural* people *or* persons

a human being

personal
ADJECTIVE

1 belonging to, or done by, one particular person and no one else ⇒ *a personal opinion*   ⇒ *a personal appearance*

2 private ⇒ *It's a personal matter.*

▸ **personality**
NOUN   *plural* personalities

1 your personality is your character and the qualities you have

2 someone with personality behaves in a way that makes a strong impression on you

3 a personality is a famous person

pet
NOUN   *plural* pets

1 a tame animal that you keep in your home ⇒ *Do you have any pets?*

2 a person who is given special attention and seems to be the favourite ⇒ *teacher's pet*

petal
NOUN   *plural* petals

one of the coloured parts of a flower

petrol
NOUN

a fuel for engines, made from oil

phone
NOUN   *plural* phones

a telephone

VERB   phones, phoning, phoned

to phone someone is to call them on the telephone

photo
NOUN   *plural* photos

a photograph

photograph
NOUN   *plural* photographs

a picture taken by a camera

VERB   photographs, photographing, photographed

to photograph something is to take a picture of it using a camera

▸ **photographer**
NOUN   *plural* photographers

someone who takes photographs

▸ **photography**
NOUN

the art of taking photographs

> **Photograph** comes from the Greek words **photo**, which means *light*, and **graphein**, which means *to draw*, so together they mean 'to draw with light'. Another word in English where you can work out that **photo** means *light* is **photosynthesis**.

piano
NOUN   *plural* pianos

a stringed instrument that you sit at and play by pressing the black and white keys on a long keyboard

pick
VERB   picks, picking, picked

1 to pick a person or thing is to choose them

2 to pick something, or pick it off, is to lift it off, using your finger and thumb

3 to pick fruit or flowers is to break or pull them off the plant they are growing on

a
b
c
d
e
f
g
h
i
j
k
l
m
n
o
p
q
r
s
t
u
v
w
x
y
z

NOUN *plural* **picks**

if you have, or take, your pick of things, you choose whichever you like

picnic

NOUN *plural* **picnics**

a meal that you have outdoors at a place that you walk or travel to

VERB **picnics, picnicking, picnicked**

to have a picnic

▸ **picnicker**

NOUN *plural* **picnickers**

a person who is having a picnic

picture

NOUN *plural* **pictures**

a painting, drawing or photograph

VERB **pictures, picturing, pictured**

to picture something is to form an image of it in your mind

ADJECTIVE

with a picture or pictures ⋧ *a picture book* ⋦

pie

NOUN *plural* **pies**

food baked in a covering of pastry

piece

NOUN *plural* **pieces**

1 a part or bit of something ⋧ *a jigsaw with 300 pieces* ⋦   ⋧ *a piece of cake* ⋦
2 something that has been written or composed ⋧ *There's a piece in the paper about our school.* ⋦   ⋧ *a piece of music* ⋦
3 one of the objects you move about the board in games like chess
4 a coin of a particular value ⋧ *a 50p piece* ⋦

The words **piece** and **peace** sound the same but remember that they have different spellings. **Peace** is quietness and calmness.

pig

NOUN *plural* **pigs**

an animal with a broad heavy body, small eyes and a snout

pigeon

NOUN *plural* **pigeons**

a bird with a plump body and a small head, often seen in cities or kept for racing

pill

NOUN *plural* **pills**

a small tablet of medicine

pillow

NOUN *plural* **pillows**

a large soft cushion that you lay your head on when you are in bed

pilot

NOUN *plural* **pilots**

someone who flies a plane, or who guides a ship into and out of a harbour

pin

NOUN *plural* **pins**

a short thin pointed piece of metal for pushing through fabric or paper to hold it in place

VERB **pins, pinning, pinned**

to pin something is to fasten it with a pin

pinafore

NOUN *plural* **pinafores**

a sleeveless dress, worn over a blouse or jumper

pine

NOUN *plural* **pines**

a tall evergreen tree with cones containing seeds and with leaves like needles

pineapple

NOUN *plural* **pineapples**

a large fruit with sweet firm yellow flesh and a tough brown skin

pink

NOUN
a pale red colour with a lot of white in it

ADJECTIVE pinker, pinkest
of the colour pink

pipe

NOUN *plural* pipes
1 a metal or plastic tube through which water or gas can flow
2 a tube with a hollow bowl at one end used for smoking tobacco

pirate

NOUN *plural* pirates
someone who robs ships and boats at sea

pitch

NOUN *plural* pitches
1 an area of ground, often with special lines marked on it, used to play games like football, rugby or cricket
2 a sound's pitch is how high or low it is

VERB pitches, pitching, pitched
to pitch a tent is to put it up

pity

NOUN
1 pity is sorrow you feel for other people's troubles or difficulties
2 you say that something is a pity if you are sorry about it

pizza

NOUN *plural* pizzas
a flat round piece of dough topped with cheese and tomatoes and baked in an oven

place

NOUN *plural* places
1 a particular area or position ⋛ *a place by the sea* ⋜ ⋛ *Put the books back in their proper place on the shelf.* ⋜
2 a seat, or a space at a table for someone to sit and eat ⋛ *Please go back to your places and sit down.* ⋜

3 a position in a series or queue ⋛ *She was in first place after the second round.* ⋜

VERB places, placing, placed
to place something somewhere is to put it there

plan

VERB plans, planning, planned
1 to plan something is to work out how it may be done or make the arrangements to do it
2 to plan something, such as a building, is to design it

NOUN *plural* plans
1 an idea of how to do something
2 a drawing showing the inside of a building as if you are looking at it from above

plane

NOUN *plural* planes
an aeroplane

planet

NOUN *plural* planets
any of the large objects in space that orbit round a sun. The planets that orbit round our sun are Mercury, Venus, Earth, Mars, Jupiter, Saturn, Uranus and Neptune

plant

NOUN *plural* plants
1 any living thing that grows from the ground and has a stem, roots and leaves
2 a factory or industrial building

VERB plants, planting, planted
to plant seeds or plants is to put them in the ground so that they grow

plaster

NOUN *plural* plasters
1 plaster is a thin paste put on walls that dries to form a hard smooth surface

a b c d e f g h i j k l m n o **p** q r s t u v w x y z

2 a plaster is a sticky dressing that you put over a wound to protect it from germs

VERB plasters, plastering, plastered

1 to apply plaster to walls

2 to plaster a surface is to cover it with thick liquid ⋗ *paper plastered with paint* ⋞

▸**plasterer**

NOUN plural plasterers

someone whose job is to plaster walls

plastic

NOUN plural plastics

a substance which can be shaped and stretched to make objects

ADJECTIVE

made of plastic ⋗ *plastic bags* ⋞

plate

NOUN plural plates

a shallow dish for holding food

play

VERB plays, playing, played

1 to play is to spend time amusing yourself with games or toys ⋗ *Are you coming out to play?* ⋞

2 you play a team game when you take part in it ⋗ *He plays cricket on Saturdays.* ⋞

3 to play a musical instrument is to make music with it

4 to play a DVD, CD or tape is to put it into the player and listen to it or watch it

NOUN plural plays

1 play is having fun with games and toys, or the action that goes on in a team game ⋗ *learning through play* ⋞

2 a play is a story acted out in the theatre or on TV or radio

▸**playful**

ADJECTIVE

full of fun or wanting to play

▸**playfully**

ADVERB

in a playful way

▸**player**

NOUN plural players

1 someone who plays a game

2 a machine for playing DVDs, CDs, tapes or records

playground

NOUN plural playgrounds

an area, for example beside a school or in a public park, where children can play

please

VERB pleases, pleasing, pleased

to please someone is to do what they want or to give them pleasure or satisfaction

ADVERB AND INTERJECTION

a polite word you use when you are asking for something or accepting an offer ⋗ *Please don't park in front of the drive.* ⋞ ⋗ *'Would you like another biscuit?' 'Yes, please'.* ⋞

plenty

NOUN

1 as much as you need ⋗ *You have plenty of time to complete the test.* ⋞

2 a large amount or number ⋗ *There's plenty more bread in the freezer if we run out.* ⋞

plug

NOUN plural plugs

1 an object attached to a piece of electrical equipment by a wire and which you fit into a socket in the wall to get electricity for it

2 an object that you use for blocking a hole, especially in a bath or sink to stop the water from running away

plum

NOUN plural plums

a soft red or yellow fruit with a smooth skin and a stone in the centre

plus

PREPOSITION

1 maths adding ⋗ *8 plus 2 is 10* ⋞

2 as well as ⋗ *There are six children, plus two adults.* ⋞

ADJECTIVE
more than zero ⫽ *plus ten degrees* ⫽

NOUN   *plural* **pluses**
maths a plus, or plus sign (+), is a symbol showing that a number is to be added to another

pocket

NOUN   *plural* **pockets**
an extra piece of cloth sewn into a piece of clothing and used for keeping small items in, like money or keys

VERB   **pockets, pocketing, pocketed**
to pocket something is to put it in your pocket, or to take it and keep it for yourself, especially dishonestly

poem

NOUN   *plural* **poems**
a piece of writing in imaginative language arranged in patterns of lines and sounds, often, but not always, rhyming

▸ **poet**
NOUN   *plural* **poets**
someone who writes poetry

▸ **poetry**
NOUN
poems as a group

point

NOUN   *plural* **points**
1 a sharp end ⫽ *the point of a needle* ⫽
2 **maths** a small dot (·) used in some numbers
3 a particular place or a particular moment ⫽ *the highest point on the British mainland* ⫽ ⫽ *At that point, we all burst out laughing.* ⫽
4 a mark used to score a competition, game or test ⫽ *Who got the highest number of points?* ⫽

VERB   **points, pointing, pointed**
to point is to stretch your finger in the direction of something to show other people what or where you mean

poison

NOUN   *plural* **poisons**
something that causes death or illness when taken into your body

VERB   **poisons, poisoning, poisoned**
1 to poison someone is to kill or harm them with poison
2 to poison something is to add poison to it

▸ **poisonous**
ADJECTIVE
1 something poisonous causes illness or death when taken into your body ⫽ *This cleaning liquid is poisonous.* ⫽
2 producing poison ⫽ *a poisonous snake* ⫽

polar bear

NOUN   *plural* **polar bears**
a large white bear that lives in the Arctic

pole[1]

NOUN   *plural* **poles**
a long thin rounded piece of wood or metal

pole[2]

NOUN   *plural* **poles**
geography the north and south pole are the two points at the very top and bottom of the Earth

police

NOUN
the police are the people whose job is to prevent crime and see that laws are kept

▸ **policeman** *or* **policewoman**
NOUN   *plural* **policemen** *or* **policewomen**
a member of the police

polite

ADJECTIVE   **politer, politest**
a polite person has good manners

▸ **politely**
ADVERB
in a well-mannered way ⫽ *'Would you like a seat?' he asked her politely.* ⫽

▸**politeness**
NOUN
being well-mannered

pond
NOUN *plural* **ponds**
a small area of water

pony
NOUN *plural* **ponies**
a type of small horse

pool
NOUN *plural* **pools**
1 a small area of still water
2 a swimming pool

poor
ADJECTIVE poorer, poorest
1 a poor person has very little money
2 of a low standard ⋛ *a poor imitation* ⋚

▸**poorly**
ADVERB
1 badly ⋛ *a poorly lit passage* ⋚
2 ill ⋛ *Gran's feeling a bit poorly.* ⋚

pop[1]
NOUN *plural* **pops**
1 a sudden sound like a small explosion
2 fizzy drink

pop[2]
NOUN
modern music that is popular at the current time

popcorn
NOUN
seeds that burst open into crisp fluffy balls when they are heated

pope
NOUN *plural* **popes**
the head of the Catholic Church

poppy
NOUN *plural* **poppies**
a tall flower that grows wild in fields and has broad, flat, red petals

popular
ADJECTIVE
something that is popular is liked by a lot of people

pore
NOUN *plural* **pores**
one of the tiny openings in your skin that sweat comes out of

position
NOUN *plural* **positions**
1 a place or situation ⋛ *Tom could see the whole garden from his position in the tree.* ⋚ ⋛ *a very difficult position* ⋚
2 a way of standing, sitting or lying ⋛ *sleeping in an awkward position* ⋚
3 a job ⋛ *Uncle Frank has applied for a position as a security guard.* ⋚

possible
ADJECTIVE
1 something that is possible can happen, or may happen ⋛ *It isn't possible for human beings to travel to the planets yet.* ⋚
2 something that is possible may be true ⋛ *It's possible I made a mistake.* ⋚

▸**possibly**
ADVERB
perhaps ⋛ *Possibly I was wrong.* ⋚

▸**possibility**
NOUN *plural* **possibilities**
something that is possible

post[1]
NOUN *plural* **posts**
a long piece of wood or metal fixed upright in the ground

post²
NOUN

the service that collects and delivers letters and parcels, or the letters and parcels sent or delivered by this service

VERB   posts, posting, posted
to send a letter or parcel in this way

post³
NOUN   *plural* posts

a job ⇒ *He was dismissed from his post.*

postcard
NOUN   *plural* postcards

a card for writing messages on that you can send through the post without an envelope

poster
NOUN   *plural* posters

a large notice in a public place advertising something or giving information

pot
NOUN   *plural* pots

a deep container, often with a lid, used for cooking, holding liquids, storing things like jam, or for growing plants in

potato
NOUN   *plural* potatoes

a round white or yellowish vegetable that grows underground

potty
NOUN   *plural* potties

a container that a small child uses as a toilet

pound
NOUN   *plural* pounds

1 the main unit of money in Britain, made up of 100 pence and usually written £
2 a unit for measuring weight, equal to 0.454 kilograms

pour
VERB   pours, pouring, poured

1 to pour a liquid is to make it flow out of a container in a stream
2 to pour is to flow out in large quantities
3 if it is pouring, it is raining heavily

power
NOUN   *plural* powers

1 power is strength or force
2 to have power is to have the ability or authority to control people or things ⇒ *political power*
3 to have the power to do something is to have the ability to do it ⇒ *He's lost the power of speech.*
4 power is any form of energy used to drive machines ⇒ *wind power*

▸ **powerless**
ADJECTIVE
unable to control or affect things

▸ **powerful**
ADJECTIVE
strong or having the ability to control other people

practice
NOUN   *plural* practices

practice is doing something often so that you get better at it ⇒ *He'll soon get the hang of the violin with a bit more practice.*

> Remember that **practice** with a **c** is a noun: *I need some* practice. **Practise** with an **s** is a verb: *You must* practise *often.*

practise
VERB   practises, practising, practised

1 to practise something is to do it again and again so that you get better at it
2 to practise something is to make it a habit or to do it ⇒ *He practises yoga.*

pram

NOUN *plural* **prams**

a small wheeled vehicle that a baby sits or lies in and which is pushed about by someone walking

pray

VERB **prays, praying, prayed**

to speak to God

▸ **prayer**

NOUN *plural* **prayers**

1 the words that you use when you pray
2 prayer is praying ⋗ *They knelt in prayer.* ⋖

> The words **pray** and **prey** sound the same, but remember that they have different spellings. **Prey** is the creatures an animal hunts.

prepare

VERB **prepares, preparing, prepared**

1 to prepare is to get ready to deal with something or do it ⋗ *The children are preparing for their end-of-term test.* ⋖
2 to prepare someone or something for something is to get them ready to do it ⋗ *The coach's job is to prepare the team.* ⋖

preposition

WORD CLASS *plural* **prepositions**

a word put before a noun or pronoun to show how it is connected to another word. For example, in the sentence *I put my books in my bag*, the word *in* is a preposition

present¹

NOUN said "**prez**-int" *plural* **presents**

something given as a gift

VERB said "pri-**zent**" **presents, presenting, presented**

1 to present someone with something is to give it to them, usually as an award for good work or high achievement

2 someone presents a radio or TV show when they introduce it

present² said "**prez**-int"

NOUN

the present is the time now

ADJECTIVE

someone is present somewhere when they are there

press

VERB **presses, pressing, pressed**

to press something is to push it or squeeze it

NOUN *plural* **presses**

newspapers and journalists are the press

pretend

VERB **pretends, pretending, pretended**

1 to make believe that something is true as part of play ⋗ *Let's pretend we're submarine captains.* ⋖
2 to try to make people believe something that is not true ⋗ *He pretended to cry.* ⋖

pretty

ADJECTIVE **prettier, prettiest**

attractive to look at ⋗ *pretty flowers* ⋖ ⋗ *a pretty little girl* ⋖

ADVERB

quite ⋗ *a pretty good mark* ⋖

▸ **prettiness**

NOUN

being attractive to look at

price

NOUN *plural* **prices**

the price of something is the amount of money it costs ⋗ *What price are your apples today?* ⋖

priest

NOUN *plural* **priests**

1 a person who is qualified to conduct services in one of the Christian churches

2 a person with official duties of various kinds in other religions

▸ **priestess**
NOUN   *plural* priestesses
a female priest in certain ancient or non-Christian religions

primary
ADJECTIVE
first or most important ⋛ *the primary route into the city* ⋚

primary school
NOUN   *plural* primary schools
a school for children between the ages of 4 and 12

prime minister
NOUN   *plural* prime ministers
the leader of the government in Britain, and many other countries of the world

prince
NOUN   *plural* princes
the son or grandson of a king or queen

princess
NOUN   *plural* princesses
the daughter or granddaughter of a king or queen, or the wife of a prince

print
VERB   prints, printing, printed
1 to print something from a computer is to make a copy of it using a computer printer ⋛ *Print five copies of the letter.* ⋚
2 you print when you write words with each letter separate from the one next to it, not joined up ⋛ *Print your name.* ⋚

NOUN   *plural* prints
1 print is the words in a book or newspaper
2 a print is a mark, picture or design made by something pressing down on a surface

▸ **printer**
NOUN   *plural* printers
a machine that prints words and pictures

prize
NOUN   *plural* prizes
something won in a competition or given as a reward for good work

problem
NOUN   *plural* problems
1 a situation, matter or person that causes difficulties, or is difficult to deal with ⋛ *There's a problem with the car.* ⋚
2 a puzzle or question that has to be solved ⋛ *the problem of calculating how much water the tank would hold* ⋚

produce
VERB   said "pro-**dyoos**"   produces, producing, produced
to produce something is to make, grow or create it ⋛ *factories producing goods for export* ⋚   ⋛ *Will the tree produce fruit this year?* ⋚   ⋛ *The sun produces both light and heat.* ⋚

NOUN   said "**prod**-yoos"
produce is things grown or produced on farms

program
NOUN   *plural* programs
ICT a set of instructions that tells a computer to do a certain task

programme
NOUN   *plural* programmes
1 a show on TV or radio
2 a leaflet or thin book that gives information and details about an event

project
NOUN   said "**pro**-jekt"   *plural* projects
a piece of work done by a pupil or student, often involving study and research

promise
VERB   promises, promising, promised
1 you promise when you say that you will, or

a b c d e f g h i j k l m n o **p** q r s t u v w x y z

will not, do something ⟩ *I promise to be good.*

2 you promise something to someone when you say that you will give them something or help them in some way ⟩ *Sorry, I promised this seat to Vishal.*

NOUN *plural* **promises**

1 something promised ⟩ *Make me a promise that you won't be late.*

2 if someone or something shows promise, they show signs of future success

▸ **promising**

ADJECTIVE

seeming likely to be good or nice in the future ⟩ *a promising student*

pronoun

WORD CLASS *plural* **pronouns**

a word that can be used in place of a noun. For example, in the sentence *Gary ate the pizza*, *Gary* and *the pizza* could be changed to pronouns and the sentence would be *He ate it*

proper

ADJECTIVE

1 right or correct ⟩ *Is this the proper way to put up a tent?*

2 complete or thorough ⟩ *Shona gave her room a proper clean.*

3 right according to rules about what is sensible or polite ⟩ *It's only proper that you should thank the teacher.*

▸ **properly**

ADVERB

correctly ⟩ *Sit up properly in your chair.*

protect

VERB protects, protecting, protected

to protect someone or something is to guard them from harm and keep them safe ⟩ *Protect the plants from frost.*

▸ **protection**

NOUN

1 the act of protecting

2 safety or shelter ⟩ *The boats were heading for the protection of the harbour.*

proud

ADJECTIVE prouder, proudest

1 feeling pleased because you have done something well

2 behaving in a way that shows you think you are more important than other people

▸ **proudly**

ADVERB

in a proud way

public

NOUN

1 the public are people generally

2 to do something in public is to do it where anyone can see it or can take part

ADJECTIVE

1 to do with all the people of a country or community ⟩ *public opinion*

2 for anyone to use ⟩ *a public park*

publicity

NOUN

advertising or anything done to make the public aware of something

pudding

NOUN *plural* **puddings**

a sweet dish that you eat at the end of dinner

puddle

NOUN *plural* **puddles**

water filling a shallow hole in the ground

pull

VERB pulls, pulling, pulled

1 to pull something is to take hold of it and bring it towards you

2 if you pull a muscle, you stretch it or strain it so that it is painful

NOUN *plural* **pulls**

a pulling movement

pulse

NOUN *plural* **pulses**

your pulse is the regular beat that you feel on your wrist or neck caused by the heart pumping blood through your arteries

punish

VERB **punishes, punishing, punished**

to punish someone is to make them suffer for something they have done wrong

▸ **punishment**

NOUN *plural* **punishments**

1 punishing someone, or being punished
2 a particular method of making someone suffer for something they have done wrong

pupil

NOUN *plural* **pupils**

1 a child or adult who is being taught
2 the pupil of your eye is the round opening in the middle of your eye through which light passes

puppet

NOUN *plural* **puppets**

a doll that can be moved by wires or strings, or fitted over your hand and moved by your fingers

▸ **puppeteer**

NOUN *plural* **puppeteers**

someone who operates puppets

puppy

NOUN *plural* **puppies**

a baby dog

purple

NOUN

a dark reddish-blue colour

ADJECTIVE

of the colour purple

purpose

NOUN *plural* **purposes**

1 you have a purpose when you are intending to do or achieve a particular thing
2 something's purpose is the job or role it is intended for

▸ **on purpose**

if you do something on purpose you mean to do it and it is not an accident

▸ **purposely**

ADVERB

on purpose

purse

NOUN *plural* **purses**

a small container for money, for carrying in a handbag or pocket

push

VERB **pushes, pushing, pushed**

to push something is to press against it with your hands or body so that it moves

NOUN *plural* **pushes**

a pushing movement

put

VERB **puts, putting, put**

to put something somewhere is to move it or place it there ⋛ *Put the shopping over there.* ⋚

pyjamas

PLURAL NOUN

a suit with a top and matching trousers that you wear in bed

Pyjamas comes from the Persian and Hindi word **payjamah**, which means 'clothing for the leg', because pyjamas have trousers.

a b c d e f g h i j k l m n o **p** q r s t u v w x y z

quack

NOUN *plural* quacks

the sound made by a duck

VERB quacks, quacking, quacked

a duck quacks when it makes this sound

quarrel

VERB quarrels, quarrelling, quarrelled

to quarrel with someone is to argue angrily with them ⟫ *I've quarrelled with my brother.* ⟫ *We often hear them quarrelling next door.*

NOUN *plural* quarrels

an angry argument ⟫*I've had a quarrel with my brother.*

▸ **quarrelsome**

ADJECTIVE

quarrelling a lot ⟫ *quarrelsome children*

quarter

NOUN *plural* quarters

1 a quarter is one of four equal parts that together make up the whole of something ⟫ *We cut the cake into quarters.*
2 **maths** the fraction ¼, equivalent to the decimal fraction 0.25, and equal to one divided by four
3 one fourth of a year, three months

VERB quarters, quartering, quartered

to quarter something is to divide it into four equal parts

queen

NOUN *plural* queens

1 a woman who rules a country ⟫ *Queen Elizabeth II*
2 the wife of a king ⟫ *the king and his queen*
3 a female bee, ant or wasp that lays eggs

question

NOUN *plural* questions

1 what you ask when you want to know something ⟫ *After the talk, some people asked questions.*
2 one of the things you have to answer or write about in an exam ⟫ *I didn't have time to answer all the questions*
3 a subject for discussion ⟫ *There is the question of how much to pay him.*
4 a suggestion or possibility ⟫ *There's no question of him leaving.*

queue

NOUN *plural* queues

a line of people waiting for something ⟫ *There was a long queue outside the cinema.*

VERB queues, queueing, queued

to stand in a line waiting for something ⟫*We had to queue for three hours to get the tickets.*

quick

ADJECTIVE quicker, quickest

1 fast ⟫ *a quick walker*

2 done in a short time ⇒ *a quick trip into town*

3 doing something without delay ⇒ *She's always quick to help.*

▸ **quickly**

ADVERB

if someone does something quickly, they do it rapidly or at great speed ⇒ *Come quickly! Someone's fallen in the river!*

▸ **quickness**

NOUN

being quick

quiet

ADJECTIVE   quieter, quietest

1 not loud ⇒ *a quiet voice*

2 calm and peaceful ⇒ *a quiet life*

NOUN

a quiet state or time ⇒ *in the quiet of the night*

▸ **quieten**

VERB   quietens, quietening, quietened

1 to quieten something or someone is to make them quiet ⇒ *Her mother was trying to quieten her.*

2 to quieten, or quieten down, is to become quiet ⇒ *Things seem to have quietened down.*

▸ **quietly**

ADVERB

with little or no sound ⇒ *She slipped quietly from the room.*

▸ **quietness**

NOUN

being quiet ⇒ *the quietness of early morning*

quite

ADVERB

1 rather ⇒ *I'm quite hungry but I don't mind waiting.*

2 completely ⇒ *I'm afraid I'm not quite ready.*

quiver

VERB   quivers, quivering, quivered

to tremble or shake ⇒ *Her lip quivered and her eyes filled with tears.*

quiz

NOUN   *plural* quizzes

a competition in which you have to answer questions on different subjects ⇒ *a TV quiz show*

VERB   quizzes, quizzing, quizzed

to quiz someone is to ask them lots of questions

Qur'an said "koo-**ran**"

NOUN

the Qur'an is the Koran, the holy book of the Islamic religion

a b c d e f g h i j k l m n o p **q** r s t u v w x y z

R

rabbi
NOUN *plural* **rabbis**
a Jewish religious minister

rabbit
NOUN *plural* **rabbits**
a long-eared furry animal that lives in holes in the ground that are called burrows

race¹
NOUN *plural* **races**
a competition to be first at something ⋛ *a two-mile horse race* ⋚

VERB **races, racing, raced**
1 to try to do something first, before anyone else ⋛ *I'll race you to the postbox.* ⋚
2 to go very fast ⋛ *The car raced along.* ⋚

race²
NOUN *plural* **races**
a large group of people who have the same ancestors and look the same in some ways, for example in the colour of their skin

racket¹
NOUN *plural* **rackets**
an oval frame with strings stretched across it that you use for hitting the ball in some games

racket²
NOUN *plural* **rackets**
a loud and disturbing noise ⋛ *Will you turn that racket down?* ⋚

radio
NOUN *plural* **radios**
1 a system of broadcasting that uses sound waves instead of wires to send messages
2 an electrical device that receives or sends messages as sound waves

rag
NOUN *plural* **rags**
an old piece of cloth ⋛ *a painting of a young girl dressed in rags* ⋚ ⋛ *Polish the wood with a soft rag.* ⋚

railway
NOUN *plural* **railways**
a track for trains to travel on ⋛ *a house by the railway* ⋚ ⋛ *a short railway journey* ⋚

rain
NOUN
drops of water falling from the clouds ⋛ *a heavy shower of rain* ⋚

VERB **rains, raining, rained**
it is raining when drops of water fall from the clouds

rainbow
NOUN *plural* **rainbows**
an arch of different colours that you can see in the sky when it is raining and the sun is shining at the same time

raise

VERB raises, raising, raised

1 to raise something is to lift it up ⋛ *Raise your hand if you know the answer.* ⋜
2 to raise an amount or number is to increase it ⋛ *They've raised prices again.* ⋜
3 to raise a subject is to mention it in a discussion ⋛ *I want to raise a matter that we all care very much about.* ⋜
4 to raise money is to get money together for a certain reason ⋛ *We're raising money for the school.* ⋜

raisin

NOUN *plural* **raisins**

a dried grape

Ramadan

NOUN

the ninth month of the Islamic calendar, when Muslims fast during the day

ran

VERB

a way of changing the verb **run** to make a past tense ⋛ *I ran all the way here.* ⋜

rang

VERB

a way of changing the verb **ring** to make a past tense ⋛ *Jane rang the doorbell.* ⋜

rash¹

ADJECTIVE rasher, rashest

a rash person does foolish things quickly without thinking first

rash²

NOUN *plural* **rashes**

an area of redness or red spots on your skin, caused by an illness or allergy

raspberry

NOUN *plural* **raspberries**

a red berry that you can eat and that grows on bushes

rat

NOUN *plural* **rats**

a small furry animal like a large mouse with a long tail

rather

ADVERB

1 a bit or somewhat ⋛ *It's rather cold in here, isn't it?* ⋜
2 you would rather do something if you would prefer to do it ⋛ *I'd rather talk about this later if you don't mind.* ⋜

reach

VERB reaches, reaching, reached

1 to reach a place is to arrive there ⋛ *We didn't reach the cottage till late.* ⋜
2 to be able to reach something is to be able to touch or get hold of it ⋛ *I can't reach the top shelf.* ⋜

read

VERB reads, reading, read

1 to look at something, such as writing, and understand it ⋛ *Read a book.* ⋜ ⋛ *I'd like to learn to read music.* ⋜
2 to say aloud what is written or printed ⋛ *Read me a story please, Mummy.* ⋜

▸ **reader**

NOUN *plural* **readers**

a person who reads, especially a particular book or newspaper ⋛ *Beano readers* ⋜

ready

ADJECTIVE

1 prepared for something ⋛ *Are the children ready for bed?* ⋜ ⋛ *Dinner's ready.* ⋜
2 willing ⋛ *Are you sure you're ready to give up chocolate for a whole week?* ⋜

a b c d e f g h i j k l m n o p q **r** s t u v w x y z

real

ADJECTIVE

1 actually existing, not invented or pretend ⋛ *real people with real problems* ⋚
2 genuine, not a copy ⋛ *The seats are made of real leather.* ⋚

▸ **realistic**

ADJECTIVE

1 very like real life
2 dealing with the real situation in a sensible way ⋛ *a realistic outlook on life* ⋚

realize *or* realise

VERB realizes, realizing, realized

to realize something is to know and understand it ⋛ *I realized I was lost.* ⋚

really

ADVERB

1 actually, in fact ⋛ *We're in the same class but we're not really friends.* ⋚
2 very ⋛ *a really lovely day* ⋚

reason

NOUN *plural* **reasons**

the reason for something is why it happened or exists ⋛ *The reason I'm worried is that I forgot to do my homework.* ⋚

▸ **reasonable**

ADJECTIVE

1 sensible and not foolish ⋛ *Please try to be reasonable.* ⋚
2 quite good, big, etc ⋛ *He has a reasonable chance of success.* ⋚

receive

VERB receives, receiving, received

to get something that someone gives or sends to you ⋛ *Did you receive my last letter?* ⋚

recipe

NOUN *plural* **recipes**

a set of instructions on how to cook a particular dish and a list of its ingredients ⋛ *a recipe for cookies* ⋚

recognize *or* recognise

VERB recognizes, recognizing, recognized

1 to recognize someone or something is to know who or what you are seeing or hearing because you have seen or heard them before ⋛ *I recognized you from your photo.* ⋚
2 to accept that something is true ⋛ *The teacher recognized that I was not to blame.* ⋚

record

VERB said "ri-**kod**" or "ri-**kord**" records, recording, recorded

1 to record something, such as music or a television programme, is to copy it on to a tape or disc so that it can be played again later ⋛ *The band recorded their first album in 1982.* ⋚
2 to record a piece of information is to write it down

NOUN said "**rek**-od" or "**rek**-ord" *plural* **records**

1 a piece of information that has been written down and stored ⋛ *We have a record of all the names of the past members.* ⋚
2 a round flat piece of plastic that music was stored on in the past ⋛ *a pile of old jazz records* ⋚
3 the highest, lowest, best or worst level or performance ⋛ *Denise is determined to beat her own record on this jump.* ⋚

▸ **recorder**

NOUN *plural* **recorders**

1 a machine that copies sounds or pictures, such as a tape recorder or video recorder
2 a wind instrument with holes that you cover with your fingers as you blow

▸ **recording**

NOUN *plural* **recordings**

a tape or video of sounds or pictures

rectangle

NOUN *plural* **rectangles**

a four-sided shape with opposite sides that are of equal length and four right angles

▸ **rectangular**

ADJECTIVE

with two pairs of straight sides and four right angles ⋛ *a rectangular table* ⋜

recycle

VERB **recycles, recycling, recycled**

to save something so that it can be used again ⋛ *We recycle our newspapers.* ⋜

▸ **recycling**

NOUN

saving things so that they can be used again

red

NOUN

1 the colour of blood, or any similar shade
2 an orangey-brown hair colour

ADJECTIVE **redder, reddest**

of the colour red

referee

NOUN *plural* **referees**

in some sports, the person who makes sure the players obey the rules

reflection

NOUN *plural* **reflections**

an image you can see in a surface like a mirror

refuse¹ said "ri-**fyooz**"

VERB **refuses, refusing, refused**

1 to decide not to take something that you are offered ⋛ *Gerry refused a cup of tea.* ⋜
2 to decide not to do something that you are asked to do ⋛ *I simply refuse to go shopping with you again.* ⋜

▸ **refusal**

NOUN *plural* **refusals**

1 a decision not to accept something ⋛ *three*

refusals and twenty acceptances for our party invitations ⋜
2 a decision not to do something ⋛ *a refusal to shake hands* ⋜

refuse² said "**ref**-yoos"

NOUN

rubbish that people throw away

rehearse

VERB **rehearses, rehearsing, rehearsed**

to practise performing something ⋛ *Can we rehearse that last bit again?* ⋜

▸ **rehearsal**

NOUN *plural* **rehearsals**

a rehearsal is a practice of a performance ⋛ *the dress rehearsal* ⋜

reindeer

NOUN *plural* **reindeer**

a large deer with large horns

relation

NOUN *plural* **relations**

1 a relation between things is some kind of connection
2 a relation is someone in your family

▸ **relationship**

NOUN *plural* **relationships**

the way people feel about each other

relative

NOUN *plural* **relatives**

a member of your family

relax

VERB **relaxes, relaxing, relaxed**

1 to become less worried or stressed ⋛ *A short holiday will help you relax.* ⋜
2 to rest completely ⋛ *The family spent the afternoon relaxing in the garden.* ⋜

religion

NOUN *plural* **religions**

1 belief in, or the worship of, a god or gods

abcdefghijklmnopqrstuvwxyz

2 a particular way of worshipping a god or gods ⇒ *the Sikh religion*

▸ **religious**
ADJECTIVE
1 to do with belief in a god or gods ⇒ *a religious service*
2 a religious person believes in a god or gods very strongly

remember

VERB remembers, remembering, remembered
1 to have something in your mind from the past ⇒ *How much of what you saw can you remember?*
2 not to forget to do something ⇒ *Remember to take your key with you.*

remind

VERB reminds, reminding, reminded
to make someone remember something ⇒ *Remind me to phone John.*

▸ **reminder**
NOUN *plural* reminders
a note that helps someone remember to do something

remove

VERB removes, removing, removed
1 to remove something is to take it away or get rid of it ⇒ *The police have removed the car that was dumped here.*
2 to remove clothes is to take them off ⇒ *Please remove your shoes before you go upstairs.*

▸ **removal**
NOUN *plural* removals
taking something away

repair

VERB repairs, repairing, repaired
to repair something that is damaged or not working is to fix it ⇒ *Can the washing-machine be repaired?*

NOUN *plural* repairs
something you do to fix something that is damaged or not working

repeat

VERB repeats, repeating, repeated
1 to say something again ⇒ *Could you repeat your name please?*
2 to do something again ⇒ *I hope this mistake will never be repeated.*

▸ **repeatedly**
ADVERB
again and again

reply

VERB replies, replying, replied
to answer ⇒ *You haven't replied to my question yet.*

NOUN *plural* replies
an answer ⇒ *We've had a number of replies to our advertisement.*

report

NOUN *plural* reports
1 an account of something that has happened ⇒ *reports of an accident*
2 a piece of writing that gives you information about someone or something, or about something that has taken place

VERB reports, reporting, reported
to tell people about what has happened ⇒ *Did you report this to the police?*

reptile

NOUN *plural* reptiles
a cold-blooded animal, such as a snake

rescue

VERB rescues, rescuing, rescued
to save someone from danger ⇒ *Firefighters rescued the people from the building.*

NOUN *plural* rescues
when someone is saved from danger ⇒ *on an island with no hope of rescue*

▸rescuer

NOUN *plural* rescuers

a person who saves someone from a dangerous situation

research

NOUN *plural* researches

to do or carry out research is to study a subject in a lot of detail, in order to find out new information ⋟ *scientific research* ⋞

VERB researches, researching, researched

to research something is to study it in a lot of detail, in order to find out new information

respect

NOUN

a feeling that a thing or person deserves your attention, admiration or consideration

VERB respects, respecting, respected

to respect someone is to treat them with kindness and attention

responsible

ADJECTIVE

1 to be responsible for something is to be the person whose job that thing is ⋟ *Who is responsible for feeding the dog?* ⋞
2 to be responsible for something like a mistake is to be the person whose fault it is
3 a responsible person is someone you can trust

rest

VERB rests, resting, rested

1 to spend time doing very little, or nothing, in order to relax ⋟ *You need rest – you've been ill.* ⋞
2 to rest against something is to lean against it ⋟ *a spade resting against a wall* ⋞

NOUN *plural* rests

1 a time when you relax or sleep ⋟ *I need a rest before I can work any more.* ⋞
2 the rest of something is what is left ⋟ *I want to spend the rest of my life here.* ⋞

restaurant

NOUN *plural* restaurants

a place where you can buy and eat a meal

This is a French word that comes from the word **restaurer**, which means *to restore*, because the food was thought to refresh you and make you feel better.

result

NOUN *plural* results

1 the result of something is what happens because of it ⋟ *Stuart failed all his exams, as a result of never doing any work.* ⋞
2 the result of a contest is the number of points each team or contestant won
3 a student's exam results are the marks they got

return

VERB returns, returning, returned

1 to return is to go back to a place ⋟ *We fly out on Monday and return on Friday.* ⋞
2 to return something is to give it, put it or send it back ⋟ *Please return your books.* ⋞

NOUN *plural* returns

1 a time when you come or go back again ⋟ *On my return to the house, I found the door wide open.* ⋞
2 a return ticket, a ticket that allows you to travel to a place and back again ⋟ *Do you want a single or a return?* ⋞

reveal

VERB reveals, revealing, revealed

1 to reveal something is to allow it to be seen
2 to reveal information is to tell it to someone ⋟ *The newspaper is claiming that it can reveal all the details.* ⋞

reward

NOUN *plural* rewards

something you get for doing something good or useful ⋟ *a £300 reward for any information that helps catch the criminal* ⋞

a b c d e f g h i j k l m n o p q r s t u v w x y z

VERB rewards, rewarding, rewarded
to give someone something for being good or useful ⋟**The class was rewarded for its good behaviour.** ⋞

rhinoceros

NOUN *plural* **rhinoceroses**
a large animal from Africa and Asia that has thick grey skin and one or two horns on its nose

> The word comes from the Greek word **rhinokeros**. This is made up of **rhinos**, which means *nose*, and **keras**, which means *horn*. A **rhinoceros** is so called because of the horn on its snout.

rhyme

VERB rhymes, rhyming, rhymed
if two words rhyme, they end with the same sound. For example, *ghost* rhymes with *toast*

NOUN *plural* **rhymes**
a rhyme is a word that sounds like another, or a pair of words that have a similar sound ⋟**Is there a rhyme for 'orange'?**⋞

rhythm

NOUN *plural* **rhythms**
a repeated pattern of sounds or movements

rice

NOUN
brown or white grains that are cooked and used as food ⋟**a bowl of boiled rice** ⋞

rich

ADJECTIVE richer, richest
1 a rich person has a lot of money or possessions
2 rich food contains a lot of sugar or fat

riddle

NOUN *plural* **riddles**
a word puzzle

ride

VERB rides, riding, rode, ridden
1 to travel on a horse or bicycle ⋟**I never learnt to ride a bike.** ⋞
2 to travel in or on a vehicle

NOUN *plural* **rides**
a journey in or on a vehicle ⋟**a bus ride** ⋞

▸**rider**
NOUN *plural* **riders**
someone sitting on and controlling a bike or horse

right

ADJECTIVE
1 correct ⋟**I got most of the answers wrong but a couple were right.** ⋞
2 good and proper ⋟**It doesn't seem right that people in the world are hungry.** ⋞
3 on the other side from the left side ⋟**I write with my right hand.** ⋞

ADVERB
1 on or towards the other side from the left ⋟**Now turn right.** ⋞
2 exactly ⋟**Don't move; stay right there.** ⋞
3 immediately ⋟**I'll be right there.** ⋞
4 correctly ⋟**Can't you do anything right?**⋞

NOUN *plural* **rights**
1 the right is the opposite side to the left side ⋟**There's a chemist on the right.** ⋞
2 a right is something that you should be allowed ⋟**the right to vote** ⋞

ring¹

NOUN *plural* **rings**
1 anything in the shape of a circle ⋟**The class**

sit in a ring around the teacher.
2 a small circle, usually made of metal, that you wear on your finger ▷ *a wedding ring*
3 the area where a performance takes place ▷ *a boxing ring* ▷ *a circus ring*

ring²

NOUN *plural* rings

1 the sound a bell makes ▷ *Did I hear a ring at the door?*
2 a telephone call ▷ *I'll give you a ring later.*

VERB rings, ringing, rang, rung

1 to make a sound like a bell ▷ *I think I heard the doorbell ring.*
2 to telephone someone ▷ *Can I ring you back?*

rinse

VERB rinses, rinsing, rinsed

to rinse something is to wash it with clean water

NOUN *plural* rinses

a wash with clean water

rip

VERB rips, ripping, ripped

to tear something roughly ▷ *Steve had ripped his trousers on the barbed wire.*

NOUN *plural* rips

a rough tear ▷ *a rip in my sleeve*

ripe

ADJECTIVE riper, ripest

ripe fruit or crops are ready to be picked or eaten ▷ *Slightly green bananas will soon be completely ripe.*

▸ **ripen**

VERB ripens, ripening, ripened

when fruit or crops ripen they become ready to pick or eat

▸ **ripeness**

NOUN

how completely ready a growing food is to pick or eat ▷ *Check the ripeness of the fruit by squeezing it very gently.*

rise

VERB rises, rising, rose, risen

1 to go upwards ▷ *Ahead, the ground rose steeply.* ▷ *The sun rises in the east.*
2 to get up ▷ *His habit was to rise early for breakfast.*

NOUN *plural* rises

an increase ▷ *a pay rise*

river

NOUN *plural* rivers

a large stream of water that flows across land ▷ *the River Thames*

road

NOUN *plural* roads

a hard, level surface for vehicles to travel along ▷ *The British drive on the left-hand side of the road.*

roar

VERB roars, roaring, roared

to make a loud, angry sound like a lion ▷ *traffic roaring past in the street below*

NOUN *plural* roars

a loud noise like the sound a lion makes

rob

VERB robs, robbing, robbed

to rob someone is to steal something from them ▷ *They stole thousands of pounds when they robbed the bank.*

▸ **robber**

NOUN *plural* robbers

a person who steals

▸ **robbery**

NOUN *plural* robberies

when something is stolen ▷ *a bank robbery*

robin

NOUN *plural* robins

a small brown bird with a red breast

a b c d e f g h i j k l m n o p q r s t u v w x y z

robot

NOUN *plural* **robots**

a machine that can do things like a person

rock¹

NOUN *plural* **rocks**

1 rock is the hard stone substance that the Earth is made of
2 a rock is a large stone
3 rock is a hard sweet that is usually in the form of a long stick

rock²

VERB **rocks, rocking, rocked**

to rock is to move gently backwards and forwards or from side to side ⋛ *She was rocking the baby in her arms.* ⋜

NOUN

a type of loud music with a deep beat

rocket

NOUN *plural* **rockets**

1 a spaceship for travelling from Earth into space
2 a type of bomb that is shot from a large gun
3 a kind of firework that explodes high in the sky

VERB **rockets, rocketing, rocketed**

to go upwards very very quickly ⋛ *rocketing prices* ⋜

rode

VERB

a way of changing the verb **ride** to make the past tense ⋛ *I rode my bike for hours at a time in those days.* ⋜

roll

VERB **rolls, rolling, rolled**

1 to move along, turning over and over ⋛ *a ball rolling down a slope* ⋜
2 to move along on wheels ⋛ *Take the brake off and let the car roll forwards.* ⋜
3 to form something into the shape of a ball or cylinder ⋛ *Roll the sleeping bag up tightly and tie the string around it.* ⋜
4 to roll something is to make it flat by crushing it under a rolling cylinder ⋛ *I am going to roll the lawn.* ⋜ ⋛ *rolled metal* ⋜

NOUN *plural* **rolls**

1 a very small loaf of bread ⋛ *a cheese roll* ⋜
2 a cylinder shape made from a large flat piece of something like carpet or paper ⋛ *We'll need 12 rolls of paper for this room.* ⋜
3 a long rumbling sound ⋛ *a drum roll* ⋜

roof

NOUN *plural* **roofs**

1 the part that covers the top of a building or vehicle ⋛ *The house has a red tiled roof.* ⋜
2 the top inside surface of your mouth

room

NOUN *plural* **rooms**

1 one of the areas a building is divided into inside ⋛ *We have three rooms downstairs and four upstairs.* ⋜
2 enough space for something ⋛ *Is there room for a grand piano on the stage?* ⋜

▶ **roomy**

ADJECTIVE **roomier, roomiest**

having a lot of space inside it

root

NOUN *plural* **roots**

1 the underground part of a plant
2 the part of a tooth or hair that attaches it to the body

VERB **roots, rooting, rooted**

to grow roots ⋛ *The seedlings rooted nicely when I planted them in the compost.* ⋜

rope

NOUN *plural* **ropes**

a very thick twisted cord ⋛ *an anchor tied on the end of a long piece of rope* ⋜

rose[1]

NOUN *plural* **roses**

1 a garden plant with prickly stems and sweet-smelling flowers
2 a pink colour

rose[2]

VERB

a way of changing the verb **rise** to make a past tense ⋝ *The temperature in the room rose steadily as the day wore on.* ⋜

Rosh Hashanah said "rosh ha-**sha**-na"

NOUN

a Jewish festival celebrating the new year

rotten

ADJECTIVE

1 going bad or decaying ⋝ *John stepped on a rotten floorboard and it gave way beneath him.* ⋜
2 bad quality ⋝ *a rotten meal* ⋜
3 unfair or unkind ⋝ *a rotten thing to say* ⋜

round

ADJECTIVE **rounder, roundest**

1 the same shape as a circle ⋝ *a round table* ⋜
2 the same shape as part of a circle ⋝ *a round archway* ⋜
3 the same shape as a ball ⋝ *The Earth is round.* ⋜

ADVERB AND PREPOSITION

1 around, or on all sides ⋝ *I glanced round at the pictures on the walls.* ⋜ ⋝ *The Moon goes round the Earth.* ⋜
2 from one person or place to another ⋝ *The news got round pretty quickly.* ⋜

NOUN *plural* **rounds**

1 a burst of something like laughing, cheering, clapping or firing ⋝ *Let's give him a round of applause.* ⋜
2 a route of calls that someone makes ⋝ *We're always last on the postman's round.* ⋜

3 a level in a contest ⋝ *a second-round match* ⋜

VERB **rounds, rounding, rounded**

to go around a corner ⋝ *As I rounded the corner, I came face to face with Sharon.* ⋜
▸ **round someone** or **something up**
to round up people or animals is to collect them together ⋝ *Farmers are rounding the animals up for the winter.* ⋜

rounders

NOUN

a team game in which one side bats and the other side tries to catch the ball

route

NOUN *plural* **routes**

a way of getting somewhere ⋝ *Terry's route to school takes him past the library.* ⋜

row[1] rhymes with "**low**"

NOUN *plural* **rows**

a number of things arranged beside each other in a line ⋝ *the front row of seats* ⋜ ⋝ *Sow the seeds in a straight row.* ⋜
▸ **in a row**
happening one after another ⋝ *They've lost five matches in a row.* ⋜

row[2] rhymes with "**low**"

VERB **rows, rowing, rowed**

to pull a boat through water using oars

row[3] rhymes with "**how**"

NOUN *plural* **rows**

1 a noisy argument or a fight
2 a loud unpleasant noise ⋝ *Why are the children making such a row?* ⋜

VERB **rows, rowing, rowed**

to argue noisily

rub

VERB **rubs, rubbing, rubbed**

1 to move your hand backwards and forwards over a surface, usually pressing

down at the same time ⟩ *He lowered his head and rubbed his eyes.*

2 to press against something and move backwards and forwards ⟩ *My shoes are rubbing and giving me blisters.*

NOUN *plural* **rubs**

a backwards and forwards movement of your hand while pressing down ⟩ *Let me give your neck a rub where it's aching.*

rubber

NOUN *plural* **rubbers**

1 rubber is a strong substance that stretches and can be man-made or made from tree juices ⟩ *rubber-soled shoes*

2 a rubber is a small block that you can use to rub on pencil marks to remove them

rubbish

NOUN

1 things that have been thrown away or should be thrown away ⟩ *a rubbish bin*

2 complete nonsense ⟩ *Her new chat show is utter rubbish.*

rucksack

NOUN *plural* **rucksacks**

a bag that you carry on your back, especially when you are walking or climbing

> This is a German word which comes from **ruck**, which means *back*, and **sack**, which means *bag*.

rude

ADJECTIVE **ruder, rudest**

1 not polite ⟩ *a rude answer*

2 embarrassing and not proper in a polite situation ⟩ *rude jokes*

3 rough and basic ⟩ *a rude stable*

▸ **rudely**

ADVERB

in a bad-mannered way, without being polite ⟩ *'Not likely!' he said rudely.*

▸ **rudeness**

NOUN

bad manners or not being polite ⟩ *I apologize for my friend's rudeness.*

rug

NOUN *plural* **rugs**

a large mat on the floor

rule

NOUN *plural* **rules**

1 an instruction about what is or what is not allowed ⟩ *It's against the rules to move your feet when you're holding the ball.*

2 government, or control by politicians or a king or queen ⟩ *a country under the rule of the military*

VERB **rules, ruling, ruled**

1 to rule something, such as a country, is to control it

2 to make an official decision ⟩ *The judge has ruled that the prisoner can go free.*

3 to rule a line is to draw a straight line ⟩ *a pad of ruled paper*

▸ **ruler**

NOUN *plural* **ruler**

1 a person who controls or governs a country

2 a strip of wood, plastic or metal that can be used to help you to draw a straight line or for measuring short lengths

run

VERB **runs, running, ran, run**

1 to move with very fast steps ⟩ *We had to run for the bus.*

2 to follow a certain route ⟩ *The number 5 bus runs every 10 minutes.* ⟩ *This road runs over the hill to the next village.*

3 to run someone somewhere is to give them a lift ⟩ *Dad runs us to school if it's raining.*

4 a liquid runs when it flows easily ⟩ *tears running down my face* ⟩ *Your nose is running.*

5 an engine or other machinery runs, or you

run it, when it works or operates ⸱ *The engine runs on diesel oil.*

6 to compete to be elected to an official job ⸱ *Mr Obama was running for president.*

▸ **run away**

to leave somewhere in secret or in a hurry

▸ **run out of something**

to have none of something left ⸱ *We've run out of vinegar.*

NOUN *plural* **runs**

1 a fast movement, quicker than a walk ⸱ *break into a run and get there faster*

2 a race or period of exercise ⸱ *a cross-country run*

3 a trip or journey in a vehicle ⸱ *a quick run into town to do the shopping*

rung¹

NOUN *plural* **rungs**

a step on a ladder

rung²

VERB

the form of the verb **ring** that is used with a helping verb to show that something hapened in the past ⸱ *I've rung all my friends and no one wants to come.*

rush

NOUN *plural* **rushes**

1 a hurry ⸱ *We were just in time but it had been a dreadful rush.*

2 a large number of people trying to get to the same place at the same time ⸱ *a rush for the door*

VERB rushes, rushing, rushed

1 to rush is to go somewhere in a hurry ⸱ *I rushed downstairs as soon as I heard the thump.*

2 to rush is to do something too quickly or in a hurry ⸱ *Don't rush it or you'll just make a mistake.*

a
b
c
d
e
f
g
h
i
j
k
l
m
n
o
p
q
r
s
t
u
v
w
x
y
z

Sabbath

NOUN

the day of the week set aside for rest and worship in certain religions. The Jewish Sabbath is Saturday, for Muslims it is Friday and for most Christians, it is Sunday

sad

ADJECTIVE sadder, saddest

1 feeling unhappy ⋑ *a sad look* ⋐
2 making you feel unhappy ⋑ *a sad film* ⋐

▸ **sadden**

VERB saddens, saddening, saddened

you are saddened if something makes you feel unhappy

▸ **sadly**

ADVERB

1 unfortunately ⋑ *Sadly, we must say goodbye to Mrs Green today.* ⋐
2 unhappily ⋑ *She looked at us sadly.* ⋐

▸ **sadness**

NOUN

a feeling of unhappiness or pity

saddle

NOUN *plural* **saddles**

a seat for a rider of a horse or a bicycle

safe

ADJECTIVE safer, safest

1 not harmed ⋑ *Thank goodness you're safe!* ⋐
2 not involving danger or risk ⋑ *That ladder doesn't look very safe to me.* ⋐

NOUN *plural* **safes**

a strong metal box for keeping valuable things in ⋑ *The safe had been opened.* ⋐

▸ **safely**

ADVERB

without risk or danger ⋑ *getting everyone home safely* ⋐   ⋑ *safely tucked up in bed* ⋐

said

VERB

a way of changing the verb **say** to make a past tense. It can be used with or without a helping verb ⋑ *They've said I can come back any time.* ⋐   ⋑ *I've told you what he said.* ⋐

sail

VERB sails, sailing, sailed

1 to travel in a ship or a boat ⋑ *My dream is to sail across the Atlantic on a yacht.* ⋐
2 to start a journey in a ship ⋑ *The ferry sails at noon.* ⋐

NOUN *plural* **sails**

a sheet of canvas on a boat that catches the wind and carries the boat along

▸ **sailor**

NOUN *plural* **sailors**

someone who works on a ship

salad

NOUN *plural* **salads**

a mixture of mostly raw vegetables that sometimes includes other foods like ham

saliva

NOUN

the watery liquid produced in your mouth

salt

NOUN *plural* **salts**

salt is small white crystals that come from the ground (**rock salt**) or the sea (**sea salt**), used for flavouring food

▶ **salty**

ADJECTIVE   saltier, saltiest

containing salt or tasting very strongly of salt ⸲ *The soup was awfully salty.* ⸱

same

ADJECTIVE

exactly alike or very similar ⸲ *I was wearing the same jacket as Barbara.* ⸱   ⸲ *The two cases are exactly the same.* ⸱

PRONOUN

something that is alike or similar ⸲*You know I'd do the same for you.* ⸱

sand

NOUN   *plural* sands

tiny grains of rock that are found on beaches, on river-beds and in deserts

sandal

NOUN   *plural* sandals

sandals are light open shoes with straps for wearing in warm weather

sandpit

NOUN   *plural* sandpits

1 a hole filled with sand
2 a small area filled with sand for children to play in

sandwich

NOUN   *plural* sandwiches

two slices of bread with a filling between them ⸲ *cucumber sandwiches* ⸱

This word comes from the name of the Earl of **Sandwich**. It is said that in the 18th century he ate sandwiches so that he would not have to stop playing cards to be served meals.

sang

VERB

a way of changing the verb **sing** to make a past tense ⸲ *We sang folk songs all night.* ⸱

sank

VERB

a way of changing the verb **sink** to make a past tense ⸲ *The Titanic sank in 1912.* ⸱

sat

VERB

a way of changing the verb **sit** to make a past tense. It can be used with or without a helping verb ⸲ *Class 3 sat quietly, waiting for their teacher.* ⸱   ⸲ *I've sat here for an hour waiting for you!* ⸱

Saturday

NOUN   *plural* Saturdays

the day of the week after Friday and before Sunday

Saturday comes from the Old English word **Sæterdæg**, which means *Saturn's day*. Saturn is the Roman god of harvest.

sauce

NOUN   *plural* sauces

a liquid that food is cooked in or served with ⸲ *I like tomato sauce with my chips.* ⸱

saucer

NOUN   *plural* saucers

a small shallow dish that is used for resting a cup on

sausage

NOUN   *plural* sausages

meat that is minced and stuffed into a skin to make long tube shapes

save

VERB   saves, saving, saved

1 to save someone or something is to rescue them from something unpleasant ⸲ *The firefighters saved everyone in the house.* ⸱
2 to save someone's life is to prevent them from dying ⸲ *There's no doubt that the safety belts saved our lives.* ⸱

a b c d e f g h i j k l m n o p q r s t u v w x y z

a b c d e f g h i j k l m n o p q r **s** t u v w x y z

3 to save something is to store it for later ⋛ *Jamie saves half his pocket money.* ⋛

4 to save time or money is to use less time or money than you would normally do ⋛ *Save 20% on all our products this week.* ⋛

NOUN *plural* **saves**

when a goalkeeper prevents the other team from scoring a goal ⋛ *a brilliant save* ⋛

▶ **savings**

PLURAL NOUN

money that you collect and keep to use at some time in the future ⋛ *Colin's going to spend all his savings on a drum kit.* ⋛

saw[1]

NOUN *plural* **saws**

a tool with a thin notched blade that can cut through wood or metal

saw[2]

VERB

a way of changing the verb **see** to make a past tense ⋛ *I saw him here last week.* ⋛

say

VERB **says, saying, said**

1 to speak words out loud ⋛ *I was just going to say 'hello'.* ⋛

2 to express in written words ⋛ *What does the notice say?* ⋛

▶ **saying**

NOUN *plural* **sayings**

a phrase or sentence that people often use and which sometimes gives wise advice ⋛ *Gran's favourite saying is 'an apple a day keeps the doctor away'.* ⋛

scare

VERB **scares, scaring, scared**

to scare someone is to frighten them

NOUN *plural* **scares**

1 a scare is a fright ⋛ *It gave us all a bit of a scare when Mother fainted.* ⋛

2 a scare is a sudden worry that lots of people have about something ⋛ *a bomb scare* ⋛

▶ **scared**

ADJECTIVE

frightened ⋛ *After the attack she was too scared to go out.* ⋛

scarecrow

NOUN *plural* **scarecrows**

a simple model of a person in a field, set up to frighten birds and stop them from eating crops

scarf

NOUN *plural* **scarves**

a long strip or square of cloth that you wear around your neck, shoulders or head to keep warm or for decoration

scene

NOUN *plural* **scenes**

1 the setting that an event takes place in ⋛ *the scene of the crime* ⋛

2 a small section of a play, a book or a film ⋛ *a fight scene* ⋛

▶ **scenery**

NOUN

the countryside around about you ⋛ *You see some wonderful scenery from the train.* ⋛

school

NOUN *plural* **schools**

1 a place where children and teenagers go to be educated ⋛ *You'll go to school when you're five years old.* ⋛

2 all the pupils and teachers in a school ⋛ *The whole school was in the playground.* ⋛

3 a large number of fish or dolphins that swim together in a group

science

NOUN   *plural* sciences

1 studying the natural world and the things that happen in it
2 a particular study about the natural world, especially chemistry, physics or biology

> The word **science** comes from the Latin word **scientia**, which means *knowledge*.

scientist

NOUN   *plural* scientists

a person who studies science or whose work involves science ⇒ *a laboratory where scientists test bacteria found in food*

scissors

PLURAL NOUN

a cutting tool that has two blades joined in the middle. You use scissors by opening and closing the blades with the fingers and thumb of one hand

score

VERB   scores, scoring, scored

1 to get a point in a game, test or competition ⇒ *Hamilton has scored again for the Rovers.*
2 to keep a record of the points that are won in a game or competition ⇒ *Who's scoring?*
3 to scratch a surface with something sharp ⇒ *Score a straight line across the card and fold it carefully.*

NOUN   *plural* scores

the number of points that you get in a game, test or competition ⇒ *What's the final score?*

scrape

VERB   scrapes, scraping, scraped

1 to remove something from a surface, using something such as a knife or a stick ⇒ *I'll have to scrape the mud off my shoes.*
2 to damage or hurt something by rubbing it against a rough surface ⇒ *Lydia had scraped her elbow when she fell.*

NOUN   *plural* scrapes

1 when something hard or rough is rubbed or scratched against a surface
2 a difficult or embarrassing situation ⇒ *You expect children to get into scrapes.*

scratch

VERB   scratches, scratching, scratched

1 to make a mark on a surface with something sharp or pointed ⇒ *Mick scratched the car when he brushed the wall.*
2 to rub your nails on your skin, usually because you feel itchy ⇒ *Try not to scratch the spots.*

NOUN   *plural* scratches

a mark left on a surface by something sharp

▶ **scratchy**

ADJECTIVE   scratchier, scratchiest

rough ⇒ *a scratchy woollen jersey*

scream

VERB   screams, screaming, screamed

to make a long high-pitched cry because you are frightened, angry or in pain ⇒ *Everyone screamed when Peter jumped out of the cupboard.*

NOUN   *plural* screams

a loud and high-pitched cry ⇒ *The neighbours came when they heard the screams.*

a b c d e f g h i j k l m n o p q r s t u v w x y z

screen

NOUN   *plural* screens

1 the part of a computer, television or cinema that you look at to see images ⋛ *You should sit two metres away from the screen.* ⋚

2 an upright frame or panel that protects people from something or makes a more private area in a room ⋛ *You have to go behind the screen to be examined.* ⋚

VERB   screens, screening, screened

1 to show a television programme or film ⋛ *They are screening the whole series for the third time.* ⋚

2 to hide something from view or shelter it ⋛ *The garden is screened by a fence.* ⋚

3 to test lots of people for a particular illness ⋛ *All the workers here should be screened for the virus.* ⋚

scribble

VERB   scribbles, scribbling, scribbled

1 to write very quickly and untidily ⋛ *I scribbled his name down before I forgot it.* ⋚

2 to draw meaningless lines in an untidy way ⋛ *The baby had a pen and was scribbling on the wall.* ⋚

NOUN   *plural* scribbles

1 handwriting that is very untidy

2 meaningless untidy lines that someone has drawn

sea

NOUN   *plural* seas

1 the salt water that covers most of the Earth's surface ⋛ *Australia is completely surrounded by sea.* ⋚

2 a large lake of salt water ⋛ *the Dead Sea* ⋚

seagull

NOUN   *plural* seagulls

a sea bird with webbed feet, short legs and long wings with grey, black or white feathers

seal¹

VERB   seals, sealing, sealed

to close something firmly ⋛ *Don't seal the envelope yet.* ⋚

seal²

NOUN   *plural* seals

an animal with a small head and a shiny coat that lives mainly in the sea

search

VERB   searches, searching, searched

to look carefully for a thing or person ⋛ *I've searched everywhere for my keys.* ⋚

NOUN   *plural* searches

an attempt to find something or someone ⋛ *a thorough search of the area* ⋚

season

NOUN   *plural* seasons

1 one of the four main periods that the year is divided into ⋛ *Spring is my favourite season.* ⋚

2 the particular period of the year that a certain activity takes place ⋛ *the football season* ⋚

VERB   seasons, seasoning, seasoned

to season food is to flavour it by putting salt, pepper or other herbs and spices into it

seat

NOUN   *plural* seats

1 a piece of furniture for sitting on ⋛ *a garden seat* ⋚ ⋛ *a theatre seat* ⋚

2 the part of a piece of clothing that covers your bottom ⋛ *the seat of my trousers* ⋚

VERB   seats, seating, seated

1 to seat a person is to give them somewhere to sit ⋛ *The host and hostess were seated at opposite ends of the table.* ⋚

2 to seat a certain number of people is to have enough room for them all to sit down ⋛ *The new theatre seats twice as many people as the old one did.* ⋚

second

ADJECTIVE AND ADVERB

next after the first ⹃ *Julia is their second daughter.* ⹁ ⹃ *Craig came second in the final exam.* ⹁

NOUN *plural* **seconds**

1 a thing or person that is number two in a series ⹃ *This programme is the second in a series of three.* ⹁
2 one sixtieth of a minute or a very short time ⹃ *one minute and thirty seconds* ⹁ ⹃ *Just wait a second.* ⹁

▸ **secondary**

ADJECTIVE

coming after the thing that is first ⹃ *Freddie had measles and then developed a secondary infection.* ⹁

secondary school

NOUN *plural* **secondary schools**

a school for pupils between the ages of 11 and 18

secret

NOUN *plural* **secrets**

1 a piece of information that must not be told to anyone else ⹃ *The birthday party was a well-kept secret.* ⹁
2 something that nobody understands or knows ⹃ *the secret of eternal youth* ⹁

ADJECTIVE

not to be told or shown to other people ⹃ *a secret passage* ⹁ ⹃ *secret messages* ⹁

▸ **secretive**

ADJECTIVE

liking to keep secrets from people ⹃ *Logan was very secretive about his past.* ⹁

see

VERB sees, seeing, saw, seen

1 to look at something and notice it ⹃ *The dog goes mad whenever he sees a cat.* ⹁ ⹃ *We're going to London to see the sights.* ⹁
2 to meet someone or spend time with them ⹃ *Have you seen Peter much lately?* ⹁

3 to understand something ⹃ *Now I see what you mean.* ⹁
4 to see someone somewhere is to go there with them ⹃ *I'll see you to the door.* ⹁

seed

NOUN *plural* **seeds**

a thing that a plant produces and that new plants grow from ⹃ *Sow the seeds about two inches deep in the soil.* ⹁

▸ **seedling**

NOUN *plural* **seedlings**

a very young plant

seek

VERB seeks, seeking, sought

1 to search for something ⹃ *We sought him high and low but never found him.* ⹁
2 to try to get or achieve something ⹃ *She's seeking fame and fortune.* ⹁

seem

VERB seems, seeming, seemed

to appear to be something or to give the impression of being something ⹃ *You didn't seem to be interested.* ⹁ ⹃ *Things seem calm at the moment.* ⹁

seen

VERB

a form of the verb **see** that is used with a helping verb to show that something happened in the past ⹃ *I haven't seen you for ages.* ⹁

seesaw

NOUN *plural* **seesaws**

a playground toy that children sit on either

a b c d e f g h i j k l m n o p q r s t u v w x y z

end of, pushing off the ground with their feet and swinging up and down

sell

VERB sells, selling, sold

to give somebody something in exchange for money *I sold my car and bought a van.*

▸ **seller**

NOUN *plural* sellers

a person who has something for sale

send

VERB sends, sending, sent

1 to make something go to a place or person *I'll send you an email.* *Our luggage was sent on the next flight.*

2 to tell someone to go somewhere *Rob was feeling sick so the school sent him home.*

▸ **sender**

NOUN *plural* senders

the person that a letter or parcel comes from *If this letter is undelivered, please return it to the sender.*

sense

NOUN *plural* senses

1 one of the five powers of sight, touch, taste, hearing and smell *Janet lost her sense of smell after an illness.*

2 an ability to understand or appreciate something *I don't think he has much of a sense of humour.*

3 a feeling *People need work that gives them a sense of achievement.*

4 sense is the ability to make sensible decisions *Someone had the sense to call an ambulance.*

5 a meaning *A single English word can have lots of different senses.*

VERB senses, sensing, sensed

to become aware of something although it is not very obvious *I sensed that not many people agreed with what I was saying.*

sent

VERB

a way of changing the verb **send** to make a past tense. It can be used with or without a helping verb *I've sent ten email messages this morning.* *Rory was sent to prison.*

sentence

NOUN *plural* sentences

1 **grammar** a sequence of words that usually includes a verb and expresses a statement, a question or a command

2 the punishment that a judge gives a person who has been found guilty of a crime *a five-year prison sentence*

VERB sentences, sentencing, sentenced

to tell a person who has been found guilty of a crime what their punishment will be *He was sentenced to life imprisonment.*

separate

ADJECTIVE said "**sep**-i-rit" *or* "**sep**-rit"

different and not joined or connected *This is a completely separate matter.* *The farm is separate from the rest of the house.*

VERB said "**sep**-i-rait" separates, separating, separated

1 to split up the people in a group or the parts of something that can be divided *Could we please separate the boys from the girls for this exercise?*

2 to decide to live apart *They are not divorced but they separated last year.*

▸ **separately**

ADVERB

not together *Each of the suspects was interviewed separately by the police.*

▸ **separation**

NOUN *plural* separations

1 when people are apart from each other *Lily found the separation from her family hard while she was working abroad.*

2 keeping things apart *I firmly believe in the separation of work from family life.*

September

NOUN

the ninth month of the year, after August and before October

> **September** was the seventh month of the Roman year and the name comes from the word **septem**, which means *seven* in Latin.

series

NOUN *plural* series

1 a number of similar things that happen one after the other ⋟ *a series of accidents* ⋞
2 a set of television or radio programmes with the same subject and characters ⋟ *a nature series* ⋞   ⋟ *an old series of 'Dr Who'* ⋞

serious

ADJECTIVE

1 important and needing proper attention ⋟ *a more serious matter* ⋞
2 very bad ⋟ *a serious accident* ⋞
3 not joking ⋟ *I can never tell when he's joking and when he's being serious.* ⋞

serve

VERB serves, serving, served

1 to work for someone ⋟ *Brown had served the family for fifty years.* ⋞
2 to hand people things they want to buy in a shop or what they want to eat ⋟ *Are you being served?* ⋞   ⋟ *Serve the soup now.* ⋞
3 to serve in tennis is to start play by throwing the ball up and hitting it

NOUN *plural* serves

in tennis, a serve is throwing the ball up and hitting it to start playing a point ⋟ *a very fast serve* ⋞

set

VERB sets, setting, set

1 to place something somewhere ⋟ *Set the tray down on the table.* ⋞   ⋟ *a house that was set back from the road* ⋞

2 to adjust a clock or control so that it is ready to work ⋟ *Don't forget to set the video to record.* ⋞
3 to become hard or firm ⋟ *Wait an hour or so for the jelly to set.* ⋞
4 the sun sets when it goes down ⋟ *watching the setting sun* ⋞
5 to set someone something to do is to give it to them to do ⋟ *The teacher didn't set us any homework.* ⋞

ADJECTIVE

1 fixed or compulsory, not something you can choose ⋟ *a set piece for this year's exam* ⋞ ⋟ *Each person had a set job to do.* ⋞
2 ready or prepared ⋟ *Are we all set to go?* ⋞

NOUN *plural* sets

1 a number of things or people that have something in common or are used together ⋟ *a set of chairs* ⋞   ⋟ *a chess set* ⋞ ⋟ *I'm in the top set for maths.* ⋞
2 a radio or television ⋟ *We have a technical problem; please do not adjust your set.* ⋞
3 a series of games that form part of a tennis match

seven

NOUN *plural* sevens

the number 7

seventeen

NOUN

the number 17

seventy

NOUN *plural* seventies

the number 70

several

ADJECTIVE

more than two but not very many ⋟ *Several people stopped to look.* ⋞   ⋟ *I've asked him several times to return my book.* ⋞

sew

VERB sews, sewing, sewed, sewn

to use a needle and thread or a machine to

a b c d e f g h i j k l m n o p q r **s** t u v w x y z

join fabric with stitches ⸗ *Could you teach me to sew?* ⸗ *I'll need some red thread to sew that button back on.* ⸗

shadow

NOUN *plural* **shadows**

1 a shadow is a dark shape on a surface caused when an object is between the surface and a bright light ⸗ *children trying to jump on each other's shadow* ⸗

2 shadow is an area darkened by the blocking out of light ⸗ *I couldn't see his face because it was in shadow.* ⸗

shake

VERB **shakes, shaking, shook, shaken**

1 to shake is to move quickly or unsteadily with very small movements ⸗ *The earth shook when the bomb landed.* ⸗

2 to shake something is to move it quickly from side to side or backwards and forwards ⸗ *The wind shook the trees and rattled the windows.* ⸗

3 to shake someone is to shock or upset them ⸗ *We were terribly shaken by the news of his death.* ⸗

NOUN *plural* **shakes**

1 a quick movement from side to side or backwards and forwards ⸗ *Give the bottle a quick shake.* ⸗

2 a very quick moment ⸗ *I'll be there in two shakes.* ⸗

3 a drink of milk and some sort of flavouring

▸ **shaky**

ADJECTIVE **shakier, shakiest**

not steady and almost crying ⸗ *Her voice was shaky as she told us the news.* ⸗

shall

VERB **should**

a helping verb that is used along with a main verb to make future tenses when the subject of the verb is **I** or **we** ⸗ *I shall never forget this moment.* ⸗

shallow

ADJECTIVE **shallower, shallowest**

not deep ⸗ *a shallow lake* ⸗

shame

NOUN

1 shame is an embarrassing feeling of guilt or foolishness, especially because you have done something wrong

2 if something brings shame on or to people, it brings them disgrace because it is bad or morally wrong

3 if you say something is a shame, you mean it is a pity ⸗ *What a shame that you can't come to the party.* ⸗

shampoo

NOUN *plural* **shampoos**

a soapy liquid for washing your hair or for cleaning carpets

VERB **shampoos, shampooing, shampooed**

to shampoo your hair, or a carpet, is to wash it using shampoo

> This word comes from the Indian language Hindi, from the word **champu**, which means *squeeze*. You use a squeezing action to wash with it.

shape

NOUN *plural* **shapes**

1 something's shape is its outline or form ⸗ *a mountain in the shape of a crown* ⸗

2 shapes are things like squares, circles, rectangles, diamonds and triangles

VERB **shapes, shaping, shaped**

to shape something is to form it or model it into a certain shape ⸗ *He shapes the clay pots on the potter's wheel.* ⸗

share

VERB shares, sharing, shared

1 to share something is to divide it among a number of people so that each person gets some ⇒ *Are you going to eat that whole pizza yourself or are you going to share it?*
2 to share something with other people is to give some of it to them or allow them to use it too ⇒ *There aren't enough books to go round so some of you will have to share.*

NOUN plural shares

1 a share is one of the parts of something that has been, or is to be, divided among several people
2 someone's share in an activity or project, which involves several people, is the part they play in it

shark

NOUN plural sharks

a large fish whose mouth is full of rows of very sharp teeth

sharp

ADJECTIVE sharper, sharpest

1 a sharp object has a thin edge that can cut or a point that can pierce ⇒ *a sharp knife*
2 a sharp fall or increase is sudden and steep ⇒ *a sharp rise in crime*
3 sharp images are clear and distinct with no blurred edges
4 a sharp pain is sudden and stabbing
5 a person or animal with sharp hearing or eyesight is good at hearing or seeing
6 something that tastes sharp tastes bitter, like lemon juice

ADVERB

1 punctually ⇒ *He was to be there at 5 o'clock sharp.*
2 with a sudden or abrupt change of direction ⇒ *Turn sharp left at the next set of traffic lights.*

▸ **sharpen**

VERB sharpens, sharpening, sharpened

to sharpen something is to make it sharp or sharper ⇒ *The leopard was sharpening its claws on a tree.*

▸ **sharpener**

NOUN plural sharpeners

a tool that you use to sharpen pencils or knives

she

PRONOUN

a word you use to talk about a woman, girl, female animal or boat that has already been mentioned or pointed out for the first time ⇒ *Madeleine is funny. She tells jokes and imitates people.* ⇒ *This boat is great for racing and she steers very easily.*

shed

NOUN plural sheds

a simple wooden or metal building used for working in or for storing things

VERB sheds, shedding, shed

1 people shed their clothes, reptiles shed their skins and birds shed their feathers when they take or cast them off and get rid of them
2 a tree sheds its leaves when they drop off in the autumn
3 to shed tears is to have tears flowing from your eyes

sheep

NOUN plural sheep

a medium-sized farm animal with a thick wool fleece

The singular and plural forms of **sheep** are the same: *a sheep in the field • two sheep in the pen.*

a b c d e f g h i j k l m n o p q r **s** t u v w x y z

sheet

NOUN *plural* sheets

1 a large piece of cloth that you put on a bed
    ⇒ *I'll just change the sheets.* ⇐
2 a single piece of paper used for writing or printing on
3 a flat piece of metal or glass
4 a layer of ice

shelf

NOUN *plural* shelves

a board fixed horizontally to a wall or as part of a cupboard, used for putting things on

shell

NOUN *plural* shells

1 a hard covering on an egg or a nut, or protecting the soft bodies of creatures like snails, crabs, shellfish and tortoises
2 an explosive bomb or bullet fired from a large gun
3 the framework of a building or other structure

shelter

NOUN *plural* shelters

1 a shelter is a building or other structure that provides protection from harm or bad weather
2 to take shelter is to go somewhere that gives protection from danger or bad weather

VERB shelters, sheltering, sheltered

1 to shelter somewhere is to stay in a place where you are protected from harm or bad weather
2 to shelter someone or something is to protect them

shin

NOUN *plural* shins

the front of your leg below the knee

shine

VERB shines, shining, shone

1 something shines when it gives off or reflects light

2 you shine a light on something when you point the light in its direction
3 you shine something when you polish it

shiny

ADJECTIVE shinier, shiniest

reflecting light or polished so as to reflect light

ship

NOUN *plural* ships

a large boat that carries passengers or things, or both, on long sea journeys

VERB ships, shipping, shipped

to ship something somewhere is to have it carried on a ship

shirt

NOUN *plural* shirts

a piece of clothing for the top half of your body, with long or short sleeves, a collar, and buttons down the front

shock

NOUN *plural* shocks

1 shock, or a shock, is a strong and unpleasant reaction you get when you have had a fright or a bad injury
2 a sudden bump or jolt that comes with great force ⇒ *The shock of the impact threw us all forward.* ⇐
3 if you get an electric shock, a current of electricity passes through your body

VERB shocks, shocking, shocked

if something shocks you, it upsets or horrifies you

▸ **shocking**

ADJECTIVE

upsetting or horrifying

shoe

NOUN *plural* shoes

shoes are the things you wear on your feet over your socks, which usually cover the area between your toes and your ankles

shoelace

NOUN *plural* **shoelaces**

a thin piece of cord threaded through the holes of a certain type of shoe to fasten it

shone

VERB

a way of changing the verb **shine** to make a past tense. It can be used with or without a helping verb ⇒ *The sun shone all day.* ⇒ *It had shone all week.*

shook

VERB

a way of changing the verb **shake** to make a past tense ⇒ *He shook his head sadly.*

shoot

VERB shoots, shooting, shot

1 to shoot a gun or other weapon is to fire it ⇒ *I shot an arrow in the air.*
2 to shoot someone or something with a gun or other weapon is to kill or wound them with it
3 a person or thing shoots somewhere when they travel there very fast ⇒ *He shot past me in his new red sports car.* ⇒ *Pain shot through his body.*
4 in games like football and hockey, a player shoots when they kick or hit the ball at the goal

> The words **shoot** and **chute** sound the same but remember that they have different spellings. A **chute** is a sloped surface.

shop

NOUN *plural* **shops**

1 a place which sells things
2 a place where work of a particular kind is done, for example in a factory

VERB shops, shopping, shopped

to buy things in shops

shore

NOUN *plural* **shores**

the area of land beside the sea or beside a lake

short

ADJECTIVE shorter, shortest

1 not very long ⇒ *a short skirt* ⇒ *a short speech*
2 small, not tall ⇒ *a short man*
3 if something is short, or in short supply, there is less than there should be, or there is not enough of it to go round ⇒ *We are two players short.*

▸ **shortage**
NOUN *plural* **shortages**
a lack of something ⇒ *food shortages*

shorts

PLURAL NOUN

shorts are a piece of clothing for the bottom half of your body, with short legs that reach down to the tops of your thighs or as far down as your knees

shot

VERB

a way of changing the verb **shoot** to make a past tense. It can be used with or without a helping verb ⇒ *The ships had shot at each other using large guns.* ⇒ *The cat shot up the tree when the dog barked.*

should

VERB

1 **should** is used as a past tense of the verb **shall** ⇒ *He said that we should all go home.*
2 ought to ⇒ *I wonder whether or not I should go.*
3 used to say what is likely to happen ⇒ *The train should be arriving soon.*
4 sometimes used with *I* or *we* to express a wish ⇒ *I should love to come to your party.*

a b c d e f g h i j k l m n o p q r **s** t u v w x y z

shoulder

NOUN *plural* shoulders

one of the top parts of your body between your neck and the tops of your arms

VERB shoulders, shouldering, shouldered

1 to shoulder something is to carry it on your shoulder or shoulders
2 to shoulder a responsibility is to accept it as something you must do

shout

VERB shouts, shouting, shouted

to say something very loudly

NOUN *plural* shouts

a loud cry or call

shove

VERB shoves, shoving, shoved

to shove something is to push it hard or roughly

NOUN *plural* shoves

a hard or rough push

show

VERB shows, showing, showed, shown

1 to show something is to allow it or cause it to be seen ⇒ **Show me your new bike.** ⇒ **There's a cartoon showing at the local cinema.**
2 something shows if it can be seen ⇒ **The scar hardly shows.**
3 to show someone something is to point it out to them or demonstrate it to them ⇒ **Can you show me how to tie this?**
4 to show someone somewhere is to guide them in that direction ⇒ **The steward showed us to our seats.**

▸ **show off**

to behave in a way that attracts attention

NOUN *plural* shows

1 an entertainment in the theatre or on radio or TV
2 an event where people or businesses can show things to the public ⇒ **a fashion show**

shower

NOUN *plural* showers

1 a short fall of rain, snow or sleet ⇒ **sunshine and showers**
2 a sudden burst or fall of things ⇒ **a shower of sparks**
3 a device that sends out water in a stream or spray and that you stand under to wash your body

VERB showers, showering, showered

to wash your body under a shower

▸ **showery**
ADJECTIVE

showery weather is when showers of rain fall between periods when it is dry

shrink

VERB shrinks, shrinking, shrank, shrunk

to get smaller ⇒ **My jumper shrank in the wash.**

shut

VERB shuts, shutting, shut

1 to close something ⇒ **Shut the door.** ⇒ **He shut his eyes and went to sleep.**
2 a shop or other business shuts when it stops being open or the staff stop working and go home

ADJECTIVE

closed ⇒ **All the shops are shut at night.**

shy

ADJECTIVE shyer, shyest

a shy person feels very uncomfortable when they have to speak or do something in front of other people, or when they meet new people

VERB shies, shying, shied

if a horse shies, it turns to the side suddenly because it has been frightened

sick

ADJECTIVE sicker, sickest

1 if you feel sick, you feel as if you are going to vomit

2 you are sick when you vomit

3 sick people or animals are ill

4 if you are sick of something, you are very tired of it

▸ **sickening**

`ADJECTIVE`

disgusting ⇒ *a sickening smell*

▸ **sickness**

`NOUN` *plural* **sicknesses**

an illness or disease

side

`NOUN` *plural* **sides**

1 the side of something is the part at or near its edge ⇒ *a house by the side of the river* ⇒ *at the side of the garden*

2 one of two or more surfaces of a figure, shape or structure, especially one of the surfaces that is not the top, bottom, front or back ⇒ *A cube has six sides.* ⇒ *Put the label on the side of the box.*

3 your sides are the left and right parts of your body ⇒ *I've got a pain in my side.*

4 one of the two teams playing in a match, or one of the two groups of people involved in an argument or battle

sight

`NOUN` *plural* **sights**

1 sight is the power of seeing things ⇒ *A very young kitten's sight is not very good.*

2 a sight is something that you see or something that is worth seeing ⇒ *It was a sight I'll never forget.* ⇒ *the sights of London*

3 something that is in sight can be seen and something that is out of sight cannot be seen

4 a person or thing that looks ridiculous, unusual or shocking ⇒ *What a sight she is with that bright blue hair!*

> The words **sight** and **site** sound the same but remember that they have different spellings. A **site** is the place where something is.

sign

`NOUN` *plural* **signs**

1 a mark or gesture with a special meaning ⇒ *He gave the sign to join him.*

2 a notice that gives information to the public ⇒ *The sign said 'No parking'.*

3 one thing is a sign of another thing when it shows what is happening or what will happen ⇒ *Leaves falling are a sign of autumn.*

`VERB` **signs, signing, signed**

1 you sign something or sign your name on something when you write your signature on it

2 to sign to someone is to make a sign or gesture to them ⇒ *He signed to me to come in.*

signature

`NOUN` *plural* **signatures**

your name, written by you in a way that you and other people can recognize

Sikh

`NOUN` *plural* **Sikhs**

someone whose religion is Sikhism

`ADJECTIVE`

to do with Sikhs or Sikhism ⇒ *a Sikh temple*

▸ **Sikhism**

`NOUN`

a religion believing in one God, founded by Guru Nanak in Punjab in North India

silence

`NOUN` *plural* **silences**

1 silence is complete quietness when no sound can be heard

a b c d e f g h i j k l m n o p q r **s** t u v w x y z

2 a silence is a time when there is no sound or no one speaks

VERB silences, silencing, silenced

1 to silence someone is to stop them speaking

2 to silence something is to stop it making a noise

▸ **silent**

ADJECTIVE

completely quiet

▸ **silently**

ADVERB

without making any sound

silly

ADJECTIVE sillier, silliest

foolish or stupid

▸ **silliness**

NOUN

silly behaviour

silver

NOUN

1 a shiny grey precious metal

2 a whitish grey colour

3 things made of silver or a silvery grey metal, such as knives and forks and coins

ADJECTIVE

silver-coloured or made of silver ⋛ *a silver cup* ⋛ ⋛ *silver hair* ⋛

▸ **silvery**

ADJECTIVE

like silver in colour ⋛ *Birch trees have silvery bark.* ⋛

simple

ADJECTIVE simpler, simplest

1 straightforward or very easy to do ⋛ *simple instructions* ⋛ ⋛ *a simple sum* ⋛

2 plain or basic ⋛ *a simple design* ⋛

▸ **simplicity**

NOUN

being simple and uncomplicated

▸ **simply**

ADVERB

1 in a straightforward, uncomplicated way ⋛ *I'll explain it simply so that you all understand.* ⋛

2 only ⋛ *Now, it's simply a question of waiting until something happens.* ⋛

3 completely or absolutely ⋛ *The concert was simply fantastic.* ⋛

sing

VERB sings, singing, sang, sung

1 people sing when they make musical sounds with their voices

2 birds and some other animals sing when they make musical calls

▸ **singer**

NOUN *plural* singers

a person who sings

▸ **singing**

NOUN

singing is making musical sounds with your voice

single

ADJECTIVE

1 a single thing is only one and no more

2 someone who is single is not married

3 for use by one person ⋛ *a single room* ⋛

NOUN *plural* singles

1 a ticket for a journey you make in one direction but not back again

2 a recording of a song that is released on its own, and not as part of an album

VERB singles, singling, singled

▸ **single someone** *or* **something out**

to pick someone or something in particular from a group of people or things

▸ **singles**

PLURAL NOUN

in games like tennis, you play singles when you play against only one other person

sink

VERB sinks, sinking, sank, sunk

1 to drop below the surface of water and go on moving downwards to the bottom ⋛ *The boat sank in a storm.* ⋛
2 to go down or get lower ⋛ *The sun was sinking towards the horizon.* ⋛

NOUN *plural* sinks

in a kitchen or bathroom, a large fixed container with taps and a drain, used for washing

sister

NOUN *plural* sisters

your sister is a girl or woman who has the same parents as you do

sit

VERB sits, sitting, sat

1 you sit or sit down when you have your weight supported on your bottom rather than your feet
2 you sit or sit down when you lower yourself into this position so that your bottom is resting on a surface
3 something sits in the place where it is resting or lying ⋛ *There was a big parcel sitting on the kitchen table.* ⋛
4 you sit an exam when you do the exam

six

NOUN *plural* sixes

the number 6

sixteen

NOUN

the number 16

sixty

NOUN *plural* sixties

the number 60

size

NOUN *plural* sizes

1 how big or small something is, or how long, wide, high, and deep it is
2 a shoe or clothes size is one that is made to fit a certain size of feet or body

skate

NOUN *plural* skates

1 a boot with a blade fitted to the bottom, used for gliding smoothly over ice
2 a **rollerskate**, a boot with a pair of wheels on the bottom

VERB skates, skating, skated

to move over ice wearing skates on your feet, or to move over the ground with rollerskates on your feet

▸ **skater**

NOUN *plural* skaters

someone who skates or rides a skateboard

▸ **skating**

NOUN

1 the sport or pastime of moving over the surface of ice wearing skates
2 skateboarding

skateboard

NOUN *plural* skateboards

a long narrow board with wheels fitted to the bottom, for riding on in a standing or crouching position

▸ **skateboarder**

NOUN *plural* skateboarders

someone who rides a skateboard

▸ **skateboarding**

NOUN

riding on skateboards

skeleton

NOUN *plural* skeletons

the frame of bones inside your body that supports all your muscles and organs

skin

NOUN *plural* skins

1 the tissue that covers the outer surface of the bodies of humans and animals

2 the thin outer covering on fruit and some vegetables

3 a layer that forms on the top of some liquids

skip

VERB skips, skipping, skipped

1 to move forward springing or hopping from one foot to the other as you go

2 to jump over a rope in a game

3 to skip something is to leave it out and go on to the next thing

4 to skip school or lessons is to not attend them

NOUN *plural* skips

a skipping movement ⟩*Off the rabbit went, with a hop, skip and a jump.* ⟨

skirt

NOUN *plural* skirts

a piece of clothing that hangs from the waist

sky

NOUN *plural* skies

the area of space above the Earth where you can see the sun, moon, stars and clouds

> **Sky** is a word from the Old Norse language, which was used long ago in countries such as Norway and Denmark. It means *cloud*.

sleep

NOUN *plural* sleeps

1 sleep is rest that you have with your eyes closed and in a natural state of unconsciousness

2 a sleep is a period of time when you rest in this way

VERB sleeps, sleeping, slept

to rest with your eyes closed and in a state of unconsciousness

▸ **sleepy**

ADJECTIVE sleepier, sleepiest

feeling tired and wanting to sleep

sleet

NOUN

a mixture of rain and snow

sleeve

NOUN *plural* sleeves

the part of a piece of clothing that covers your arm or part of your arm

▸ **sleeveless**

ADJECTIVE

having no sleeves

slept

VERB

a way of changing the verb **sleep** to make a past tense. It can be used with or without a helping verb ⟩ *He slept for ten hours.* ⟨ ⟩ *He had slept all morning.* ⟨

slide

VERB slides, sliding, slid

to slip or move over a surface quickly and smoothly

NOUN *plural* slides

a piece of play equipment with a smooth sloping surface for children to slide down

slip

VERB slips, slipping, slipped

1 to slide accidentally and lose your balance

2 to slip in or out of a place, or to slip away, is to go in or out, or go away, quietly and without anyone noticing you

3 to slip something somewhere is to slide it there or put it there quickly

NOUN *plural* slips

1 an accidental slide

2 a small mistake

3 a small piece of paper ⟩ *Fill in the green slip and give it back to me.* ⟨

▸ **slipper**

NOUN *plural* slippers

a soft shoe for wearing indoors

▸ **slippery**

ADJECTIVE

smooth, wet or shiny and not easy to balance on or hold

slow

ADJECTIVE   slower, slowest

1 not fast or not moving quickly ⋗ *a slow march* ⋖   ⋗ *Our progress was slow.* ⋖
2 if a clock or watch is slow, it shows a time earlier than the correct time

VERB   slows, slowing, slowed

to slow, or to slow down, is to become slower or to make something slower

▸ **slowly**

ADVERB

in a slow way ⋗ *He walks very slowly.* ⋖

slug

NOUN   *plural* slugs

a creature with a long soft body like a snail, but with no shell

small

ADJECTIVE   smaller, smallest

1 little ⋗ *a small country* ⋖   ⋗ *This coat is too small for you.* ⋖   ⋗ *a small problem* ⋖
2 if something makes you feel small, it makes you feel silly and unimportant
3 a small voice is soft and difficult to hear

▸ **smallness**

NOUN

how small something is compared to other things

smart

ADJECTIVE   smarter, smartest

1 neat ⋗ *my smartest clothes* ⋖
2 clever and quick
3 fast ⋗ *a smart pace* ⋖

VERB   smarts, smarting, smarted

if a part of your body smarts, you feel a stinging pain there

▸ **smarten**

VERB   smartens, smartening, smartened

to smarten, or smarten up, is to make a person or place look neater ⋗ *Smarten up a bit before you go to school.* ⋖

▸ **smartly**

ADVERB

1 neatly and fashionably ⋗ *smartly dressed businessmen* ⋖
2 quickly or briskly ⋗ *You'll have to walk smartly if you want to catch the train.* ⋖

▸ **smartness**

NOUN

being smart

smash

VERB   smashes, smashing, smashed

1 to break, or break something into pieces ⋗ *He kicked the ball and it smashed the window.* ⋖   ⋗ *The vase fell off the table and smashed.* ⋖
2 to smash something, or smash into it, is to hit or crash into it with great force

NOUN   *plural* smashes

1 the sound of something breaking
2 a road accident in which two vehicles hit each other and are damaged

▸ **smashing**

ADJECTIVE

great or splendid ⋗ *a smashing film* ⋖

smell

NOUN   *plural* smells

1 smell is the power or sense of being aware of things through your nose
2 a smell is something you notice using this sense ⋗ *a strong smell of garlic* ⋖
3 a sniff at something ⋗ *Have a smell at this milk and tell me if you think it's off.* ⋖

VERB   smells, smelling, smelled *or* smelt

1 to smell something is to notice it through your nose
2 something that smells gives off a smell of some kind

a b c d e f g h i j k l m n o p q r s t u v w x y z

▸**smelly**

ADJECTIVE smellier, smelliest

giving off a strong or bad smell

smile

VERB smiles, smiling, smiled

to show pleasure or amusement by turning up the corners of your mouth

NOUN plural smiles

an expression of pleasure or amusement in which you turn up the corners of your mouth

smirk

VERB smirks, smirking, smirked

to smile in a cheeky or silly way

NOUN plural smirks

a cheeky or silly smile

smoke

NOUN

the cloud of gases and bits of soot given off by something that is burning

VERB smokes, smoking, smoked

1 something smokes when it gives off smoke
2 someone who smokes puts a lit cigarette, cigar or pipe in their mouth and breathes in the smoke

▸**smoker**

NOUN plural smokers

someone who smokes cigarettes, cigars or a pipe

▸**smoking**

NOUN

the habit of smoking cigarettes, cigars or a pipe

▸**smoky**

ADJECTIVE smokier, smokiest

filled with smoke

smooth

ADJECTIVE smoother, smoothest

1 something smooth has an even surface that is not rough or bumpy

2 a smooth substance has no lumps

VERB smoothes, smoothing, smoothed

to smooth something is to make it smooth or flat ▸***She smoothed the bed covers and tidied her bedroom.**￼*

▸**smoothly**

ADVERB

in a smooth way

▸**smoothness**

NOUN

being smooth

snack

NOUN plural snacks

a small meal, or something like a biscuit or piece of fruit eaten between meals

snail

NOUN plural snails

a small creature with a soft body and a shell on its back that it can draw its body into for protection

snake

NOUN plural snakes

a type of reptile with a long thin body and no legs, which moves along the ground with twisting movements

snap

VERB snaps, snapping, snapped

1 to break with a sudden sharp noise
2 something snaps shut when it closes with a sudden sharp noise
3 you snap your fingers when you rub your thumb and finger together in a quick movement, making a cracking noise

4 if someone snaps at you, they speak to you in a sharp angry way

5 an animal snaps when it makes a biting movement with its jaws

NOUN *plural* **snaps**

1 the sound of something breaking or of an animal bringing its teeth together quickly

2 a photograph ⟩ *holiday snaps* ⟨

sneak

NOUN *plural* **sneaks**

someone who tells tales or is deceitful

VERB **sneaks, sneaking, sneaked**

1 to go somewhere quietly and secretly

2 to tell tales to someone in authority such as a teacher

▶ **sneak up on someone**

to creep up behind someone, to surprise them or give them a fright

▶ **sneakily**

ADVERB

in a sneaky way

▶ **sneaky**

ADJECTIVE **sneakier, sneakiest**

deceitful or secretive

sneeze

VERB **sneezes, sneezing, sneezed**

to suddenly and uncontrollably blow out air from your nose and mouth

NOUN *plural* **sneezes**

this action and sound

snore

VERB **snores, snoring, snored**

to make a noise like a snort while you are sleeping, when you breathe in

snow

NOUN

water that has frozen into soft white pieces called flakes that falls from the sky
⟩ *The children loved playing in the snow.* ⟨
⟩ *Snow had blocked the road.* ⟨

VERB **snows, snowing, snowed**

when it snows, snow falls from the sky ⟩ *It's been snowing all night.* ⟨

snowman

NOUN *plural* **snowmen**

a figure of a person, made of snow

so

ADVERB

1 to such an extent or to a great extent ⟩ *I was so relieved to hear her voice.* ⟨ ⟩ *The box was so heavy he could not lift it.* ⟨ ⟩ *Thank you so much for all your help.* ⟨

2 you can use **so** when you are talking about something mentioned, or shown by a gesture ⟩ *a little boy about so high* ⟨ ⟩ *'Is Ann coming to the party?' 'I hope so.'* ⟨

3 also ⟩ *Jane's ten and so am I.* ⟨

4 in this way or that way ⟩ *Stretch your leg out so.* ⟨

▶ **so far**

up to now ⟩ *I've enjoyed his lessons so far.* ⟨

CONJUNCTION

therefore ⟩ *He asked me to come, so I did.* ⟨ ⟩ *So they got married and lived happily ever after.* ⟨

soap

NOUN *plural* **soaps**

a substance that you use to wash yourself and other things ⟩ *a bar of soap* ⟨

▶ **soapy**

ADJECTIVE **soapier, soapiest**

covered in or full of soap bubbles ⟩ *soapy water* ⟨

sob

VERB **sobs, sobbing, sobbed**

to cry noisily ⟩ *Lisa lay on her bed, sobbing.* ⟨

NOUN *plural* **sobs**

the sound of someone sobbing

a b c d e f g h i j k l m n o p q r s t u v w x y z

sock

NOUN *plural* **socks**

a covering for your foot that you wear inside your shoe ⇒ *a pair of socks*

▸ **pull your socks up**

to try harder to do something better than before ⇒ *You'll have to pull your socks up if you want to pass this exam.*

sofa

NOUN *plural* **sofas**

a long comfortable chair for two or three people

soft

ADJECTIVE softer, softest

1 not hard or firm ⇒ *a nice soft cushion* ⇒ *soft silky hair*
2 not strict or tough ⇒ *He's far too soft with his children.* ⇒ *Ben's too soft to get into a fight.*
3 not loud ⇒ *a soft voice*
4 not too bright ⇒ *Her bedroom is decorated in soft colours.*

▸ **soften**

VERB softens, softening, softened

1 to soften something is to make it become soft ⇒ *Soften the plasticine by working it with your hands.*
2 to soften is to become soft ⇒ *Her voice softened as she looked at the baby.*

▸ **softly**

ADVERB

gently or quietly ⇒ *Snow was falling softly in the moonlight.* ⇒ *She stroked the cat softly.*

▸ **softness**

NOUN

being soft, gentle, or quiet ⇒ *the softness of the pillows*

soil

NOUN

the top layer of the ground, which you can grow plants in ⇒ *sandy soil*

VERB soils, soiling, soiled

to soil something is to make it dirty ⇒ *soiled linen*

sold

VERB

a way of changing the verb **sell** to make a past tense. It can be used with or without a helping verb ⇒ *Tom sold me his old bike.* ⇒ *Have your parents sold their house yet?*

soldier

NOUN *plural* **soldiers**

someone who is in the army

sole[1]

ADJECTIVE

1 only ⇒ *Her sole ambition was to be famous.*
2 belonging to one person alone ⇒ *He has sole ownership of the company.*

sole[2]

NOUN *plural* **soles**

1 the bottom side of your foot
2 the bottom side of your shoe

sole[3]

NOUN *plural* **soles** *or* **sole**

a flat fish that people can eat

solid

ADJECTIVE

1 **science** with a fixed shape, not in the form of a liquid or a gas
2 not hollow ⇒ *a solid chocolate teddy*
3 firm and strong ⇒ *a solid piece of furniture*
4 **maths** a solid shape is flat and has length, height and width you can measure ⇒ *A cube is a solid figure.*
5 with no pauses in between ⇒ *I've been working for six solid hours.*

NOUN *plural* **solids**

1 **science** something that is not a liquid or a gas
2 **maths** a shape that has length, width, and height

some

ADJECTIVE

1 quite a large number or amount *> It's all right; I've got some money.*
2 a small number or amount *> There's some soup left.* *> Some people agreed but others didn't.*
3 certain *> You're like your father in some ways.*

PRONOUN

part of a number or amount *> I've made a cake – would you like some?*

somebody

PRONOUN

1 a person that you do not know or name *> Somebody pushed me.*
2 an important person *> He really thinks he's somebody in that big car.*

somehow

ADVERB

in some way *> Don't worry, we'll manage somehow.*

someone

PRONOUN

a person that you do not know or name *> Is there someone there?*

something

PRONOUN

1 a thing that is not known or stated *> Let's have something to eat before we go.*
2 a slight amount or degree *> There is something in what he says.*

sometimes

ADVERB

at times *> I still see him sometimes.*

somewhere

ADVERB

1 in or to some place *> They live somewhere near Oxford.*
2 used when you are not sure of an amount, time or number *> She must be somewhere between 35 and 40.*

son

NOUN   *plural* **sons**

someone's male child

song

NOUN   *plural* **songs**

1 a piece of music with words that you can sing *> a pop song*
2 the activity of singing *> A blackbird suddenly burst into song.*

soon

ADVERB   sooner, soonest

1 in a short time from now *> It will soon be Christmas.*
2 early *> It's too soon to tell whether she'll recover.*

▸ **as soon as**

when *> We ate as soon as they arrived.*

sore

ADJECTIVE   sorer, sorest

red and painful *> a sore finger*

NOUN   *plural* **sores**

a red, painful spot on your skin

▸ **soreness**

NOUN

being painful

sorry

ADJECTIVE   sorrier, sorriest

1 **sorry** is a word you use when you are apologizing or saying you regret something *> I'm sorry I upset you.*
2 if you are sorry for someone, you feel pity for them *> I felt so sorry for Lizzie when she failed her exam.*

INTERJECTION

you say 'sorry' when you are apologizing to someone *> Sorry, I didn't mean to shout.*

a b c d e f g h i j k l m n o p q r s t u v w x y z

sort

NOUN *plural* sorts

a type or kind of person or thing ⋛ *What sort of books do you read?*⋛ ⋛ *You meet all sorts of people at school.* ⋛

▶ **sort of**

slightly ⋛ *It was sort of strange, seeing dad at school.* ⋛

VERB sorts, sorting, sorted

▶ **sort something out**

1 if you sort out one type of thing from a group of things, you separate it from them ⋛ *Sort out the books that have to go back to the library.* ⋛
2 if you sort out a problem, you deal with it ⋛ *There are a lot of things to sort out before we go on holiday.* ⋛

sound

NOUN *plural* sounds

1 something that you can hear ⋛ *There isn't a sound coming from the children's bedroom.* ⋛ ⋛ *the sound of crying* ⋛
2 the way that something such as a description or piece of news seems from what you have heard ⋛ *I don't like the sound of your new teacher.* ⋛

VERB sounds, sounding, sounded

1 if something sounds good or bad, it seems that way from what you have heard about it ⋛ *Tom's holiday sounds wonderful.* ⋛
2 if something sounds like something else the two sounds are very similar ⋛ *That sounds like Zoe's voice in the kitchen.* ⋛

ADJECTIVE sounder, soundest

1 strong, firm, or healthy ⋛ *The walls of the old church were still sound.* ⋛ ⋛ *a sound heart* ⋛
2 a sound sleep is deep and difficult to wake up from

soup

NOUN *plural* soups

a liquid food made from meat, fish, or vegetables

south

NOUN

1 the direction on your right when you are facing towards the rising sun
2 the part of a country or the world that is in the south

ADJECTIVE

in, from, or towards the south ⋛ *the south coast* ⋛ ⋛ *the south wind* ⋛

ADVERB

to the south ⋛ *The river flows south into the sea.* ⋛

sow[1] rhymes with "**low**"

VERB sows, sowing, sowed, sown

to sow seeds is to scatter them on or in the ground so that they will grow

sow[2] rhymes with "**how**"

NOUN *plural* sows

a female pig

space

NOUN *plural* spaces

1 a gap or empty place ⋛ *a parking space* ⋛ ⋛ *Fill in the spaces on your answer sheet.* ⋛
2 the area available to use or do something ⋛ *Can you make space for one more person?*⋛
3 the empty area beyond the Earth's atmosphere, where the planets and stars are ⋛ *exploring space* ⋛

VERB spaces, spacing, spaced

if you space things or space them out, you leave gaps between them ⋛ *Try to space your work out neatly.* ⋛

spaceship

NOUN *plural* spaceships

a vehicle that can travel into space

spade

NOUN *plural* spades

1 a tool with a broad blade that you use for digging

2 spades is one of the four suits of playing cards, which have the symbol ♠ printed on them

spaghetti
NOUN

a type of pasta that is like long thin string ⋛ *Eve ordered a plate of spaghetti with tomato sauce.* ⋚

sparrow
NOUN   *plural* sparrows

a small brown bird

spat
VERB

a way of changing the verb **spit** to make a past tense. It can be used with or without a helping verb ⋛ *Jenny spat out the sweet.* ⋚ ⋛ *The man had spat on the ground.* ⋚

speak
VERB   speaks, speaking, spoke, spoken

1 to say something ⋛ *Could I speak to you for a moment?*⋚ ⋛ *She was so tired she could hardly speak.* ⋚
2 to be able to talk in a particular language ⋛ *Do you speak Greek?*⋚
3 to make a speech ⋛ *The headmaster spoke for almost an hour.* ⋚

▸ **speaker**
NOUN   *plural* speakers

1 someone who is speaking
2 a piece of equipment that increases the sound coming out of a radio, CD player or cassette player

special
ADJECTIVE

1 unusual and different from others ⋛ *my special friend* ⋚ ⋛ *I stayed up late because it was a special occasion.* ⋚
2 meant for or having a specific purpose ⋛ *Special trains will take fans to the match.* ⋚

speech
NOUN   *plural* speeches

1 speech is the ability to speak ⋛ *He seemed to have lost the power of speech.* ⋚
2 speech is the way that you speak ⋛ *Her speech was slurred.* ⋚
3 a speech is a talk that you give in front of a lot of people ⋛ *The bride's father usually makes a speech.* ⋚

▸ **speechless**
ADJECTIVE

if you are speechless, you cannot talk because you are so surprised or shocked ⋛ *His remarks left her speechless.* ⋚

speed
NOUN   *plural* speeds

1 the rate at which someone or something is moving ⋛ *He was driving at a speed of about 30 miles per hour.* ⋚
2 quickness ⋛ *Speed is important in this job.* ⋚

VERB   speeds, speeding, sped *or* speeded

1 to move quickly or hurry ⋛ *I'll speed through my homework, then watch TV.* ⋚
2 to drive faster than the law says you can ⋛ *Dad didn't think he was speeding until he saw the police car.* ⋚

▸ **speeding**
NOUN

driving faster than the law says you can

spell¹
VERB   spells, spelling, spelt *or* spelled

1 to say or write the letters of a word in the correct order ⋛ *Could you spell your name for me?*⋚
2 to make up a word ⋛ *C-A-T spells 'cat'.* ⋚

spell²
NOUN   *plural* spells

a short period of time ⋛ *The weather will be dull with sunny spells.* ⋚

spell³

NOUN *plural* **spells**

a set of words that are supposed to make something magic happen ⋛ *The wicked witch cast a spell on Snow White.* ⋛

spend

VERB spends, spending, spent

1 to use money to buy things ⋛ *Adam spends all his pocket money on sweets.* ⋛
2 to pass time ⋛ *I used to spend hours reading in my room.* ⋛

spent

VERB

a way of changing the verb **spend** to make a past tense. It can be used with or without a helping verb ⋛ *Mum spent weeks making that sweater.* ⋛ ⋛ *Have you spent your birthday money yet?* ⋛

spider

NOUN *plural* **spiders**

a small creature with eight legs that spins a web made of very fine threads

spin

VERB spins, spinning, spun

1 to turn round and round very quickly ⋛ *The ballerina spun around on her toes.* ⋛
2 to make long, thin threads out of cotton or wool by pulling it and twisting it

spine

NOUN *plural* **spines**

1 the line of bones down the back of a person or animal
2 a stiff spike that grows on animals, such as the hedgehog, or on plants ⋛ *the spines of a cactus* ⋛

spit

NOUN *plural* **spits**

the watery liquid inside your mouth

VERB spits, spitting, spat

if you spit, you push liquid or food out of your mouth ⋛ *She took one mouthful and then spat it out on to her plate.* ⋛

split

VERB splits, splitting, split

1 if something splits, it breaks or tears apart ⋛ *My skirt has split down the back.* ⋛
2 if you split something, you break it or tear it apart ⋛ *Lightning split the tree in two.* ⋛
3 to divide a group of people into smaller groups ⋛ *The teacher split us up into groups of six to do the experiment.* ⋛

NOUN *plural* **splits**

a crack, tear or break in something ⋛ *There's a long split in your sleeve.* ⋛

spoil

VERB spoils, spoiling, spoilt *or* spoiled

1 to spoil something is to damage or ruin it ⋛ *Tommy scribbled on my picture and spoilt it.* ⋛
2 if food spoils, it starts to go bad ⋛ *If you don't put it in the fridge, it will spoil.* ⋛
3 to spoil someone is to give them too much of what they want so that they do not appreciate it

spoke¹

NOUN *plural* **spokes**

one of the thin pieces that come out from the centre of the wheel to the edge

spoke²

VERB

a way of changing the verb **speak** to make a past tense ⋛ *He spoke so fast that I couldn't understand him.* ⋛

▸ **spoken**

VERB

a form of the verb **speak** that is used with

a helping verb to show that something happened in the past ⇒ *I've spoken to your teacher, and everything's fine.*

sponge

NOUN *plural* sponges

1 a soft object, made from natural or artificial material, that you use to wash your body
2 a light cake or pudding ⇒ *a sponge pudding*

▸ **spongy**

ADJECTIVE spongier, spongiest

feeling soft like a sponge ⇒ *spongy grass*

spoon

NOUN *plural* spoons

an object with a thin handle and a shallow bowl at one end that you use for eating food

▸ **spoonful**

NOUN *plural* spoonfuls

the amount a spoon will hold

sport

NOUN *plural* sports

1 sport is games and physical activities like football, tennis and swimming ⇒ *Adam loves all kinds of sport.*
2 a sport is a particular game or activity ⇒ *Alex particularly enjoys winter sports.*
3 a kind and helpful person ⇒ *Max will give us a hand – he's a good sport.*

spot

NOUN *plural* spots

1 a small mark or stain on something
2 a round shape that is part of a pattern ⇒ *a pink dress with white spots*
3 a red raised mark on your skin ⇒ *Teenagers often suffer from spots.*
4 a place ⇒ *a lovely spot for a picnic*

VERB spots, spotting, spotted

to notice something or someone ⇒ *I suddenly spotted Ian over by the window.*

▸ **spotless**

ADJECTIVE

totally clean ⇒ *The room was spotless.*

sprain

VERB sprains, spraining, sprained

to sprain a joint, such as your ankle or wrist, is to twist it and hurt yourself ⇒ *a sprained ankle*

NOUN *plural* sprains

a painful injury when you twist a joint such as your ankle or wrist ⇒ *Her wrist isn't broken; it's just a bad strain.*

sprang

VERB

a way of changing the verb **spring** to make a past tense ⇒ *The cat sprang on to the mouse.*

spread

VERB spreads, spreading, spread

1 to put a layer of something onto a surface ⇒ *She spread her toast thickly with butter.*
2 to spread something or to spread something out is to open something out flat or to make it cover a surface ⇒ *Spread the map out so that we can see it.*
3 if news spreads, it becomes known by a lot of different people ⇒ *Rumours spread very quickly in this little village.*
4 to spread things or spread things out is to space them over a period of time so they do not all happen at once ⇒ *The exams were spread out over two whole weeks.*

spring

VERB springs, springing, sprang, sprung

1 to jump quickly, usually up ⇒ *He springs out of bed in the morning.*
2 to develop from something else ⇒ *His confidence springs from his background.*

NOUN *plural* springs

1 a coil of wire ⇒ *a chair with a broken spring*

a b c d e f g h i j k l m n o p q r s t u v w x y z

2 the season of the year between winter and summer when plants start to grow ⋛ *the first day of spring* ⋚

3 a jump or quick movement

4 a small stream that flows up out of the ground ⋛ *a mountain spring* ⋚

spun

VERB

a way of changing the verb **spin** to make a past tense. It can be used with or without a helping verb ⋛ *When the door opened he spun around.* ⋚ ⋛ *They had spun the finest thread possible.* ⋚

spy

NOUN *plural* **spies**

someone who is employed by the government of their country to find out information secretly about another country

VERB spies, spying, spied

1 to spy is to work as a spy

2 to spy someone or something is to see or notice them ⋛ *I spy, with my little eye, something beginning with S.* ⋚

square

NOUN *plural* **squares**

1 a flat shape with four equal sides and four right angles

2 an open space with buildings on all four sides ⋛ *Trafalgar Square* ⋚

3 **maths** the square of a number is the number you get when you multiply the number by itself, for example the square of 3 is 3 × 3, which is 9. Look up and compare **cube**

ADJECTIVE

1 shaped like a square ⋛ *a square seat* ⋚

2 measuring a particular amount on each side ⋛ *The room was about 3 metres square.* ⋚

3 **maths** a square number is a number that has been multiplied by itself, for example 3 × 3, which is written as 3^2

VERB squares, squaring, squared

maths to square a number is to multiply it by itself ⋛ *Four squared is sixteen.* ⋚

squash

VERB squashes, squashing, squashed

to press, squeeze or crush someone or something ⋛ *We were all squashed into the back of the car.* ⋚

NOUN *plural* **squashes**

1 a squash is a situation when people or things are squashed ⋛ *It was a bit of squash fitting everyone in his car.* ⋚

2 a sweet drink with a fruit flavour ⋛ *an orange squash* ⋚

3 squash is a game in which you hit a small rubber ball against the walls of a court with a racket

▸ **squashy**

ADJECTIVE squashier, squashiest

soft and easy to squash

squeak

VERB squeaks, squeaking, squeaked

to make a small, high-pitched sound ⋛ *That door squeaks when you open it.* ⋚

NOUN *plural* **squeaks**

a small, high-pitched sound

▸ **squeaky**

ADJECTIVE squeakier, squeakiest

making a noise like a squeak ⋛ *a squeaky floorboard* ⋚

stable

ADJECTIVE

1 firm and steady ⋛ *This bracket will help to keep the shelf stable.* ⋚

2 a stable person is sensible and calm

NOUN *plural* **stables**

1 a building to keep a horse in

2 a place where you can learn to ride a horse ⋛ *a riding stables* ⋚

staff

NOUN *plural* staffs

1 the people who work in a particular place ⋮ *The company has a staff of 150.* ⋮
2 a stick ⋮ *a wooden staff* ⋮

stage

NOUN *plural* stages

1 the raised platform in a theatre where the actors perform
2 a step in a process or series of developments ⋮ *The work is still in its early stages.* ⋮

VERB stages, staging, staged

to put a play or other performance on in a theatre ⋮ *an opera staged in Verona* ⋮

stain

VERB stains, staining, stained

1 to leave a permanent coloured mark on something ⋮ *The coffee you spilt has stained the carpet.* ⋮
2 to dye wood a different colour

NOUN *plural* stains

a dirty mark that is hard to remove from something ⋮ *overalls covered in oil stains* ⋮

stair *or* stairs

NOUN *plural* stairs

1 a set of steps that lead to another level in a building ⋮ *A flight of stairs led down to the cellar.* ⋮
2 one of these steps

staircase

NOUN *plural* staircases

a set of stairs ⋮ *a marble staircase* ⋮

stale

ADJECTIVE staler, stalest

not fresh but dry, tasteless and unpleasant ⋮ *stale bread*   ⋮ *The air smelt stale.* ⋮

stamp

VERB stamps, stamping, stamped

1 to bring your foot down firmly on the ground ⋮ *She stamped her feet to keep them warm.* ⋮
2 to stick a stamp on a letter
3 to print letters, numbers or a design on something ⋮ *Each letter is stamped with the date we receive it.* ⋮

NOUN *plural* stamps

1 a small printed label put on a letter or parcel to show that you have paid for it to be sent by post ⋮ *first-class stamps* ⋮
2 the movement or sound of a foot being brought down hard on the ground
3 an object that you put into ink and press onto a surface to print words, numbers, or a design ⋮ *a date stamp* ⋮
4 a design or mark that you make with this object ⋮ *a manufacturer's stamp* ⋮

stand

VERB stands, standing, stood

1 to be upright on your feet, not sitting or lying ⋮ *The horse was standing on three legs.* ⋮ *I was too tired to stand.* ⋮
2 to get up onto your feet ⋮ *Stand up and let me look at you.* ⋮
3 to be or stay in a particular position or way ⋮ *The train stood at the platform.* ⋮ *Durham stands on the River Wear.* ⋮
4 to bear ⋮ *I can't stand her brother, Mark.* ⋮

▶ **stand in for someone**
to do someone else's job for a short time ⋮ *Emma will stand in for Mrs Harris while she is on holiday.* ⋮

▶ **stand up to someone**
to fight back when someone attacks you or says horrible things to you ⋮ *You've got to learn to stand up to bullies.* ⋮

NOUN *plural* stands

1 something that an object stands on ⋮ *a television stand* ⋮
2 rows of seats where people sit to watch a game or event ⋮ *Spectators were cheering from the stands.* ⋮

stank

VERB

a way of changing the verb **stink** to make a

a b c d e f g h i j k l m n o p q r **s** t u v w x y z

past tense ⟫ *The room stank of wet dog.* ⟪

star

NOUN *plural* stars

1 a mass of burning gas in the sky that you can see at night as a point of light
2 a shape with five or six points
3 a famous actor, singer, or performer ⟫ *a film star* ⟪ ⟫ *a pop star* ⟪

VERB stars, starring, starred

1 if an actor stars in something, they play one of the main parts in it ⟫ *Tom Cruise is to star in the sequel.* ⟪
2 if a film or play stars someone, they have one of the main parts in it ⟫ *the new film starring Kate Winslet* ⟪

stare

VERB stares, staring, stared

to look at someone or something for a long time ⟫ *Gemma spends her days staring out of the window.* ⟪

NOUN *plural* stares

a long look at someone or something

start

VERB starts, starting, started

1 to begin ⟫ *Suddenly, a bird started to sing.* ⟪ ⟫ *What time did you start working this morning?* ⟪ ⟫ *Children may start school when they are four.* ⟪
2 to start a machine is to make it begin to work ⟫ *Start the car and drive off.* ⟪
3 to jump because you are surprised ⟫ *The thunder made me start.* ⟪

NOUN *plural* starts

1 the beginning ⟫ *I liked him from the start.* ⟪ ⟫ *the start of the race* ⟪
2 a sudden movement or shock ⟫ *Her news gave me quite a start.* ⟪

starve

VERB starves, starving, starved

to die or suffer because you have not got enough to eat

▸ starving

ADJECTIVE

informal very hungry

station

NOUN *plural* stations

1 a building where trains, buses or coaches stop to let people get on or off
2 a place where police officers, fire officers or ambulance drivers work ⟫ *The police station is at the top of the High Street.* ⟪
3 a radio or television station is a company that makes or broadcasts programmes

statue

NOUN *plural* statues

a figure of a person or animal carved out of stone, metal or wood ⟫ *a statue of Napoleon* ⟪

stay

VERB stays, staying, stayed

1 to remain in a place ⟫ *I stayed in Padua for three years.* ⟪ ⟫ *Would you like to stay for dinner?* ⟪
2 to continue to be in a particular state ⟫ *She tried to stay calm as they waited.* ⟪

NOUN *plural* stays

time spent in a place ⟫ *The trip includes an overnight stay in Bangkok.* ⟪

steal

VERB steals, stealing, stole, stolen

1 to take something without the owner's permission ⟫ *The thieves stole money and jewellery.* ⟪ ⟫ *It's wrong to steal.* ⟪
2 to move quietly ⟫ *The fox stole away.* ⟪

steam

NOUN

1 the clouds of tiny drops of liquid that rise from boiling water
2 power produced by steam ⟫ *Diesel fuel has replaced steam on the railways.* ⟪

VERB steams, steaming, steamed

1 to give off steam ⇒ *A kettle was steaming on the stove.*
2 to steam food is to cook it by steam ⇒ *steamed vegetables*

stem

NOUN plural stems

1 the part of a plant from which the leaves and flowers grow
2 the narrow part of various objects, for example of a wine glass

step

NOUN plural steps

1 the action of lifting your foot off the ground and putting in down again in walking, running or dancing ⇒ *He took a step back.*
2 the sound made by someone's foot coming down on the ground when they walk etc ⇒ *I'm sure I heard steps outside.*
3 a particular movement of the feet, for example in dancing ⇒ *Try to learn these simple steps.*
4 the flat part of a stair that you put your foot on when going up or down ⇒ *The postman left the parcel on the front step.*

VERB steps, stepping, stepped

1 to take a step ⇒ *He opened the door and stepped out.*
2 to walk ⇒ *Please step this way.*

stew

VERB stews, stewing, stewed

to stew something is to cook it by boiling it slowly ⇒ *First she stewed the apples to make the tart.*

NOUN plural stews

a mixture of vegetables, or meat and vegetables, cooked slowly together in liquid in a pan ⇒ *beef stew and dumplings*

stick¹

NOUN plural sticks

1 a branch or twig from a tree ⇒ *We searched for sticks to make a fire.*

2 a long thin piece of wood shaped for a special purpose ⇒ *a walking stick* ⇒ *a hockey stick* ⇒ *a drumstick*
3 a long piece of something ⇒ *a stick of rhubarb* ⇒ *a stick of rock*

stick²

VERB sticks, sticking, stuck

1 to stick something in or into something is to push it in ⇒ *Stop sticking your elbows into me!* ⇒ *Stick the knife in your belt.*
2 to stick something is to fix it with something like glue ⇒ *Never mind, we can always stick the pieces back together.*
3 to stick is to become fixed and unable to move ⇒ *The car stuck in the mud.*
4 to stick to something is to become attached firmly to it ⇒ *These seeds stick to your clothes.*

sticky

ADJECTIVE stickier, stickiest

1 designed or likely to stick to something else ⇒ *Mend the book with some sticky tape.* ⇒ *sticky fingers*
2 difficult ⇒ *a sticky situation*

still

ADJECTIVE stiller, stillest

1 without movement or noise ⇒ *Keep still while I brush your hair!* ⇒ *The city seems very still in the early morning.*
2 not fizzy ⇒ *still lemonade*

ADVERB

1 up to the present time or the time mentioned ⇒ *Are you still working for the same company?* ⇒ *By Sunday she still hadn't replied to the invitation.*
2 even so, nevertheless ⇒ *It's difficult but we must still try.*
3 even ⇒ *Still more people were arriving.*

▶ **stillness**

NOUN

being still ⇒ *the stillness of early morning*

a b c d e f g h i j k l m n o p q r s t u v w x y z

sting

NOUN *plural* **stings**

1 the part of some animals and plants, such as the wasp or nettle, which can prick the skin and cause pain or irritation ⇒ *Bees usually leave their stings in the wound.*
2 the wound or pain caused by a sting

VERB **stings, stinging, stung**

1 if an insect or plant stings you, they prick your skin and put poison into the wound ⇒ *The child was badly stung by nettles.* ⇒ *Do these insects sting?*
2 if something stings, it is painful ⇒ *The salt water made his eyes sting.*

stink

NOUN *plural* **stinks**

a bad smell ⇒ *the stink of rotting fish*

VERB **stinks, stinking, stank** *or* **stunk, stunk**

to have a bad smell ⇒ *The house stinks.*

stir

VERB **stirs, stirring, stirred**

1 to stir something is to mix it with a circular movement ⇒ *He put sugar in his tea and stirred it.*
2 to stir is to move ⇒ *The baby stirred in its sleep.* ⇒ *The breeze stirred her hair.*

NOUN *plural* **stirs**

1 an act of stirring ⇒ *Now give the paint a stir.*
2 a fuss ⇒ *Their arrival caused quite a stir.*

stole

VERB

a way of changing the verb **steal** to make a past tense ⇒ *How can you be sure that she stole the money?*

stomach

NOUN *plural* **stomachs**

the bag-like part inside the body where food goes when it is swallowed, and where it is digested

stone

NOUN *plural* **stones** *or* **stone**

1 stone is the hard material that rocks are made of ⇒ *a house built of stone*
2 a stone is a piece of this ⇒ *The boys were throwing stones into the water.*
3 a piece of this shaped for a special purpose, for example a tombstone or paving stones
4 a gem or jewel ⇒ *diamonds, rubies and other stones*
5 the hard shell around the seed in some fruits, for example peaches and cherries
6 a measure of weight equal to 6.35 kilograms ⇒ *My dad weighs twelve stone.*

VERB **stones, stoning, stoned**

to stone someone is to throw stones at them

ADJECTIVE

made of stone ⇒ *stone tools*

▸ **stony**

ADJECTIVE **stonier, stoniest**

1 hard like stone
2 full of, or covered with, stones ⇒ *a stony beach*

> The plural of **stone** is **stones**, except when it means a measure of weight. Then you use the plural **stone**.

stood

VERB

a way of changing the verb **stand** to make a past tense. It can be used with or without a helping verb ⇒ *She stood quietly in the corner.* ⇒ *He had stood there all day.*

stool

NOUN *plural* **stools**

a seat without a back

stop

VERB **stops, stopping, stopped**

1 to stop is to come to a halt or come to an end ⇒ *The car stopped in front of our house.* ⇒ *The rain stopped.*

2 to stop something is to bring it to a halt or bring it to an end ⇒ *Stop the car now!* ⇒ *Please stop this nonsense.*

3 to stop doing something is to finish doing it or not do it any longer ⇒ *We stopped talking and listened.*

4 to stop someone doing something is to prevent them from doing it ⇒ *Can't you stop her working so hard?*

NOUN *plural* **stops**

1 the act of stopping ⇒ *We made two stops on our journey.*

2 a place where something, such as a bus, stops

▸ **stopper**

NOUN *plural* **stoppers**

something, such as a cork, that is put into the neck of a bottle or jar to close it

store

NOUN *plural* **stores**

1 a supply of goods from which things are taken as they are needed ⇒ *Squirrels keep a store of food.*

2 a place where things are kept ⇒ *a store for books*

3 a shop ⇒ *the village store*

VERB **stores, storing, stored**

to store something is to keep it somewhere for use in the future ⇒ *Store the wine in a cool dry place.*

storm

NOUN *plural* **storms**

a sudden burst of bad weather with strong winds, rain or snow, and sometimes thunder and lightning

VERB **storms, storming, stormed**

1 to storm is to shout or move in an angry way ⇒ *She stormed out of the room.* ⇒ *'How dare you!' he stormed.*

2 to storm a place is to attack it suddenly and violently in order to capture it ⇒ *Troops stormed the embassy.*

▸ **stormy**

ADJECTIVE **stormier, stormiest**

1 stormy weather is weather with strong winds, rain or snow, and sometimes thunder and lightning

2 full of anger ⇒ *a stormy meeting*

story

NOUN *plural* **stories**

a description of an event or events, which can be real or invented

straight

ADJECTIVE **straighter, straightest**

1 not bent, curved or curly ⇒ *a straight line* ⇒ *straight hair*

2 honest ⇒ *Give me a straight answer!*

3 in the proper position, not crooked ⇒ *That picture isn't straight.*

4 tidy, sorted out ⇒ *I'll never get this room straight* ⇒ *Get the facts straight!*

5 not smiling or laughing ⇒ *You should keep a straight face when you tell a joke.*

ADVERB

1 in a straight line, without changing direction ⇒ *Turn right, then go straight on.*

2 at once, without any delay ⇒ *I came straight here.*

▸ **straight away**

immediately ⇒ *Could you sign this for me straight away?*

▸ **straighten**

VERB **straightens, straightening, straightened**

to become or make something straight ⇒ *The road curved then straightened.*

strange

ADJECTIVE **stranger, strangest**

1 unusual or odd ⇒ *a strange noise coming from the engine*

2 not familiar, not known or seen before ⇒ *a strange land*

▸ **strangely**

ADVERB

in a strange way ⟫ *Mum looked at me strangely.* ⟪

▸ **strangeness**

NOUN

being strange ⟫ *the strangeness of the situation* ⟪

▸ **stranger**

NOUN *plural* strangers

1 a person you do not know
2 a person who is in a place they do not know

straw

NOUN *plural* straws

1 straw is dried stalks of grain ⟫ *The cows need fresh straw.* ⟪
2 a straw is a thin tube, usually made of plastic, for sucking up a drink

strawberry

NOUN *plural* strawberries

a soft red fruit with many tiny seeds on its skin

stream

NOUN *plural* streams

1 a small river ⟫ *He managed to jump across the stream.* ⟪
2 a flow of something ⟫ *streams of people* ⟪ ⟫ *a stream of traffic* ⟪

▸ **streamer**

NOUN *plural* streamers

a long narrow strip of paper or ribbon, used as a decoration

street

NOUN *plural* streets

a road with buildings, such as houses and shops, on one or both sides ⟫ *I live at 32 Montgomery Street.* ⟪

strength

NOUN *plural* strengths

1 strength is being strong ⟫ *He didn't have the strength to lift the box.* ⟪

2 a person's strengths are the good things about them ⟫ *Her greatest strength is her sense of humour.* ⟪

▸ **strengthen**

VERB strengthens, strengthening, strengthened

1 to strengthen something is to make it strong or stronger ⟫ *He did exercises to strengthen his muscles.* ⟪
2 to strengthen is to become strong or stronger ⟫ *The wind strengthened.* ⟪

stretch

VERB stretches, stretching, stretched

1 to stretch something is to make it longer or wider, especially by pulling ⟫ *Stretch this rope between the two posts.* ⟪
2 to stretch is to become longer or wider ⟫ *This material stretches.* ⟪
3 to stretch from one place to another is to cover the distance between them ⟫ *The mountains stretch from the north to the south of the country.* ⟪

NOUN *plural* stretches

1 the action of stretching ⟫ *I always have a good stretch when I get out of bed.* ⟪
2 a length in distance or time ⟫ *a stretch of road* ⟪ ⟫ *a three-year stretch* ⟪

▸ **stretchy**

ADJECTIVE stretchier, stretchiest

able to stretch easily ⟫ *jeans made of stretchy denim* ⟪

string

NOUN *plural* strings

1 thick thread used for tying things ⟫ *a ball of string* ⟪
2 the strings of a musical instrument, such as a guitar, are the pieces of wire or other material that are stretched across it
3 a string of things is a number of things coming one after the other ⟫ *a string of disasters* ⟪

VERB strings, stringing, strung

1 to string something is to tie it and hang it

with string ⋽ *Coloured lights were strung across the ceiling.* ⋽

2 to string something such as beads is to put them on a string ⋽ *She took the pearls to a jeweller to be strung.* ⋽

▸ **stringy**
ADJECTIVE   stringier, stringiest
something that is stringy is long and thin and looks like string ⋽ *stringy hair* ⋽

strip¹
NOUN   *plural* strips
1 a long narrow piece ⋽ *a strip of paper* ⋽
2 an outfit worn by a sports team

strip²
VERB   strips, stripping, stripped
1 to strip something is to take the covering off it ⋽ *I asked you to strip your bed.* ⋽
2 to strip is to undress ⋽ *He stripped and dived into the water.* ⋽

stripe
NOUN   *plural* stripes
a band of colour ⋽ *a blue suit with thin white stripes* ⋽

▸ **striped**
ADJECTIVE
having stripes ⋽ *striped wallpaper* ⋽

▸ **stripy**
ADJECTIVE   stripier, stripiest
having stripes ⋽ *a stripy T-shirt* ⋽

strong
ADJECTIVE   stronger, strongest
1 powerful, not weak ⋽ *a strong young man* ⋽ ⋽ *a strong wind* ⋽
2 not easily worn away or broken ⋽ *strong cloth* ⋽   ⋽ *fastened with a strong chain* ⋽

▸ **strongly**
ADVERB
1 in a strong way ⋽ *The boxer fought back strongly at the end of the fight.* ⋽
2 very much ⋽ *I strongly recommend that you follow the instructions.* ⋽

stuck
VERB
a way of changing the verb **stick** to make a past tense. It can be used with or without a helping verb ⋽ *He stuck the stamp on the envelope.* ⋽   ⋽ *I've stuck the broken vase together again.* ⋽

study
VERB   studies, studying, studied
1 to study is to spend time learning about a subject ⋽ *I'm studying French language.* ⋽ ⋽ *She's studying to be a teacher.* ⋽
2 to study something is to look at it carefully ⋽ *He studied the railway timetable.* ⋽

NOUN   *plural* studies
1 study is reading and learning about something ⋽ *the study of history* ⋽
2 a room used for studying or quiet work

stuff
NOUN
1 a substance or material of any kind ⋽ *What's that black oily stuff all over the beach?* ⋽
2 things or objects ⋽ *There's far too much stuff in this cupboard.* ⋽

VERB   stuffs, stuffing, stuffed
1 to stuff something is to pack it or fill it tightly ⋽ *We need to stuff the turkey before we cook it.* ⋽
2 to stuff something into a place is to push it in carelessly ⋽ *He stuffed the papers into his pocket.* ⋽

▸ **stuffing**
NOUN   *plural* stuffings
1 material used for stuffing things such as cushions or soft toys
2 a savoury mixture used to stuff meat such as turkeys and chickens before cooking ⋽ *sage and onion stuffing* ⋽

stung

VERB

a way of changing the verb **sting** to make a past tense. It can be used with or without a helping verb ⇒ *The wasp stung him on the finger.* ⇒ *Ouch! It's stung me.*

stunk

VERB

a way of changing the verb **stink** to make a past tense. It can be used with or without a helping verb ⇒ *The room stunk of cigar smoke.* ⇒ *If the dead mouse hadn't stunk so much, I'd never have found it.*

stupid

ADJECTIVE stupider, stupidest

not clever, slow at understanding ⇒ *a stupid mistake* ⇒ *You stupid boy!*

▸ **stupidity**

NOUN

being stupid ⇒ *His stupidity cost us first prize.*

▸ **stupidly**

ADVERB

in a stupid way ⇒ *Stupidly, I agreed to go.*

subject said "sub-jikt"

NOUN plural subjects

1 something that you learn about, for example science or art
2 the subject of a story or conversation is the person or thing that it is about ⇒ *Can we change the subject please?*
3 **grammar** the subject of a sentence is the word or words that stand for the person or thing doing the action of the verb, for example *He* in *He hit me*

subtract

VERB subtracts, subtracting, subtracted

maths to take one number away from another ⇒ *If you subtract 4 from 6, you get 2.*

▸ **subtraction**

NOUN plural subtractions

maths the act of taking one number away from another

sudden

ADJECTIVE

happening quickly without being expected ⇒ *a sudden attack*

▸ **suddenly**

ADVERB

quickly and unexpectedly ⇒ *He suddenly woke up.*

▸ **suddenness**

NOUN

being sudden ⇒ *We were shocked by the suddenness of the events.*

sugar

NOUN

1 a sweet substance that is obtained from the plants sugar cane and sugar beet
2 grains of sugar that you add to food and drink to make them taste sweeter ⇒ *Do you take sugar in your coffee?*

▸ **sugary**

ADJECTIVE

very sweet ⇒ *a cup of hot, sugary tea*

suit

NOUN plural suits

1 a set of clothes, for example a jacket and trousers, made to be worn together ⇒ *Our teacher always wears a suit and tie.*
2 a piece of clothing worn for a particular activity ⇒ *a bathing suit*
3 one of the four sets (spades, hearts, diamonds, clubs) of playing cards

VERB suits, suiting, suited

1 something such as a colour, hairstyle or piece of clothing suits you when it makes you look nice ⇒ *Blue really suits her.*
2 something suits you when you are happy to agree to it ⇒ *Would it suit you if I called round this evening?*

suitable

ADJECTIVE

something is suitable when it is right for a purpose or occasion ⇒ *Those shoes aren't suitable for walking in the country.* ⇒ *a suitable time for our meeting*

sum

NOUN *plural* sums

1 the total made by two or more things or numbers added together ⇒ *The sum of 2, 3 and 4 is 9.*
2 a problem in arithmetic ⇒ *I'm better at sums than my mum.*
3 an amount of money ⇒ *It will cost a huge sum to repair the roof.*

summer

NOUN *plural* summers

the warmest season of the year, between spring and autumn

sun

NOUN *plural* suns

1 the star in the sky that you see as a huge white disc, and which gives light and heat to the Earth ⇒ *The Earth goes round the sun.*
2 sunshine ⇒ *We sat in the sun.*

Sunday

NOUN *plural* Sundays

the day of the week after Saturday and before Monday ⇒ *My parents always go to church on Sundays.*

> **Sunday** comes from the Old English word **Sunnandæg**, which means *day of the sun.*

sunflower

NOUN *plural* sunflowers

a tall yellow flower whose seeds provide oil

sung

VERB

the form of the verb **sing** that is used with a helping verb to tell you that something happened in the past ⇒ *I've sung that song all day.*

sunk

VERB

the form of the verb **sink** that is used with a helping verb to tell you that something happened in the past ⇒ *The ship had sunk in minutes.*

▸ **sunken**

ADJECTIVE

1 under water ⇒ *sunken treasure*
2 lower than the surrounding area ⇒ *a sunken bath*

sunny

ADJECTIVE sunnier, sunniest

1 full of sunshine ⇒ *It's a lovely sunny day.*
2 cheerful ⇒ *her sunny nature*

sunset

NOUN *plural* sunsets

the setting of the sun in the evening, or the time of this ⇒ *a beautiful sunset* ⇒ *The baby was in bed by sunset.*

sunshine

NOUN

the light and heat of the sun ⇒ *The cat was enjoying the warm sunshine.*

super

ADJECTIVE

extremely good or excellent ⇒ *We had a super time at the funfair.*

superb

ADJECTIVE

magnificent or excellent ⇒ *a superb meal*

a b c d e f g h i j k l m n o p q r s t u v w x y z

supermarket

NOUN *plural* **supermarkets**

a large self-service shop that sells food and other goods

supper

NOUN *plural* **supper**

a meal that you eat in the evening

sure

ADJECTIVE

1 you are sure of something when you have no doubts about it ⫸ *I'm sure I gave him the book.* ⫷
2 certain to do or get something ⫸ *He's sure to win.* ⫷

surface

NOUN *plural* **surfaces**

the outside or top part of something ⫸ *This road has a very bumpy surface.* ⫷

surname

NOUN *plural* **surnames**

your last name or family name ⫸ *Smith is a common British surname.* ⫷

surprise

NOUN *plural* **surprises**

1 something sudden or unexpected ⫸ *Your letter was a nice surprise.* ⫷
2 the feeling caused by something sudden or unexpected

VERB surprises, surprising, surprised

to surprise someone is to cause them to feel surprise ⫸ *The news surprised me.* ⫷

surround

VERB surrounds, surrounding, surrounded

1 to surround someone or something is to be or come all round them ⫸ *Enemy troops surrounded the town.* ⫷
2 to surround something is to enclose it or put something round it ⫸ *He surrounded the castle with a high wall.* ⫷

▸ **surroundings**

PLURAL NOUN

the area around a person or place ⫸ *The hotel is set in beautiful surroundings.* ⫷

swallow¹

VERB swallows, swallowing, swallowed

to swallow food or drink is to make it pass down your throat to your stomach ⫸ *Try to swallow the pill.* ⫷

swallow²

NOUN

a small bird with long pointed wings and a forked tail

swam

VERB

a way of changing the verb **swim** to make the past tense. ⫸ *Michael swam as far as he could before he got too tired.* ⫷

swan

NOUN *plural* **swans**

a large, usually white, water bird with a long neck

swap

VERB swaps, swapping, swapped

to exchange one thing for another ⫸ *She swapped her bike for a scooter.* ⫷

swear

VERB swears, swearing, swore, sworn

1 to promise ⫸ *I swear to tell the truth.* ⫷
2 to use words that are offensive or rude ⫸ *He swore under his breath.* ⫷

sweat

NOUN

the salty liquid that comes out of your skin when you are hot ⫸ *He was dripping with sweat after his run.* ⫷

VERB sweats, sweating, sweated

to give out sweat ⫸ *Exercise makes you sweat.* ⫷

▸ **sweaty**

ADJECTIVE sweatier, sweatiest

wet with sweat

sweatshirt

NOUN *plural* sweatshirts

a type of thick jersey

sweep

VERB sweeps, sweeping, swept

1 to sweep something is to clean it using a brush or broom ⋛ *He swept the floor.* ⋚
2 to sweep is to move quickly or forcefully ⋛ *The disease is sweeping through the country.* ⋚ ⋛ *She swept into my room without knocking.* ⋚
3 to sweep someone or something is to move them with a sweeping movement ⋛ *The wind nearly swept me off my feet.* ⋚ ⋛ *Cars were swept away by the flood.* ⋚

NOUN *plural* sweeps

1 the action of sweeping ⋛ *She gave the room a sweep.* ⋚
2 a sweeping movement ⋛ *He indicated the damage with a sweep of his hand.* ⋚
3 a person who cleans chimneys

sweet

ADJECTIVE sweeter, sweetest

1 tasting like sugar ⋛ *strong sweet tea* ⋚
2 pleasant ⋛ *the sweet smell of roses* ⋚ ⋛ *the sweet song of the nightingale* ⋚
3 attractive or nice ⋛ *a sweet baby* ⋚

NOUN *plural* sweets

1 a small piece of sweet food, for example chocolate or toffee ⋛ *a packet of sweets* ⋚
2 something sweet served at the end of a meal

▸ **sweeten**

VERB sweetens, sweetening, sweetened

to sweeten something is to make it sweet ⋛ *Sweeten the raspberries with sugar.* ⋚

▸ **sweetly**

ADVERB

in a sweet way ⋛ *She smiled sweetly.* ⋚

▸ **sweetness**

NOUN

being sweet

sweetcorn

NOUN

sweetcorn is the yellow grains of a cereal crop called maize, that are eaten as a vegetable

swept

VERB

a way of changing the verb **sweep** to make a past tense. It can be used with or without a helping verb ⋛ *He swept up the crumbs.* ⋚ ⋛ *She has swept the floor, just as you asked.* ⋚

swim

VERB swims, swimming, swam, swum

1 to swim is to move through water ⋛ *I learned to swim when I was five.* ⋚
2 to swim something is to cross it by swimming ⋛ *Her ambition is to swim the Channel.* ⋚

NOUN *plural* swims

an act of swimming ⋛ *Let's go for a swim.* ⋚

▸ **swimmer**

NOUN *plural* swimmers

someone or something that swims ⋛ *Penguins are excellent swimmers.* ⋚

swimsuit

NOUN *plural* swimsuits

a piece of clothing worn for swimming, usually by women and girls

swing

VERB swings, swinging, swung

1 to move from side to side, or forwards and backwards, from a fixed point ⋛ *You swing your arms when you walk.* ⋚ ⋛ *The children were swinging on a rope.* ⋚
2 to turn suddenly ⋛ *He swung round and stared at us.* ⋚

a b c d e f g h i j k l m n o p q r s t u v w x y z

NOUN *plural* swings

a seat for swinging, hung on ropes or chains from a support ⟩ *I like playing on the swings in the park.*

switch

NOUN *plural* switches

a device for turning power on and off ⟩ *I can't find the light-switch.*

VERB switches, switching, switched

to switch something on or off is to turn it on or off using a switch

swop

VERB swops, swopping, swopped

another spelling of **swap**

sword

NOUN *plural* swords

a weapon with a long blade

swore

VERB

a way of changing the verb **swear** to make a past tense ⟩ *She swore to tell the truth.*

sworn

VERB

the form of the verb **swear** that is used with a helping verb to show that something happened in the past ⟩ *He has sworn he will never tell anyone.*

ADJECTIVE

promised always to be something ⟩*They are sworn enemies.*

swum

VERB

a form of the verb **swim** that is used with a helping verb to show that something happened in the past ⟩ *She has swum out to those rocks over there.*

swung

VERB

a way of changing the verb **swing** to make a past tense. It can be used with or without a helping verb ⟩ *Tarzan swung through the trees.* ⟩ *Anna had swung the skipping rope as she had walked along.*

synagogue said "sin-a-gog"

NOUN *plural* synagogues

a place where Jewish people go to worship

system

NOUN *plural* systems

1 an arrangement of many parts that work together ⟩ *the railway system*
2 a way of organizing something ⟩ *a system of education*

T

table

NOUN *plural* **tables**

1 a piece of furniture with a flat top that is supported on legs
2 a list of sums and the answers, which you learn by heart ⋛ *the five times table* ⋛

tadpole

NOUN *plural* **tadpoles**

a young frog or toad with a rounded head and long tail. The tail eventually disappears as it develops legs

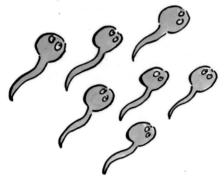

tail

NOUN *plural* **tails**

1 an animal's, bird's or fish's tail is the part of its body that sticks out from the end of its spine or at the end of its body
2 any part that sticks out, or hangs down, at the back of an object ⋛ *The aeroplane had a red symbol painted on its tail.* ⋛

take

VERB takes, taking, took, taken

1 you take something when you reach out and get it or get it for yourself ⋛ *Take my hand.* ⋛ ⋛ *Someone's taken my ruler.* ⋛
2 to take someone or something to a place is to bring them or it with you when you go there ⋛ *Take me to your leader.* ⋛ ⋛ *I took the parcel to the post office.* ⋛
3 you take one number from another when you subtract the first one from the second one ⋛ *If you take 5 from 16, you are left with 11.* ⋛
4 you take something when you eat it, drink it or swallow it ⋛ *You must take your medicine if you want to get better.* ⋛
5 to take something is to accept it ⋛ *Take my advice. Wear a warm jumper when you go out.* ⋛ ⋛ *He cannot take criticism.* ⋛
6 to take something such as a form of transport or a route is to use it ⋛ *We usually take the bus.* ⋛ ⋛ *Take the next left after the town hall.* ⋛
7 you take an exam or test when you do it
8 to take a photograph is to use a camera to record an image
9 something takes a certain length of time if it lasts for that length of time or you need that amount of time to do it ⋛ *The journey took hours and hours.* ⋛

▸ **take part**

to take part in some activity is to do it or become involved in it

tale

NOUN *plural* **tales**

a story ⋛ *tales of great adventures* ⋛

talent

NOUN *plural* **talents**

you have talent, or a talent, when you have special skill or natural ability to do something well

▸ **talented**

ADJECTIVE

having the skill or ability to do something well

talk

VERB talks, talking, talked

1 to say words out loud
2 to talk to someone is to have a conversation with them

NOUN plural talks

1 talk is speech or conversation
2 if someone gives a talk, they talk about some subject to an audience

▸ **talkative**

ADJECTIVE

a talkative person talks a lot

tall

ADJECTIVE taller, tallest

1 big, or bigger than average, in height ⋛ *He's tall for his age.* ⋚ ⋛ *a tall building* ⋚
2 how big someone or something is in height ⋛ *He's only three feet tall.* ⋚

Talmud

NOUN

a book of religious laws written by rabbis, used by members of the Jewish faith

tambourine

NOUN plural tambourines

an instrument made up of a circular frame with skin stretched tightly across it and small round pieces of metal set into the frame in pairs

tame

ADJECTIVE tamer, tamest

a tame animal is used to being with humans and is not dangerous

VERB tames, taming, tamed

to tame a wild animal is to train it so that it is used to living or working with humans

tangerine

NOUN plural tangerines

a type of small orange with skin that is loose and easy to peel

tank

NOUN plural tanks

1 a large container for holding liquids
2 a large heavy army vehicle covered with metal plates and with a long gun on the top

tap¹

NOUN plural taps

a device fitted to a water or gas pipe used to turn the water or gas on and off and control the flow

tap²

NOUN plural taps

a light quick knock

VERB taps, tapping, tapped

to knock lightly ⋛ *He tapped on the window to get my attention.* ⋚

target

NOUN plural targets

1 a mark or object that people aim at when they are shooting
2 something or someone being aimed at ⋛ *My savings target is £100.* ⋚

taste

NOUN plural tastes

1 taste is the sense by which you recognize different flavours or foods when you touch them with your tongue
2 something's taste is the particular flavour it has when it touches your tongue
3 to have a taste of something is to put a little bit of it in your mouth to find out what its flavour is like
4 your taste or tastes are the kinds of things you like

VERB tastes, tasting, tasted

1 you taste something when you put it in your mouth so that you can find out what sort of flavour it has ⋛ *Have you tasted this cheese?* ⋚
2 food tastes a certain way if it has that

flavour ⋗ *This sauce tastes salty.* ⋖

3 if you taste something, you experience it briefly ⋗ *They'd tasted victory for the first time and wanted more.* ⋖

▸ **tasty**

ADJECTIVE tastier, tastiest

having a good flavour

tea

NOUN *plural* teas

1 tea is a drink made by pouring boiling water on dried leaves that come from a small tree or shrub that grows in Asia
2 a cup of tea ⋗ *Two teas please.* ⋖
3 a light meal, with tea and sandwiches, that some people have between lunch and their evening meal
4 the name some people give to the meal that they have in the early evening

teach

VERB teaches, teaching, taught

1 to teach is to pass the knowledge and experience you have on to other people to help them learn new things ⋗ *Will you teach me how to sail a dinghy?* ⋖ ⋗ *He taught in the local school.* ⋖
2 to teach a particular subject is to give people lessons in that subject ⋗ *He teaches violin.* ⋖

▸ **teacher**

NOUN *plural* teachers

someone who teaches, usually as their job

▸ **teaching**

NOUN

the work of a teacher

team

NOUN *plural* teams

1 a side in a game ⋗ *the England cricket team* ⋖ ⋗ *Which football team do you support?* ⋖
2 a group of people working together ⋗ *a team of engineers* ⋖

The words **team** and **teem** sound the same but remember that they have different spellings. If something **teems**, there is a lot of it.

teapot

NOUN *plural* teapots

a pot with a spout and a handle, used for making and pouring tea

tear¹ said "tair"

VERB tears, tearing, torn

1 to tear something is to make a hole or split in it ⋗ *You've torn your sleeve.* ⋖
2 to tear something is to pull it using force ⋗ *The old buildings were torn down and new ones built in their place.* ⋖
3 to tear somewhere is to rush there

NOUN *plural* tears

a hole or split made in something

tear² said "teer"

NOUN *plural* tears

1 a drop of liquid that forms in, and drops from, your eyes when you cry
2 if someone is in tears, they are crying

▸ **tearful**

ADJECTIVE

crying or almost crying

tease

VERB teases, teasing, teased

1 to tease a person or animal is to annoy them or it on purpose ⋗ *Stop teasing the dog!* ⋖
2 to tease someone is to make fun of them or joke with them ⋗ *I didn't mean what I said. I was only teasing.* ⋖

teddy *or* teddy bear

NOUN *plural* teddies *or* teddy bears

a toy bear with soft fur

a b c d e f g h i j k l m n o p q r s **t** u v w x y z

teeth

NOUN

the plural of **tooth** ⋗ *He got fillings in two back teeth.* ⋖

telephone

NOUN   *plural* telephones

a device that allows you to speak to someone at a distance, using electrical wires or radio

VERB   telephones, telephoning, telephoned

to telephone someone is to contact them using the telephone

Telephone comes from the Greek words **tele**, which means *far*, and **phone**, which means *a sound*, so together they mean 'sound at a distance'. Another word in English beginning with **tele** is **television**.

television

NOUN   *plural* televisions

1 television is a system for sending images and sounds in the form of radio waves from a transmitter to a receiver, which changes the radio signals back into pictures and sounds
2 a television, or television set, is the equipment that receives these pictures and sounds

tell

VERB   tells, telling, told

1 to tell someone something is to give them information by speaking to them ⋗ *Why won't you tell me your name?* ⋖
2 to tell someone to do something is to order them to do it ⋗ *I told you to be quiet.* ⋖
3 you can tell what something is, or what is happening, if you know what it is, or understand what is happening ⋗ *I couldn't tell if it was a boat or a whale.* ⋖
4 to tell the truth or a lie is to give true or untrue information to someone
5 someone who tells gives away a secret

telly

NOUN   *plural* tellies

an informal word for **television**

temper

NOUN   *plural* tempers

a person's mood ⋗ *Don't ask him until he's in a better temper.* ⋖
▸ **lose your temper**
to get angry suddenly

temperature

NOUN   *plural* temperatures

1 something's temperature is how hot or cold it is
2 if someone has a temperature, their body is hotter than it should be, usually because they are ill

temple

NOUN   *plural* temples

a building in which the members of some religions worship

ten

NOUN   *plural* tens

the number 10

tend[1]

VERB   tends, tending, tended

to tend someone or something is to look after them ⋗ *doctors and nurses tending the sick and injured* ⋖

tend²
VERB   tends, tending, tended

something tends to happen when it is likely to happen, or often happens ⋟ *She tends to be a bit moody.* ⋞

▸ **tendency**
NOUN   *plural* tendencies

if someone or something has a tendency to do something, they are likely to act in that way

tennis
NOUN

a game played on a court that has a net stretched across the middle. Tennis is played by two or four players who use rackets to hit a ball to and fro across the net

tense¹
NOUN   *plural* tenses

a verb's tense is the form of the verb that shows whether the action of the verb happens here and now (the **present tense**: for example, *Today I am painting the wall*), in the past (the **past tense**: for example, *I painted the shed yesterday*), or in the future (the **future tense**: for example, *I will paint the garage tomorrow*)

tense²
ADJECTIVE   tenser, tensest

nervous and unable to relax

tent
NOUN   *plural* tents

a temporary shelter made of canvas or nylon supported by a frame

term
NOUN   *plural* terms

1 one of the periods of time that the school or college year is divided into ⋟ *the autumn term* ⋞

2 any limited period of time ⋟ *the president's term of office* ⋞

3 a word or expression with a particular meaning, or used in a particular subject area ⋟ *What is the term for someone who collects old coins?* ⋞   ⋟ *complicated medical terms* ⋞

terrible
ADJECTIVE

very bad ⋟ *a terrible smell* ⋞   ⋟ *a terrible shock* ⋞   ⋟ *Your writing is really terrible.* ⋞

▸ **terribly**
ADVERB

extremely ⋟ *I'm terribly sorry I am late.* ⋞

test
NOUN   *plural* tests

1 a set of questions or a short examination to find out your ability or knowledge ⋟ *a spelling test* ⋞

2 something done to find out whether something is in good condition or is working well ⋟ *medical tests* ⋞

VERB   tests, testing, tested

to test someone or something is to give them a short examination or to carry out tests on them

than
CONJUNCTION

than is used when you are making comparisons ⋟ *The test was easier than I thought it would be.* ⋞   ⋟ *He can run faster than his big brother.* ⋞

thank
VERB   thanks, thanking, thanked

you thank someone when you let them know you are grateful for something they have done for you or have given you

a b c d e f g h i j k l m n o p q r s **t** u v w x y z

▸**thank you**

you say 'thank you' to someone to tell them you are grateful for something they have done

▸**thankful**

ADJECTIVE

happy, relieved and grateful

▸**thanks**

PLURAL NOUN

you say 'thanks' to someone, or express your thanks to them, when you express your gratitude or appreciation

that

ADJECTIVE   those

the word **that** is used before a noun to refer to a person or thing that is some distance away from you, or that has already been mentioned ⧽ *Who is that girl over there?*⧼ ⧽ *Pass me that towel, please.* ⧼

PRONOUN   those

the word **that** is used instead of a noun to refer to a person or thing that is some distance away from you, or that has already been mentioned ⧽*I don't want to know that.* ⧼ ⧽ *Who is that at the door?*⧼ ⧽ *That's my friend, Gerry.* ⧼

ADVERB

to the extent or degree mentioned ⧽*I didn't think I'd run that far.* ⧼   ⧽*The film wasn't that bad.* ⧼

CONJUNCTION

that is used after verbs that have to do with saying, thinking or feeling, and to connect clauses ⧽*He said that he hated sports.* ⧼   ⧽*I'm afraid that I can't help.* ⧼

the

ADJECTIVE

the is used before nouns to refer to a particular person, thing or group ⧽ *The bus arrived late, as usual.* ⧼ ⧽ *Is it on the right or the left side of the road?*⧼ ⧽ *The men rode on horses and the women rode in carriages.* ⧼

theatre

NOUN   *plural* **theatres**

1 a theatre is a building where plays, operas or musicals are performed
2 a special room in a hospital where operations are done

their

ADJECTIVE

belonging to them ⧽ *They told me where their house was.* ⧼

▸**theirs**

PRONOUN

a word you use to talk about something belonging to a group of people or things that have already been mentioned ⧽ *They say it belongs to them but I know it's not theirs.* ⧼

> Be careful not to confuse the spellings of **their**, **there** and **they're**. **There** points something out: *Put this box over* there.
> • There *is nothing to do here.* **They're** is short for **they are**: They're *late.*

them

PRONOUN

a word you use to talk about two or more people or things that have already been mentioned ⧽ *The girls waved to me and I waved back to them.* ⧼ ⧽ *'Do you like your new boots?' 'Yes, I like them a lot'.* ⧼

themselves

PRONOUN

1 you use **themselves** after a verb or preposition when the people who perform the action are affected by it ⧽ *They'd made themselves a cosy little shelter.* ⧼
2 **themselves** is also used to show that a group of people do something without any help from other people ⧽ *They'll have to work it out for themselves.* ⧼
3 you can use **themselves** to show more clearly who you mean ⧽ *They themselves are innocent.* ⧼

then

ADVERB

1 at that time, in the past or future ⇾ *I didn't know you then.* ⇽ ⇾ *The rest of the kids should be here by then.* ⇽
2 after that time, or next ⇾ *I went for a swim and then I went home.* ⇽

CONJUNCTION

as a result, or in that case ⇾ *If you have been eating sweets, then you must brush your teeth.* ⇽

there

ADVERB

at, in, or to that place ⇾ *Don't stop there. I was just beginning to enjoy the story.* ⇽ ⇾ *My granny lives there.* ⇽ ⇾ *I'm going there tomorrow.* ⇽

PRONOUN

you use **there** with *is* or *are* to draw attention to what is going to follow ⇾ *There is a mouse somewhere in this house.* ⇽

> Be careful not to confuse the spellings of **there**, **their** and **they're**. **Their** shows you someone owns something: *They have brought* their *exercise books*. **They're** is short for **they are**: *They're* late.

therefore

ADVERB

for that reason or because of that ⇾ *She had been awake all that night and therefore was very tired the next day.* ⇽

these

ADJECTIVE

these is used before a noun to refer to people or things nearby or which are being mentioned ⇾ *Both these cups are dirty.* ⇽ ⇾ *On these cold winter days, you have to wrap up warmly.* ⇽ ⇾ *Can you make me a pair of these gloves?* ⇽

PRONOUN

these is used instead of a noun to refer to people or things nearby or which are being mentioned ⇾ *Are these the same as the ones you had yesterday?* ⇽ ⇾ *These are difficult times for everyone.* ⇽

they

PRONOUN

you use **they** to talk about two or more people or things that have already been mentioned or pointed out for the first time ⇾ *Apes are not monkeys. They don't have tails.* ⇽ ⇾ *What did they think of your idea?* ⇽

thick

ADJECTIVE thicker, thickest

1 quite wide from one side to the other ⇾ *a thick piece of rope* ⇽
2 something is a certain measurement thick when it measures that distance between one side and the other ⇾ *The ice was two feet thick.* ⇽
3 made up of parts that are very close together or densely packed ⇾ *thick wool* ⇽
4 not having a lot of liquid in it or not flowing easily ⇾ *thick gravy* ⇽
5 thick smoke or fog is dense and difficult to see through

▸ **thicken**

VERB thickens, thickening, thickened
to make or become thicker

▸ **thickness**

NOUN *plural* thicknesses
how thick something is, especially compared with other things

thief

NOUN *plural* thieves
someone who steals

▸ **thieving**

NOUN
stealing

a b c d e f g h i j k l m n o p q r s **t** u v w x y z

thigh

NOUN   *plural* thighs

your thighs are the top parts of your legs above your knees

thin

ADJECTIVE   thinner, thinnest

1 not wide from one side to the other
2 a thin person doesn't have much fat on their body
3 not dense or thick ⋨ **His hair is getting a bit thin.** ⋨   ⋨ **a thin porridge** ⋨

VERB   thins, thinning, thinned

to make something thin or thinner, for example by adding water or liquid to it

thing

NOUN   *plural* things

1 an object, or something that is not alive ⋨ **I bought a few things for the party when I was in town.** ⋨   ⋨ **Where's the thing for opening bottles?** ⋨
2 a fact, item, action or event ⋨ **We've got lots of things to discuss.** ⋨   ⋨ **I hope I haven't done the wrong thing.** ⋨

think

VERB   thinks, thinking, thought

1 to think is to have or form ideas in your mind ⋨ **Don't disturb him. He's thinking.** ⋨
2 what you think about something is the opinion you have of it ⋨ **I don't think much of their new album.** ⋨
3 if you are thinking of doing something, you are planning to do it

third

ADJECTIVE AND ADVERB

after second and before fourth ⋨ **That's the third time he's fallen off his bike.** ⋨

NOUN   *plural* thirds

the fraction ⅓, which means one of three equal parts of something ⋨ **The bottle holds a third of a litre.** ⋨

thirst

NOUN

thirst is the feeling that you must have something to drink

▸ **thirsty**

ADJECTIVE   thirstier, thirstiest

feeling you must have something to drink

thirteen

NOUN

the number 13

thirty

NOUN   *plural* thirties

the number 30

this

ADJECTIVE   these

the word **this** is used before a noun to refer to a person or thing nearby or which is being mentioned ⋨ **This apple is sour.** ⋨   ⋨ **We have got PE this afternoon.** ⋨

PRONOUN

the word **this** is used instead of a noun to refer to a person or thing nearby or which is being mentioned ⋨ **I can't eat this.** ⋨   ⋨ **Where are you going after this?** ⋨

ADVERB

to the extent or degree mentioned ⋨ **It was this long and this wide.** ⋨   ⋨ **We've come this far. Don't let's give up now.** ⋨

thorn

NOUN   *plural* thorns

a hard sharp point that sticks out from the stems of some plants

those

ADJECTIVE

those is used before a noun to refer to people or things at a distance from you or which are being mentioned ⋨ **Who are those two boys?** ⋨   ⋨ **In those days, people didn't have cars.** ⋨

PRONOUN

those is used instead of a noun to refer to people or things at a distance from you or which are being mentioned ⇒*What are those?* ⇒*Those are just some of the coins in his collection.*

though

CONJUNCTION

in spite of the fact that ⇒ *We only waited for half an hour, though it seemed like hours.* ⇒ *He went out, though I told him not to.*

ADVERB

however ⇒*It's a pity we didn't win. It was an exciting match, though.*

▸ **as though**

as if ⇒ *He looks as though he needs a good meal.*

thought

VERB

a way of changing the verb **think** to make a past tense. It can be used with or without a helping verb ⇒ *I thought I heard a noise.* ⇒ *He had thought about the problem all day.*

NOUN *plural* **thoughts**

1 thought is thinking

2 a thought is an idea or something you think

▸ **thoughtless**

ADJECTIVE

a thoughtless person does things without first thinking about how they or other people will be affected by their actions

▸ **thoughtful**

ADJECTIVE

1 if someone looks thoughtful, they look as if they are thinking

2 a thoughtful person is kind and thinks of other people

thousand

NOUN *plural* **thousands**

the number 1000

▸ **thousandth**

ADJECTIVE AND ADVERB

coming last in a series of one thousand things ⇒ *the thousandth customer in the shop today*

NOUN *plural* **thousandths**

one of a thousand equal parts of something

thread

NOUN *plural* **threads**

a thin strand of cotton, wool or silk used for sewing

VERB **threads, threading, threaded**

to thread a needle is to push a strand of thread through the hole in the top of a sewing needle

three

NOUN *plural* **threes**

the number 3

threw

VERB

a way of changing the verb **throw** to make a past tense ⇒ *He threw the ball hard.*

throat

NOUN *plural* **throats**

1 your throat is the top part of the tube that goes from your mouth down to your stomach

2 your throat is also the front part of your neck

throne

NOUN *plural* **thrones**

a special chair that a king or queen, or a bishop, sits on

through

PREPOSITION

1 entering at one side and coming out at the other ⇒ *He walked through the door.*

2 from end to end ⇒ *She was flicking through a magazine.*

3 because of, or by means of ⇒ *He ended up*

in hospital through his own stupidity. ≳ ≳ *I heard about it through a friend.* ≳

ADVERB

1 entering at one side and coming out at the other ≳ *He opened the hatch and stuck his head through.* ≳
2 from end to end ≳ *Take this booklet away and read it through.* ≳

> The words **through** and **threw** sound the same but remember that they have different spellings. **Threw** is the past tense of **throw**.

throw

VERB   throws, throwing, threw, thrown

1 to throw something is to send it through the air with force ≳ *He threw the ball into the scrum.* ≳ ≳ *She threw her schoolbag down and rushed to switch on the TV.* ≳
2 a horse throws its rider when it makes the rider fall off its back

NOUN   *plural* throws

a throwing movement ≳*That was a great throw!*≳

thumb

NOUN   *plural* thumbs

the short thick finger that is at a different angle from the other four fingers on your hand

thunder

NOUN

the loud and deep rumbling sound that you hear after a flash of lightning

VERB   thunders, thundering, thundered

to make a loud rumbling sound, or to talk in a very loud, angry voice

▸**thunderstorm**

NOUN   *plural* thunderstorms

a storm with thunder and lightning

Thursday

NOUN   *plural* Thursdays

the day of the week after Wednesday and before Friday

> **Thursday** comes from the Old English word **Thursdæg**, which means *Thor's day*. Thor is the Norse god of thunder.

tick

NOUN   *plural* ticks

1 a small mark (✔) used to show that something is correct or to mark off the things on a list that you have dealt with
2 the soft regular tapping or clicking noise that a clock makes
3 a very short time ≳ *Can you wait a tick while I get my coat?*≳

VERB   ticks, ticking, ticked

1 to tick something is to mark it with a tick
2 a clock ticks when it makes regular tapping or clicking noises

ticket

NOUN   *plural* tickets

a small piece of printed paper or card that shows you have paid a fare on a bus, train or aeroplane, or that allows you to get into a concert or other event

tickle

VERB   tickles, tickling, tickled

1 to tickle someone is to touch part of their body lightly so that they get a tingling or prickly feeling that makes them laugh
2 something tickles when it causes this tingling or prickly feeling on your skin

NOUN   *plural* tickles

a tickling movement

▸**ticklish**

ADJECTIVE

if you are ticklish, you are sensitive to tickling

▶**tickly**

ADJECTIVE   ticklier, tickliest

causing a tingling or prickly feeling

tidy

ADJECTIVE   tidier, tidiest

1 a place is tidy when it is neat and everything is in its proper place
2 a tidy person likes to keep things neat and in their proper place

VERB   tidies, tidying, tidied

to put things back in their proper places and make everything neat

tie

VERB   ties, tying, tied

1 to tie one thing to another is to join them or fasten them together, using string, rope or wire
2 to tie a knot or bow is to make loops that you twist round each other to form a knot or bow
3 two teams or competitors tie when they each have the same number of points ⋗ **They tied for second place.** ⋖

NOUN   plural ties

1 a narrow strip of material that goes round your neck under your shirt collar and is tied in a knot just under your chin
2 a situation in which two teams or competitors each have the same number of points
3 a match between two teams in a competition

tiger

NOUN   plural tigers

a large striped wild animal related to the cat

tight

ADJECTIVE   tighter, tightest

1 fitting very closely or too closely ⋗ **a tight shirt** ⋖   ⋗ **The top on this jar is very tight.** ⋖
2 very firm ⋗ **Have you got a tight grip on that rope?** ⋖
3 not leaving much room or space for movement ⋗ **a tight bend** ⋖

▶**tighten**

VERB   tightens, tightening, tightened

to make or become tight or tighter

▶**tightly** or **tight**

ADVERB

1 closely ⋗ **She held her doll tightly.** ⋖
2 firmly ⋗ **Hold tight to your hat.** ⋖

tights

PLURAL NOUN

tights are a one-piece covering for your feet, legs and bottom made of thin stretchy material

tile

NOUN   plural tiles

a piece of baked clay of various sizes, used for putting on roofs, walls or floors

VERB   tiles, tiling, tiled

to tile a roof, wall or floor is to put tiles on it

tilt

VERB   tilts, tilting, tilted

to tilt is to lean to one side ⋗ **She tilted her head.** ⋖   ⋗ **The floor tilted slightly.** ⋖

time

NOUN   plural times

1 time is the passing of days, weeks, months and years
2 the time is the hour of the day ⋗ **What's the time?** ⋖
3 the time of something is when it happens or is done ⋗ **Do you know the times of the trains to Edinburgh?** ⋖
4 the number of minutes, hours, days or years that something takes to do or happen ⋗ **It**

a b c d e f g h i j k l m n o p q r s t u v w x y z

takes a long time for water to wear down rocks. ⟩

5 one of several occasions ⟩ *They've won the cup four times.* ⟩

6 a particular period ⟩ *in olden times* ⟩

7 a suitable or right moment ⟩ *Now is not a good time to ask for more money.* ⟩

VERB times, timing, timed

1 to time something is to use a clock or watch to find out how long it takes or when it will be ready

2 to time something well is to choose a good time to do it

▸ **in** *or* **on time**

to be in time, or on time, is to arrive or happen at the right time and not be late, or too late

▸ **timer**

NOUN *plural* timers

a device for timing something

times

PLURAL NOUN

maths 'times' is used in multiplication between the numbers you are multiplying ⟩ *Two times four is eight.* ⟩

tin

NOUN *plural* tins

1 tin is a soft, silvery metal

2 a tin is a metal container for food ⟩ *Let's just open a tin of soup for lunch.* ⟩

tiny

ADJECTIVE tinier, tiniest

very, very small ⟩ *a baby's tiny hands and feet* ⟩ ⟩ *the tiniest handwriting you ever saw* ⟩

tip¹

NOUN *plural* tips

the point at the end or the top of something ⟩ *arrows with poison tips* ⟩ ⟩ *Point to it with the tip of your finger.* ⟩

tip²

VERB tips, tipping, tipped

1 to tip something is to tilt it

2 if something tips, it tilts

NOUN *plural* tips

a place where you can dump rubbish

tip³

NOUN *plural* tips

1 a small extra amount of money for someone who has done a job for you ⟩ *They left almost ten dollars tip.* ⟩

2 a small piece of helpful advice ⟩ *useful tips on studying for an exam* ⟩

VERB tips, tipping, tipped

to give someone a small gift of money when they have done a good job for you ⟩ *How much did you tip the taxi driver?* ⟩

tiptoe

VERB tiptoes, tiptoeing, tiptoed

to walk somewhere very quietly or carefully on your toes ⟩ *tiptoeing along the corridor, trying not to wake the other guests* ⟩

NOUN

▸ **on tiptoe**

standing or walking balanced on your toes ⟩ *I can just see the sea if I stand on tiptoe.* ⟩

tire

VERB tires, tiring, tired

1 to run out of energy and need a rest ⟩ *Auntie tires easily nowadays and has a rest every afternoon.* ⟩

2 to tire of something is to get bored of it ⟩ *I'm beginning to tire of Nigel's stories.* ⟩

▸ **tired**

ADJECTIVE

1 needing a rest ⟩ *You must be tired after your journey.* ⟩

2 if you are tired of something, you are bored with it ⟩ *I'm tired of wearing the same clothes every day.* ⟩

a b c d e f g h i j k l m n o p q r s t u v w x y z

▸ **tiring**

ADJECTIVE

making you feel that you need a rest or sleep ⋛ *a tiring climb up the hill* ⋚

> The words **tire** and **tyre** sound the same but remember that they have different spellings. A **tyre** is the covering of a wheel. However, in North America these words are both spelt **tire**.

tissue

NOUN   *plural* **tissues**

1 a tissue is a paper handkerchief
2 tissue is very thin paper that is used for protecting delicate objects
3 tissue is the substance that animals and plants are made of ⋛ *muscle tissue* ⋚ ⋛ *plant tissue* ⋚

title

NOUN   *plural* **titles**

1 the name of something like a book, song or film ⋛ *What's the title of your poem?* ⋚
2 a word that you can use before your name ⋛ *Her title is 'Doctor', not 'Mrs'.* ⋚

to

PREPOSITION

1 towards ⋛ *walking to the shops* ⋚
2 as far as ⋛ *a mile from the house to the station* ⋚
3 compared with ⋛ *win by two goals to one* ⋚

ADVERB

1 almost closed ⋛ *Would you pull the door to?* ⋚
2 awake ⋛ *He came to in a few moments.* ⋚

▸ **to and fro**
backwards and forwards

toad

NOUN   *plural* **toads**

an animal like a large frog

toadstool

NOUN   *plural* **toadstools**

a plant like a large mushroom that is often poisonous

toast

NOUN   *plural* **toasts**

1 toast is bread that has been made crisp by being sliced and heated ⋛ *toast and marmalade for breakfast* ⋚
2 a toast is when people drink together to express a good wish for someone ⋛ *a toast to the bride and groom* ⋚

VERB   **toasts, toasting, toasted**

1 to toast food is to cook it under a grill or at a fire
2 to toast a person is to have a drink and wish them well

▸ **toaster**
NOUN   *plural* **toasters**

a machine for heating slices of bread to make them crisp to eat

today

NOUN

this day ⋛ *Today is Tuesday.* ⋚

ADVERB

1 on this day ⋛ *I can't come today.* ⋚
2 nowadays, at the present time ⋛ *People are taller today than they were a hundred years ago.* ⋚

toddler

NOUN   *plural* **toddlers**

a very young child who has just learned to walk

toe

NOUN   *plural* **toes**

1 one of the five jointed parts at the end of your foot ⋛ *reach up high, standing on your toes* ⋚
2 the closed end of a shoe or sock ⋛ *a hole in the toe of my sock* ⋚

a b c d e f g h i j k l m n o p q r s **t** u v w x y z

toffee

NOUN *plural* **toffees**

a sticky sweet that may be chewy or hard ⋗ *a piece of toffee* ⋖ ⋗ *a bag of toffees* ⋖

together

ADVERB

with each other ⋗ *The two friends always walk to school together.* ⋖ ⋗ *Mix the sugar and eggs together in a bowl.* ⋖

toilet

NOUN *plural* **toilets**

1 a large bowl-shaped piece of furniture where human waste can be washed away
2 a room with a toilet in it

▸ **toiletries**

PLURAL NOUN

products that people use to keep clean and to look and smell nice ⋗ *Perfume, toothpaste and hairspray are all toiletries.* ⋖

told

VERB

the way of changing the verb **tell** to make a past tense. It can be used with or without a helping verb ⋗ *Every day the teacher told us a story.* ⋖ ⋗ *Has Sarah told you her news yet?* ⋖

tomato

NOUN *plural* **tomatoes**

a juicy red-skinned fruit that is used like a vegetable in salads, sauces and sandwiches

tomorrow

NOUN

the day after today ⋗ *Tomorrow is Sunday.* ⋖

ADVERB

on the day after today ⋗ *We've got PE tomorrow.* ⋖

tongue

NOUN *plural* **tongues**

1 the fleshy part of your mouth that you can move and that you use to lick, speak, eat and taste ⋗ *Callum bit his tongue when he fell off the wall.* ⋖
2 a language ⋗ *speaking in a foreign tongue* ⋖
3 the leather flap underneath the opening of a shoe or boot

tonight

NOUN

the night or evening of today ⋗ *I'll have to miss tonight's class, I'm afraid.* ⋖

ADVERB

on the night or evening of today ⋗ *I'm going to bed early tonight.* ⋖

too

ADVERB

1 also ⋗ *Can I come too?* ⋖
2 more than necessary or more than is sensible ⋗ *If the water is too hot, add some cold.* ⋖ ⋗ *You're driving much too fast!* ⋖

took

VERB

a way of changing the verb **take** to make a past tense ⋗ *Fran took me to a concert on my birthday.* ⋖ ⋗ *The shopping took all morning.* ⋖

tool

NOUN *plural* **tools**

1 a piece of equipment that you hold to do a certain job ⋗ *Dad's plumbing tools are in the boot of the car.* ⋖
2 **ICT** something that a computer program can do ⋗ *This program features a drawing tool.* ⋖

tooth

NOUN *plural* **teeth**

1 one of the hard, white, bony parts of the jaw that are used for biting and chewing.
2 one of the sharp points of something like a saw or a comb

toothpaste

NOUN

a cream that you use to clean your teeth

top¹

NOUN *plural* tops

1 the highest point or part of something *≳ climbing to the top of the tower ≲ ≳ waiting at the top of the steps ≲*
2 the upper surface of something *≳ a vase on the top of the television ≲*
3 the lid or cap of a container *≳ Screw the top back on tightly. ≲*
4 a piece of clothing for the upper half of your body *≳ green trousers and a black top ≲*

ADJECTIVE

highest or most important *≳ Our flat is on the top floor. ≲ ≳ a top fashion designer ≲*

ADVERB

with the highest marks or score *≳ Ellie comes top in maths every term. ≲*

VERB tops, topping, topped

1 to top something is to cover its upper surface *≳ Top the cake with fruit and whipped cream. ≲*
2 to come first in a list *≳ This album is expected to top the charts. ≲*

top²

NOUN *plural* tops

a toy that spins around on a point

topic

NOUN *plural* topics

a subject or theme to study, write or talk about *≳ Choose one of the topics below as the title of your essay. ≲*

Torah

NOUN

the holy book of the Jewish people

torch

NOUN *plural* torches

1 a small electric light with batteries in it that you can hold in one hand and switch on and off
2 a big stick with something burning on the end that is carried as a light in a procession

tore

VERB

a way of changing the verb **tear** to make a past tense *≳ Heidi tore the parcel open to see what was inside. ≲*

torn

VERB

the form of the verb **tear** that is used with a helping verb to show that something happened in the past *≳ The photograph had been torn right down the middle. ≲*

tortoise

NOUN *plural* tortoises

a slow-moving animal with a hard shell that covers its body

total

NOUN *plural* totals

the number you get when you add everything together *≳ We've got a total of fifteen cats. ≲ ≳ thirty people in total ≲*

VERB totals, totalling, totalled

to come to a certain amount when added together *≳ Our collection totalled £320. ≲*

ADJECTIVE

complete or absolute *≳ a total eclipse of the sun ≲ ≳ The job must be done in total secrecy. ≲*

▸totally

ADVERB

completely *≳ Is she totally deaf? ≲ ≳ I agree with you totally. ≲*

a b c d e f g h i j k l m n o p q r s t u v w x y z

touch

VERB touches, touching, touched

1 to put your hand or fingers on something ⋮ *Please do not touch the items on the shelf.* ⋮ *Can you touch the ceiling?*
2 to make contact with a thing or person ⋮ *We stood in a long line with our shoulders touching.* ⋮ *The car came close, but fortunately didn't actually touch us.*
3 to interfere with something ⋮ *Don't let anyone touch my desk while I'm away.*
4 to be touched by something is to be affected emotionally by it ⋮ *I was touched by your kind letter.*

NOUN *plural* touches

1 touch is the sense that tells you what things feel like ⋮ *The fur was smooth to the touch.*
2 putting a hand or finger on something ⋮ *You can start the engine at the touch of a button.*
3 a small thing that you add to improve something ⋮ *Fiona was adding the finishing touches to the display.*
4 communication with someone ⋮ *Get in touch with me.* ⋮ *I have lost touch with Sally.*

tough

ADJECTIVE tougher, toughest

1 strong and not easily worn out ⋮ *You'll need a tough pair of shoes for climbing.*
2 strong, fit and not easily beaten ⋮ *a tough businesswoman*
3 difficult to deal with ⋮ *a tough customer* ⋮ *a tough decision*
4 hard to chew ⋮ *tough meat*
5 firm or strict ⋮ *It's time to get tough with football hooligans.*

▸**toughen**

VERB toughens, toughening, toughened

to toughen or toughen up a thing or person is to make them stronger

▸**toughness**

NOUN

being strong and not easily beaten or worn out

towards *or* toward

PREPOSITION

1 in a certain direction ⋮ *walking towards the gate* ⋮ *leaning over towards Bill*
2 in connection with ⋮ *Nothing has been done towards organizing the prize giving.*
3 helping to pay for something ⋮ *a donation towards the new roof*

towel

NOUN *plural* towels

a piece of thick cloth for drying yourself ⋮ *a bath towel*

VERB towels, towelling, towelled

to dry a thing or person with a towel ⋮ *Towel your hair dry before applying the cream.*

▸**towelling**

NOUN

thick cotton material that absorbs water well and so is good for drying things ⋮ *a bath robe made of towelling*

tower

NOUN *plural* towers

a tall narrow building or part of a building ⋮ *the clocktower of the church* ⋮ *the Eiffel Tower*

VERB towers, towering, towered

▸**tower over** *or* **above something** *or* **someone**

to be much taller than other things or people ⋮ *William towers over all his classmates.*

▸**towering**

ADJECTIVE

very tall ⋮ *towering office blocks in the city centre*

a b c d e f g h i j k l m n o p q r s **t** u v w x y z

town

`NOUN` *plural* towns

a place where people live and work, which has streets, buildings and a name

> **Town** comes from the Old English word **tun**, which means 'an enclosed area'.

toy

`NOUN` *plural* toys

an object made for a child to play with

`VERB` toys, toying, toyed

▸ **toy with something**

1 to push something around for no real reason ⋛ *toying with her food but not eating it* ⋚
2 to toy with an idea is to consider it, but not very seriously

track

`NOUN` *plural* tracks

1 a mark on the ground left by a person, animal or thing that has passed ⋛ *following the bear's tracks through the forest* ⋚
2 a rough path or road ⋛ *a narrow track around the edge of the field* ⋚
3 a piece of ground on which races are run
4 a set of rails that a train or tram runs on
5 one of the songs or pieces of music on a CD or tape

`VERB` tracks, tracking, tracked

to follow the marks that an animal, person or thing leaves as they pass ⋛ *It was impossible to track anyone over such stony ground.* ⋚

tracksuit

`NOUN` *plural* tracksuits

a warm suit with a loose top and trousers that you can wear when exercising or to keep your body warm before or after exercise

tractor

`NOUN` *plural* tractors

a slow vehicle with two large rear wheels that

is used for pulling heavy loads, for example on a farm

traffic

`NOUN`

travelling vehicles ⋛ *air traffic controllers* ⋚ ⋛ *road traffic reports* ⋚

train¹

`NOUN` *plural* trains

1 a series of railway carriages or trucks that are pulled by an engine
2 the back part of a long dress that trails on the floor ⋛ *The bride's gown had a long train made of lace.* ⋚

train²

`VERB` trains, training, trained

1 to train a person or animal is to teach them to do something ⋛ *Veronica has trained her dog to carry her handbag.* ⋚
2 to train as something is to learn to do that job ⋛ *Andrew trained as a nurse as soon as he left school.* ⋚
3 to prepare for a sporting event ⋛ *The team trains for three hours every day.* ⋚
4 to point a camera or gun in a certain direction ⋛ *The enemy's guns are trained on the airport.* ⋚

▸ **trainer**

`NOUN` *plural* trainers

1 a person who teaches people or animals to improve their skills
2 trainers are soft shoes that are designed for sports use

▸ **training**

`NOUN`

1 practice and instruction in doing a certain job ⋛ *training in computing* ⋚
2 preparation for a sports event ⋛ *The team will be in training for the next year.* ⋚

trampoline

`NOUN` *plural* trampolines

a piece of canvas that is stretched across a

frame for acrobats, gymnasts and children to jump on

transport

NOUN said "**trans**-port"

1 the vehicles that you travel in, such as cars, trains, aircraft and boats ⋛ *travel by public transport* ⋚

2 moving people or things from one place to another ⋛ *This includes the cost of transport.* ⋚

VERB said "trans-**port**" transports, transporting, transported

to transport something is to move it from one place to another

travel

VERB travels, travelling, travelled

to go from one place to another, especially abroad or far from home ⋛ *Holly spent the summer travelling in the United States.* ⋚ ⋛ *How fast does sound travel?* ⋚

NOUN *plural* travels

1 travel is going from one place to another, especially far from home

2 your travels are the journeys you make ⋛ *Did you have good weather on your travels?* ⋚

▶ **traveller**

NOUN *plural* travellers

1 a person who is on a journey ⋛ *a hostel for travellers* ⋚

2 a person who lives in a vehicle and does not stay in one place

treasure

NOUN *plural* treasures

1 valuable things, especially if they have been hidden ⋛ *looking for where the treasure is buried* ⋚

2 a precious thing ⋛ *the treasures in our museums* ⋚

VERB treasures, treasuring, treasured

to think that something is very precious ⋛ *Mother treasured all the memories of those family outings for the rest of her life.* ⋚

treat

VERB treats, treating, treated

1 to deal with someone or behave towards them in a certain way ⋛ *I think Debbie treated Steve really badly.* ⋚ ⋛ *You should not treat a mistake like this as a joke.* ⋚

2 to give a person who is ill some medicine or medical help ⋛ *Our doctors use all the latest methods to treat their patients.* ⋚

3 to apply some sort of layer or protection to a surface ⋛ *The material is treated with a waterproofing spray.* ⋚

4 to pay for something special for someone else ⋛ *Dad treated us all to a pizza on the way home.* ⋚

NOUN *plural* treats

1 an unexpected present for someone that you pay for ⋛ *How would you like a treat?* ⋚

2 an enjoyable outing that someone organizes for you ⋛ *We went to the theatre as a treat.* ⋚

▶ **treatment**

NOUN *plural* treatments

1 the way you deal with someone or behave towards them ⋛ *Will I get special treatment if I offer to pay more?* ⋚

2 the medical care that a patient gets ⋛ *My treatment will last for about a month.* ⋚

tree

NOUN *plural* trees

a tall plant with a hard trunk and branches

triangle

NOUN *plural* triangles

1 a flat shape with three sides and three angles ⋛ *a right-angled triangle.* ⋚

2 a musical instrument that is a three-sided metal bar that you tap with a short metal stick

▸ **triangular**

ADJECTIVE

in the shape of a triangle ⧽ *a triangular scarf* ⧼

trick

NOUN *plural* tricks

1 something that you do or say to fool someone ⧽ *a nasty trick to get all her money* ⧼ ⧽ *a card trick* ⧼
2 a clever special way of doing something ⧽ *There's a trick to opening that door quietly.* ⧼

ADJECTIVE

▸ **a trick question**

a question that is cleverly worded so that you probably give the wrong answer

VERB tricks, tricking, tricked

to trick someone is to fool them, especially by making them do something they do not want to do ⧽ *They tricked her into agreeing to help.* ⧼

tried

VERB

a way of changing the verb **try** to make a past tense. It can be used with or without a helping verb ⧽ *I've tried and tried but I still don't understand.* ⧼ ⧽ *Rita tried not to giggle.* ⧼

tries

VERB

the form of the verb **try** in the present tense that you use with **he, she** or **it** ⧽ *He tries to be like his big brother.* ⧼

NOUN

the plural of the noun **try**

trip

NOUN *plural* trips

a short journey to a place and back again ⧽ *a shopping trip* ⧼ ⧽ *a trip to the zoo* ⧼

VERB trips, tripping, tripped

1 to trip is to catch your foot on something and fall, or nearly fall over ⧽ *Caroline tripped over the edge of the carpet.* ⧼

⧽ *Mind you don't trip on the step.* ⧼
2 to trip someone or trip someone up is to make them fall or stumble ⧽ *One of the boys tripped me up.* ⧼

trouble

NOUN *plural* troubles

1 something that gives you a lot of work or problems ⧽ *A washing machine would save you a lot of trouble.* ⧼ ⧽ *You'd have no trouble finding a better job.* ⧼
2 your troubles are your worries and problems

VERB troubles, troubling, troubled

1 to trouble someone is to bother or disturb them ⧽ *I'm sorry to trouble you, but can you help me please?* ⧼
2 to trouble to do something is to make an effort or be bothered to do it ⧽ *He didn't even trouble to say where he was going.* ⧼
3 to be troubled by something is to worry about it or to suffer from it ⧽ *What's troubling you?* ⧼

▸ **troublesome**

ADJECTIVE

causing worry or problems

trousers

PLURAL NOUN

a garment for the lower half of the body that covers each leg separately

truck

NOUN *plural* trucks

1 a lorry
2 an open railway wagon for transporting goods or animals

trumpet

NOUN *plural* trumpets

a brass musical instrument that you blow into to make a loud, high, clear sound

VERB trumpets, trumpeting, trumpeted

an elephant trumpets when it makes a loud noise

a b c d e f g h i j k l m n o p q r s t u v w x y z

trunks

PLURAL NOUN

trunks are short trousers or pants worn by men or boys for swimming

trust

VERB trusts, trusting, trusted

1 to believe that someone is honest and loyal ⇒ **The colonel picked out ten men he knew he could trust.**
2 to rely on someone to do something properly and not cause damage ⇒ **I know I can trust you not to make any mistakes.** ⇒ **Can I trust you with my new camera?**

NOUN

1 the belief that someone is honest and loyal ⇒ **It can be difficult to get a new pet's trust.**
2 a responsibility to look after something or do something properly ⇒ **The children had been placed in my trust.**

▸ **trusting**
ADJECTIVE
believing that other people are honest and good

▸ **trustworthy**
ADJECTIVE
honest

truth

NOUN *plural* truths

1 what is true and real ⇒ **Please try to tell the truth.** ⇒ **The truth is that she never really loved him.**
2 being true ⇒ **There is no truth in his story.**

▸ **truthful**
ADJECTIVE
1 a truthful person tells the truth
2 truthful information is not false

▸ **truthfully**
ADVERB
without lying ⇒ **Answer the questions as truthfully as you can.**

try

VERB tries, trying, tried

1 to make an effort or an attempt to do something ⇒ **Please try to understand.** ⇒ **I'm trying to call John but he's not answering the phone.**
2 to do or use something to see if you like it or if it is good ⇒ **Try this powder for a cleaner wash.** ⇒ **My son tried karate for a while but didn't like it.**
3 to find out if someone committed a crime by hearing all the evidence in a court ⇒ **They will be tried in the European Court of Human Rights.**

NOUN *plural* tries

1 an attempt to do something ⇒ **That was a good try. Better luck next time.**
2 in rugby, a successful attempt to put the ball over the other team's goal line ⇒ **Scotland scored three tries in the match.**

T-shirt or **tee-shirt**

NOUN *plural* T-shirts *or* tee-shirts

a loose shirt with short sleeves that you pull on over your head

Tuesday

NOUN *plural* Tuesdays

the day of the week after Monday and before Wednesday

> **Tuesday** comes from the Old English word **Tiwesdæg**, which means *Tiw's day*. Tiw is the Norse god of war and of the sky.

tummy

NOUN *plural* tummies

a word children use for their stomach ⇒ **Mummy, my tummy aches.**

tuna

NOUN *plural* tuna

a large fish that is used as food

tune

NOUN *plural* tunes

a series of musical notes that sound nice together

▶ **in tune**

1 a musical note is in tune if it is exactly the right note
2 a musical instrument is in tune if it produces the right notes

VERB tunes, tuning, tuned

1 to adjust a musical instrument so that it sounds right
2 to adjust a television or radio to a certain channel or station
3 to adjust an engine so that it works smoothly

▶ **tuneful**

ADJECTIVE

having a pleasant melody

tunnel

NOUN *plural* tunnels

a long underground passage

VERB tunnels, tunnelling, tunnelled

to make an underground passage ⋟ *Will they tunnel under the river or build a bridge over it?* ⋞

turkey

NOUN *plural* turkeys

a large bird that is used as food

turn

VERB turns, turning, turned

1 to move or to move something to face in another direction ⋟ *He turned and walked away.* ⋞ ⋟ *Why have you turned that picture towards the wall?* ⋞
2 to spin around or twist ⋟ *a turning wheel* ⋞ ⋟ *Turn the handle to the right.* ⋞
3 to change ⋟ *She took one look and turned pale.* ⋞ ⋟ *The frog turned into a prince.* ⋞

▶ **turn someone** or **something down**

to refuse an offer that someone makes

▶ **turn something down**

to reduce the noise or heat that something is making ⋟ *Turn the television down. It's too loud.* ⋞

▶ **turn out**

1 to turn out a certain way is to finish or end up like that ⋟ *Everything turned out well in the end.* ⋞
2 to come out to see or do something ⋟ *Not many people turned out for the local election.* ⋞

▶ **turn something up**

to increase the sound or heat which something is making ⋟ *Can you turn the volume up a bit?* ⋞

NOUN *plural* turns

1 a curve, bend or change of direction ⋟ *Take the first turn on the right.* ⋞
2 something that people do one after the other ⋟ *It's your turn next.* ⋞
3 a short performance in a show ⋟ *Jolly Jack will be the star turn at the Christmas show this year.* ⋞

▶ **a good turn**

a favour that you do for someone

▶ **in turn**

if you do things in turn, you do them one after the other

turtle

NOUN *plural* turtles

a large reptile with a hard shell and flippers for swimming

TV

NOUN *plural* TVs

1 a television set ⋟ *We've got a new TV.* ⋞
2 television broadcasts ⋟ *I think the children watch too much TV.* ⋞

twelve

NOUN *plural* twelves

the number 12

twenty

NOUN *plural* twenties

the number 20

twice

ADVERB

two times ⟩ *You've done that twice now so don't do it again.* ⟩ *I could eat twice that amount.*

twig

NOUN   *plural* twigs

a small thin piece that grows from a branch of a tree or bush ⟩ *We need a pile of dry twigs to start the fire.*

VERB   twigs, twigging, twigged

informal to realize something suddenly ⟩ *Then I twigged what he was talking about.*

twinkle

VERB   twinkles, twinkling, twinkled

1 lights twinkle when they glitter brightly ⟩ *lights twinkling along the shoreline*
2 someone's eyes twinkle when they are bright with excitement or humour

NOUN   *plural* twinkles

a bright shining light

two

NOUN   *plural* twos

the number 2

tying

VERB

a form of the verb **tie** that is used with another verb to make different tenses ⟩ *I was tying my laces and I fell over.* ⟩ *We need to start tying up some parcels.*

type

NOUN   *plural* types

1 a sort or kind of thing or person ⟩ *What type of person would write a letter like this?* ⟩ *Choose the right type of shampoo for your hair.*
2 letters and figures that are used in printing ⟩ *The title should be in bold type.*

VERB   types, typing, typed

to write using a keyboard on a computer or typewriter ⟩ *Type your name and then your password.*

tyre

NOUN   *plural* tyres

a thick rubber ring that is filled with air and covers the edge of a wheel ⟩ *The car had a flat tyre.*

a b c d e f g h i j k l m n o p q r s **t** u v w x y z

ugly

ADJECTIVE   uglier, ugliest

not very nice to look at ⋛ *an ugly man* ⋛ ⋛ *an ugly building* ⋛

▸ **ugliness**

NOUN

being ugly

umbrella

NOUN   *plural* **umbrellas**

something you put up and shelter under when it rains, which consists of a frame with cloth over it

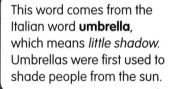

This word comes from the Italian word **umbrella**, which means *little shadow*. Umbrellas were first used to shade people from the sun.

uncle

NOUN   *plural* **uncles**

1 the brother of one of your parents
2 your aunt's husband

unconscious

ADJECTIVE

in a state like sleep when you are not aware of what is happening around you, because you are seriously ill or injured ⋛ *A brick fell on his head and he was knocked unconscious.* ⋛

under

PREPOSITION

1 below or beneath ⋛ *The bag is under the table.* ⋛

2 less than ⋛ *All the clothes are under £20.* ⋛
3 working for ⋛ *a manager with three members of staff under her* ⋛
4 in a state of ⋛ *The fire is now under control.* ⋛
5 in the section called ⋛ *To find a dictionary, look in the library under 'reference'.* ⋛

▸ **under way**

if something gets under way, it starts

ADVERB

in or to a lower place ⋛ *We watched the divers go under.* ⋛

underneath

ADJECTIVE AND PREPOSITION

under something ⋛ *Look underneath the table!* ⋛ ⋛ *He was wearing a jumper with a shirt underneath.* ⋛

understand

VERB   understands, understanding, understood

1 to know what something means ⋛ *I can't understand the instructions.* ⋛ ⋛ *Do you understand German?* ⋛
2 to know about something ⋛ *Doctors still don't understand how the disease is spread.* ⋛
3 to know why someone behaves and feels the way they do ⋛ *I'll never understand him.* ⋛
4 to think something is true ⋛ *I understood that you weren't coming.* ⋛

▸ **understandable**

ADJECTIVE

reasonable in a particular situation ⋛ *His disappointment is understandable.* ⋛

▸ **understanding**

ADJECTIVE

able to understand other people's feelings and treat them in a kind way

NOUN   *plural* **understandings**

1 the ability to see the meaning of something ⋛ *I have no understanding of chemistry.* ⋚

2 an agreement ⋛ *We have an understanding that we will stand up for each other.* ⋚

underwater

ADJECTIVE AND ADVERB

under the surface of water ⋛ *an underwater creature* ⋚   ⋛ *Can you swim underwater?* ⋚

underwear

NOUN

clothes you wear next to your skin and under your other clothes

undress

VERB   **undresses, undressing, undressed**

to take your clothes off

▸ **undressed**

ADJECTIVE

not wearing any clothes ⋛ *He was getting undressed.* ⋚

uniform

NOUN   *plural* **uniforms**

a set of clothes that someone must wear for school or for their job

unit

NOUN   *plural* **units**

1 a single thing, person or group that can be part of a larger thing ⋛ *an army unit* ⋚ ⋛ *The book is divided into ten units.* ⋚

2 a fixed quantity that is used for measuring something ⋛ *A metre is a unit of length.* ⋚

3 a department in a hospital that provides a particular type of treatment ⋛ *a burns unit* ⋚

universe

NOUN

everything that exists anywhere, including the Earth, the sun and all the other planets and stars in space ⋛ *Somewhere in the universe there might be another world like ours.* ⋚

unless

CONJUNCTION

except when or except if ⋛ *We always go for a walk on Sundays, unless it's raining.* ⋚ ⋛ *Don't come unless I phone you.* ⋚

until

PREPOSITION

up to the time of ⋛ *We waited until ten o'clock.* ⋚

CONJUNCTION

up to the time when ⋛ *Keep walking until you come to the station.* ⋚

unusual

ADJECTIVE

not normal or not ordinary ⋛ *It's unusual for him to arrive late.* ⋚ ⋛ *That's an unusual necklace.* ⋚

▸ **unusually**

ADVERB

to an unusual degree ⋛ *unusually cold for the time of year* ⋚

up

ADVERB

1 towards or in a higher position ⋛ *Prices have gone up again.* ⋚ ⋛ *Stand up!* ⋚

2 completely, so that something is finished ⋛ **Drink up your milk.** ⋚
3 out of bed ⋛ **I got up at five o'clock this morning.** ⋚
4 as far as something or someone ⋛ **He came up to me and shook my hand.** ⋚

PREPOSITION

1 to or at a higher part of ⋛ **He climbed up the tree.** ⋚ ⋛ **She's up the ladder.** ⋚
2 along ⋛ **walking up the road** ⋚

ADJECTIVE

1 going up ⋛ **the up escalator** ⋚
2 out of bed ⋛ **He's not up yet.** ⋚
3 ahead ⋛ **two goals up at the end of the first half** ⋚
4 if the sun is up it has risen
5 finished ⋛ **Your time is up.** ⋚
6 an informal way of saying 'wrong' ⋛ **What's up with you today?** ⋚

▸ **up to**

1 if you are up to something you are doing that thing, especially in a secretive way ⋛ **My little brother is up to no good again.** ⋚
2 if you are up to a task, then you have the ability to do it ⋛ **Do you think you are up to winning the race?** ⋚
3 if a choice is up to you, then you have to decide what to do or have ⋛ **Whether we go swimming or just go home is up to you.** ⋚

▸ **up to date**

with all the information or features available just now ⋛ **I want to bring my diary up to date.** ⋚ ⋛ **I need a computer that is more up to date.** ⋚

▸ **ups and downs**

good and bad times

upper

ADJECTIVE

higher ⋛ **the upper floors of the building** ⋚

NOUN *plural* **uppers**

the part of a shoe above the sole ⋛ **These shoes have leather uppers.** ⋚

upset

VERB upsets, upsetting, upset

1 to make someone sad, angry or worried ⋛ **His friend's death upset him very much.** ⋚
2 to spoil something ⋛ **Her illness has upset our holiday plans.** ⋚
3 to knock something over ⋛ **The dog upset a vase of flowers.** ⋚

ADJECTIVE

sad, angry or worried ⋛ **He's upset about failing his exam.** ⋚

NOUN *plural* **upsets**

1 sadness or worry ⋛ **Her sudden departure caused a lot of upset.** ⋚
2 something that causes feelings such as unhappiness and worry ⋛ **Losing the match to such a poor team was quite an upset.** ⋚
3 a slight disturbance ⋛ **a stomach upset** ⋚

upside-down

ADJECTIVE AND ADVERB

1 with the top part where the bottom should be and the bottom part where the top should be ⋛ **I knew he wasn't really reading – he was holding the book upside-down.** ⋚
2 in or into confusion ⋛ **The burglars turned the house upside-down.** ⋚

us

PRONOUN

a word you use when you are talking about yourself and at least one other person ⋛ **His happy face surprised all of us.** ⋚ ⋛ **Do you want to come with us?** ⋚

use

VERB uses, using, used

1 to use something is to put it to a purpose ⋛ **Use a knife to open it.** ⋚ ⋛ **Use your common sense!** ⋚
2 to take an amount of something from a supply ⋛ **Who's used all the cheese?** ⋚

a b c d e f g h i j k l m n o p q r s t **u** v w x y z

▸ **use something up**

to use something up is to use all of it so that there is none left ⟩ *He used up all the milk.* ⟨

NOUN *plural* uses

1 the using of something ⟩ *We cannot allow the use of guns.* ⟨
2 the purpose for which something can be used ⟩ *This knife has a lot of uses.* ⟨
3 the value or advantage of something ⟩ *Is this coat of any use to you?* ⟨ ⟩ *What's the use of crying?* ⟨

▸ **used**

ADJECTIVE

not new ⟩ *a used car* ⟨

▸ **used to**

1 to be used to something is to know it well, or to have done it lots of times ⟩ *She soon got used to her new school.* ⟨
2 if you used to do something, you did it often or regularly in the past ⟩ *We used to go to the seaside every summer.* ⟨

useful

ADJECTIVE

helpful or able to do what needs doing ⟩ *She made herself useful by washing the dishes.* ⟨ ⟩ *a useful tool* ⟨

▸ **usefulness**

NOUN

being useful

usual

ADJECTIVE

done or happening most often ⟩ *I took my usual route to school this morning.* ⟨ ⟩ *He was late as usual.* ⟨

▸ **usually**

ADVERB

normally, on most occasions ⟩ *We usually go on holiday in June.* ⟨

Vaisakhi
NOUN
another word for **Baisakhi**

value
NOUN *plural* **values**
1 the amount that something is worth
2 usefulness and importance

VERB **values, valuing valued**
1 to value something is to think it is important
2 to say how much something is worth

▸ **valuable**
ADJECTIVE
1 worth a lot of money
2 very useful ⋛ *a valuable member of the team* ⋚

van
NOUN *plural* **vans**
a road vehicle, smaller than a lorry, for carrying goods

vandal
NOUN *plural* **vandals**
someone who deliberately damages buildings and other things

▸ **vandalism**
NOUN
the crime of deliberately damaging something such as a public building

▸ **vandalize** *or* **vandalise**
VERB **vandalizes, vandalizing, vandalized**
to damage something on purpose

vanish
VERB **vanishes, vanishing, vanished**
to disappear and leave nothing behind

various
ADJECTIVE
different ⋛ *There were various things to choose from.* ⋚

vase
NOUN *plural* **vases**
a container for flowers that is often kept as an ornament

vast
ADJECTIVE
extremely big ⋛ *vast desert lands* ⋚

Veda
NOUN
the most ancient holy writings of the Hindu religion

vegetable
NOUN *plural* **vegetables**
a plant that you can eat, especially one that is not sweet ⋛ *Potatoes and carrots are vegetables.* ⋚

vegetarian
NOUN *plural* **vegetarians**
someone who does not eat meat

ADJECTIVE
not containing meat ⋛ *vegetarian foods* ⋚

vehicle
NOUN *plural* **vehicles**
something that carries people or goods, for example a car or lorry

verse

NOUN *plural* **verses**

1 a verse is a set of lines that form one part of a song or poem
2 verse is poetry rather than writing

very

ADVERB

to a great degree ⋧ *I'm very tired.* ⋦

ADJECTIVE

exact ⋧ *At that very moment, the telephone rang.* ⋦

Vesak said "**ves**-ak"

NOUN

an important Buddhist festival that takes place in May

vest

NOUN *plural* **vests**

a piece of underwear that covers the top part of your body

vet

NOUN *plural* **vets**

a **veterinary surgeon**, someone whose job is to treat animals who are ill or injured

vibrate

VERB **vibrates, vibrating, vibrated**

to shake very quickly

▸ **vibration**

NOUN *plural* **vibrations**

1 shaking very quickly
2 a quick shaking movement

vicar

NOUN *plural* **vicars**

a priest in the Church of England

victory

NOUN *plural* **victories**

winning a battle or competition ⋧ *victory in the Cup Final* ⋦

▸ **victorious**

ADJECTIVE

successful in a battle or competition

video

NOUN *plural* **videos**

1 a recording of a film or television programme
2 a recording of an event on a cassette
3 a machine for playing videos

VERB **videos, videoing, videoed**

1 to record a television programme
2 to film an event

> **Video** was taken from the Latin word **videre**, which means *to see*.

view

NOUN *plural* **views**

1 the things you can see from a place ⋧ *There's a fantastic view from the top of the hill.* ⋦
2 your ability to see things from a place ⋧ *The pillar spoilt my view of the concert.* ⋦
3 someone's opinion ⋧ *What's your view on the new school uniform?* ⋦

▸ **in view of**

considering something ⋧ *In view of the weather, we have cancelled the game.* ⋦

▸ **on view**

being shown for people to look at ⋧ *Several classic cars will be on view.* ⋦

▸ **with a view to**

with the intention of ⋧ *My grandparents visited apartments in Spain with a view to buying one.* ⋦

VERB **views, viewing, viewed**

1 to look at something ⋧ *Parents can view the plans for the new school buildings.* ⋦
2 to think about someone or something in a particular way ⋧ *Maths is often viewed as a difficult subject.* ⋦

▸ **viewer**

NOUN *plural* **viewers**

someone who watches television ⋧ *The*

programme attracted over ten million viewers.

village

NOUN   *plural* villages

a small place in a country area, which is not as big as a town

▸ **villager**

NOUN   *plural* villagers

someone who lives in a village

violence

NOUN

behaviour that is rough and intended to hurt someone

▸ **violent**

ADJECTIVE

1 behaving in a rough way that is intended to hurt someone
2 very sudden and strong ▹ *a violent storm*

▸ **violently**

ADVERB

in a violent way

violin

NOUN   *plural* violins

music a musical instrument with four strings, which you hold under your chin and play by drawing a bow across the strings

▸ **violinist**

NOUN   *plural* violinists

someone who plays the violin

visible

ADJECTIVE

able to be seen ▹ *The house is not visible from the road.*

▸ **visibly**

ADVERB

in a way that is easy to see ▹ *He was visibly upset.*

▸ **visibility**

NOUN

1 how far and well you can see ▹ *poor visibility*
2 the fact of being easy to see

vision

NOUN   *plural* visions

1 your ability to see
2 something that you see or imagine might happen

visit

VERB   visits, visiting, visited

to go and see a place or person

NOUN   *plural* visits

the act of visiting a place or person ▹ *I'm going to pay him a visit.*

▸ **visitor**

NOUN   *plural* visitors

someone who visits a person or place

voice

NOUN   *plural* voices

1 the sound you make when you speak or sing ▹ *'Hello!' he said in a loud voice.*
2 your ability to make speaking or singing sounds ▹ *I had a sore throat and lost my voice.*

VERB   voices, voicing, voiced

to express an opinion ▹ *Many people have voiced their concerns.*

volcano

NOUN   *plural* volcanoes

geography a mountain with a hole at the top which hot lava sometimes comes out of

a b c d e f g h i j k l m n o p q r s t u **v** w x y z

▸ **volcanic**

ADJECTIVE

relating to volcanoes

> Volcanoes are named after **Vulcan**, the ancient Roman god of fire.

volume

NOUN *plural* **volumes**

1 **science** the space that something takes up or the amount of space that a container has
2 the amount of sound that something makes ⫶ **Can you turn the volume down on the TV, please?**
3 the amount of something ⫶ **The volume of trade has increased.**
4 a book, especially a book that is part of a set

vomit

VERB **vomits, vomiting, vomited**

to bring food back up from your stomach through your mouth

NOUN

food that a person or animal has brought back from their stomach through their mouth

vote

VERB votes, voting, voted

1 to choose someone for an official job or choose something by secretly marking a piece of paper or putting your hand up to be counted ⫶ **Which party did you vote for?**
2 to decide something by voting ⫶ **He was voted best actor.**

NOUN *plural* votes

1 a choice you make by marking a piece of paper or putting your hand up to be counted
2 the right you have to vote in elections

▸ **voter**

NOUN *plural* **voters**

someone who votes in an election

vowel

NOUN *plural* **vowels**

1 one of the letters of the alphabet **a, e, i, o** or **u**
2 a speech sound you make that does not use your lips, teeth, or tongue to stop the flow of air

waddle

VERB waddles, waddling, waddled

to walk moving from side to side, like a duck

waist

NOUN *plural* waists

the narrow part of your body between your chest and your hips

wait

VERB waits, waiting, waited

1 to wait or wait for someone or something is to stay in a place until they arrive ⋙ *Several people were waiting for the bus.* ⋘

2 to wait, or wait until something happens, is to not do an action until that thing happens ⋙ *I will wait until it stops raining before I leave.* ⋘

NOUN *plural* waits

a delay or period of waiting ⋙ *It seemed like a long wait for the show to start.* ⋘

wake

VERB wakes, waking, woke, woken

1 if you wake or wake up, you stop sleeping ⋙ *She suddenly woke up and looked around.* ⋘

2 to wake someone is to make them stop sleeping ⋙ *Please don't wake the baby!* ⋘

walk

VERB walks, walking, walked

1 to move on foot fairly slowly ⋙ *The door opened and Simon walked in.* ⋘ ⋙ *I think I'll walk to work today.* ⋘

2 to travel on foot because you enjoy it ⋙ *We go walking on the moors at weekends.* ⋘

NOUN *plural* walks

1 a journey on foot ⋙ *It's just a short walk to the newsagent's.* ⋘

2 a way of walking ⋙ *I recognised Ann by her walk.* ⋘

3 a path that you can walk along for pleasure ⋙ *a book of local walks* ⋘

wall

NOUN *plural* walls

1 a structure made of brick or stone that separates or goes around an area ⋙ *Hadrian's Wall* ⋘ ⋙ *A high wall surrounds the school.* ⋘

2 any of the sides of a room or building ⋙ *She hung the new clock on the kitchen wall.* ⋘

wallet

NOUN *plural* wallets

a small folding holder for banknotes and cards that you can put in your pocket ⋙ *a leather wallet* ⋘

wand

NOUN *plural* wands

a long thin stick such as the one a magician or fairy uses when doing magic spells or tricks ⋙ *The fairy waved her magic wand and turned a pumpkin into a coach.* ⋘

want

VERB wants, wanting, wanted

1 to wish for something ⋙ *Do you want some cake?* ⋘ ⋙ *Someone wants to speak to you.* ⋘

2 to need or lack something ⋙ *Your hands want a good wash.* ⋘

NOUN *plural* wants

1 something that you want ⋙ *a long list of wants* ⋘

2 a lack of something ⋛ *He failed the test, but not for want of trying.* ⋛

war

NOUN *plural* **wars**

armed fighting between two countries or groups ⋛ *the war in Afghanistan* ⋛

wardrobe

NOUN *plural* **wardrobes**

1 a tall cupboard that you can hang clothes inside
2 all of the clothes someone owns ⋛ *her summer wardrobe* ⋛

warm

ADJECTIVE **warmer, warmest**

1 pleasantly hot ⋛ *a warm bath* ⋛ ⋛ *As the sun rose we felt warmer.* ⋛
2 warm clothes make you feel warm ⋛ *a warm winter coat* ⋛
3 kind and friendly ⋛ *a warm welcome* ⋛

VERB **warms, warming, warmed**

to warm someone or something, or warm them up, is to make them warm ⋛ *She warmed her hands on the radiator.* ⋛

▸ **warmly**

ADVERB

in a warm way ⋛ *Make sure you're warmly dressed for the hike.* ⋛ ⋛ *She smiled warmly.* ⋛

▸ **warmth**

NOUN

1 pleasant heat, or being pleasantly warm
2 being kind and friendly

warn

VERB **warns, warning, warned**

to tell someone that something is dangerous or bad before it happens ⋛ *I warned her about the icy roads.* ⋛

▸ **warning**

NOUN *plural* **warnings**

an event or something that you say to warn someone ⋛ *The volcano erupted without any warning.* ⋛

was

VERB

the past tense of the verb **be** that you use with **I**, **he**, **she** or **it** ⋛ *I was surprised to see Rosie there.* ⋛ ⋛ *Mr Brock was my favourite teacher.* ⋛

wash

VERB **washes, washing, washed**

1 to wash something is to clean it with water and soap ⋛ *Wash your hands and face before we eat.* ⋛
2 if water washes against something, it flows against it ⋛ *Gentle waves were washing against the boat.* ⋛

▸ **wash up**

to wash the dishes after you have eaten ⋛ *It's your turn to wash up, Adam.* ⋛

NOUN *plural* **washes**

1 the act of washing someone or something
2 all the clothes that need to be washed ⋛ *Your red shirt is in the wash.* ⋛
3 the waves that a boat causes as it moves

▸ **washing**

NOUN

all the clothes that need to be washed ⋛ *a pile of dirty washing* ⋛

wasp

NOUN *plural* **wasps**

an insect with a thin black and yellow striped body that can sting you

waste

VERB wastes, wasting, wasted

1 to waste something is to use more of it than you need ⋗ **Try not to waste any paper.**
2 if you waste time or money, you spend it in a way that is not useful ⋗ **You're wasting your time trying to fix the television.**

NOUN plural wastes

1 waste is rubbish or things that are not needed ⋗ **industrial waste**
2 a bad use of something ⋗ **The computer turned out to be a waste of money.**

ADJECTIVE

1 waste products or materials are useless and thrown away ⋗ **waste paper**
2 waste land has no buildings or crops on it

▶ **wasteful**

ADJECTIVE

involving or causing waste ⋗ **It's very wasteful, throwing all this food away.**

watch

VERB watches, watching, watched

1 to look at someone or something ⋗ **Roy's watching the football in the other room.**
2 to be careful about something ⋗ **Watch you don't trip over that root.**
3 to look after someone or something ⋗ **Could you watch the baby for me?**

NOUN plural watches

a small clock that you wear on your wrist

water

NOUN

a clear liquid with no taste that falls from the sky as rain

VERB waters, watering, watered

1 to water a plant is to give water to it
2 if your eyes water, they produce tears ⋗ **The thick smoke made her eyes water.**
3 if your mouth waters, it produces saliva because you see something good to eat

waterfall

NOUN plural waterfalls

a place where a river or stream falls over a high rock or cliff

wave

NOUN plural waves

1 a moving ridge of water in the sea ⋗ **Surfers were jumping into the waves.**
2 a curving shape in your hair ⋗ **Your hair has a natural wave.**
3 a movement of the hand to say hello or goodbye or attract someone's attention ⋗ **She gave a cheery wave as the train pulled out of the station.**

VERB waves, waving, waved

1 to move your hand backwards and forwards ⋗ **Wave bye-bye to granny.**
2 to move in the wind ⋗ **flags waving in the breeze**

wax

NOUN

1 the sticky, fatty substance that bees make their cells out of
2 a sticky, yellow substance that forms in your ears
3 a substance used to make candles and crayons, which melts when it is hot

way

NOUN plural ways

1 a method or manner of doing something ⋗ **She's got a funny way of walking.** ⋗ **a way to make new friends**
2 a road or path ⋗ **22 Purley Way**
3 a route or direction ⋗ **Could you tell me the way to the cinema?**
4 a distance ⋗ **It's quite a long way to the coast.**

▶ **by the way**

you say 'by the way' when you are mentioning another subject ⋗ **By the way, I met John in town today.**

▶ **in the way**

if something is in the way, it is blocking your

progress or movement ⟩ *Am I in the way if I sit here?*⟨

we

PRONOUN

a word you use when you are talking about yourself and at least one other person ⟩ *We left home at about nine o'clock.* ⟨

weak

ADJECTIVE   weaker, weakest

1 feeble and not physically strong ⟩ *His illness has left him feeling very weak.* ⟨ ⟩ *a weak heart* ⟨
2 not strong in character ⟩ *She's too weak to stand up to her boss.* ⟨
3 someone who is weak at a subject or activity is not good at it ⟩ *I was always weak at maths.* ⟨
4 a weak drink or mixture has too much water in it ⟩ *a cup of weak tea* ⟨

▸ **weaken**

VERB   weakens, weakening, weakened

1 to weaken is to become weak ⟩ *His determination to leave weakened when Jenny arrived.* ⟨
2 to weaken something or someone is to make them weaker ⟩ *The bout of flu had weakened her.* ⟨

▸ **weakly**

ADVERB

in a way that is not strong or determined ⟩ *She smiled weakly at his joke.* ⟨

▸ **weakness**

NOUN   *plural* weaknesses

1 lack of strength ⟩ *the weakness of an argument* ⟨
2 a fault or something that you cannot help liking ⟩ *Chocolate is my only weakness.* ⟨

wealth

NOUN

1 riches ⟩ *a businessman of great wealth* ⟨
2 a wealth of something is a lot of it ⟩ *a sports team with a wealth of talent* ⟨

▸ **wealthy**

ADJECTIVE   wealthier, wealthiest

rich ⟩ *a wealthy landowner* ⟨

weapon

NOUN   *plural* weapons

something that you use to fight someone ⟩ *weapons of war* ⟨   ⟩ *Our best weapon was surprise.* ⟨

wear

VERB   wears, wearing, wore, worn

1 to be dressed in clothes or carrying something on your body ⟩ *Ann was wearing her school uniform.* ⟨   ⟩ *How long have you worn glasses?* ⟨
2 to arrange your hair in a particular style ⟩ *She usually wears her hair in a ponytail.* ⟨
3 to have a particular expression on your face ⟩ *Ted wore an angry frown.* ⟨

NOUN

1 clothes ⟩ *evening wear* ⟨
2 damage caused by being used or rubbed ⟩ *The carpet was showing signs of wear.* ⟨

▸ **wearer**

NOUN   *plural* wearers

someone who is wearing something

weather

NOUN

how hot, cold, wet or dry it is outside ⟩ *The weather's very warm for October.* ⟨

VERB   weathers, weathering, weathered

1 to change gradually because of being exposed to the weather ⟩ *buildings weathered by the wind and rain* ⟨
2 to survive a bad situation safely ⟩ *John weathered the difficulties more easily than his brother.* ⟨

Wednesday

NOUN   *plural* Wednesdays

the day of the week after Tuesday and before Thursday

Wednesday comes from the Old English word **Wodnesdæg**, which means *Woden's day*. Woden is the old German god of war and of wisdom.

weed

NOUN *plural* **weeds**

a wild plant that is growing where you do not want it to ⇒ *The garden was overgrown with weeds.*

VERB **weeds, weeding, weeded**

to remove the weeds from a place ⇒ *I offered to weed the garden for my dad.*

▸ **weedy**

ADJECTIVE **weedier, weediest**

1 full of weeds
2 someone who is weedy is thin and weak

week

NOUN *plural* **weeks**

1 a period of seven days, often from Sunday to Saturday ⇒ *I have dance lessons twice a week.*
2 the five days from Monday to Friday when many people go to work ⇒ *I don't go out much during the week.*

▸ **weekly**

ADJECTIVE

happening or produced once a week ⇒ *a weekly magazine*

ADVERB

once a week ⇒ *I visit my Grandma weekly.*

weekend

NOUN *plural* **weekends**

Saturday and Sunday ⇒ *We're going to Oxford for the weekend.*

weep

VERB **weeps, weeping, wept**

to cry tears ⇒ *Mother wept when she heard the terrible news.*

weight

NOUN *plural* **weights**

1 the amount that something or someone weighs ⇒ *What weight are you?*
2 a piece of solid material that is used to hold things down or weigh things on scales
3 a load or burden ⇒ *Getting a job took a weight off his mind.*

well¹

ADVERB **better, best**

1 in a satisfactory, successful or correct way ⇒ *Janet speaks French very well.*
2 thoroughly ⇒ *Mix the butter and sugar well before adding the flour.*

▸ **as well**

too ⇒ *I'd like an ice cream as well.*

ADJECTIVE **better, best**

healthy ⇒ *I don't feel well today.*

well²

NOUN *plural* **wells**

a deep hole in the ground where you can get water, oil or gas ⇒ *an oil well*

VERB **wells, welling, welled**

▸ **well up**

if tears well up in your eyes, they begin to flow

wellingtons *or* wellington boots

PLURAL NOUN

high rubber boots that cover your lower leg

These boots were named after the Duke of **Wellington**, a British army general who wore boots like them.

went

VERB

a way of changing the verb **go** to make a past tense ⇒ *Bill went out at about 6 o'clock.*

were

VERB

the past tense of the verb **be** that you use with **you**, **we** or **they** ⇒ *We were so relieved*

a b c d e f g h i j k l m n o p q r s t u v **w** x y z

to see him. ⮥   ⮧ *The children were playing in the garden when we arrived.* ⮥

> Be careful not to confuse the spellings of **were** and **where**. **Where** means to, from or in what place: Where *are you going?*

west

NOUN

1 the direction in which the sun sets, opposite to east ⮧ *the west of England* ⮥
2 the West is a name for the countries in Europe and North America

ADJECTIVE

in, from, or towards the west ⮧ *the west coast of America* ⮥

ADVERB

to the west ⮧ *We travelled west as far as the motorway.* ⮥

wet

ADJECTIVE   wetter, wettest

1 full of water or covered with water ⮧ *wet clothes* ⮥ ⮧ *It's easy to skid on wet roads.* ⮥
2 not dried ⮧ *wet paint* ⮥
3 rainy ⮧ *a wet afternoon* ⮥

VERB   wets, wetting, wet

to wet something is to make it wet ⮧ *He wet his hair to flatten it down.* ⮥

whale

NOUN   *plural* **whales**

a very large mammal that lives in the sea

▸whaling

NOUN

hunting and killing whales

what

ADJECTIVE AND PRONOUN

1 **what** is used to ask questions about things ⮧ *What day is it today?* ⮥ ⮧ *What's your brother's name?* ⮥
2 you can say **what** in exclamations to emphasize something ⮧ *What a beautiful view!* ⮥
3 the thing or things ⮧ *I hope you find what you're looking for.* ⮥ ⮧ *This bag is just what I wanted.* ⮥

wheel

NOUN   *plural* **wheels**

one of the round things under a vehicle that turns around as it moves ⮧ *The spare wheel is in the boot.* ⮥

VERB   wheels, wheeling, wheeled

to wheel something is to push it along on wheels ⮧ *He got a puncture and had to wheel his bike home.* ⮥

when

ADVERB

at what time ⮧ *When did you arrive?* ⮥

CONJUNCTION

1 at the time at which, or during the time at which ⮧ *I was just going out when the phone rang.* ⮥
2 in spite of the fact that ⮧ *How is it that you don't even have 10p when you've only just got your pocket money?* ⮥

where

ADVERB

to, from or in what place ⮧ *Where are we going?* ⮥ ⮧ *Where did you get that hat?* ⮥

CONJUNCTION

to, from or in what place ⮧ *I have no idea where we are.* ⮥

Be careful not to confuse the spellings of **where** and **were**. **Were** is the past tense of the verb **be** that you use with **you**, **we** or **they**: Were *you sleeping?*

whether

CONJUNCTION

whether is used to show that there is a choice between two possibilities ⟫ *Whether we like it or not, we have to get up early.*

which

ADJECTIVE

what one or ones ⟫ *Which hand do you think the coin is in?*

PRONOUN

1 what one or ones ⟫ *Which of these books is yours and which is mine?*
2 you use **which** to talk about the person or thing that has been mentioned in the earlier part of a sentence ⟫ *I had eaten four chocolate bars, which made me feel sick.*

while

CONJUNCTION

1 during the time that ⟫ *Will you be going to Disneyland while you are in Florida?*
2 although ⟫ *While I understand why you got angry, I think you should try to control your temper.*

NOUN

a period of time ⟫ *We waited inside for a while but the rain didn't stop.*

whisper

VERB whispers, whispering, whispered

to talk very quietly under your breath so that only people near you can hear what you are saying

NOUN *plural* whispers

a very quiet voice ⟫ *She hung her head and answered in a whisper.*

whistle

VERB whistles, whistling, whistled

1 to make a high-pitched sound or a musical note by blowing air through your teeth and lips
2 if something whistles, it makes a high-pitched sound

NOUN *plural* whistles

1 a whistling sound
2 a small device that you blow into to make a high-pitched sound ⟫ *The referee blew his whistle.*
3 a simple musical instrument that you blow into and which makes high-pitched sounds

white

NOUN

1 the very pale colour of milk or snow
2 the white of an egg is the clear substance around the yolk, which turns white if it is cooked

ADJECTIVE whiter, whitest

of the colour white

▸ **whiten**

VERB whitens, whitening, whitened

to make something white or whiter

whiteboard

NOUN *plural* whiteboards

1 a board with a white plastic surface that you can write on with marker pens
2 a white plastic board in a classroom that you can use with a computer to do things such as move words and pictures around

who

PRONOUN

1 which person or people ⟫ *Who is your favourite pop star?*
2 you use **who** when you want to say something else about a person or people you have just mentioned, or to explain which person you mean ⟫ *Emily, who lives next door, is 12 years old.* ⟫ *It was Malcolm who told me the news.*

a b c d e f g h i j k l m n o p q r s t u v **w** x y z

whole

ADJECTIVE

all of something ⋗ *a whole carton of milk* ⋖

NOUN

a whole is a complete thing, especially one that is made up of different parts ⋗*Two halves make a whole.* ⋖

whom

PRONOUN

whom is used as the object of a verb or preposition, and means the same as **who** ⋗ *He phoned his friend Andrew, whom he hadn't seen for years.* ⋖ ⋗ *To whom should I address the letter?* ⋖

> Nowadays, people often use **who** instead of **whom**: *He phoned his friend Andrew, who he hasn't seen for years.*

whose

ADJECTIVE

1 you use **whose** before a noun when you are asking which person or people something belongs to ⋗ *Whose bike is this?* ⋖
2 you use **whose** before a noun to mean 'of which' or 'of whom' ⋗ *the boy whose family owns the castle on the hill* ⋖

PRONOUN

you use **whose** when you are asking or talking about which person or people something belongs to ⋗ *Whose is this?* ⋖ ⋗ *It must be someone's dog but I don't know whose.* ⋖

who's

a short way to say and write **who is** or **who has** ⋗ *Who's there?* ⋖ ⋗ *Who's got my keys?* ⋖

> Be careful not to confuse the spellings of **who's** and **whose**. **Who's** is a short form of **who is** or **who has**: Who's *in the bathroom?* **Whose** tells you something belongs to someone: Whose *shoes are these?*

why

ADVERB

for what reason ⋗ *Why did it have to rain today?* ⋖

wide

ADJECTIVE   wider, widest

1 measuring a great distance from side to side ⋗ *across the wide Missouri river* ⋖
2 having a certain width ⋗ *The river is nearly a mile wide at some points.* ⋖
3 covering a great range or amount ⋗ *a wide knowledge of history* ⋖

ADVERB   wider, widest

1 with a great distance from top to bottom or side to side ⋗ *The tiger opened his mouth wide, showing his enormous fangs.* ⋖
2 if you are wide awake, you are completely awake and alert

▶ **widely**

ADVERB

something that is widely known or widely admired is known or admired by a lot of people

▶ **widen**

VERB   widens, widening, widened

to make or cause to be wide or wider

wife

NOUN   *plural* **wives**

a man's wife is the woman he has married

wiggle

VERB   wiggles, wiggling, wiggled

to move from side to side, or backwards and forwards ⋗ *Look! I can wiggle my front tooth.* ⋖

NOUN   *plural* **wiggles**

1 a movement from side to side or backwards and forwards
2 a line that has lots of bends and curves

▶ **wiggly**

ADJECTIVE   wigglier, wiggliest

1 a wiggly line has lots of bends and curves

2 something wiggly moves, or can be moved, by wiggling ⇒ *a wiggly tooth* ⇐

wild

ADJECTIVE wilder, wildest

1 wild animals or plants live in their natural surroundings and are not kept by human beings ⇒ *a wild goat* ⇐ ⇒ *wild rice* ⇐

2 a wild area of land is in a natural state and has not been farmed or built on

3 wild behaviour is not controlled and sometimes violent ⇒ *The fans went wild with excitement.* ⇐

4 wild weather is windy and stormy

NOUN *plural* wilds

animals that live in the wild live in their natural environment and are not kept as pets or in zoos

will¹

VERB would

1 **will** is used to talk about the future ⇒ *It will be winter soon.* ⇐

2 you use **will** to ask someone to do something, or to tell them to do something, or to ask them what they would like ⇒ *Will you hold this for me?* ⇐ ⇒ *Will you please stop making that racket!* ⇐ ⇒ *Will you have tea or coffee?* ⇐

will²

NOUN *plural* wills

1 your will is the control you have over your own actions and decisions

2 your will is what you want to do and your desire or determination to do it

3 a will is a legal document written by someone saying who they want their property and money to be given to after their death

VERB wills, willing, willed

if you will something to happen, you try to make it happen by using the power of your thoughts

willing

ADJECTIVE

if you are willing, you are ready or happy to do what is asked or needed ⇒ *a willing helper* ⇐ ⇒ *He's willing to work hard.* ⇐

win

VERB wins, winning, won

1 to win is to beat all the others in a competition and get first place or first prize

2 to win something is to get it as a prize

NOUN *plural* wins

a victory

wind¹ rhymes with "**tinned**"

NOUN *plural* winds

1 wind, or a wind, is a strong current of air

2 if someone has wind, they have gas trapped in their stomach, which makes them feel uncomfortable

3 your wind is your breath or your ability to breathe easily

wind² rhymes with "**find**"

VERB winds, winding, wound

1 to wind something is to twist it round and round in loops or coils ⇒ *A turban is a long piece of cloth that is wound round the head.* ⇐

2 to wind or wind up a watch or clock is to turn the screw or key that tightens the spring inside and makes it work

3 a road, path or river winds if it twists and turns

▸ **wind up**

to wind up somewhere is to end up in that place or situation, especially one that is unpleasant or uncomfortable

▸ **wind someone up**

to make someone believe something is true when it isn't, as a joke or to annoy them

▸ **wind something up**

to end something such as a meeting or activity

a b c d e f g h i j k l m n o p q r s t u v **w** x y z

window

NOUN *plural* **windows**

1 an opening in the wall of a building or in a vehicle, with glass fitted in it so that you can see through it, and which can usually be opened to let in air
2 **ICT** an area on a computer screen where you can view or work with information or a computer file

wing

NOUN *plural* **wings**

1 a bird's or insect's wings are the parts of its body that it uses to fly with
2 an aeroplane's wings are the two long flat parts that stick out at either side of its body
3 a wing of a building is a part that sticks out from the main building
4 in games like football and hockey, the wings are the two long sides of the pitch, or the players whose position is at either side of the field ⋛ *He's dribbling the ball down the wing.* ⋚ ⋛ *She's the best right wing we've ever had in our team.* ⋚

wink

VERB winks, winking, winked

1 to shut one of your eyes and open it again quickly, as a friendly or secret sign to someone
2 lights wink when they twinkle or go off and on again quickly

NOUN *plural* **winks**

a sign you make by closing and opening one of your eyes quickly

winter

NOUN *plural* **winters**

the coldest season of the year, between autumn and spring

ADJECTIVE

happening or used during winter ⋛ *a warm winter coat* ⋚ ⋛ *the winter months* ⋚

▸ **wintry**
ADJECTIVE
cold, like winter

wipe

VERB wipes, wiping, wiped

1 to wipe something is to rub its surface to clean it or dry it
2 **ICT** to wipe a computer disk, or a sound or video tape, is to remove all the information, sound or images on it

▸ **wipe something** *or* **someone out**
to destroy someone or something and get rid of them completely

NOUN *plural* **wipes**

1 an act of wiping ⋛ *I need to give my glasses a wipe.* ⋚
2 a piece of cloth or tissue used to wipe things with

wire

NOUN *plural* **wires**

1 metal that has been pulled into a long narrow strand that bends easily
2 a length of wire, or several pieces of it twisted into a cable for carrying electricity or telephone signals

VERB wires, wiring, wired

1 to wire a house is to fit the cables that are needed to carry electricity to lights and plugs
2 to wire or wire up a piece of equipment is to fit it with electrical cables or a plug so that it can be connected to the power supply

wise

ADJECTIVE wiser, wisest

1 sensible ⋛ *a wise decision* ⋚ ⋛ *She was wise enough not to say anything to him.* ⋚
2 if you are wise to something, you know about it

wish

VERB wishes, wishing, wished

1 to want something and hope that it will happen ⋛ *I wish it would stop raining.* ⋚ ⋛ *What did you wish for when you blew out the candles on your cake?* ⋚

a b c d e f g h i j k l m n o p q r s t u v w x y z

2 to want to do something or want it to be done ⇒ *Do you wish to pay now or later?*

3 you wish someone something when you say that you hope they will have it ⇒ *We all wish you luck.*

NOUN *plural* wishes

something you wish for or want ⇒ *Make a wish.*

witch

NOUN *plural* witches

a woman or girl who is supposed to have special magic powers

▶ **witchcraft**
NOUN

the magic and spells that witches do, especially to make something bad happen

with

PREPOSITION

1 in the company of or in the same place as ⇒ *Come with me.* ⇒ *She keeps her diary on the shelf with her school books.*

2 using ⇒ *We stuck it down with glue.*

3 having ⇒ *a house with a green door*

4 going in the same direction ⇒ *drifting with the tide*

5 as the result of ⇒ *He was doubled up with pain.*

6 against ⇒ *They've argued with each other since they were small children.*

7 **with** is used after verbs about covering, filling or mixing ⇒ *He covered the table with a sheet.* ⇒ *Mix the dry ingredients with the milk in a large bowl.*

8 **with** is used after verbs about separating or finishing ⇒ *I parted with them at the station.* ⇒ *Have you finished with this magazine?*

without

PREPOSITION

not with or not having ⇒ *They left without me.* ⇒ *Do you take coffee with or without milk?*

wizard

NOUN *plural* wizards

a man or boy who is supposed to have special magic powers

▶ **wizardry**
NOUN

1 magic performed by a wizard

2 clever or surprising things, especially done using machines ⇒ *technical wizardry*

woke

VERB

a way of changing the verb **wake** to make a past tense ⇒ *He woke with a start.*

woken

VERB

the form of the verb **wake** that is used with a helping verb to show that something happened in the past ⇒ *He had woken with a start.*

wolf

NOUN *plural* wolves

a wild animal like a dog, which lives in family groups called packs

▶ **cry wolf**

to cry wolf is to give a warning of danger when there is no danger

VERB wolfs, wolfing, wolfed

to wolf food or wolf it down is to eat it very quickly and greedily

a b c d e f g h i j k l m n o p q r s t u v w x y z

woman

NOUN   *plural* **women**

an adult female human being

won

VERB

a way of changing the verb **win** to make a past tense. It can be used with or without a helping verb ⋛ *We won the cup.* ⋚ ⋛ *We'd won it for four years running.* ⋚

wonder

VERB   wonders, wondering, wondered

1 you wonder about things when you are curious about them or cannot decide about them ⋛ *I wonder what Jack has bought me for Christmas.* ⋚
2 you wonder at something when you are surprised by it
3 you use 'I wonder if' when you are asking someone politely about or for something ⋛ *I wonder if you could tell me the time?* ⋚

NOUN   *plural* **wonders**

1 wonder is the feeling you get when you see something extraordinary or surprising ⋛ *The comet filled people who saw it with wonder.* ⋚
2 a wonder is something unexpected or extraordinary ⋛ *It's a wonder you didn't freeze to death out in that blizzard.* ⋚

▶ **wonderful**

ADJECTIVE

extraordinary or marvellous ⋛ *a wonderful view of the mountains* ⋚

wood

NOUN   *plural* **woods**

1 wood is the hard material that forms the trunks and branches of trees. It is cut up to make furniture, buildings and paper
2 a wood or the woods is an area with many trees

▶ **wooden**

ADJECTIVE

1 made of wood ⋛ *wooden toys* ⋚

2 a wooden action, expression or behaviour is stiff and unnatural

wool

NOUN

1 the soft fibre that grows on the bodies of sheep
2 a thread made from this fibre, used for knitting and making cloth ⋛ *a ball of wool.* ⋚

▶ **woollen**

ADJECTIVE

made of wool ⋛ *a woollen blanket* ⋚

▶ **woolly**

ADJECTIVE   woollier, woolliest

covered with wool or with hair that is dense and curly like wool

word

NOUN   *plural* **words**

1 a unit of language that is written as a group of letters with spaces on either side
2 to get word about something is to get news about it ⋛ *Her family got word that she had got married in Mexico.* ⋚
3 if you give your word, you give your solemn promise that you will do something

VERB   words, wording, worded

you word something in a certain way when you choose words to express it

▶ **wording**

NOUN

the wording of something is which words have been used to express it

word class

NOUN   *plural* **word classes**

word classes are the various groups that words belong to depending on the job they do. The word classes you will find in this dictionary are noun, pronoun, verb, adjective, adverb, preposition, conjunction and interjection

wore

VERB

a way of changing the verb **wear** to make a past tense ⋗ *She wore an old pair of jeans.*

work

NOUN   *plural* **works**

1 someone's work is their job or employment ⋗ *Dad leaves for work about 8 o'clock in the morning.*
2 work is something you do that needs effort ⋗ *It was hard work climbing to the top with heavy packs on our backs.*
3 your work is what you create by working ⋗ *The teacher marked my work.*
4 a work is something produced by an artist or composer
5 a works is a factory or workshop
6 the works of a machine or clock are the parts inside it that make it operate

VERB   works, working, worked

1 you work when you do something that needs effort or energy
2 people who work have a job
3 a machine that works operates properly
4 a plan works when it is successful
5 to work something is to make it operate

▸ **work out**

something works out a certain way when it turns out that way at the end

▸ **work something out**

you work out something such as a problem when you think about it carefully until you find the answer

▸ **worker**

NOUN   *plural* **workers**

someone who works for a living, especially in a particular industry ⋗ *steel workers*

worksheet

NOUN   *plural* **worksheets**

a sheet listing work that has to be done or that has been done

world

NOUN   *plural* **worlds**

1 the Earth or all the people living on it ⋗ *The whole world is affected by global warming.*
2 a planet ⋗ *a creature from another world*
3 all the people and things that are connected with an activity or subject ⋗ *the world of sport*

worm

NOUN   *plural* **worms**

a small creature with a long, soft body and no legs

VERB   worms, worming, wormed

to worm your way somewhere is to get there by wriggling through small spaces

▸ **worm something out of someone**

to get information from someone gradually and with great difficulty

worn

VERB

the form of the verb **wear** that is used with a helping verb to show that something happened in the past ⋗ *She had worn the dress before.*

ADJECTIVE

worn things are damaged by rubbing or wearing ⋗ *The carpet is worn and dirty.*

▸ **worn out**

very tired

worry

VERB   worries, worrying, worried

1 to worry about a problem is to keep thinking about it in an anxious way because you are not sure how to deal with it or how it will turn out
2 to worry someone is to disturb them and make them anxious or upset

NOUN   *plural* **worries**

1 worry is being anxious
2 a worry is something that makes you anxious

a b c d e f g h i j k l m n o p q r s t u v **w** x y z

▸ **worried**

ADJECTIVE

anxious

▸ **worrier**

NOUN   *plural* **worriers**

a person who worries, especially all the time

worse

ADJECTIVE

worse is a form of the adjective **bad**, which you use when you are comparing how bad things are ⊰ *My brother's room is a worse mess than mine.* ⊱

ADVERB

more badly, or more severely ⊰ *It was raining worse than ever.* ⊱

▸ **worsen**

VERB   worsens, worsening, worsened

1 something worsens when it becomes worse than it was before
2 to worsen something is to make it worse

worship

VERB   worships, worshipping, worshipped

1 to honour a god or gods by praising them and praying to them
2 to love or admire someone or something, especially in a way that stops you seeing their faults

NOUN

religious services and other ways of worshipping ⊰ *a place of worship* ⊱

worst

ADJECTIVE

worst is a form of the adjective **bad**, which you use when you are describing something as the most bad ⊰ *It was the worst storm we'd ever seen.* ⊱

ADVERB

badly to the greatest degree ⊰ *I did worst in the test.* ⊱

would

VERB

1 a way of changing the verb **will** to make a past tense ⊰ *She said she would be in touch later.* ⊱
2 you use **would** to ask people if they want something or if they will do something ⊰ *Would you like a new bike for your birthday?* ⊱ ⊰ *Would you close the door behind you, please.* ⊱

wound[1] rhymes with "**pound**"

VERB

a way of changing the verb **wind** to make a past tense. It can be used with or without a helping verb ⊰ *She wound a long, red, knitted scarf around her neck.* ⊱ ⊰ *He had wound the old grandfather clock in the hall.* ⊱

wound[2] said "**woond**"

NOUN   *plural* **wounds**

an injury to a person's or animal's body in which the skin has been damaged by a cut

VERB   wounds, wounding, wounded

1 to wound a person or animal is to cause an injury to their body
2 to wound someone is to hurt their feelings

▸ **wounded**

ADJECTIVE

a wounded person or animal has been injured

wrap

VERB   wraps, wrapping, wrapped

1 to wrap something, or to wrap something up, is to put a covering of paper or other material round it
2 to put something like paper or cloth round another thing to cover it ⊰ *She wrapped the bandage round my knee.* ⊱

▸ **wrapper**

NOUN   *plural* **wrappers**

a piece of paper or plastic that something is wrapped in

wreck

VERB wrecks, wrecking, wrecked

1 to wreck something is to damage it or destroy it
2 a ship is wrecked when it is badly damaged, for example by hitting rocks, and can no longer sail

NOUN *plural* wrecks

a badly damaged ship or an aeroplane or vehicle that has crashed

▸ **wreckage**
NOUN

the broken or damaged pieces left after something has been wrecked

wrist

NOUN *plural* wrists

one of the two parts of your body where your arms join your hands

write

VERB writes, writing, wrote, written

1 to form letters and words, usually on paper using a pen or pencil
2 you write to someone when you write or type a letter and send it to them
3 to write a story, article, play or music is to create it and write it down

▸ **writer**
NOUN *plural* writers

someone who writes books, plays, film scripts or newspaper articles

▸ **writing**
NOUN *plural* writings

1 writing is forming letters and words on paper or some other surface so that they can be read
2 your writing is the way you write
3 an author's writings are the things he or she has written

wrong

ADJECTIVE

1 not right or not satisfactory ⋛ *Is there something wrong with David? He doesn't look happy.* ⋚ ⋛ *Cheating in examinations is wrong.* ⋚
2 not correct ⋛ *That was the wrong answer.* ⋚
3 not suitable ⋛ *He has decided he's in the wrong job.* ⋚

ADVERB

wrongly or incorrectly ⋛*I think I have spelt your name wrong.* ⋚

▸ **wrongly**
ADVERB

not correctly or accurately ⋛ *The plug had been fitted wrongly so the machine did not work.* ⋚

wrote

VERB

a way of changing the verb **write** to make a past tense ⋛ *He wrote a letter to his pen friend.* ⋚

a b c d e f g h i j k l m n o p q r s t u v **w** x y z

xylophone

NOUN *plural* **xylophones**

a musical instrument made up of a set of wooden bars that make different notes when you hit them with hammers

> This word comes from the Greek word **xylon**, which means *wood*, together with the ending **phone**, which means *sound*, because the instrument has wooden keys. Other words in which **phone** means *sound* are **telephone** and **headphones**.

yard¹

NOUN *plural* **yards**

a unit for measuring length, equal to 91 centimetres

yard²

NOUN *plural* **yards**

1 an enclosed area of land used for a particular purpose ⋛ *a builders' yard* ⋚
2 an American English word for **garden**

yawn

VERB yawns, yawning, yawned

to open your mouth very wide and breathe in, because you are feeling tired or bored

NOUN *plural* **yawns**

the sound or action of someone yawning

year

NOUN *plural* **years**

a period of 365 days, or 366 days in a leap year, especially the period from 1 January to 31 December. It is based on the length of time it takes for the Earth to go around the sun

▸ yearly

ADJECTIVE

happening every year ⋛ *our yearly holiday* ⋚

yell

VERB yells, yelling, yelled

to shout or scream ⋛ *'Let me go!' she yelled.* ⋚

NOUN *plural* **yells**

a shout or scream

yellow

NOUN

the colour of the sun or the middle of an egg

ADJECTIVE yellower, yellowest

of the colour yellow

yes

ADVERB

a word you say when you agree with someone or something

yesterday

NOUN

the day before today

ADVERB

on the day before today

yet

ADVERB

1 by now, by this time ⋛ *Have you read her new book yet?* ⋚
2 before something is finished, still ⋛ *We might win this game yet.* ⋚
3 in addition, besides ⋛ *After London, we visited yet more places.* ⋚

a b c d e f g h i j k l m n o p q r s t u v w x y z

CONJUCTION

however, nevertheless ⇒ *He seemed friendly, yet I did not trust him.*

▸ **as yet**

up till now ⇒ *I would like to go to Paris but I haven't been as yet.*

yogurt *or* yoghurt

NOUN *plural* yogurts *or* yoghurts

1 a runny food with a slightly sour taste that is made from milk
2 a pot of this food ⇒ *a strawberry yogurt*

yolk

NOUN *plural* yolks

the yellow part in the middle of an egg

Yom Kippur

NOUN

a Jewish religious day when people do not eat. It is also called the Day of Atonement

you

PRONOUN

a word you use to the person or people that you are talking to ⇒ *Do you like pizza?* ⇒ *Max is taller than you.*

young

ADJECTIVE younger, youngest

not old ⇒ *a young boy*

NOUN

1 the babies that an animal or bird has ⇒ *a sparrow feeding its young*
2 the young are young people

▸ **youngster**

NOUN *plural* youngsters

a young person

your

ADJECTIVE

belonging to the person or people you are talking to ⇒ *Can I borrow your ruler?*

Be careful not to confuse the spellings of **your** and **you're**. **Your** means something belongs to the person you are talking to: *I like* your *shoes*. **You're** is short for **you are**: *You're* my best friend.

yours

PRONOUN

a word you use to talk about something belonging to a person or people you are talking to ⇒ *Which glass is yours?*

▸ **Yours faithfully, Yours sincerely** *or* **Yours truly** words that you write before your name at the end of a formal letter

yourself

PRONOUN *plural* yourselves

1 you use the word **yourself** (or **yourselves**) when the person (or people) you are talking to performs the action of a verb but is also affected by it ⇒ *Careful you don't cut yourself on that knife.* ⇒ *You'll have to dry yourselves on your T-shirts.*
2 on your own, without any help from anyone else ⇒ *Did you really make that skirt yourself?*

youth

NOUN *plural* youths

1 the time in your life when you are young ⇒ *She spent most of her youth abroad.*
2 a young man aged between about 15 and 20 ⇒ *a gang of youths*
3 young people as a group ⇒ *the youth of today*

▸ **youthful**

ADJECTIVE

young ⇒ *a youthful-looking fifty-year-old.*

yo-yo

NOUN *plural* yo-yos

a toy that is made up of a circular object on a piece of string that you have to try to keep spinning up and down

a b c d e f g h i j k l m n o p q r s t u v w x y z

zebra

NOUN *plural* **zebras**

an animal like a horse with black and white stripes

zero

NOUN *plural* **zeros**

nothing, or the number 0 ⋗ *There are six zeros in one million.* ⋖

zip

NOUN *plural* **zips**

a fastener on clothes or bags that has two rows of metal or plastic teeth that fit tightly together when a sliding piece is pulled along them

VERB **zips, zipping, zipped**

1 to fasten something with a zip ⋗ *Zip up your jacket, it's cold.* ⋖
2 to move somewhere very quickly ⋗ *The bullet zipped by his head.* ⋖

zoo

NOUN *plural* **zoos**

a place where people keep wild animals to breed them and study them, and where you can go to see these animals

> The word **zoo** comes from the Greek word **zoion**, which means *animal*.